Houses for All

Houses for All is the story of the struggle for social housing in Vancouver between 1919 and 1950. It argues that, however temporary or limited their achievements, local activists played a significant role in the introduction, implementation, or continuation of many early national housing programs. Ottawa's housing initiatives were not always unilateral actions in the development of the welfare state. The drive for social housing in Vancouver complemented the tradition of housing activism that already existed in the United Kingdom and, to a lesser degree, in the United States.

Jill Wade analyzes the housing problem that developed in Vancouver in the first half of this century: the chronic shortage of decent living conditions for those of low income, and the occasional serious crisis in owned and rented dwellings for others of middle income. Beginning in 1919 with the Better Housing Scheme and concluding in the early 1950s with the construction of Little Mountain, the first public housing project in Vancouver, the book also chronicles the responses of governments and activists alike to the city's residential conditions. It highlights the spirited, yet frustrated, campaign for low-rental housing in the late 1930s and the more successful, sometimes militant, drive for relief during the housing emergency of the 1940s. Fascinating and informative, *Houses for All* repairs the curious rupture in the collective historical memory that has left Vancouverites of the 1990s unaware of previous housing crises and past activism and achievements.

Jill Wade teaches British Columbia history in the university program at the Open Learning Agency in Burnaby, British Columbia.

Jill Wade

Houses for All: The Struggle for Social Housing in Vancouver, 1919-50

UBCPress / Vancouver

ISBN 0-7748-0454-8 (hardcover)
ISBN 0-7748-0495-5 (paperback)

Canadian Cataloguing in Publication Data

Wade, Catherine Jill, 1942-
  Houses for all

  Includes bibliographical references and index.
  ISBN 0-7748-0454-8 (bound)
  ISBN 0-7748-0495-5 (pbk)

1. Public housing — British Columbia — Vancouver — History. 2. Housing policy
— British Columbia — Vancouver — History. I. Title.

HD7288.78.C32V382 1994   363.5′09711′33   C94-910091-9

This book has been published with the help of a grant from the Social Science
Federation of Canada, using funds provided by the Social Sciences and Humanities
Research Council of Canada.

UBC Press also gratefully acknowledges the ongoing support to its publishing
program from the Canada Council, the Province of British Columbia Cultural
Services Branch, and the Department of Communications of the Government of
Canada.

UBC Press
University of British Columbia
6344 Memorial Road
Vancouver, BC V6T 1Z2
(604) 822-3259
Fax: (604) 822-6083

To 71 Claremont Avenue and 769 Sawyer's Lane

Contents

Illustrations and Tables / ix

Acknowledgments / xi

Abbreviations / xiii

Introduction / 3

1 Housing and Reform in Pre-Depression Vancouver / 8

2 'Slum Dwellings': The Housing Problem in the 1930s / 38

3 Responding to the Housing Problem in the 1930s: The Campaign for Low-Rent Housing / 62

4 'A Camp Existence': The Housing Problem in the 1940s / 93

5 Responding to the Housing Problem in the 1940s: The War on Canada's 'Number One Emergency' / 115

6 Conclusion / 162

Notes / 173

Index / 231

Illustrations and Tables

Illustrations

1 Map of Vancouver. Map by Eric Leinberger / 14-15
2 East end cabins. Courtesy National Archives of Canada, PA-154626 / 18
3 Encampment of native people. Courtesy BC Archives and Records Service, HP 35623 / 19
4 Chinese boardinghouse room. Courtesy BC Archives and Records Service, HP 59639 / 20
5 Central City Mission dormitory. Courtesy BC Archives and Records Service, HP-66178 / 22
6 Better Housing Scheme home, South Vancouver. Photograph by the author / 33
7 Better Housing Scheme home, Kitsilano. Photograph by the author / 35
8 Prior Street jungle. Courtesy City of Vancouver Archives, RE P 12, N 3 #1 / 44
9 False Creek shacks. Courtesy City of Vancouver Archives, WAT P 128 / 51
10 First DHA house, Vancouver. Photograph by the author / 75
11 The 'down east' DHA style / 76
12 B.C. Binning home, West Vancouver. Courtesy National Archives of Canada, PA-132040 / 77
13 Strathcona houses. National Archives of Canada, PA-154630 / 107
14 WHL subdivision in North Vancouver. Courtesy National Archives of Canada, PA-111586 / 121
15 WHL standard house types / 122
16 WHL home, North Vancouver. Courtesy National Archives of Canada, PA-148472 / 123

17 Burkeville. Photographed by Charles Wishart, Vancouver. Courtesy City of Richmond Archives Photograph Collection, P84-17-84 / 124

18 Veterans' housing on Broadway Avenue. Courtesy G. Warrington/ National Archives of Canada, PA-154627 / 130

19 Veterans' housing built by WHL. Courtesy City of Vancouver Archives, 150-1 / 143

20 Picket line outside the old Hotel Vancouver / 145

21 Aerial view of Renfrew Heights. Courtesy Aero Surveys Limited/National Archives of Canada, PA-148474 / 148

22 Fraserview house type / 152

23 Little Mountain public housing. Courtesy National Archives of Canada, PA-154628 / 158

Tables

1 Housing Canadians in selected cities, 1921, by percentage / 11

2 Summary of building permits for all new construction in Vancouver, 1902-24 / 24

3 Summary of building permits for dwellings in Vancouver, 1920-55 / 39

4 Business licences for contractors, real estate dealers, and operators of apartment and lodging houses, Vancouver, 1930-7 / 40

5 Relief cases of the City of Vancouver Public Welfare and Relief Department, 31 December 1931 to 31 December 1938 / 42

6 Unemployment, personal income, and rental costs in Canada, 1926-40 / 43

7 Average rents in dollars in Vancouver and Canada, December 1929 to December 1939 / 43

8 Owner-occupied dwellings in selected cities, 1931, 1941, and 1951, by percentage / 46

9 Relief tenants, classified according to rent, in Vancouver, 8 April 1936 / 47

10 Monthly shelter allowances in dollars, City of Vancouver, effective September 1932 and January 1936 / 47

11 Home ownership in selected cities, 1931 / 52

12 Value of tax arrears and tax sale properties, in dollars, City of Vancouver, 1930-40 / 53

13 Housing conditions in selected cities, 1941, by percentage / 56

14 Vital statistics for the City of Vancouver, 1930-50 / 96

15 Facilities, conveniences, disrepair, and overcrowding in Vancouver (1941 and 1951) and Strathcona (ca. 1950) / 108

Houses for All

2

Introduction

Vancouver today is in the grip of a chronic housing problem. The homeless live quietly on the street, the beach and the park, under bridges, or in cheap lodgings and hostels.[1] The declining supply of inexpensive rental accommodation cannot provide enough decent shelter for those of lowest income. Even potential middle-income owners and renters are frustrated by the unavailability of affordable homes.

The community and governments respond to this distressing predicament sometimes with constructive measures and often with nothing at all. Tenant groups send an endless parade of delegations to city council. On occasion, they have engaged in rent strikes or demolition blockages. A few youthful militants have squatted in vacant houses, receiving wide media coverage and community support, and then been evicted. Organizations such as the Downtown Eastside Residents' Association (DERA), St. James Social Services, and the First United Church Social Housing Society bring aid to their homeless constituency in innovative ways and raise public awareness about core area housing conditions. Several social housing agencies and DERA have built nonprofit housing with federal and provincial funding. Voters and politicians made housing and neighbourhoods the major issues of the 1990 civic election. The City of Vancouver assists a limited dividend company to develop medium-priced rental units. Yet in its 1992 budget, the federal government axed the national cooperative housing program, which has worked very well in Vancouver for two decades. In the 1993 budget, it withdrew support from the construction of new social housing.

The present situation is not Vancouver's first experience of acute and chronic difficulties in residential conditions or of efforts to ameliorate them. Indeed, records held in archives in Ottawa, Victoria, and

Vancouver reveal a housing problem extending back into the early years of the twentieth century and an equally persistent response emerging from citizens and governments alike. In particular, the housing hardships of the 1930s and 1940s generated a reaction of great vigour and lasting impact. Unfortunately, the history of this activism has until now remained unwritten, and a 'rupture in historical memory' has left the activists of the 1990s (with some exceptions) unaware of previous crises and older struggles and achievements.[2] What was the nature of the earlier problem, and how did local activists and governments respond? Does the past furnish any general lessons for meeting today's crisis? Finally, what contributions does this study make towards the history of housing in Canada, Britain, and the United States?

To some, any discussion of a housing problem in Vancouver before the post-Second World War years may seem unwarranted. The city compared favourably with other major Canadian cities in the 1931 and 1941 census figures. The percentage of home ownership remained at about the same comparatively high rate of 50 per cent in those two censuses, and rose sharply by 1951. Furthermore, the commonly held image of the city as a place of homes and gardens makes it difficult to accept the idea of a housing problem, especially before 1929.[3]

Still, the available primary sources disclose a long-standing housing problem characterized by two separate elements. On the one hand, a lack of satisfactory low-rental residential space plagued the core area throughout the first half of the century. On the other hand, crises in the availability and affordability of middle-income dwellings beyond downtown occurred intermittently before 1950, and placed additional pressure on the inadequate low-income housing supply. Although the problem in both its aspects existed before 1929, it later worsened because of conditions associated with depression, wartime, and reconstruction.

Efforts to improve the housing situation in Vancouver began before the First World War and continued into, and after, the 1950s. The federal government played an important role by creating national programs meant to be introduced at the local level across Canada. Its intention was to generate construction, increase employment, stimulate the economy, and encourage home ownership. The housing industry in Vancouver actively supported the implementation of the national market housing programs. At the same time, a drive for publicly assisted social housing programs emerged in Vancouver.

For the purposes of this book, the term 'market housing programs' refers to those plans in which the private sector built owned or rented dwellings with federal assistance. 'Social housing programs' are defined as schemes in which the federal government aided the construction of accommodation for people of low or moderate incomes who could not afford homes provided by the housing industry.[4] The public sector and a third sector of public, private, or cooperative non-profit groups have built social housing since 1950 in Canadian cities. Public housing, housing cooperatives, and seniors' housing are examples of social housing.

Attempts to ameliorate Vancouver's housing problem through government-assisted housing plans may be found as early as the First World War. Three levels of government cooperated in the introduction of the first market housing initiative, the Better Housing Scheme, during the post-First World War housing shortages. Labour, women's, and veterans' groups – the beginnings of a local housing movement – supported the plan. During the Depression, the federal government implemented national market programs for home ownership and rehabilitation. As well, a spirited campaign by groups of local activists to obtain subsidized public housing in Vancouver began in earnest but fell far short of its goal. In the 1940s, Ottawa again stepped in with emergency measures to regulate the housing market and to meet war workers' needs. New legislation was passed to promote postwar home ownership. Despite federal intervention, however, the housing situation deteriorated. Consequently, activist organizations in the community applied intense pressure to all governments, especially Ottawa, for programs to relieve both the temporary and the lasting aspects of the housing problem. By the early 1950s, they had secured short-lived improvements such as an evictions freeze, emergency shelter, continuation of rent controls, and construction of hundreds of veterans' dwelling units. Out of this action came a more permanent achievement, the Little Mountain public housing project, which was the first of many social housing complexes developed in Vancouver in subsequent decades.

Obviously, any complete analysis of the housing problem in Vancouver before 1950 and the response to it requires the integration of local and national primary and secondary evidence. This study combines local and national perspectives on Canadian housing history and therefore goes beyond the work of those historians who have investigated events only in specific cities or policy-making only at the federal level. It reinforces the studies of others who have already fused the local and national dimensions of our housing history.[5]

Any attempt to merge local and national perspectives departs from the two recent major historiographical traditions in Canada. In the postwar years, historical writing was national, political, biographical, and descriptive in character. With the arrival of the 'new social history' around 1970, historians tended to concern themselves with social issues more than with political events, with theory, methodology, or historiography more than with narration, with ordinary Canadians more than with prominent elites, and with cities, regions, and provinces more than with the nation. Yet the shift in historiographical approach was never as dramatic as it appeared. In June 1986, for example, a product of the 'new social history,' the *Urban History Review/Revue d'histoire urbaine*, published several articles on the topic of national policy-making in housing.[6] Moreover, many contemporary historians have continued to describe twentieth-century Canada from a national perspective, and have viewed federal housing initiatives as unilateral actions in the development of the welfare state.[7] Still, much historical writing, particularly in the area of housing policy history, demands an amalgamation of the two traditions. Two decades beyond the shift of the early 1970s, it is time to consider blending various elements of postwar historiography: the local and the national; the social and the political; the ordinary Canadian and the federal elite; and the historio-graphical and the narrative.

In fusing the local and national dimensions in Vancouver's housing history, this book adds to the growing British and American literature about the role of local agitation in national housing policy-making.[8] It argues that the initiation, implementation, or continuation of some improvements devised by the federal government often came about under pressure from groups of 'citizens in action' in Vancouver and, apparently, in other Canadian cities.[9] The participation of these organizations complemented a tradition of housing activism that already existed in the United Kingdom and, to a lesser degree, in the United States.

This work, then, emphasizes the emergence of a drive for social housing in Vancouver. It takes a different course from housing histories that stress residential arrangements for working-class households, social control of workers through housing reform, state provision of low-income dwellings, or conditions in the housing market.[10] Similarly, it is not preoccupied with the relationship between tenure, class, and social mobility, the phenomenon of suburbanization, and the implications of gender, family, ethnicity, and race for housing and its design.[11] Yet in following a different path, the book aims to contribute significantly to housing history in Canada. It clearly shows that conditions in Vancouver were not as agreeable as the census suggested and that many households did live in slum dwellings in the city's downtown area and along its shorelines. As well, it asserts that, while bureaucrats and members of the business community led the drive to bring market housing schemes to Vancouver before 1950, local activists played an effective role in introducing social housing programs to this West Coast city. The study offers some inspiration to housing advocates who deal with today's housing problem, and it allows the story of Vancouver's early social housing movement to assume its proper place in the housing history of Canada.

1
Housing and Reform in Pre-Depression Vancouver

Historical geographer Deryck Holdsworth has described Vancouver in the years before the Great Depression as a 'unique urban landscape.'[1] It was 'a city of single family homes peacefully situated on a peninsula on the edge of the Pacific and at the foot of coastal mountains' without 'a dense concentration of workers' housing on expensive inner city land next to the workplace.' Working- and middle-class residents could take advantage of cheap land, inexpensive building materials, good wages, and spreading street railway lines in buying or building their own suburban homes, whether a 'cottage' in Grimmett or a 'castle' in Shaughnessy Heights. The home-owning aspirations of immigrants recently arrived from places where they had been tenants rather than owners matched the sales rhetoric of Vancouver's real estate agents. Thus, in 1928-9, 72 per cent of the city's houses were single dwellings. Despite a broad spatial sorting into the working-class east side and the middle-class west side, with overlapping in suburbs such as Kitsilano, Mount Pleasant, and Grandview, the wage-earning population generally lived in their own homes, which might be scaled-down versions of the California bungalow or Tudor Revival mansions. In working-class South Vancouver, single homes made up 75 per cent of all residential types, and home owners occupied 84 per cent of houses. A few tenements close to docks, mills, and foundries presented only potential slum conditions. Satisfactory housing contributed to the contentment and stability of the local labour force. 'Little reform rhetoric' existed 'in the minds of civic leaders and embryonic planners' because 'there were few tenements and few areas of abject poverty, overcrowding or disease.' According to Holdsworth, 'for nearly all men and women the city seemed to offer adequate shelter together with the hint of further affluence.'

More recent writing has tempered this sanguine interpretation of Vancouver's residential situation before 1929. Another historical geographer, Donna McCririck, has argued that the city before the First World War did not represent a place of opportunity for all people.[2] Land assembly practices left little room for people without surplus capital, and job insecurity and high living costs deterred many from home ownership. By 1911, between one-quarter and one-third of suburban wage earners rented accommodation, and between 10 and 15 per cent of the population lived in crowded, substandard housing in Chinatown and in the immigrant quarters of the east end. The city's distinctiveness lay in its natural surroundings rather than in its streetscape of detached dwellings, which was not very different from that of other Canadian cities, such as Winnipeg. Furthermore, in a review of a Holdsworth paper, historian John Weaver has questioned whether land was any less available elsewhere in Canada and whether home ownership levels in cities and municipalities west of the Province of Quebec were greatly different from Vancouver's.[3] He has also observed that high rents, inflation, and speculation affected this West Coast city as much or more than other Canadian urban areas between 1905 and 1913, when the big building boom occurred.

Some historians have noted the contrasts in housing conditions in Vancouver. R.A.J. McDonald has juxtaposed Holdsworth's description of 'a suburban environment of detached residences with surrounding gardens rather than a dense concentration of tenements' with Margaret Andrews's evidence of 'the higher incidence of death from disease and the deplorable tenement and rooming conditions in the east-side waterfront area.'[4] McDonald has emphasized 'the need to differentiate between the domestic circumstances of seasonal migrants and ... of more stable urban workers.' As well, Jean Barman has pointed out the residential differences between the boardinghouses and tenements of the east end and the middle- and working-class suburbs east, south, and west of False Creek.[5]

A more accurate assessment of Vancouver's pre-1929 accommodation would take into consideration those circumstances that Holdsworth has not examined in detail: statistics about housing conditions; development of downtown neighbourhoods over time; house types other than single-family dwellings; and residents other than middle- or working-class home owners mainly of British ethnicity. Such an investigation paints a less optimistic picture of Vancouver's housing than the one that Holdsworth has given us. Certainly, Point Grey, South Vancouver, and the city of Vancouver generally supplied newer, better quality accommodation than did older industrial cities in North America and Europe, particularly for skilled working people. Still, the scarcity of adequate, affordable rental units for low-income households already presented a small problem in the downtown area. Furthermore, periods of depression, war, or inflation temporarily affected the supply and price of houses for suburban owners. By 1929, a pattern of chronic shortage of satisfactory, low-income rented premises and occasional crises in middle- and working-class ownership had appeared. As well, the first steps to ameliorate the housing problem in Vancouver had been taken at the local, provincial, and national levels, and the beginnings of a movement to improve residential conditions existed.

The statistics upon which Holdsworth based his exposition of pre-Depression housing in Vancouver came from the plan for the city submitted in 1929 by the St. Louis, Missouri firm of Harland Bartholomew and Associates.[6] Bartholomew's figures in turn came from the South Vancouver voters' list and other, unidentified sources. The plan offered little or no statistical material about dwellings, particularly tenements, cheap hotels, lodgings, shacks, and floathouses. Indeed, it appears to have dismissed tenements, or 'cabins,' simply by recommending that they no longer be permitted.

The 1921 census of Canada furnishes more information than the Bartholomew plan, but its analysis is incomplete compared to later censuses. Moreover, its division of the pre-amalgamation city into Vancouver, Point Grey, and South Vancouver makes difficult any comparison of the 1921 and 1931 census data (these areas were amalgamated in 1929). Yet the 1921 statistics indicate that, in all probability, housing in Vancouver differed in no drastic way from that in Toronto, Hamilton, Winnipeg, Edmonton, or Victoria in terms of numbers of detached houses, ownership rates, rents, overcrowding, and construction materials.

In 1921, single houses made up 88.7 per cent of Vancouver's 21,489 dwellings. Of the rest, 6.4 per cent were apartments, 1.6 per cent row or terraced housing, and 2.6 per cent semi-detached units.[7] If one includes the municipalities of South Vancouver and Point Grey, where detached dwellings predominated, then the percentage of single houses for the entire Vancouver area exceeded 88.7 per cent. This high proportion compared to 93.7, 95.5, and 89 per cent in Victoria, Edmonton, and Winnipeg respectively. Although semi-detached and row or terraced houses prevailed in Toronto, single houses outnumbered other residential types in Hamilton (Table 1). During the 1920s in Vancouver, the number of apartment houses rose substantially. Consequently, by 1931, the proportion of single houses to all dwelling types decreased to 80.4 per cent.[8] Like Victoria and Edmonton, Vancouver in 1921 had a higher percentage of one-room dwellings than Winnipeg, Toronto, or Hamilton. No doubt most of these 238 homes took the form of shacks along the Burrard Inlet and False Creek foreshores or in the city's uncleared outskirts (Table 1).

Table 1

Housing Canadians in selected cities, 1921, by percentage

	Single houses	One-room dwellings	Renting families	Owning families	Rooms per person
Toronto	35.6	0.2	53.1	46.9 (42)*	1.29 (1.41)
Hamilton	73.8	0.2	49.6	50.4 (44)	1.40 (1.41)
Winnipeg	89.0	0.3	57.4	42.6 (43)	1.11 (1.19)
Edmonton	95.5	1.3	52.3	47.7 (50)	1.21 (1.22)
Vancouver	88.7	1.1	65.5	34.5 (48)	1.22 (1.30)
Victoria	93.7	1.4	58.6	41.4 (44)	1.39 (1.53)

* 1931 percentages are in parentheses. The percentages for owning families are rounded.
Sources: Canada, Dominion Bureau of Statistics, *Sixth Census of Canada, 1921* (Ottawa: King's Printer 1927), vol. 3, *Population*, 39, table 11, 53, table 14, 57-9, table 17, 66-7, table 21; idem, *Seventh Census of Canada, 1931: Census Monograph no. 8, Housing in Canada*, prepared by Harold F. Greenway (Ottawa: King's Printer 1941), 51, 93.

As well, the 1921 census data contradict Holdsworth's assertions about unusually high home ownership levels in the Vancouver area (Table 1). Before amalgamation, the percentage of owning families (34.5 per cent) in Vancouver lagged far behind the figures for Toronto, Winnipeg, Edmonton, Hamilton, and Victoria. Of course, the addition of ownership figures for Point Grey and South Vancouver would have increased this 1921 statistic. Nonetheless, McCririck has used evidence from the voters' list for 1911 to conclude that tenancy rates already amounted to 38, 25.2, and 48 per cent in the east end, Mount Pleasant, and West End respectively, and that 25 per cent of registered voters were not property owners. Finally, the 1931 census figure of 48 per cent for owning families in the amalgamated municipality does not differ radically from that of other Canadian cities (Table 1).

Vancouver's rents, overcrowding, and construction materials were not unique. In 1921, monthly rents averaged about the same in Vancouver as in Toronto, although the concentration of seasonal workers living in hotels and rooms meant that more West Coast families paid very low rents (under $9).[9] Using the accepted standard that anything less than one room per person demonstrates overcrowding, Vancouver's crowding rate matched that of other Canadian cities in 1921 and showed the same general improvement over the next decade (Table 1). Without doubt, however, the average of 1.2 rooms per person obscures the poor housing conditions of those who lived under the standard because they lacked sufficient income, just as the figures for other cities do.[10] In the area of construction materials, the city's homes were not unusual in comparison to residences in many parts of Canada. In 1931, 83.9 per cent of all dwellings were of wooden construction. The same trend existed in Victoria, Edmonton, and Winnipeg, while builders in Toronto and Hamilton favoured brick and stone.

Holdsworth has also given us a static impression of Vancouver's residential landscape. Following the 1929 amalgamation of the City of Vancouver with the municipalities of Point Grey and South Vancouver, the landscape could be broken down into the east and west sides and the downtown core. Ontario Street was the dividing line between east-side neighbourhoods, such as Grandview, East Hastings, and Mount Pleasant, and west-side ones, such as Fairview, Kitsilano, Shaughnessy Heights, and Kerrisdale (Figure 1). These suburban neighbourhoods occupied the area between Burrard Inlet or False Creek and the Fraser River, and were bordered by Burnaby on the east and Georgia Strait on the west. In the downtown peninsula, the West End extended from Stanley Park to Burrard Street, the business district from Burrard to Carrall Street (including Yaletown), and the east end (including Strathcona and Chinatown) from Carrall to Clark Drive along Terminal Avenue. More recently, the area encompassing the business district and the east end has been called the downtown east side.

Holdsworth depicted the housing of the city's various neighbourhoods when it was new, not as it altered. The homes of the suburban east and west sides had not experienced excessive modification before 1929. In fact, construction of new units in those areas expanded in the 1920s. By contrast, the residential conditions of the West End, business district, and east end had changed noticeably by the time of the Depression. In many cases, the Yaletown cottages for Canadian Pacific Railway (CPR) workers, the West End mansions for railway management, and the east end one- and two-storey houses had become multiple family dwellings by the 1920s. At the end of the decade, the shift was significant enough for the Bartholomew report to recommend zoning the core area into six-storey multiple dwelling, general business, heavy industrial, six-storey light industrial, and six-storey commercial districts.

The conversion of the core neighbourhoods into multiple dwelling areas began before 1900 in the business district and the east end and later spread to the West End. By 1901, dollar-a-day hotels with saloons, where proprietors and bartenders watched out for 'good and drunk' loggers on a spree 'after hard days and weeks of work in the woods,' had become concentrated in parts of the business district and the east end.[11] The Vancouver health department had also initiated inspections of lodging houses. The migration of some original residents to other neighbourhoods and the arrival of European immigrants in the early 1900s transformed the east end into a mixed single-family and boardinghouse area. According to the medical health officer, many male immigrants, especially unmarried Italian labourers, rented small east end houses and lived communally in crowded conditions. In the three years from 1911 to 1913, lodging-house inspections increased from 480 to 1,326 and then 2,513 units. In those years, the city granted 71, 346, and 333 lodging-house licences and rejected 113, 119, and 127 applications because of inadequate lighting, ventilation, toilet and bathing facilities, fire exits, and sanitation. Overcrowding greatly disturbed health department officials. In 1912, the lodging-house inspector and his assistant conducted nocturnal visits 'with good results' to flush out unauthorized tenants. The unknown number of unlicensed dwellings of perhaps five to seven rooms with one to twelve lodgers also worried health officials.[12]

As its residents gradually moved to Shaughnessy Heights and other west-side neighbourhoods in the 1910s, the West End began its transformation into a lodging and apartment-house area. During the 1920s, the health department produced three reports on overcrowding in rental accommodation located in the West End and the business district, roughly within the square formed by Cambie, Thurlow, Pender, and Robson streets.[13] At the decade's end, the City of Vancouver issued 380 business licences to lodging-house operators and 732 to block managers, mostly for buildings situated in the core area.[14]

Despite the great number of single-family, owner-occupied homes in 1929 in Vancouver, rented houses, lodgings, 'cabins,' apartments, shacks, floathouses, and even tents accommodated a sizable minority of the city's households. An investigation of the character of these other

Figure 1 Map of Vancouver showing government-assisted housing schemes (1919-53) and problematic housing types (ca. 1930-50)

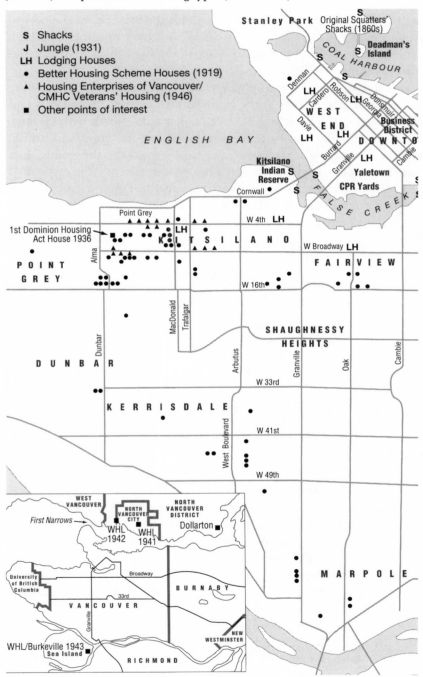

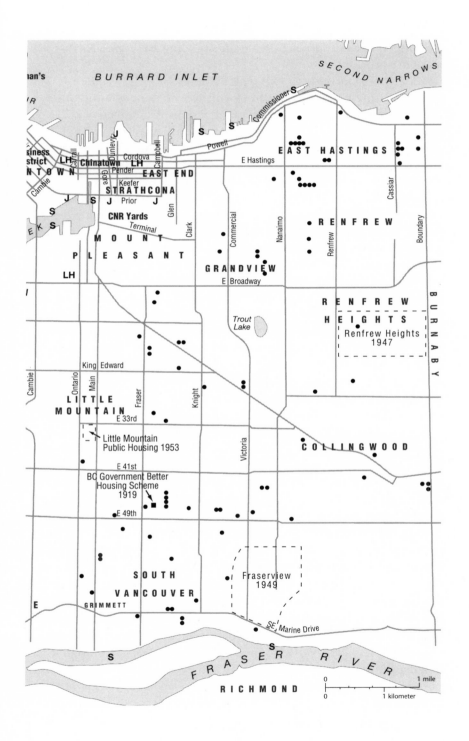

SECOND NARROWS

BURRARD INLET

Commissioner S

Powell

EAST HASTINGS

E Hastings

Cassiar

Boundary

BURNABY

RENFREW

Renfrew

RENFREW
HEIGHTS
Renfrew Heights
1947

ısiness
strict
NTOWN

LH
Chinatown   LH
Cordova
Pender
Keefer
Prior

Carrall
Dunlevy
Campbell
Gore
Cambie

EAST END
STRATHCONA

J   S J   J

Glen

Clark

Commercial

Nanaimo

CNR Yards
Terminal

M O U N T

P L E A S A N T

LH

GRANDVIEW
E Broadway

Trout
Lake

King Edward

Cambie

Ontario

Main

Fraser

Knight

Victoria

COLLINGWOOD

LITTLE
MOUNTAIN
E 33rd

Little Mountain
Public Housing 1953

E 41st

BC Government Better
Housing Scheme
1919

E 49th

Fraserview
1949

SOUTH
VANCOUVER

GRIMMETT

SE Marine Drive

S

F R A S E R   R I V E R

RICHMOND

0   1 mile

0   1 kilometer

dwelling types permits a fuller understanding of Vancouver's early residential conditions.

Probably we know least about rented houses. In 1921, as much as 88.7 per cent of the city's housing stock consisted of single-family homes. Tenants represented 65.5 per cent of families in Vancouver in 1921 and 52 per cent of those in the amalgamated municipalities in 1931. The census does not reveal the distribution of families between leased detached residences and other types of rental quarters. Still, in 1921, 40.5 per cent of tenant families occupied more than five rooms, and they more likely lived in houses than in lodgings or apartments.[15]

More complete information is available about house rents before the First World War. According to the 1915 report of the Board of Inquiry into the Cost of Living in Canada, despite two depressions, rents rose 40 per cent in Vancouver in the period 1900-1910 owing to increased building costs and taxation, housing shortages brought on by rapid population growth, demands for additional conveniences, and specula- tion on vacant suburban properties. Rents for a typical six-room dwell- ing with sanitary facilities in a working-class district jumped from $12-$15 in 1900 to $25-$30 in 1912, and fell to $20-$25 in 1913. Rents for the same sized home without those conveniences followed the same pattern of rise and fall, at $3 to $5 less. These rents were slightly lower than ones for similar accommodation in Prairie cities and much higher than in Toronto or Montreal.[16]

The dispersal of lodging houses throughout the West End and the business district had occurred by the 1920s. The health department documented 111 in its 1920, 1922, and 1927 surveys. A manager, who was usually a woman either renting or owning a whole dwelling, let rooms and housekeeping suites to single men or women, couples, and families. The building itself, which might be a Yaletown version of pattern-book Gothic Revival domestic architecture, consisted of perhaps six, twelve, or even twenty-two rooms. The manager supplied gas plates or coal or gas ranges in rooms and suites and, frequently, central heating. During the housing crisis following the First World War, lodging places tended to be overcrowded. Outward migration from Vancouver in the hard economic times of 1921-2 and a subsequent upswing in construc- tion, however, slowly reduced the congestion. By 1927, a handful of the houses had actually reverted to single-family residences. Although some lodging houses were well kept, many suffered from bad repair, damp- ness, insufficient sanitary facilities, filth, flooded basements, and a lack of heat, natural light, and hot water. All too often, children lived in lodgings. After 1904, rooms and suites in lodging houses usually furnished tenants with cooking fixtures fuelled by gas manufactured at the British Columbia Electric Company plant on False Creek. Within a few years, the medical health officer's reports expressed grave reservations about the installation, inspection, and maintenance of these fixtures, and noted cases of asphyxiation and complaints about odours.[17]

According to the health department, lodging houses included both 'rooms' and cheap hotels located in the business district and the east end. Although companies ordinarily ran the hotels, individuals tended to operate the rooms. Premises such as the Powell Rooms or Grand Union Rooms would have twenty to thirty-five rooms.[18] Some of these buildings had a dumbbell design with a deep, narrow light well that provided the only source of daylight and ventilation for bedrooms and toilets. As early as 1912, this design greatly troubled health officials. By 1925, they described ten dumbbell structures as 'a menace to the health of the occupants.'[19]

The health department considered 'cabins' to be 'the worst [lodging houses] with which we have to contend' (Figure 2).[20] Many 'rooms' were, in fact, cabins: two- or three-storey frame buildings containing single rooms that opened off a porch running along one side of the structure from street to lane. Usually, cabins covered most of a lot. Closer to the city centre, large neighbouring industrial plants or warehouses surrounded them and cut off natural light and ventilation.[21] The construction of cabins had started by 1900 in the east end. Within a decade, lodging-house inspectors declared them 'a great menace to the public health.' Although recently built and structurally sound, they suffered serious deficiencies in venting and lighting. Moreover, they not only accommodated single working men but also frequently families with small children. Late in 1912, the health department inspected sixty-two cabins near the old city hall at Main and Hastings streets and found in them 1,167 men, 198 women, and 120 children. Inadequate lighting, ventilation, and cleanliness afflicted one-half to three-quarters of the cabins. A similar survey of sixty-eight cabins made a year later produced the same results.

Apartment houses became an increasingly popular form of dwelling over time, and although most offered more satisfactory accommodation than lodging houses some did not. Between the 1921 and 1931 census enumerations, the percentage of apartment blocks compared to all residential types rose from 6.4 to 11.8 per cent.[22] Some blocks had been erected before the First World War. In 1913, health department officials inspected 101 blocks and indicated their apprehension about both

Figure 2 By about 1960, some Vancouverites referred to these east end cabins as 'the black hole of Calcutta.' Yet the occupants of other cabins were content with their modest but comfortable surroundings.

dumbbell design and uncertain lines of demarcation between lodging and apartment houses.[23] By the 1920s, many better quality blocks had been built, including the Devonshire Apartment Hotel, Englesea Lodge, Sylvia Court, Manhattan Apartments, and Gilford Court. The number of licensed blocks rose every year, and total suites amounted to 6,100 by 1927.[24] Two years later, the City of Vancouver issued 732 licences to apartment managers.[25] Although 120 companies – such as Pemberton and Sons Limited and Royal Trust Company – managed many blocks, individuals operated 173 premises.

Shacks, floathouses, and tents along the foreshore functioned as less permanent types of housing in early Vancouver. Waterfront dwellings were remnants of the frontier, resource-based settlement built in the 1860s around Burrard Inlet, when squatters with colourful names like Aunt Sally, Portuguese Joe, and Portuguese Pete occupied the shoreline of what is now Stanley Park (Figure 1).[26]

Shacks and floathouses proved to be amazingly resilient. After every demolition by the city, they sprang up again with renewed vigour. In

Figure 3 An encampment of native people fills the shoreline with tents and boats between Burrard Inlet and downtown in Vancouver's early days.

the mid-1800s, unemployed Chinese railway workers threw up huts on the marshes between Pender Street and False Creek. Ten years later, the city razed the shacks because they were overcrowded and lacked sewerage, but it neglected to plan for new housing in Chinatown. As a result, congestion and poor sanitation worsened for single Chinese labouring men.[27] In addition, by 1894, at least 380 shacks lined the Burrard Inlet and False Creek shorelines.[28] Unemployment, high land values, and rising rents augmented squatting during the depression of the 1890s. The city handed out eviction notices and eventually destroyed the waterfront shanties. Yet the shacks came back. In 1911, the health department once again cleared the Burrard Inlet foreshore of about eighty shacks and forty floathouses. Still, waterfront habitation must have contributed substantially to the 238 one-room dwellings noted in the 1921 census.[29] Before the First World War, tents also concerned the health department. Like shacks, they were holdovers from the past. Native people often camped along the shoreline of the business district, and non-natives regularly summered or avoided high rents by tenting along English Bay (Figure 3).[30]

Holdsworth's interpretation of Vancouver housing overlooks the accommodation of post-1900 residents of the east end and the business district. These residents tended to be European or Asian in ethnic origin, elderly, single, unskilled, and frequently underemployed or unemployed. Holdsworth focuses instead on the family homes of middle- and skilled working-class property owners of British ethnicity, who occupied the downtown area before 1900 and the suburban east and west sides after the 1890s. His most obvious omission is the housing of single male Chinese labourers, who worked in canneries or on the railroad in summer and lived in town when jobless in winter. Conditions for these men were extremely bad throughout the pre-Depression years. They experienced dilapidated, unclean, dark, and unventilated surroundings, overcrowding, and exposure to environmentally related diseases such as tuberculosis and typhoid. They inhabited shacks at first, and later lodged in boardinghouses in cellars, mezzanines, or upper floors of commercial or society buildings and in leased houses (Figure 4). The boardinghouses were run by Chinese associations or business owners.

Figure 4 In the early 1900s, single male Chinese labourers lived in small, crowded rooms, where they shared cooking facilities and slept on low bunks with cotton quilts and mats. The men who lived in this room supported themselves by laundering and repairing clothes.

Usually, groups of men from the same family, village, or district in China shared premises. Much to the consternation of health officials, the men partitioned off whole floors of large structures into small rooms and cubicles for privacy, accentuating the problems of crowding, ventilation, lighting, and disease.[31] They prepared meals in communal cooking facilities and slept on low bunks with cotton quilts and Chinese mats. Boardinghouses like the one in the two-storey Sam Kee Building at Pender and Carrall were extremely small; narrow cots, a cast-iron stove, and a coal box were ranged along a six-foot wide room.[32] Others, managed by the Lun Yick Company Limited at 507 Shanghai Alley and 15 Canton Alley, had seventy-two and forty-two rooms respectively.[33] According to Yun Ho Chang, who arrived in Vancouver in 1908, 'the places where Chinese people lived were small and overcrowded. They'd cram 4 bunkbeds into a small room. All the cooking was done on a wood-burner and there were never enough pots and pans.'[34] City Health Inspector Robert Marrion reported to the 1902 Royal Commission on Chinese and Japanese Immigration that the

Armstrong lodging house was a two storey brick building with 27 rooms upstairs. The rooms were 20 feet long, 13 feet wide, and 10 feet high, and were capable of holding six persons in each, according to the bylaw. This was one of the best lodging houses in the city. When visited the other night all the rooms but two exceptions were occupied by more than six people. The furniture of a room would consist of a table, six bunks, and a stove: no more. As a rule, the six occupants would rent that room from a keeper who leased the building from the owner. The amount paid was $3 per month, or fifty cents per month for each occupant, provided no more than the proper number were allowed to use it. This was a fair example of the manner of living among the working Chinamen.[35]

Living arrangements for Chinese families differed from those for single men. Some families rented homes in the downtown area, and others resided in comfortable quarters at a place of business.[36]

Other ethnic groups fared a little better than or the same as the Chinese. Families of Japanese origin adapted to Vancouver's housing situation more easily than some other groups. Single East Indians and Italians lived communally in houses rented by one man for many, while the health department complained about overcrowding and cleanliness.[37] At the same time, the women in Italian and other European

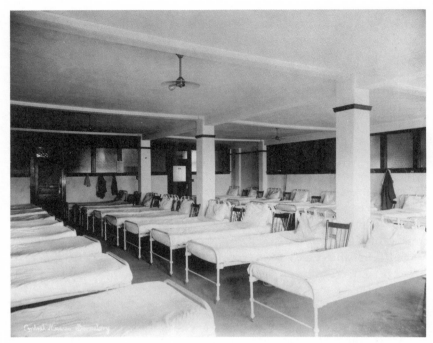

Figure 5 The poor turned to bleak shelters such as the dormitory at the Central City Mission when other options failed.

families supplemented family incomes by supplying probably the best living conditions for labouring bachelors in the way of room, board, and washing.[38]

Lodging houses, rooms, cheap hotels, shacks, and tents represented a first choice for the poor, the jobless, and the elderly. When these options failed, the homeless turned to hostels operated by the Salvation Army, the Central City Mission, the British and Foreign Sailors Society, the Anglican church, and other groups (Figure 5).[39] Although initially the city government depended upon charities to carry the major responsibility, by the early 1900s it began to develop a variety of solutions, usually demeaning and deficient, to assist those in need of affordable housing: rent allowances for families; municipal grants to one or two hostels; and bed tickets for single males to be used in missions, hotels, or lodgings. In hard times, the city used institutions such as the first public library or the jail and facilities such as the Hastings Park camp to provide the transient single unemployed with shelter in return for work.[40] Working or jobless unmarried women remained virtually without any civic or charitable housing assistance unless they were unwed mothers or former prostitutes. During recessions, the health department also decided for reasons of 'common humanity' not to close down lodging houses that it considered unfit for human habitation.[41] In 1907, the department began to care to some extent for the elderly who were unable to look after themselves and had no relatives, first in a former hospital building and six years later in the Old People's Home (later Taylor Manor) on Boundary Road.[42] This early system of resources failed, especially in desperate economic times, to meet the shelter needs of the indigent, the unemployed, and the aged.

Low-income households in the downtown area thus faced a continuing shortage of adequate, inexpensive dwellings, long before the Great Depression. Middle- and skilled working-class families located in East Vancouver, South Vancouver, and Point Grey, however, also experienced intermittent hardships over housing. Even in the best of times, home owners and carpenter-builders engaged in a risky financial venture when they took out a mortgage on a house, despite their relative security in contrast to the needy. They wrestled with mortgages when faced with unemployment, labour disputes, high living costs, rising taxes, soaring land prices, and illness.[43] They maintained their mortgage payments only by taking in boarders, renting out cottages in the backyard, managing rooms or apartment blocks, sending children to work, and keeping gardens, chickens, rabbits, and cows. Not surprisingly, many wage earners rented rather than owned a house.

Although some contractors worked on a grand scale in companies such as the Bungalow Finance and Building Company or Vancouver Freehomes Limited, most were small operators, usually carpenter-builders who erected at most a handful of units, including their own homes. Because they needed only limited capital to enter the industry, the operations initiated by members of the building trades frequently met with financial difficulty. Ernest Winch, for example, the carpenter-builder who in time became provincial leader of the Co-operative Commonwealth Federation (CCF), lost through foreclosure several heavily mortgaged dwellings that he had built in Burnaby and White Rock.[44]

In addition, the First World War, the 1913-15 depression, and the inflation of the early 1920s brought sporadic difficulties in housing. The number of building permits issued for all new construction fluctuated between 1911 and 1921, revealing the impact of macro-economic and political conditions on the Vancouver accommodation supply for mid-

dle- and skilled working-class owners (Table 2). The reduction in building operations during the prewar depression and the war itself, together
with the return of veterans from overseas, created by 1919 an enormous
demand for homes. Shortages in accommodation drove many middle-
and skilled working-class families into cheaper lodgings in the downtown area, and caused doubling up and overcrowding that diminished
only as supply increased in the mid-1920s (Table 2, and see also Chapter
2, Table 3). Postwar inflation also proved troublesome for some new
home owners struggling to meet their mortgage payments. Between
1923 and 1925, 18 per cent of the 153 residences built under the
government-sponsored Better Housing Scheme were sold to new owners
or quitclaimed when prices suddenly fell after the inflationary peak of
1919-22.[45] Owners' equity vanished, and rented quarters of the same
quality became available at rates cheaper than mortgage payments
contracted a few years previously.[46]

Table 2

**Summary of building permits for all new construction
in Vancouver, 1902-24**

Year	Permits	Year	Permits
1902	417	1914	1,314
1903	580	1915	615
1904	836	1916	444
1905	940	1917	561
1906	1,006	1918	829
1907	1,772	1919	1,233
1908	1,697	1920*	1,767 (338 dwellings)
1909	2,052	1921	2,451 (639 dwellings)
1910	2,260	1922	2,520 (644 dwellings)
1911	2,775	1923	2,183 (407 dwellings)
1912	3,221	1924	2,628 (639 dwellings)
1913	2,020		

* In 1920, the City began to summarize the number of permits issued for new dwellings.
See Table 3.
Source: City of Vancouver, *Financial Statements and Annual Reports, 1924*, 101.

In 1929, Vancouver was not an idyllic urban landscape for all its
citizens. Although its housing problems did not rival those of New York,
Chicago, London, and Glasgow, or even Toronto and Montreal,[47] the
long-term burden of sheltering low-income households in the core area
and the occasional difficulty of accommodating middle- and working-

class families in suburban districts already commanded the attention of local activists.

Although Holdsworth has stated that 'little reform rhetoric' regarding housing existed in Vancouver before the 1930s depression, some activity on the part of city bureaucrats, planners, and local community groups did in fact occur. Furthermore, several institutions and associations had developed the organizational skills necessary to undertake the improvement of society in many areas, including housing. In addition, between 1919 and 1923, the City of Vancouver and the municipalities of South Vancouver and Point Grey implemented the federally initiated and assisted Better Housing Scheme for the construction of veterans' homes.

Early in Vancouver's history, health department officials became seriously concerned about housing conditions in the downtown area and suggested rectifying them through better regulation. By 1895, the department had employed Robert Marrion, a master plumber, whose duties included lodging-house inspections.[48] Nine years later, the city decided to professionalize the department by appointing Dr. Frederick T. Underhill, who had been trained in Edinburgh in both medicine and public health, as its first full-time medical health officer.

Underhill directed a campaign to improve Vancouver's public health, including the regulation of rental accommodation. In 1911, under his guidance, the city created the position of lodging-house and restaurant inspector. The department vigorously inspected and licensed lodgings, condemned and demolished buildings deemed unfit for human habitation, and investigated cabins in the east end area. Underhill himself urged a single, consolidated model bylaw for housing and planning throughout British Columbia. He intended that the bylaw should apply to rental accommodation of all types, provide for the proper installation of gas fixtures, and contain a clause to ease demolition procedures.[49] In 1913, the provincial secretary, Dr. H.E. Young, asked Underhill to draft a concise bylaw, but the outbreak of the First World War terminated this undertaking.[50] The trades and licence inspector for the City of Vancouver took over supervision of the lodging-house and restaurant inspector's position in 1914, but returned it to the health department in 1931. During those seventeen years, the department maintained its interest in housing conditions; it prepared three surveys of overcrowding in the downtown area and one report about the use of dumbbell design in hotels and lodging houses.

Those involved in efforts to plan Vancouver in the 1920s played an important role as guardians of the suburban single-family dwelling. The Vancouver Board of Trade, founded in 1887 to promote trade and development, acted as the instrument of the city's business and professional elite in obtaining the 1925 town planning legislation under which both Vancouver and Point Grey set up town planning commissions.[51] The outcome of these efforts was the 1929 master plan for Vancouver, Point Grey, and South Vancouver proposed by Harland Bartholomew and Associates. The plan recommended using the 1928 Vancouver zoning bylaw as a model in establishing zoning to protect the amalgamated city's suburbs from downtown blight.[52]

The planning exercise involved several individuals who later became prominent in the housing debate of the 1930s and 1940s. J. Alexander Walker, a civil engineer educated at the University of Toronto, acted as engineer and secretary to Vancouver's town planning commission between 1926 and 1952. Walker helped to establish the Vancouver branch of the Town Planning Institute of Canada (TPIC), drafted the 1928 zoning bylaw, and acted as a consultant in the preparation of the 1929 South Vancouver plan. George L. Thornton Sharp, an architect with Sharp and Thompson who was active with the Vancouver TPIC and the Architectural Institute of British Columbia, served on both the Vancouver and the Point Grey town planning commissions. Frank E. Buck, a horticulturalist from McGill and Cornell universities and later a faculty member at the University of British Columbia, conceived an interest in planning when he worked in Ottawa for the federal government. He sat first on Point Grey's town planning commission and eventually on the Vancouver commission. Dorothy Gretchen Steeves, who took a law degree in Holland before coming to Vancouver as a war bride in 1919, also occupied a seat on the Point Grey commission.[53] In the next two decades, Steeves became a well-known housing activist as a member of the CCF; Buck played an important part in drafting the 1937 Vancouver housing survey; Sharp designed plans for an unexecuted public housing project at Trout Lake; and Walker, representing the town planning commission, acted as an adviser to city council on housing matters for many years.

Local organizations also began to take some interest in housing issues before the Depression. Prompted by an Ottawa official in 1913 to cooperate in ensuring 'properly built [i.e., sanitary and uncrowded] houses,' the Vancouver Council of Women pressed the city to resolve housing problems before they grew any larger. The council urged its national organization to investigate the accommodation of urban 'masses of people' and to lobby for legislation regulating apartment and lodging construction.[54] A year later, the Vancouver council addressed a resolution to the provincial government and the civic health committee calling for residential design that would incorporate sufficient light and surrounding open space. In addition, during the period of economic readjustment following the First World War, numerous groups and individual veterans kept up a constant pressure on municipal governments in Vancouver and South Vancouver and on the federal government for additional veterans' homes and, in particular, more Better Housing Scheme units.[55] The British Columbia Mainland United Soldiers, the Vancouver branch of the Grand Army United Veterans, the Amputation Club of British Columbia, and the Great War Veterans' Association of Canada and its women's auxiliary were all involved in this effort. Finally, the Vancouver Trades and Labour Council and the University Club of Vancouver both sent telegrams in 1921 to Prime Minister Arthur Meighen advocating expansion of the national housing program.[56]

Not unexpectedly, city officials, planners, and community organizations kept in touch with the broader housing reform movement. Having emigrated from Britain to Vancouver, Underhill was aware of the 'gross errors' that had been made in accommodating Europeans. He communicated with the Commission of Conservation medical health officer, Dr. Charles A. Hodgetts, who had an interest in the housing problem. He also knew the work of Lawrence Veiller on New York City's slums.[57] As well, the initiators of the planning process in Vancouver felt the impact of the Commission of Conservation through the frequent visits of its internationally respected town planning adviser, Thomas Adams, following his appointment in 1914.[58] At the time, Adams was perhaps the country's most qualified authority on housing matters. He advised the federal government on its post-First World War program to direct and fund the Better Housing Scheme undertaken in Vancouver, South Vancouver, and Point Grey. Finally, groups such as the Local Council of Women (LCW) and the Great War Veterans' Association of Canada had links with national executives that responded to accommodation problems on a country-wide basis.[59]

By 1929, many groups in the community stood ready to take up the housing cause: the Vancouver Trades and Labour Council, founded in 1889; the various socialist and labourist political parties, established from the 1890s on; the Communist Party of Canada (CPC), constituted in the 1920s; the Family Welfare Bureau of Greater Vancouver, organized in the late 1920s; the east end social services programs of First United Church, set up after 1914-16 by the First Presbyterian and Central Methodist churches; and the University Women's Club and New Era League, started in 1907 and 1916.[60] In addition, several individuals were poised to become vocal promoters of social housing as elected members of the CCF at all three governmental levels: Helena Gutteridge, the indefatigable suffragist and trade unionist; Angus MacInnis, the socialist representative of labour on city council; and Laura Jamieson, the juvenile court judge and another energetic clubwoman.[61] At the same time, the groups that organized the various branches of the housing industry and eventually opposed the housing activists had also formed. These included the Builders' Exchange, the local branch of the Dominion Mortgage and Investments Association, the Lumbermen's Association, the Real Estate Exchange, and the Associated Property Owners.[62] Whether critics or advocates, all these groups played roles in the future struggle over social housing.

The major reform effort in pre-1929 Vancouver was the Better Housing Scheme. Dwellings built under this market housing scheme represented the city's portion of a federal program designed to respond to the post-First World War housing problem. An acute accommodation shortage was brought on by the cessation of building operations during the war and the return from overseas of soldiers eager to re-establish themselves and their families in civilian life. This shortage prompted proposals for state action from members of parliament, Ontario government members, labour, and organizations such as the Great War Veterans' Association, the Canadian Manufacturers' Association, and the Toronto Board of Trade.[63] In July 1918, the Ontario government set up a scheme under which it made loans to municipalities to be used as mortgage money for individual home buyers. Later that year, Ontario and the federal government negotiated a program of federal loans for the provincial scheme. When the issue of housing congestion arose at the Dominion Provincial Conference in Ottawa in November, Acting Prime Minister and Minister of Finance Sir Thomas White offered to make such loans available to all provincial governments.[64]

The federal government next devised the machinery needed to implement a housing program. An order-in-council in December 1918 authorized the disbursement of $25 million to the provinces under the War Measures Act, to be apportioned by population size.[65] The allotment took the form of a twenty-year loan at 5 per cent annual interest, secured in provincial bonds or debentures. The federal government expected each province to negotiate an agreement for a housing scheme financed by the loan.

A subsequent order-in-council established a Cabinet committee to determine the nature and the objectives of the program.[66] Chaired by N.W. Rowell, president of the Privy Council, the committee included G.D. Robertson, the minister of labour, A.K. Maclean, the vice-chairman of the Reconstruction and Development Committee of Canada, and T.A. Crerar, the minister of agriculture. Thomas Adams acted as adviser and largely drafted the housing plan. The committee also worked with representatives of the Ontario scheme to define federal and provincial responsibilities.

According to the committee report of February 1919, the program objectives were to relieve shortages through construction, to give working people, especially veterans, the opportunity to own homes at a fair price, and to promote community health and well-being through planning and housing projects. Under the program, a province had to submit for federal approval a proposal explaining the guidelines for local schemes. Federal regulations permitted the maximum cost of houses to range between $3,000 and $4,500, depending on size and building material, and allowed the land to be owned by province or municipality, limited dividend societies or companies, or individual home owners. The committee strongly recommended using large sites for 'good planning and economy,' limiting loans to purchasers or renters with incomes below $3,000, and imposing minimum standards of services, space, and sanitation. Ottawa made the expertise of Thomas Adams available to the provinces. In October 1919, Adams and the administration of the program moved from the Cabinet committee to the newly created housing branch of the federal Department of Health.

In addition to their stated objectives, those who supported, approved, and fashioned the federal housing program appear to have had a less visible motive. Sir Thomas White, who was at first cool to the proposed scheme, eventually offered loans for housing to the provinces because he expected that residential construction would contribute to post-war social stability.[67] In May and June of 1919, the Winnipeg General Strike and the strikes accompanying it elsewhere in the country made clear to all governments the importance of implementing the program. The June 1919 report of the Royal Commission of Industrial Relations, prepared by the Honourable Chief Justice T.G. Mathers of Manitoba, stressed that insufficient and poor housing represented one of the chief causes of industrial unrest across Canada.[68] For the same reason, the program received strong support from the National Industrial Conference, from business in general, and from labour and veterans. Thus, the execution of the program in the turbulent context of 1919 may be seen as insurance against social unrest, much like the contemporary British 'homes fit for heroes' program.[69]

The federal housing program of 1919-23 stimulated the construction of 6,244 dwellings in 179 municipalities scattered across all provinces except Alberta and Saskatchewan.[70] Ontario passed enabling legislation in 1919 and quickly put its scheme into operation under a Bureau of Municipal Affairs housing branch. Its eligibility requirements tended to favour veterans who were provincial residents of modest means. Municipalities appointed housing commissions to administer local projects. While the Quebec scheme offered no preference for ex-servicemen, other provinces, including British Columbia, followed the Ontario model.

As in Britain, federal interest in the program faded after 1919, as the economy slumped and the threat of social disorder declined.[71] At first, the government reduced the size of the Department of Health's housing branch. Despite an additional advance of money in 1920-1 under pressure from veterans, provincial and municipal governments, boards of trade, labour, businesses, and community groups, the federal government then discontinued funding in the fiscal year 1923-4. A.E. Jones has offered two further reasons for the abandonment of the program. First, the government viewed the program as a temporary solution to a temporary problem, rather than the beginning of permanent involvement. Housing remained the responsibility of provincial and municipal governments and, in particular, the private sector. Second, the political context of the program changed as sympathetic politicians such as N.W. Rowell, T.A. Crerar, and A.K. Maclean left the scene and other, lukewarm ones such as Arthur Meighen and William Lyon Mackenzie King arrived.

British Columbia was one of the first provinces to participate in the federal housing program. Its Better Housing Act received royal assent on 29 March 1919.[72] This legislation enabled the provincial government to borrow federal money using debentures as security and to lend funds to municipalities at 5 per cent annual interest repayable in twenty years. The act also allowed municipalities to make available sums of money to soldiers for housing. Any agreement or contract made under the legislation had to include a fair wage clause. The provincial Department of Lands assumed administrative responsibility for the act. British Columbia promptly submitted a proposal to the federal committee and Thomas Adams, and on May Day, 1919, Cabinet approved the Better Housing Scheme.[73] The province then applied for a $1,500,000 loan and issued debentures as security for advances. Eventually, additional funding pushed the total loan to $1,701,500. British Columbia was the only province to spend its entire allotment.[74]

In the spring of 1919, Vancouver experienced serious housing congestion, characterized by rising rents, diminishing vacancies, and doubling up. The wartime construction slow-down, veterans' new families, the migration of Prairie people to the West Coast (especially during winter), and the problem of material shortages, rising costs, and severe unemployment in the building trades produced the crisis.[75] The City of Vancouver was therefore eager to share in the Better Housing Scheme. It set up a special committee to work out details for a civic proposal, and in May it contracted an agreement with the BC government. The city borrowed $300,000 from the province, repayable in twenty years at 5 per cent annual interest, and issued debentures as security for the loan. The agreement included a fair wage clause and a preference for employing ex-servicemen, and it gave priority to soldiers or their families in obtaining loans or purchasing dwellings. It also made a $300 rebate available if families remained in their houses for ten years. The scheme provided for detached dwellings of frame, stucco on frame, or brick veneer, complying with municipal building bylaws and costing $3,000 maximum for four to five rooms or $4,500 maximum for six to seven rooms. It also allowed the province, the city, or an individual to own the site of a house.

The special civic committee did not obtain all of its objectives in negotiations.[76] Significantly, in terms of subsequent developments, it could not convince the province to make guarantees against losses in the scheme. Minister of Lands Duff Pattullo argued that the federal government had similarly declined to assume liability against loss for the provinces and that the city should share equal responsibility with British Columbia for the Vancouver project. As well, the committee unsuccessfully pressed the province to set up a central administration to direct the entire Better Housing Scheme in the interests of continuity and economy. Some committee members also believed that the Vancouver proposal should have gone to the voters in the form of a plebiscite before implementation.

The City of Vancouver set up an administrative committee consisting of three council members and three civic officials, and formulated a series of rules to guide the execution of the scheme.[77] An allotment subcommittee accepted applications and $10 fees from individual citizens, all of whom were investigated by the Civic Employment Bureau. No applicant received consideration unless she or he had been domiciled for at least six months prior to enlistment for overseas service and had an income of under $3,000. Top priority went to widows of soldiers and disabled veterans burdened with dependants and few material resources. The city building inspector, who sat on the administrative committee, played an important role in the scheme. He approved plans and specifications for all houses, and supervised the tenders and contracts for construction, the expenditures and progress estimates of the contractors, and the erection of every dwelling. City council itself approved all loans and extended written permission to owners to sublet, vacate, or transfer houses.

The municipalities of Point Grey and South Vancouver also entered into agreements with the provincial government under the Better Housing Scheme. By February 1920, the allotments amounted to $54,000 for Point Grey and $65,000 for South Vancouver, and a year later they had increased to $94,000 and $90,000 respectively.[78] (After amalgamation in 1929, the City of Vancouver assumed responsibility for the homes erected by the Point Grey and South Vancouver municipalities.) In 1919, the provincial Department of Lands purchased fifty lots from South Vancouver municipality between 47th and 49th avenues near Fraser Street (Figure 1). It combined several lots into 50' x 120' 'homesites' and built ten soldiers' houses costing a maximum $2,500 each and following plans drawn up by the provincial architect (Figure 6).[79] The province continued to administer this housing even after the South Vancouver municipality itself decided to participate in the scheme and to set up a housing commission composed of representatives from various veterans' groups.[80]

Over the years, various critics have offered negative assessments of the 1919 federal program. The 1935 report of a special parliamentary committee on housing presented a bleak picture of mismanagement, loss of owners' equity, and poor construction. According to one witness, the Ottawa scheme, which comprised 29 houses on city lots and 142 in the Adams-designed community of Lindenlea, represented 'a hopeless mess' and 'a gross failure.'[81] Incompetent administration led to embezzlement and mishandling of funds, substandard construction and thus vacant houses, and additional city funding to cover tax and mortgage arrears and extra building costs. In Winnipeg, better control by city

Figure 6 In 1919, this Better Housing Scheme home on Windsor Street, South Vancouver, was built in the Dutch colonial style under supervising architect Henry Whittaker of the British Columbia Department of Lands.

council produced 712 units of superior quality and a small surplus. As inflation came and went in the postwar period, many owners across the country, who had bought houses when prices peaked, lost their equity when values declined and faced foreclosure when they could not meet their mortgage payments. Three studies of the 1930s and 1940s – the housing monograph of the 1931 census, the final report of the housing and community planning subcommittee of the federal advisory committee on reconstruction, and A.E. Grauer's housing study written for the Royal Commission on Dominion-Provincial Relations – repeated the theme of mismanagement.[82]

More recent evaluations are even less flattering than the older ones, but for different reasons. Applying the objectives of the program itself, A.E. Jones charged that the scheme was too limited in scope to relieve congestion, that it did not systematically favour low-income people, and that it failed completely as a demonstration of good planning and housing principles.[83] In his biography of Thomas Adams, Michael Simpson characterized the federal program as short-term and market oriented; its aim was to diffuse social unrest, stimulate the private sector, and generate employment without sounding too collectivistic.[84] The housing never reached those of lowest income, who most desperately needed it. Simpson mentioned other difficulties with the program: projects did not fulfil the standards set by Adams; no government surveyed actual accommodation needs at the municipal level; funding represented a token sum; some provinces did not participate; and regulations excluded rural housing. Simpson, too, called the program 'a dismal failure.'

More recently, Michael Doucet and John Weaver have examined the program within the context of government intervention in the mortgage market.[85] In their minds, the plan's major 'blunder' was to offer high ratio loans, that is, low downpayment and high monthly installment mortgages, without insuring repayment. Inevitably, many buyers were foreclosed either when the housing market weakened after the post-First World War inflationary period or during the 1930s depression. Thus, Doucet and Weaver argue that the plan offered significant lessons to government in subsequent innovations in mortgage lending.

An analysis of the operation of Vancouver's Better Housing Scheme confirms general impressions of this nation-wide program but also offers new perspectives. The scheme never signified a model housing or planning project to Vancouverites. Rather, since the houses consisted of detached dwellings on city lots, they conformed to the city's unplanned suburban development patterns and to its predilection for bungalow styles (Figure 7). Even supervising architect Henry Whittaker missed the opportunity to design a garden suburb for the bungalows and Dutch colonial houses built by the Department of Lands (Figure 6).

The Better Housing Scheme had very little impact as an instrument of social control. It built or added to only 153 houses in Vancouver, Point Grey, and South Vancouver.[86] Furthermore, the scheme proved itself a poor stimulus to the economy and employment, since contractors were reluctant to tender for houses.[87] They resisted depositing 10 per cent of the contract value as security when they could use it to better advantage in other ways, and they were loath to bid for small houses.

More importantly, the scheme failed to reach people of low income living downtown in congested conditions like those described in the 1920 housing survey.[88] Only one house was located in the core area. The remainder were situated in suburban areas, about 60 per cent on the east side and 40 per cent on the west side of the amalgamated city.[89] In addition, the allotment subcommittee gave the housing only to those applicants with the financial ability to repay their loans. Blue- and white-collar workers with up to $3,000 yearly income made up almost 80 per cent of mortgagors between 1919 and 1929. Some level of

Figure 7 In 1920, this house on West 13th Avenue in Kitsilano was built for about $3,500 under the City of Vancouver's Better Housing Scheme. A bakery employee, a plasterer, and a carpenter successively owned the California bungalow-style home. In 1942, the carpenter still owed the city $660 on the mortgage.

government employed about 30 per cent of mortgagors in those years, and professionals, business people, and agricultural workers accounted for about 20 per cent of those who held mortgages.[90] In 1919-23, only eleven mortgagors were female; they appear to have been soldiers' widows. The value of about three-quarters of the east-side loans fell short of $3,000, while about three-quarters of those on the west side exceeded $3,000.

The city government and community groups had no input into the design of the overall program. Federal and provincial bureaucrats apparently never consulted civic officials such as Underhill, who had extensive knowledge of local housing conditions. Not surprisingly, assistance went to moderate-income households rather than low-income ones. Moreover, the scheme's organizers at every level ignored groups outside government that might have offered sound advice, excepting veterans' organizations. The women's department of the Canadian Reconstruction Association, for example, which quickly became aware of the omission of women from any housing commission set up by May 1919, suggested that recommendations from women be sent either directly to the federal government or indirectly under its auspices.[91] Vancouver city council similarly ignored the women's department of the local reconstruction league.[92]

Finally, the administrative and financial structure of the federal program and the Better Housing Scheme created great problems in both the short- and the long-term for the City of Vancouver. The senior governments expected municipalities to carry the burden of executing the program. In Vancouver, the city had to hire extra staff to assist the building inspector, who carefully supervised all contractors' work in order to prevent shoddy construction or financial liability on the part of the taxpayers.[93] As well, the city comptroller and finance department officials had to assume the heavy responsibility for allotment and administration when the load became too cumbersome for a special civic committee.[94] Eventually, they also directed the Point Grey and South Vancouver schemes. Whatever the pressures on city staff, Vancouver, like Winnipeg, never experienced any hint of mismanagement of funds.

The greatest difficulty with the Better Housing Scheme in Vancouver emerged from its financial structure. As Weaver and Doucet point out, uninsured high ratio mortgage lending elsewhere in the national plan was based on small downpayments and large monthly installments. By contrast, the Vancouver scheme, which was also uninsured, offered more varied arrangements. The downpayment on a $4,900 Point Grey house with lot might be $50, with monthly payments of $30. On the east side, a downpayment for a $2,380 house including lot could be $52, with a monthly charge of $14.[95] Still, as elsewhere in Canada, the chain of lending arrangements too easily broke down during a weak economy. If an individual home owner failed to meet his or her obligations, the house reverted to the city, which then had to subsidize arrears in taxes and mortgage, rent or sell the unit, and pay off the provincial loan.

The scheme worked reasonably well in the 1920s with the exception of the three years following the postwar inflationary peak, when owners' equity vanished and high monthly installments often remained. Yet although the records show forty-five transfers to new owners between 1923 and 1926, they reveal only three quitclaims and no foreclosures for the entire decade. The real problem arose during the Depression, when many more mortgagors could not meet their house payments and taxes and when the City of Vancouver could not repay the BC government. The Better Housing Scheme thus left a terrible legacy to the social housing movement that grew up in the late 1930s. By then, city council was struggling with the consequences of the scheme's financial organization without any federal or provincial support. It therefore distrusted any nationally initiated public housing proposal in which the city might have to bear unwanted costs.

Yet in a more positive sense, the story of the Better Housing Scheme and the actions of city bureaucrats, planners, and community organizations attest to the emergence of housing reform before 1929 in Vancouver. Although local groups were not instrumental in the introduction of Better Housing, they were successful in pressing the three levels of government to continue the program longer than originally planned. As well, civic officials, professionals, and labour, veterans', and women's organizations had already started the work of ameliorating the housing problem in Vancouver. Indeed, they laid the groundwork for the more mature social housing movement of the following decades.

2

'Slum Dwellings': The Housing Problem in the 1930s

In Vancouver in the 1930s, 'the central housing issue of the day' was 'the inability of many urban residents to afford adequate housing.'[1] Contemporary surveys of Toronto, Montreal, Winnipeg, and Halifax attributed deplorable residential conditions to 'the inability of the lowest wage earners to pay rents sufficiently high to obtain adequate housing accommodation.'[2] By 1939, Vancouver's social activists also blamed 'slum growth' upon 'a chronic shortage of low rental housing.'[3] These early studies concentrated upon the predicament of the low-income tenant household and overlooked the plight of the homeless single unemployed and the jobless home owner. To define Vancouver's problem with accuracy and depth, it is thus necessary to investigate the availability, affordability, and quality of shelter for transients without means and for renters and home owners of reduced earnings. By the 1930s, the problem represented, on the one hand, a continuing scarcity of low-cost accommodation located in the downtown area and, on the other hand, a short-term crisis in housing for working- and middle-class households acutely affected by the Depression.

In his inaugural address in January 1930, Mayor W.H. Malkin looked forward to 'a year of activity and prosperity for Vancouver.'[4] He expected building permits for all types of construction to total about $50 million. With the erection over the previous year of a few towers (such as the present Hotel Vancouver), several new apartment buildings, and many houses, real estate appeared healthy. Then construction of dwellings plummeted. By 1933 and 1934, it had ground almost to a halt; the city licence department issued only 199 and 190 building permits for new residences (Table 3). Conditions improved very slowly through the rest of the decade. Permit issues reached 1930 levels again only in 1940. The

Table 3

Summary of building permits for dwellings in Vancouver, 1920-55

	New		Alterations	
	Permits	Value ($)	Permits	Value ($)
1920	338	1,039,744	1,268	690,245
1921	639	1,550,280	429	169,030
1922	644	1,550,810	516	178,037
1923	407	1,068,900	412	150,811
1924	639	1,585,475	444	153,585
1925	855	2,243,850	533	177,745
1926	1,051	2,695,110	538	181,195
1927	1,188	3,179,125	538	169,317
1928	1,074	2,904,184	532	176,474
1929	1,964	6,665,250	1,009	396,405
1930	1,579	4,978,625	1,231	330,497
1931	1,298	3,868,760	1,046	240,255
1932	402	992,950	687	171,710
1933	199	440,000	467	96,317
1934	190	460,000	497	128,027
1935	285	750,000	560	143,445
1936	559	1,604,800	704	188,945
1937	862	2,515,155	865	253,295
1938	1,197	3,418,535	869	229,565
1939	1,042	2,819,575	789	228,609
1940	1,552	4,263,720	907	274,155
1941	2,130	6,168,375	868	250,960
1942	1,028	2,665,165	784	244,575
1943	1,042	2,596,495	1,294	294,070
1944	2,487	8,121,970	1,334	447,053
1945	2,687	10,087,305	1,743	636,710
1946	3,307	14,555,950	1,454	741,740
1947	2,128	10,022,500	1,623	876,100
1948	3,367	18,469,230	1,417	826,340
1949	2,180	13,369,240	1,598	874,145
1950	1,781	11,919,360	1,377	854,740
1951	1,092	8,236,710	1,165	891,890
1952	1,737	13,449,848	1,215	863,270
1953	1,443	11,399,100	3,103	1,123,338
1954	1,125	9,415,450	2,996	1,137,785
1955	1,083	10,533,300	1,337	965,905

Sources: City of Vancouver, *Financial Statements and Annual Reports*, 1920-36; City of Vancouver Archives, Records of the Department of Permits and Licenses, Building Department, Building Reports, 1929-56, 125-A-1, files 2-5.

yearly licensing of contractors and real estate dealers followed a parallel pattern of sudden reduction and gradual expansion (Table 4).

Table 4

Business licences for contractors, real estate dealers, and operators of apartment and lodging houses, Vancouver, 1930-7

	Contractors	Real estate dealers	Apartments, flats	Lodging houses, hotels
1930	572	177	745	404
1931	470	154	809	652
1932	174	138	877	1,125
1933	113	128	905	587
1934	88	120	818	664
1935	131	148	902	1,406
1936	166	125	921	1,585
1937	269	183	1,267	1,678

Source: City of Vancouver Archives, Records of the Department of Permits and Licenses, Business License Registers, 126-B-13 (1930), 126-B-15 (1931), 126-C-2 (1932), 126-C-4 (1933), 126-C-6 (1934), 127-G-1 (1935), and 127-G-2 (1936-7).

The number of new dwellings in Vancouver increased by less than 10,000 from 1931 to 1941. Although the 1941 census reported 10,586 additional sets of living quarters over the 1931 census, building permit records showed an increase of 9,716 homes. Federal market housing legislation contributed 2,711 of these units between 1938 and 1941.[5] By contrast, the number of permits granted for 1921-31 and 1941-51 amounted to 11,338 and 23,229 respectively. In 1937, the city council's special housing committee estimated that the Depression had produced a backlog of about 6,000 houses.[6]

As the house-building industry lagged, population growth inched upwards. The numbers of marriages and births dropped in the early 1930s before climbing later in the decade, while in general the number of deaths continued to advance slightly (see Chapter 4, Table 14).[7] At the same time, migration to British Columbia, particularly from drought-stricken Prairie provinces like Saskatchewan, contributed to a population increase.[8] The population of Vancouver rose from 240,421 in 1929 to 269,454 in 1939.[9]

Vacancies expanded and contracted with the economy. According to surveys prepared by H.A. Roberts Limited, apartment house vacancy rates were probably 10 per cent or higher in the worst years of the

Depression, when many households crowded into cheaper accommodation.[10] These rates exceeded the national average of 6.7 per cent in 1933,[11] but diminished after 1935 as the local economy improved slightly and the population began to grow again. By the outbreak of the Second World War, occupancy of houses and suites was almost 100 per cent.[12] Thus, until the very end of the decade, availability alone was not the major housing problem. Nonetheless, the full occupancy rate of 1939 – resulting from an earlier lapse in construction, a swelling population, and better economic conditions – created a troublesome legacy for Vancouver's residents in the 1940s.

Early in the Depression, a civic relief officer reported the 'hopeless condition' of several unemployed single loggers of Swedish and Finnish origin who occupied an upper floor of a Cordova Street hotel.[13] They were 'honest and hard working' men eager 'to earn a living and pay their debts.' Lagging far behind with payments, they did without food, sold off their clothing, and expected to be evicted at any moment. Another officer investigating the relief cases of unemployed married couples in South Vancouver described their 'brave fight to overcome their distressing circumstances' and their 'equally hard fight to keep up the standard of decency' in their 'nice homes' with 'well-kept gardens.'[14] How extensive, then, was unemployment in Vancouver during the Depression, and how did loss of income affect the affordability of housing for transient single men, tenant households, and property owners?

Available statistics provide an imprecise reckoning of the city's unemployment. On 1 June 1931, census takers found 25,042 (or 30.2 per cent) of wage earners aged twenty and over of both sexes without either a permanent or a temporary job.[15] The next complete enumeration of the jobless did not occur until the 1941 census. Still, according to the average annual unemployment rates for Canada, conditions worsened in 1932 and 1933 and then meliorated between 1934 and 1939.[16] The national rates probably remained below those in a city such as Vancouver, where the transient single unemployed gathered.[17] The 1931 census also confirms the impact of the Depression upon Vancouver's building industry: in 1930-1, 77 per cent of male construction workers aged ten and over lost work time.[18]

Other statistics suggest the magnitude of the unemployment problem. The Employment Service of Canada listed 25,643 jobless persons in the City of Vancouver for the nine months prior to 30 April 1932.[19] A total of 22,515 registrations for unemployment and relief occurred over eleven months in 1931-2.[20] In May 1934, Vancouver had 7,455 and 1,116 unemployment relief cases respectively of domiciled residents and of transient families and single women, involving almost 31,000 dependents, and 9,098 single, homeless men. In addition, over 14,000 individuals, mostly on Vancouver's east side, relied upon workers' compensation or mothers', old age, or war pensions. Still other figures for cases of civic relief indicate the extent of unemployment in Vancouver over several years (Table 5). Their sudden fluctuations in volume reflect the movement of single men in and out of relief camps and the return to the city in 1938 of the administrative burden for welfare.

Table 5

Relief cases of the City of Vancouver Public Welfare and Relief Department, 31 December 1931 to 31 December 1938

	Indigent relief		Unemployment relief		
	Family, single women	Single men	Married men	Single men	Women
1931	807	646	2,588	4,664	175
1932	493	593	6,247	3,443	636
1933	250	566	7,062	85	496
1934	207	487	6,741	89	419
1935	301	439	6,574	84	433
1936	305	350	5,948	86	390
1937	423	264	4,884	67	373
1938	1,513	1,604	4,719	1,955	181

Source: City of Vancouver Archives, Records of the Mayor's Office, 33-F-1, Relief file [Report of the Social Services Committee, 1938], 3 January 1939.

Personal income and rents rose and fell with employment in Vancouver according to national patterns.[21] In 1933, employment and personal income declined across the country to their lowest levels in the decade. Rents reached bottom a year later, as landlords lagged behind in adjusting to economic dislocation (Table 6). Conditions improved somewhat later in the 1930s. In Vancouver, where personal income and employment followed the national example, average rents in the city plunged to a low in 1934-5 and then moved upwards during the 1936 Golden Jubilee celebrations (Table 7).[22]

The most visible unemployed group in the community was the 'floating population' of jobless and homeless single men who wandered

Table 6

Unemployment, personal income, and rental costs in Canada, 1926-40

	Civilian jobless seeking work (thousands)	Personal income (millions)	Rent component of the cost-of-living index (1935 = 100)
1926	108	4,057	116.7
1927	67	4,281	115.3
1928	65	4,600	118.1
1929	116	4,665	120.5
1930	371	4,392	123.6
1931	481	3,669	120.2
1932	741	3,063	110.6
1933	826	2,840	99.3
1934	631	3,175	93.4
1935	625	3,398	94.0
1936	571	3,602	96.1
1937	411	4,070	99.7
1938	522	4,126	103.1
1939	529	4,350	103.8
1940	423	4,972	106.3

Source: F.H. Leacy, ed., *Historical Statistics of Canada*, 2nd ed. (Ottawa: Statistics Canada and Social Science Federation of Canada 1983), D132, F81, K4.

Table 7

Average rents in Vancouver and Canada (in dollars per month), December 1929 to December 1939

	6-room house with modern conveniences		6-room house with incomplete modern conveniences	
	Canada	Vancouver	Canada	Vancouver
1929	27.909	29.00	20.007	25.00
1930	28.280	29.00	20.164	25.00
1931	27.095	27.50	19.261	24.00
1932	23.950	23.50	15.850	20.00
1933	22.262	17.00-22.00	15.877	14.00-18.00
1934	22.174	15.00-22.00	15.900	13.00-17.00
1935	22.515	16.00-22.00	16.262	13.00-18.00
1936	23.083	20.00-25.00	16.769	15.00-20.00
1937	23.773	22.00-27.00	17.485	17.00-22.00
1938	24.197	22.00-27.00	17.800	17.00-22.00
1939	24.235	22.00-27.00	17.823	16.00-22.00

Source: *Labour Gazette*, 30-40 (January 1930-January 1940).

Figure 8 By the summer of 1931, 450 men lived in a jungle, or hobo camp, bordering Prior Street and the CNR yards. They built shacks from boxes, boards, and old cars found in the adjacent city dump.

in and out of Vancouver according to the season, work opportunities, relief conditions, and political protests about their predicament.[23] The city and private charities applied strategies developed in earlier years to cope with the high unemployment and the transiency. As it had in previous depressions, the civic public welfare and relief department distributed bed tickets worth 20 cents per day per individual for use in cheap hotels and lodging houses.[24] Still, hundreds of disheartened men, whom the hotels and lodgings could not accommodate, spent their days in pool rooms, department stores, libraries, streets, and railway stations and their nights in refuges, parks, and jungles, or hobo camps.[25]

By the summer of 1931, about 1,000 homeless men occupied four east end jungles (see Chapter 1, Figure 1).[26] The jungle bordering Prior Street close to Campbell Avenue and the Canadian National Railway (CNR) yards grew from under 100 men in late June to 450 by early September (Figure 8). Many were Swedes, Finns, and Norwegians normally employed in logging and other primary industries. Another jungle under the Georgia Viaduct attracted between 75 and 250 men over the summer of 1931. Although at least fifty of these men had problems with alcohol, the majority searched for work. A third jungle, located on National Harbour Board property near Dunlevy Avenue, accommodated about 200 young men generally 'of a good type.' Approximately 100 men inhabited shacks scattered around the fourth jungle, situated at the Great Northern Railway sidings.

In 1932, nine hostels, including the Central City Mission and the Vancouver Emergency Refuge, provided 1,033 beds to single unemployed men.[27] As well, they supplied facilities for personal hygiene, meals, and clothing and, in varying degrees, medical care, laundry, fumigation of bedding and clothing, and religious and educational programs. Funding came from church aid, per capita civic and provincial subsidies, Vancouver Welfare Foundation grants, and sometimes small charges to the men.

The burden for housing the transient, single unemployed men of Vancouver rested with the senior and local governments. Under the national relief legislation of 1931 and 1932, the provincial and federal governments assumed administrative responsibility for the men and shared financial costs equally.[28] As a result, thousands of transient homeless men went first to provincial road camps and later to Department of National Defence relief camps, including Point Grey Camp No. 200 on the UBC endowment lands.[29] By contrast, single unemployed residents of Vancouver received shelter vouchers through the city, funded with contributions from all three governments.[30] Men who quit the relief camps and returned to Vancouver did not qualify for bed tickets, although they frequently won temporary support for themselves through protests and demonstrations.[31] By the late 1930s, the BC government had turned over its administrative role in sheltering all the single unemployed to the civic social service department, with funding shared by the city and senior governments.[32] By then, single men and women who were indigent or unemployed received a monthly shelter allowance rather than a daily bed voucher.[33]

Unemployment and reduced income affected the affordability of rental housing for tenants as well as transients, although aggregate census figures suggest otherwise. Rented and owner-occupied units represented 49 and 51 per cent respectively of the total number of dwellings in the 1931 enumeration and 49.9 and 50.1 per cent in 1941 (Table 8).[34] Tenants made an average monthly rental payment of about $26 in both 1931 and 1941. By 1941, however, a greater proportion of tenant households, especially ones on relief, paid under $15 per month for their living quarters than did in 1931. As well, an expansion in the

Table 8

Owner-occupied dwellings in selected cities, 1931, 1941, and 1951, by percentage

	1931	1941	1951
Toronto	46.5	43.8	62.2
Hamilton	48.0	44.0	65.2
Winnipeg	47.0	43.9	53.0
Edmonton	53.0	46.3	61.3
Vancouver	51.0	50.1	63.0
Victoria	46.8	45.8	58.2

Sources: Canada, Advisory Committee on Reconstruction, Subcommittee on Housing and Community Planning [chaired by C.A. Curtis], *Final Report of the Subcommittee, March 24, 1944 (Ottawa: King's Printer 1946)*, 244, table 57; *Canada, Dominion Bureau of Statistics, Ninth Census of Canada, 1951*, vol. 3, *Housing and Families*, 7-2 and 7-3.

shelter allowance system, in the conversion of single houses into rooms and flats renting at low rates, in the occupancy of waterfront shacks and houseboats, and in the number of evictions attested to a heightened need for affordable housing.

The shelter allowance system grew rapidly during the Depression. In 1932, the civic public welfare and relief department handled perhaps 1,100 cases per month.[35] By April 1936, it dealt with more than four times that number every month (Table 9). Still, although close to two-thirds of tenants on relief sought rental assistance, less than one-third of them received a weekly, biweekly, or monthly shelter allowance. Relief Officer W. Rupert Bone and the relief and employment committee of city council managed to reduce expenditures by delaying grants to clients until they remained on the welfare rolls for at least a month, built up large arrears, or faced eviction. This mean-spirited, shortsighted method of saving civic funds placed tremendous pressure on tenants and landlords alike. Landlords faced mounting deficits in managing rental accommodation and sometimes refused to accept a shelter allowance if it fell short of the requested rent. In addition, they cut off tenants' water supply, locked them out of their homes, and even withheld their belongings. As well, relief officials begrudged, or even refused to grant, allowances to families of activists such as relief camp striker Arthur 'Slim' Evans and the longshoremen of the 1935 Vancouver waterfront strike.[36]

Guided by the relief and employment committee and funded by contributions from all three governments, the public welfare and relief department provided a man, woman, and two children with about $8 for unfurnished or $11 for furnished accommodation per month.[37] The

Table 9

Relief tenants, classified according to rent, in Vancouver, 8 April 1936

Tenants in furnished units		Tenants in unfurnished units	
Cases	Monthly rent ($)	Cases	Monthly rent ($)
913*	8.00	640	5.00
486	9.00	745	6.00
24	10.00	12	7.00
224	11.00	1,045	7.50
44	12.00	304*	8.00
5	13.00		
2	14.00		
1	15.00		
1,699 (total)		2,746 (total)	

* These figures are approximate.
Source: City of Vancouver Archives, Records of the City Clerk, 16-E-7, file 17, W.R. Bone to Acting City Clerk, 4 May 1936.

shelter allowance scale, which gave slightly less money to a couple and somewhat more to a larger family, actually became less generous by the mid-1930s (Table 10). Occasionally, relief supplied assistance for fuel, electricity, water supply, furnishings, or appliance repairs. Clients received rent relief cheques upon producing a receipt from the landlord for the previous month's payment. To ensure delivery, a civic official wrote the landlord's name on the reverse side of the cheque. Because it did not wish to assume the role of legal tenant, the city refused to pay landlords directly or to place clients in dwellings. The main relief office

Table 10

Monthly shelter allowances (in dollars), City of Vancouver, effective September 1932 and January 1936

	Household size	Furnished unit	Unfurnished unit
1932	2 adults	9.00	5.00
	2 adults and one or more children	10.00-14.00	6.00-12.00
1936	2 adults	8.00	5.00
	2 adults and 1-7 children	9.00-14.00	6.00-8.00

Sources: City of Vancouver Archives, Records of the City Clerk, 15-F-1, file 4, W.R. Bone to L.D. Taylor, 21 September 1932; Records of the Mayor's Office, 33-C-6, Relief Department, 1936 file, Bone to A. Davison, 17 January 1936.

at 530 Cambie Street accepted applications for rent allowances and eventually distributed cheques through four subdepots in the South Vancouver, Collingwood, East Hastings, and Grandview areas. In 1936, the city adopted a standard cash relief system and issued monthly rather than weekly or biweekly rent cheques. Despite variations in the scale of payments, Vancouver's churlish shelter allowance program conformed to ones in other Canadian cities.

Single unemployed women also received rental assistance. Initially, the city issued bed tickets worth 20 cents per day to between 175 and 600 single women a year for use in housekeeping suites or rooms.[38] Because many respectable downtown lodging houses, hostels, and even the YWCA charged rates that were too high for relief recipients, many women lived in 'very unsatisfactory localities and associations.'[39] A hostel such as 'Dunromin,' which the Vancouver Police Women's division had opened as a relief refuge, soon sheltered prostitutes more than the unemployed.[40] By the late 1930s, the city gave single women a monthly rent allowance rather than bed tickets.

Single Asian men encountered blatant discrimination in the distribution of relief to the unemployed. Senior governments excluded them from camps because 'no special accommodation' was available to them.[41] As well, in an attempt to discourage applications for assistance, provincial government officials allocated bed tickets to Asians on a different scale of relief than to whites: Chinese men received vouchers worth 60 cents per week rather than 20 cents per day. They had no choice but to sleep in overcrowded, insanitary, and disease-infested 'dens.' Few Asians went on relief, most struggled to stay off it, and some met with refusals from the city in any case. The larger Chinese community cared for many destitute men on and off relief. In particular, the Yip family accommodated a great many old, indigent men in a building on Canton Alley leased from the city.

Although some low-income tenants may have rented small houses or apartments, others became lodgers. The 1931 census recorded 17,634 individuals and 3,363 families dwelling with other households in both owned and rented homes.[42] An increasing number of tenants, whether on relief or with reduced earnings, could not afford more expensive rental accommodation and turned to the cheaper lodging houses of the downtown area or to converted residences in neighbourhoods such as Kitsilano, Fairview, and Mount Pleasant, where rates were likely to be under $15 a week. Conversions occurred 'by force of circumstances,' as desperate owners remodelled their 'very good large houses' to generate sufficient income to keep their property.[43] A home owner whose husband's death in 1930 caused her 'to live altogether a changed life,' for example, raised a daughter, paid her taxes, and avoided relief by operating a lodging house in Kitsilano.[44]

In the 1930s, many operators and owners failed to apply for licences to alter or manage lodging houses, as they had been accustomed to do for several decades. They saved themselves fee payments to the city, and they installed appliances and undertook renovations at less cost. By 1940, Vancouver had 1,816 licensed lodging houses, but the number of unlicensed ones is unknown.[45] Contemporary observers used figures like 3,000 and 'thousands,' although the city's sanitary inspector reported fewer than a thousand inspections of unlicensed places in 1931. Moreover, the statistics for licensed lodging houses and hotels indicate that such premises frequently became unlicensed in the 1930s (Table 4). The number of business licenses rose in the first years of the Depression as rental accommodation expanded to absorb households with lower incomes.[46] Then, when the economic decline reached bottom in 1933-4, operators suddenly stopped purchasing licenses, only to take out licences once more as conditions improved somewhat after 1935.

The contradictions inherent in Vancouver's bylaws in the 1930s permitted a huge increase in house conversion to occur outside proper licensing practice. The 1928 zoning bylaw attempted to eliminate lodging houses in which individuals or families lived in a single room equipped with a gas plate and sink and shared toilet and bathing facilities with other tenants.[47] Yet a building bylaw allowed dwellings to be remodelled into lodging houses that provided no more than fifteen sleeping rooms for five or more persons and no cooking facilities. These houses usually offered illegally installed gas or electric plates or stoves in rooms since tenants could not afford to eat in restaurants and owners refused to supply board. City council did not pass a bylaw controlling the installation of gas appliances in rooming houses until 1938. The licence inspector also issued business permits without notifying the health officer, building inspector, or fire warden. Staff cutbacks at city hall in the 1930s meant that lodging houses were effectively unregulated.

Converted houses were widespread in the West End, the business district, and certain parts of Kitsilano and Mount Pleasant. In a 1934 survey of the West End, the Vancouver town planning commission noted the frequent renovation of large dwellings into suites and of smaller ones into sleeping or housekeeping rooms.[48] The commission reported 127 licensed apartment blocks, 83 licensed apartment houses converted from other buildings, and 550 lodging houses, of which only 155 had paid-up licences. A 1938 study detailed in map form the number of housekeeping rooms in parts of Kitsilano and Mount Pleasant. Another report in 1941 described the lodging situation in the West End and the business district. Here, the most congestion and the cheapest rentals occurred in the centre of the West End, between Jervis and Denman streets, and in the old Yaletown area, south of Helmcken and east of Burrard. Less crowding and higher rates typified lodging houses south of Davie and west of Burrard, where older residents sublet one or two floors. The better rooms lay west of Denman and around St. Paul's Hospital. Fairly dense housing extended north of Robson Street, with the higher quality dwellings near Georgia Street.

Other low-income people increasingly found shelter in the waterfront shacks and houseboats of the Fraser River, Burrard Inlet, and False Creek. Some, like the descendants of the original squatters in Stanley Park, lived on the shoreline by choice, but the majority were on the foreshore because they were unable to find suitable housing at affordable rents.[49] 'Shackers' were people 'of small means and of independent spirit' who survived the depression by fishing, by beachcombing and selling cut wood at the Main Street public market, or by collecting relief and small pensions.[50]

In 1937, a total of 538 people inhabited the waterfront.[51] On Burrard Inlet, 93 houseboats, 56 shacks on piles, and 10 more on land stretched from Coal Harbour to the Second Narrows and sheltered 239 adults and 54 children. Two years later, the number had climbed from 159 to 205 dwellings. In False Creek in 1937, 167 adults and 21 children occupied 108 boats on water and 18 shacks on land (Figure 9). Along the Fraser River from Main Street to Boundary Road, 62 shacks housed 117 adults and 50 children. A 1940 report showed that an enclave of 30 residences built largely in the 1930s over the Fraser or along its shoreline contained 26 households, 11 families, and 81 people ranging in age from one week to 91 years.

Throughout the Depression, reform-minded city officials threatened 'shackers' with removal, and landlords evicted large numbers of tenants from suites and rooms. Concerned about sewage and garbage disposal, water supply, petty crime, and fire hazards, the city attempted in 1937 to rid the Kitsilano Indian Reserve on False Creek of shacks, but their efforts resulted in a movement of foreshore people to the area east of

Figure 9 With a floathouse and a houseboat behind him, a 'shacker' saws driftwood on the False Creek shoreline. In 1934, earnings from selling the cut wood may have kept him off relief or supplemented his pension.

Burrard Bridge.[52] In 1938, the Parks Board cleared and 'beautified' the Windermere bathing pool area on Burrard Inlet. Tenants found themselves evicted because they had insufficient income to pay the rent or because their shelter allowances fell short of the amount demanded by the manager.[53] Frequently, a relief household that could not find living quarters at allowance rates remained shelterless for several days while the city put their belongings into storage. In early 1936, when rents rose dramatically during Vancouver's Golden Jubilee celebrations, the courts ejected forty-seven relief tenants. Nine evictions were pending, and in four cases the relief department had placed household goods in a local storage company. Rank discrimination sometimes determined the removal of relief recipients. In 1934, the sheriff ousted the wife and daughter of activist 'Slim' Evans from a house owned by a city alderman, William Tiss, who refused to accept the shelter allowance set by council.[54]

Although hard data are limited, they suggest that not only tenants but also many home owners encountered difficulty affording housing during the Depression. The near constancy of the statistics for home ownership given in the 1931 and 1941 censuses hides the struggle of many Vancouver residents, particularly wage earners, to keep possession of their property (Table 8). Although Vancouver wage earners received a lower average income than their counterparts in Toronto, Hamilton, or Winnipeg, for example, many had been able to purchase a house before the Depression because the proportion of lower valued dwellings was greater than in those other cities (Table 11). In fact, as many wage earners owned as rented in Vancouver.[55] In the 1930s, many owners found themselves with limited incomes as well as with taxes and mortgages on homes assessed or financed at pre-1929 levels. Civic records dealing with Better Housing Scheme defaults, tax arrears, 'work for taxes' schemes, and shelter allowances suggest the desperate predicament of many of the city's home owners.

Table 11

Home ownership in selected cities, 1931

	% of homes owned	% of homes valued less than $5,000	Average value of owned homes	Average annual earnings/ wage earner
Toronto	46.5	42.6	$6,500	$1,227
Hamilton	48.0	67.1	4,800	1,022
Winnipeg	47.0	64.4	5,000	1,120
Edmonton	53.0	82.0	3,400	1,097
Vancouver	51.0	77.7	4,100	947
Victoria	46.9	79.9	3,900	953

Source: Canada, Dominion Bureau of Statistics, *Seventh Census of Canada, 1931: Census Monograph no. 8, Housing in Canada*, prepared by Harold F. Greenway (Ottawa: King's Printer 1941), 117, 173-4, table 33.

The 1941 census figures for outstanding mortgages hide the difficulty that an unknown number of property owners in Vancouver must have had in paying off their debts. Although average payments on principal and interest were higher on the West Coast, 59 per cent of Vancouver's owner-occupied dwellings had no mortgage to pay off in 1941, compared to 40.5 per cent in Toronto, and the average outstanding loan amounted to several hundred dollars less.[56] Nevertheless, if the failure of the Better Housing Scheme in Vancouver is any indication, many white- and blue-collar Vancouverites were probably in arrears on their mortgages. According to a civic summary of the scheme's financial position, 29.8 per cent (45 of 151 properties) had reverted to the city by January 1937, and fifty agreement holders (33.1 per cent) were in arrears.[57] Completed agreements numbered twenty-seven (17.9 per cent), and twenty-nine holders had up-to-date payments. The total outstanding balance amounted to $229,084.59. Thirty-two quitclaims and seventeen foreclosures occurred in the 1930s, compared to three quitclaims and no foreclosures in the 1920s. In 1941-2, fifty-one agreement holders still continued to make payments.[58]

Although many Vancouverites owned their houses outright in the 1930s, some received insufficient income to pay the city's property taxes. Assessments remained at pre-Depression levels. Consequently, tax arrears rose from about $2,285 million in 1930 to $8,327 million in 1935, before dropping to $2,712 million in 1940 (Table 12). No breakdown for residential or improved property is available. Many properties of all types, particularly on the east side, reverted to the city after arrears mounted for a few years, and eventually ended up in tax sale. As a result, the total value of sale properties increased as well (Table 12). Since few people had sufficient capital to buy, most lots fell to the city, although owners had a redemption privilege within one or two years of sale. The total number of properties held by the city grew from about 17,600 in 1932 to over 31,000 in 1936, and fell to 28,000 in 1939.[59] A significant but unknown number of these properties were probably residential. When, in response to the crisis, the city suspended the 1934 and 1935 sales, it initiated a widely advertised tax consolidation scheme especially aimed at defaulting home owners. Brochures described the plan as 'a

Table 12

Value of tax arrears and tax sale properties (in dollars), City of Vancouver, 1930-40

	Tax arrears	Tax sale properties
1930	2,285,317	2,000,329
1931	3,105,028	2,028,107
1932	5,024,576	2,468,643
1933	6,871,636	2,587,088
1934	8,167,442	2,739,260
1935	8,327,141	2,631,385
1936	6,273,940	4,126,621
1937	5,947,985	4,043,261
1938	3,818,223	5,633,459
1939	3,290,572	5,595,257
1940	2,712,972	5,453,796

Source: City of Vancouver, *Financial Statements and Annual Reports, 1930-40.*

real "new deal" – one which gives the ordinary man a chance to rehabilitate himself as a citizen taxpayer.'[60]

Many home owners, including elderly ones, did all they could to hold onto their property. A seventy-six-year-old widow, 'a very fine type of old pioneer' according to a city official, owned a small cottage and several sheds 'all looking their age' on Victoria Drive.[61] She had no electricity and no water supply. The city overassessed her property at $100, and her tax arrears amounted to $640 plus interest. She borrowed money to pay her taxes and her husband's funeral expenses. Receiving a $15 monthly old age pension, she lived on one dollar and the product of ten hens and used the rest to pay off her debts. Another woman on West 14th Avenue, who owed $138 in tax arrears (and had no other debts), used up insurance money to keep her house and then tried to sell it 'at a great sacrifice' rather than lose it at tax sale.[62]

Between 1936 and 1939, the City of Vancouver sponsored 'work for taxes' schemes for delinquent owners not on relief but in danger of losing their homes at the next sale. Under these programs, successful applicants received manual work from the city worth up to a total of $60 at 50 cents an hour. In 1936, 427 persons applied to work off their taxes, and 318 received work orders.[63]

The application forms of those who participated in the 1937 'work for taxes' scheme reveal the conditions under which many people attempted to keep their property.[64] The majority of the successful 153 applicants were unemployed males with dependants, who lived east of Ontario Street, had blue-collar occupations, had resided in Vancouver since long before the Depression, and required less than $100 to prevent their property from going to the 1937 tax sale. Their property represented their life's work. Over half of them still carried mortgages held by private individuals, real estate, trust, loan, or insurance companies, banks, legal firms, or the CPR. Of these, many owed sizable amounts of principal and three months to eight years of interest. Still, whether they felt 'pressed' or 'not unduly pressed' by the mortgagees – who appear to have been remarkably lenient owing to the inactive housing market – all the mortgagors were faced with the loss of their homes in the 1937 tax sale. Some applicants also had other debts and medical bills. Many had resorted to relief at some time in the 1930s or had worked on the previous 'work for taxes' scheme. Most had incomes under $400, compared to the average annual earnings of Vancouver wage earners in 1931 of $947. In recent years, their sources of income had included temporary employment, wages of working family members, rents from stores, shacks, or land, pensions, relief payments, public works employment, work for taxes, odd jobs such as gardening or sewing, savings, superannuation, the sale of assets such as trucks or cars, and neighbours' help. The city rejected an additional ninety-four applicants who had already either lost property in the 1936 sale or consolidated their taxes, or who were on relief or physically unable to work.

While home owners qualified for food relief, they did not initially receive shelter allowances. According to the city solicitor, property owners could not be described as indigent or destitute under the statutory provisions for relief.[65] In 1935, a regulation of the unemployment relief branch of the BC Department of Labour granted the shelter allowance to home-owning relief recipients to assist in the payment of delinquent taxes and mortgage interest. City council, however, only made this concession to property owners after a year of public pressure.

In sum, many Vancouverites who experienced loss of employment and income during the Depression simply could not afford to rent lodgings or own property as they had previously done. Although dwellings were available until the end of the decade, they were too costly for anyone on little or no income.

Unsatisfactory living conditions flourished where the need for lower-priced homes was greatest. Although 1931 and 1941 census data indicate that the quality of Vancouver housing remained generally good in those years, they tend to hide the substandard rental accommodation situated in the downtown area between Stanley Park and Clark Drive and in some parts of Kitsilano, Fairview, and Mount Pleasant. Substandard conditions included overcrowding, inadequate or defective sanitary facilities, interior and exterior disrepair, and a variety of other problems such as insufficient light and ventilation or faulty gas fixtures. The censuses also ignore the predicament of shack dwellers in waterfront colonies and transient, single unemployed men who lived through force of circumstance in hostels, jungles, and camps.

Despite aggregate census figures that showed little overcrowding in Vancouver, many individual low-income renters of less expensive dwellings in the downtown area and its adjacent neighbourhoods experienced serious congestion. In the 1931 census, the average number of rooms per person was 1.3, and owners and tenants averaged 1.4 and 1.2 rooms per person.[66] Nevertheless, one-quarter of tenant households and 17 per cent of owning ones encountered overcrowding. If a renting household earned less than $800 annually, paid under $15 a month for rent, or consisted of two or more families, then it probably lived in congested circumstances. In 1941, as well, the city average of 1.4 rooms per person appeared favourable,[67] but 13.2 per cent of all households were crowded, and 8.5 per cent doubled up (Table 13). Anywhere from about one-fifth to one-third of wage-earning households in which the head earned under $1,500 averaged less than one room per person.[68]

Table 13

Housing conditions in selected cities, 1941, by percentage

	Doubled-up households	Overcrowded households	Dwellings needing external repairs	Dwellings with shared use of or without	
				Flush toilet	Bathtub/ shower
Toronto	19.1 (8.4)*	12.4	13.0	16.8	18.6
Hamilton	12.4 (7.8)	10.7	17.8	7.4	13.0
Winnipeg	15.1 (7.3)	19.0	21.8	14.5	24.4
Edmonton	7.6 (4.3)	22.2	24.8	29.0	35.7
Vancouver	8.5 (5.1)	13.2	18.2	9.7	13.3
Victoria	10.5 (4.9)	11.1	16.7	9.5	13.0

* 1931 percentages are in parentheses.
Sources: National Archives of Canada, Records of the Wartime Prices and Trade Board, RG 64, vol. 89, file 106, 'Preliminary Report on the Housing Situation in Canada and Suggestions for Its Improvement,' prepared by Leslie R. Thomson (Ottawa: Department of Munitions and Supply 1942), 56B, table 5; Canada, Dominion Bureau of Statistics, *Eighth Census of Canada, 1941*, vol. 9, *Housing*, 182, table 36; Canada, Advisory Committee on Reconstruction, Subcommittee on Housing and Community Planning [chaired by C.A. Curtis], *Final Report of the Subcommittee, March 24, 1944* (Ottawa: King's Printer 1946), 105, table 24.

Two local housing surveys confirmed the congestion in specific parts of the city. The 1939 housing study prepared by the Vancouver Housing Association (VHA) reported extensive overcrowding in the area bordered by Burrard, Beatty, and Dunsmuir streets and False Creek, in east Kitsilano, and in the east end.[69] A partial survey conducted the next year by the city health department's Inspector R. Startup found that crowding was common among those who were most poorly housed.[70] In over 199 lodging houses, 2,307 adults and children occupied 1,733 rooms for an average 0.8 rooms per person.

By the 1941 census, Vancouver on the whole seemed well advanced in its adoption of modern sanitary facilities. Most dwellings had exclusive use of a flush toilet and of a bath or shower, although tenants shared facilities more often than owners did (Table 13). Running water was available to almost all homes.[71] Still, downtown area housing for those of lowest income offered the worst facilities. In Startup's survey, one toilet and one bath, for example, served 8.2 and 11.3 people respectively. He usually described plumbing as bad, poor, or fair but seldom as good. Thirty-two of 199 lodging houses had no bathtub or shower, and one provided no toilet. Startup found instances of twenty-five people sharing a bathroom with one toilet and one bath.

The 1939 VHA report also presented a dismal picture of sanitary facilities in the downtown area. In the business district, under 10 per cent of rented rooms had sinks or wash basins. Only 5 per cent of multiple occupancy dwellings offered more than one bath, and in some instances twenty, forty, or even fifty people shared a bathroom. North of Dunsmuir between Burrard and Dunlevy, 16 per cent of premises provided no bathroom. Between Dunlevy and Clark Drive, 17 per cent of houses lacked baths, and 4 per cent still used outside toilets. The majority of cabins furnished only outside taps and common toilets and supplied no bathtubs or showers. The VHA survey noted that sanitary facilities were not only overused but also, in many cases, filthy, leaking, broken, and unvented.

By 1941, when almost three-quarters of Vancouver's dwellings had wooden exteriors, the housing stock was generally in good shape.[72] Only 18.2 per cent of all dwellings needed external repairs, and the homes of renters compared very well to those of owners.[73] Structures were fifty-five years old at the most, and many newer ones resulted from a construction boom in the 1920s (see Chapter 1, Table 2).

Nevertheless, the aggregate figures conceal cases of disrepair found in the cabins and lodging houses of the downtown area.[74] Leaking roofs, defective eavestroughs and downpipes, dilapidated front porches or stairs, settling foundations, and rotting woodwork required attention on the outside. Inside, cracked walls, loose wallpaper, old paint, missing hardware, dim, dirty halls and stairways, and decaying wood were major areas of concern. The VHA report asserted that the most serious deterioration occurred in very old housing located between Main Street and Dunlevy Avenue. It claimed that 15 per cent of homes between Dunlevy and Clark Drive needed major structural work and that probably half of those dwellings were beyond repair.

Other problems plagued low-priced rental accommodation in Vancouver.[75] An estimated 200 inside rooms without either natural light or ventilation existed between Burrard, Dunlevy, and Dunsmuir streets and Burrard Inlet, and at least two-thirds of all rooms in this area lacked adequate light and ventilation as a result of poor planning and excessive lot coverage. The Chinese boardinghouses on Market Alley and Shanghai Alley were so dark that city officials used matches to find their way to upper storeys. Basements and attics refinished into rooms and suites, especially in the West End, had low ceilings, as well as insufficient light, ventilation, fire escape provisions, and sanitary conveniences. Leaks, poor ventilation, low pressure, and faulty connections associated with the installation and maintenance of gas plates, stoves, and heaters endangered the lives of many tenants occupying small housekeeping suites or rooms. Bedbugs, cockroaches, and rats commonly infested less expensive, substandard rental premises. Overcrowded converted residences with paper-covered partitions and woodwork close to heating and hot water apparatus frequently needed proper fire escape provisions. Although by 1941 many tenant-occupied dwellings in Vancouver had radios, telephones, or even electric vacuum cleaners, most lacked proper food storage in comparison to those in other Canadian cities.[76] In the temperate West Coast climate, more than half of the housing was without refrigeration of any type. Slightly more than one-quarter had mechanical refrigeration, and about 14 per cent used ice.

The censuses of 1931 and 1941 did not include foreshore shacks or houseboats. Moreover, the biases of contemporaneous accounts make difficult any investigation of the adequacy of this type of cheap accommodation. On the one hand, observers tended to romanticize waterfront living. In Coal Harbour, the 'Shaughnessy' of the shoreline, a 'neat little house boat' became known as the city hall and its resident of twenty years as the mayor.[77] As well, a contented 'shacker' wrote to Vancouver mayor Lyle Telford praising his 'roomy' accommodation in False Creek, with its views in three directions, all 'the Amenities of life,' and 'an abundance of light, fresh air and sunshine' that gave him 'the best of health.'[78] His alternative was a dreary rooming house or cabin. On the other hand, a critic of the 'Slums of the Water Front,' Frank Buck, deplored the 'shambles indescribable' on or near water, fed by 'a fountain of continuous pollution' (a sewer outlet).[79] He described the residents of these 'pigsties' as the 'Flotsam and the Jetsam' of humanity, 'Wrecks of lives,' 'Prostitutes, whore-mongers, thieves, and ne'er-do-wells,' and 'gaunt, weary, depressed [people], accepting the environment with a deep feeling of resentment.'

A more realistic assessment reveals that foreshore conditions were neither as corrupt nor as healthy as some contemporaries would have us believe. According to several civic surveys, some colonies of shacks and houseboats provided better living conditions than others. On Burrard Inlet, enclaves at Coal Harbour and at the northern end of Kaslo and Renfrew streets sheltered more prosperous occupants, living in decent circumstances. Others, 'the worst of their type,' between Cardero and Broughton streets and at the north foot of Clark Drive near the sewer outfall, offered 'a very unsatisfactory condition.'[80] On False Creek, the area at the foot of Columbia Street among the old Great Northern Railway track pilings represented 'the filthiest and most distressful portion,' while another part east of Cambie Street bridge was 'a fairly bright and cheerful neighboorood.'[81] Along the Fraser River, the resident 'fisher folk' and mill workers set standards of health for their community, and a 'better atmosphere' pervaded the area.[82]

Access to water supply and electricity, as well as tenure, differentiated conditions in the various waterfront colonies.[83] The 'shackers' living in better situations had water connections or the use of taps or wells on adjacent property. They frequently received power directly in their homes and often supplied neighbours with electricity. Many owned their own shacks or boats and thus enjoyed greater security of tenure.

Still, sewage disposal and fire hazards represented major problems for all foreshore dwellers. Toilets placed over tidal flats and sewer outfalls from city homes or private operations such as the CPR yards or the Granville Island industrial shops discharged effluent into False Creek, English Bay, Burrard Inlet, and the Fraser River, heightening the risk of typhoid epidemics.[84] In addition, the air pollution from eleven large sawmills on False Creek created an unhealthy atmosphere. Old, abandoned timberwork or boat hulls, as well as refuse dumps, were probably more unsightly than unhygienic.

Census materials also overlooked the predicament of homeless single men. Yet contemporary local accounts give us only impressionistic assessments of hostel conditions encountered by the men. City officials defended the cleanliness, sanitation, and comfort of the Vancouver Emergency Refuge and Central City Mission (see Chapter 1, Figure 5).[85] The residents, however, described some 'pogies' as 'beyond a shadow of doubt unfit for human habitation, and a menace to the health of all men compelled to live in these places.'[86] Reliefers so resented the emergency refuge at 37 West Pender Street, a huge warehouse with a second floor made into 'military-looking sleeping quarters' accommodating 300 men in bunkbeds, that they wrecked its interior in mass protest.[87] In 1934, another city refuge at 1038 Hamilton Street met the same fate.[88]

Conditions at Point Grey Camp improved little upon those of the 'pogies.' In investigating the Department of National Defence camp system in British Columbia, the Macdonald Commission apparently approved of the camp's dining room, kitchen, bunkhouse, and store-rooms, but it also noted the rat menace in the buildings, the insanitary latrines and cesspools, the 'crude, unsightly, and dirty' washhouses and showers, and the worn, chipped sinks in need of replacement.[89]

City records and other sources reveal the plight of the men in Vancouver's jungles.[90] Near Prior Street, the men used packing boxes, corrugated iron, tar paper, barrels, tea boxes, and even old Ford cars found in the nearby dump to construct huts supposedly 'as healthful as in camplife' (Figure 8). They arranged their shacks along trails named after Vancouver's major streets.[91] Water came from a tap on adjacent city property, and the men exercised care in the disposal of human waste. In the Georgia Viaduct jungle, conditions could only be described as bad. Some men built temporary cover against the British Columbia Electric Railway fence, and others slept under the floor of an old warehouse. All the residents of this jungle used one privy, left over from the construction of the British Columbia Electric gas tank. They obtained water at a nearby gas station. The Dunlevy Avenue jungle resembled the Georgia Viaduct one but offered better lavatory facilities. City officials regarded these clusters of homeless men as 'a hot-bed for every form of disease, physical, moral and social.'[92] When one man was found dead of suspected typhoid at the Dunlevy site in early September 1931, Relief Officer H.W. Cooper used the 'grave danger of an epidemic' as an excuse to raze all the jungles.[93] He issued 879 bed tickets to the displaced men and sent them to the Pender Street refuge and a tempo-rary hostel in the old automobile building at Hastings Park.[94] Neverthe-less, the men reoccupied the old jungle locations within two weeks.

By the late 1930s, contemporary observers such as the British housing and planning expert Sir Raymond Unwin recognized that, although Vancouver was not a city of slums, some of its parts did suffer from 'slum dwellings and conditions of overcrowding and bad sanitation which should be removed and which at present are within a manage-able scale.'[95] Indeed, a scarcity of adequate housing for low-income households existed in the downtown area and in some parts of its neighbouring districts. Already visible in the years before 1929, the shortage had become chronic by the time of the Depression. As the decade of the 1930s ended, local activists took up Unwin's challenge to remove Vancouver's 'slum dwellings' and provide good quality, low-cost housing.

3
Responding to the Housing Problem in the 1930s: The Campaign for Low-Rent Housing

During the Depression, the housing problem in Vancouver gave rise to a variety of responses from government and from elements in the community. For its part, the federal government under prime ministers R.B. Bennett and William Lyon Mackenzie King provided national market housing initiatives to stimulate the ailing building industry and to create employment for construction workers. Although local builders, suppliers, and realtors actively promoted this approach, it did not resolve the problem on the West Coast or, for that matter, elsewhere in Canada. Shaped by diverse local, national, and international forces, a dynamic social housing movement emerged in Vancouver to address the shortage of decent low-income shelter and to press governments at all levels for a low-rental project. The federal government eventually designed a rental plan for the country's low-income households, but despite the efforts of groups of local activists the scheme proved unworkable in Vancouver. In the end, neither market programs nor social activism resolved the city's housing problem during the decade of the Depression.

In the mid-1930s, Ottawa intervened in the national housing market with measures to stimulate the economy and to generate employment. While these federal programs encouraged the construction and renovation of owner-occupied, single houses, they provided no low-rental housing for individuals and families devastated by the Depression. The failure of national schemes to ameliorate residential conditions for many financially disadvantaged Vancouverites contributed to the formation of a vigorous local social housing movement.

The federal market housing program implemented in the 1930s resulted partly from the demands of groups in several cities for improved

accommodation for low-income households.[1] In Toronto, at the insti-
gation of Dr. H.A. Bruce, the lieutenant governor of Ontario, the local
board of control conducted a survey of poor housing conditions with
the assistance of volunteers from the University of Toronto, the League
for Social Reconstruction (LSR), and community organizations like the
LCW. Harry M. Cassidy, an assistant professor in sociology at the
university, acted as secretary of the survey committee. In 1934, the final
report, popularly known as the Bruce report, recognized the responsibility of the community to provide 'satisfactory dwellings for those who
are too poor to afford them.'[2] It recommended the establishment of a
city planning commission, the demolition of slums, the construction
of low-cost accommodation, and the cooperation of senior governments
in passing legislation, financing projects, and creating a national housing commission and program. Organizations in Montreal, Halifax,
Ottawa, and Winnipeg also undertook surveys and prepared reports in
the early 1930s. A 'common strain' exposing the 'serious shortage of
low-rent dwellings with modern conveniences' and calling for the
assistance of senior governments ran through all the reports.[3]

At about the same time, various sectors of the construction industry
and some members of parliament began to press the Bennett government for a national low-cost housing scheme.[4] In 1934, the National
Construction Council conducted a housing survey in various localities
and came out in support of such a program to reverse the industry's
slowdown. (The council had been formed a year earlier by the Engineering Institute of Canada, the Canadian Manufacturers' Association, the
Trades and Labour Congress of Canada, the national Chamber of
Commerce, and various suppliers' organizations in order to deal with
the building crisis.) The Trades and Labour Congress, the Canadian
Construction Association, and some trades and labour councils and
provincial labour federations also independently called for improvement in residential conditions and for a national house-building policy
to stimulate economic recovery. Bennett's maverick minister of trade
and commerce from British Columbia, the Honourable H.H. Stevens,
also urged a federal housing scheme to generate employment. Several
CCF and Conservative members of parliament placed additional pressure on Bennett.

In mid-February 1935, Bennett appointed a parliamentary special
committee on housing 'to consider and report upon the inauguration
of a national policy of house building' that would have the intention
of creating employment as well as dwellings.[5] The committee's instruc-

tions were to hear evidence about the housing issue and to recommend both a policy and the means of implementing it. Member of Parliament Arthur Ganong chaired the committee. Submissions came from a variety of individuals and organizations, including prominent architects and planners from across Canada, civic officials from several large cities, Deputy Minister of Finance W.C. Clark, and representatives of the Dominion Mortgage and Investment Association and the National Construction Council. The committee presented its final report to Parliament in mid-April. Its recommendations were numerous: the establishment of a national authority to initiate and implement policies and programs; the authorization of the federal government to negotiate agreements with a province, municipality, society, corporation, or individual to construct, renovate, or repair houses; the extension of federal financial assistance for home construction; and the formulation of a national housing policy to increase employment and to coordinate the activities of government and private interests.

Legislation introduced in the House of Commons in June 1935 for the most part disregarded both the report and the demands of community groups for better low-cost accommodation. Instead, it reflected the interests of Deputy Minister of Finance Clark and Dominion Mortgage and Investment Association solicitor T. D'Arcy Leonard, both of whom had appeared before the committee on the last day of its hearings.[6] Clark wished to delay any government commitment to slum clearance and low-rental projects, preferring an indirect federal role through a central housing corporation that would assume some of the mortgage risk in the low-cost schemes of limited dividend companies. Leonard opposed a national public housing plan but supported a government-subsidized mortgage scheme to foster home ownership and economic recovery. The idea of a government role limited to mortgage assistance appealed to both Clark and Leonard. For two months, as the specifics of the draft legislation took shape, they negotiated behind the scenes on behalf of the government and the lending institutions.[7] The housing bill reached the House of Commons in June with the mortgage industry's approval.[8] Although a contract formalized cooperation between government and the mortgage industry following the proclamation of the Dominion Housing Act (DHA) in July 1935, the two parties did not work out the details of lending operations to their mutual satisfaction until almost the end of 1936.[9]

In its first part, the DHA promised further investigation of the accommodation issue. In its second part, it provided for mortgage assistance to owners and builders.[10] Under the DHA plan, an owner or builder made a downpayment worth 20 per cent of the value of a dwelling, and the federal government and the lender supplied 20 and 60 per cent respectively of the mortgage. The owner made monthly payments covering principal and 5 per cent interest over a twenty-year period. The act therefore skirted contemporary regulations in which lenders could make available no more than 60 per cent of a house's value and in which 5.5 or 6 per cent mortgages came due in short terms of perhaps five years. In implementing the act, the government designated the lending institutions able to participate in the plan and left supervision of operations to the federal Department of Finance. Representatives of the architectural profession, the mortgage industry, and Finance worked out minimum housing standards for the plan. In addition, the department sponsored two architectural competitions leading to a book of DHA house plans and to a selection of drawings available for a small fee to prospective home owners (see Chapter 3, Figure 11).[11]

In guiding the legislation through Parliament, the Bennett government explicitly stated its intention of assisting house construction in order to foster a recovery of the building industry and to stimulate employment. The CCF, some Liberals, and H.H. Stevens vigorously attacked the bill for failing to address the problem of shelter for the low-income wage earner or, for that matter, the recommendations of the special parliamentary committee's final report. Some critics speculated that the lending institutions would find the act's terms too distasteful for their participation.[12]

The DHA complemented the 'New Deal' program that R.B. Bennett introduced to Parliament in the months prior to the October 1935 general election. Like the other innovations of this program, the act seemed to herald the displacement of a 'laissez-faire' economic system by a more interventionist 'welfare state.'[13] In fact, Bennett was reacting to a political threat from the left – from the CCF and the Communist party – and his 'New Deal' was 'an act of sheer opportunism born out of political desperation.'[14] Like the rest of Bennett's initiatives, the DHA was moderate compared to what the British or even the Americans had already implemented in the housing area. Unlike the 'New Deal' legislation in general, the act never generated a constitutional challenge. When Bennett did decide to intervene in the housing field, he agreed with Deputy Minister of Finance Clark and the mortgage industry that the government should play an indirect role. He thereby prevented any substantial change in the market's operation.

The application of the DHA plan across Canada proved to be ineffective. Contemporary professionals and insurers, authors of important housing reports, and recent historians have found much to criticize in the legislation's implementation.[15] All have noted that the DHA made possible the construction of dwellings for middle-income owners rather than for low-income tenants as demanded by community groups. In fact, two-thirds of DHA houses had a value exceeding $3,000 at a time when a low-priced house cost below $2,500. Most could have been erected without the act's assistance and did little to foster the recovery of the construction industry.

Moreover, many of the corporations designated as lenders under the act were reluctant to participate. They complained of high administrative costs and excessive risks. The companies that did cooperate discriminated against applicants living in low-income urban districts or in remote smaller cities and towns. Late in 1936, amendments to the agreement with the lenders attempted to minimize undue risks and costs falling to the corporations, but few applicants from outlying communities or from low-income neighbourhoods ever received loans.[16] Indeed, some believed that lending institutions agreed to the DHA plan only to stop the federal government from direct lending.[17]

The act was eventually responsible for the construction of just 4,903 houses across Canada between 1935 and 1938, valued at $19,619,442. Ontario absorbed 48 per cent of the built units, and Quebec and British Columbia accounted for 23 and 17 per cent of the total respectively. Alberta and Saskatchewan constructed nothing at all under what a contemporary historian has called this 'bad program.'[18]

When William Lyon Mackenzie King and the Liberal party formed the government following the 1935 election, they decided to continue with the barely operational DHA. The prime minister apparently viewed the act as having the potential to generate employment. Furthermore, when King established the National Employment Commission (NEC) in April 1936 under the chairmanship of Montreal industrialist Arthur B. Purvis, it developed a job-creation initiative, the Home Improvement Plan (HIP), to put construction workers back into the labour force. The HIP was a repair and rehabilitation scheme modelled upon the United States Federal Housing Administration's 'modernization' program.[19] Under the HIP, home owners could take a bank loan of up to $2,000 for a maximum of five years at 3.25 per cent per year, repayable in equal monthly installments. No collateral or note endorsement was necessary, and the federal government guaranteed losses of up to 15 per cent of the loan. The Canadian Bankers' Association gave quick approval of the plan and permitted it to go ahead as a test project in Windsor before passage of the Home Improvement Loans Guarantee Act.[20] The federal Department of Finance administered the HIP once the NEC was disbanded in 1938.[21] A sum of $50 million carried HIP operations from October 1936 to October 1940, when the government ended the scheme because of the Second World War.

The NEC developed an effective advertising drive to promote the HIP. It hired Cockfield, Brown, and Company Limited to direct the campaign and gave the firm a budget for advertising through publications, displays, films, and radio broadcasts.[22] The NEC also depended upon national business and industry organizations such as the Canadian Construction Association to carry a large part of the task, particularly in the area of fundraising. It appointed provincial chairs of HIP campaigns, who in turn organized local committees. On 3 December 1936, a radio broadcast from Ottawa featuring a keynote speech by Prime Minister King introduced the plan to the country. Then, in March, an intensive three-month promotion began with the new building year. Another public relations effort in the autumn reinforced the campaign's work.

Ottawa fed these operations with brochures, press releases, and advertisements, trailers for movie theatres, and radio speeches. Supported by the NEC women's committee, chaired by British Columbian Mary Sutherland and endorsed by the National Council of Women, the advertising specifically targeted housewives. It reminded them of the opportunity 'to improve their homes, better their communities, and help the country as a whole' by putting people back to work.[23] Following the dissolution of the NEC, the HIP campaign merged with a drive to foster the DHA. Joint committees of volunteers carried on the work despite funding difficulties.

The HIP represented a more successful program than the DHA scheme.[24] By October 1940, the plan had resulted in 125,652 loans worth $49,990,620, with a very low default rate. Ontario again received the most loans, while British Columbia came a poor third. Once more, home owners with comfortable incomes, rather than tenants and owners with modest earnings, benefited most from the plan. As well, judging from promotional literature, the HIP's initiators intended it to be used for the 'modernization' of dwellings rather than the major structural repairs badly needed in many homes during the Depression. The plan supplied more employment for construction workers and labourers than the DHA, although it could not provide enough stimulus to ensure recovery. By February 1940, Ottawa estimated that the plan had furnished 25.3 million hours of direct labour across Canada and consumed $19 million of materials.

In July 1938, the federal government extended the DHA in the new National Housing Act (NHA), and set up a national housing administration within the Department of Finance to supervise operations.[25] Again, its objective was to increase employment, to revive the construction industry, and to expand the supply of moderately priced dwellings. Under Part I of the new act, the government and the lending institution would provide either an 80 per cent loan on a house worth over $2,500 or a 90 per cent loan on one valued under $2,500, with the government portion not exceeding 20 or 25 per cent respectively. The government established a $20 million fund for the NHA plan, of which borrowers had used all but $1 million by 1941.

Like the HIP, the new legislation functioned more efficiently than the DHA.[26] Those with more moderate income or residence in remote communities participated more frequently under the NHA. Nevertheless, the value of units between 1938 and 1941 averaged $3,947, almost $1,500 more than the price of a low-cost house. Only 20.7 per cent of NHA homes were worth below $2,999. In addition, a household head living in an NHA unit earned an average yearly income of $2,069. She or he was therefore 'somewhat better off' than the average male wage earner or salaried worker, whose 1938 annual earnings amounted to $956 and $1,719, respectively.

As well, the act led to an expansion in employment and sales of supplies. According to the federal government's estimates, by February 1940 the NHA had provided thirty-three million hours of direct labour and produced expenditures of $36 million on materials. Yet the heightened NHA activity of 1939 and 1940 came too late to assist in the recovery of the economy during its worst years.

Thus, the national programs established under the NHA, Part I, the Home Improvement Loans Guarantee Act, and the DHA all failed to address the nationwide problem of adequate accommodation for low-income households as defined in local surveys and as recommended by parliamentary report. The application of these programs in Vancouver similarly disregarded the city's housing needs.

The DHA program started slowly on the West Coast. The first loan in Vancouver was approved in May 1936, almost nine months after the act became operable.[27] In fact, its introduction came only a few months before the issue in November 1936 of the first HIP loan.[28] The protracted negotiations between Finance officials and the lending institutions initially delayed the DHA's implementation. Later, the designated lenders in Vancouver simply refused to participate in the plan.[29] In March 1936, the Mortgage and Trust Companies Association of British Columbia declared that local branches still awaited loan-issuing instructions from their central Canadian head offices and that the latter wished to assess the program's performance in the East before advancing money in the West.[30] The association itself desired revisions to the contract between government and industry. The companies feared the financial risk inherent in the DHA's low interest rate and long amortization period and the size of administrative costs over twenty years. Other problems included the aversion of branches to risk-taking, the reluctance of head offices to delegate authority to branches, the absence of application forms for potential borrowers, and the already saturated market.[31]

Nevertheless, national and local promoters of the house-building industry began to press for immediate implementation of the DHA in Vancouver.[32] In a visit to the city late in 1935, the National Construction Council vice-president, Laurence I. Anthes, called for the plan to be put into swift execution and expanded to include low-cost housing and 'modernization.' In February 1936, when the program remained inoperative west of Winnipeg, a delegation from Vancouver's business community composed of Colonel J.F. Keen, Fred J. Hale, and R.J. Lecky attended the Canadian Construction Association convention in Hamilton. They requested that the association urge Ottawa to introduce the DHA in the western provinces and to broaden it to embrace home renovation and repair. A month later, Premier Duff Pattullo announced that he would pursue the DHA issue on a forthcoming visit to Ottawa. To many of Vancouver's business leaders, the act represented 'a fifty-million dollar plum waiting to be picked.'[33]

After much lobbying, two lending institutions, the Canada Permanent Mortgage Corporation and the Mutual Life of Canada, began to accept DHA loan applications in April 1936. Yet they advanced only eight loans to builders before September. The DHA seemed 'a great disappointment' to the local construction industry.[34]

The industry's major motivation in supporting the DHA was to revive house-building activity in the city. Men such as Keen, who worked for the Ryan Contracting Company, and Hale and Lecky, who were president and executive secretary of the Building and Construction Industries Exchange, had both a financial and a career interest in recovery.[35]

Members of the local building industry also recognized the devastating economic impact of the Depression on construction workers and labourers. Lecky, for example, was secretary of the citizens' group that operated the Vancouver Emergency Refuge for unemployed transient men, and he chaired the committee on homeless men set up by the Vancouver Council of Social Agencies (VCSA), an umbrella organization for social services bureaus and groups.[36]

In all probability, a strong desire for social control also persuaded builders like Lecky to support the DHA plan. In its report of July 1932, the committee on homeless men concluded that a work system had to be found to 'preserve or restore [the men's] self-respect, maintain their morale, and prevent citizens of Vancouver or any other city from bearing more than their rightful share of the financial burden.'[37] The committee stressed that 'the temper of the unemployed and their attitude to society as a whole will become increasingly violent and anti-social if those immediately responsible for caring for them treat them in such a way that the unemployed feel that they must, in their own interest, be antagonistic and grasping, rather than co-operative and anxious to help themselves in any way possible.'[38] No doubt social control acquired more urgency between 1935 and 1938 with the On-to-Ottawa Trek and the occupation of the main post office, the Georgia Hotel, and the Vancouver Art Gallery.

In contrast to the DHA, the Home Improvement Plan became almost instantly operative in Vancouver. Ready to stimulate construction without creating more housing in a saturated market, banks made loans under the plan even before the BC promotional committee was established in January 1937. By March, the HIP – with 103 loans in three months – had surpassed the 'dormant but not dead' DHA program, which had given fifteen mortgages over seventeen months.[39]

To many, the Home Improvement Plan seemed 'a first-class scheme.'[40] In early 1937, the Building and Construction Industries Exchange and the Real Estate Exchange endorsed the plan, the city council delegated one of its members to sit on the BC committee for HIP, and the Vancouver Council of Women fostered the organization of a HIP women's council. The popularity of the scheme among business interests partly derived from a desire for economic recovery. The program also offered 'an immediate way of taking men off relief rolls and putting them on pay rolls,' at a time when the unemployed seriously threatened social order in the city.[41] A Royal Bank newspaper advertisement for the HIP in the spring of 1937 depicted a preferable world, in which a youngster with an ice-cream cone stood outside a Cape Cod cottage, waving an arm and shouting 'Dad's Got a Job Again!'[42]

The BC HIP committee directed an energetic campaign that complemented the nationwide promotional drive. The committee solicited financial contributions from trades and industries as well as from community-minded citizens. It also received some funding from the national HIP committee, which had raised $200,000.[43] The committee established a Vancouver office, managed by Lecky, to organize local activities and disseminate information.

The HIP newspaper campaign in the city was a spirited one. For months, the *Vancouver Sun*'s real estate page announced, '1937 Is Home Improvement Year: The Year for Putting Men Back to Work.' Articles inspired by Ottawa's press releases boosted the plan with suggestions for modernizing bathrooms and kitchens and for converting basements and attics into usable space.[44] On the premise that to 'have deferred payments applied to home improvement is the answer to a homemaker's prayer,' these articles followed the national example and focused heavily on women as consumers.[45] As well, banks and suppliers advertised the easy accessibility of loans and the virtues of BC products like red cedar shingles. Local papers gave extensive coverage to HIP committee luncheons for the business community at the Georgia Hotel.[46]

The HIP campaign reinforced other drives and displays intended to encourage home repairs.[47] In late April, it coincided with a junior board of trade 'Clean Up, Paint Up' promotion, which exhorted 'Make a New Home with Paint!' Later, it encouraged HIP exhibitions in various communities around the city. In May, for instance, the Grandview Chamber of Commerce sponsored a display in the local Masonic hall featuring music, entertainment, an opening ceremony with Mayor G.C. Miller, and speeches by Lecky and the local Canadian Bank of Commerce manager. In the fall, the interior decoration section of the Hudson's Bay Company department store remodelled for public viewing an older house at 52nd Avenue and Hudson Street in order to demonstrate the plan's application.

In 1938, the HIP committee in British Columbia resolved to promote the DHA and NHA programs as well as the modernization scheme.[48] Many of the people who had called for the extension of the DHA to western Canada, including Lecky, Keen, and Hale, were active members of the committee. After creating a system of subcommittees to deal with financing, lending institutions, speakers, meetings, exhibitions, and advertising, the committee went on to establish the contacts necessary to promote the federal plans. Connections were formed with local service clubs, the Architectural Institute of British Columbia, the Lower Mainland reeves, and the Associated Boards of Trade of the Fraser Valley.

The 1938 HIP/NHA campaign continued on the lines of the 1937 drive. Newspapers ran advertisements placed by builders, realtors, and suppliers, as well as drawings of NHA house designs offered by the National Housing Administration in Ottawa.[49] Once again, HIP displays attended by 'throngs' of people went up in several neighbourhoods, and Vancouver's junior board of trade sponsored another week-long 'Clean Up, Paint Up, Modernize' campaign. The Hudson's Bay Company department store exhibited submissions to a national DHA architectural competition.

By 1939, the committee for HIP and NHA heavily represented the builders, suppliers, and realtors of Vancouver and their organizations, including the newly formed BC Building Contractors' Association, the BC Lumber and Shingle Manufacturers' Association, and the Vancouver Real Estate Exchange.[50] Nevertheless, the committee's campaign appealed to a broader community. The supplier Byron Johnson, later a BC premier, outlined to a Kiwanis Club luncheon at the Hotel Vancouver the advantages of the government's housing plans to the community. The plans would create a domestic market for the province's lumber, reinvest local wealth, expand employment and purchasing power, encourage home ownership, allow the private sector to act as watchdog over a government scheme, give youth the opportunity to learn construction trades, and produce houses of an appropriate standard. With this broad orientation, the committee attracted delegates from the city council, the board of trade and junior board of trade, the trades and labour council, the Vancouver Loan and Mortgage Association, the British Columbia Underwriters' Association, and the LCW. Even the VHA, a major proponent of a low-rental scheme for the city, sent a representative to the committee. In May 1939, the BC committee for HIP and NHA, in conjunction with the West End Chamber of Commerce, sponsored a home-building show in the Hotel Vancouver's Crystal Ballroom. Booths and displays featured all aspects of renovation and construction, from loan arrangements to garden landscaping,[51] and several hundred people attended every day. The onset of war diverted finances, materials, and labour away from the house-building industry, however, and the committee and its campaigns vanished in the fall of 1939.

In the end, these federal housing programs did stimulate construction in Vancouver. Despite limited participation in the DHA plan, more owners and builders took advantage of the other schemes as the HIP/NHA committee became active.[52] By May 1938, builders such as S.D. Buzelle and J. Sexton had erected rows of houses for sale in Point Grey. By September, NHA activity exceeded that of the HIP. Between August 1938 and December 1941, the NHA program in Vancouver was responsible for 2,440 loans, worth $8,059,729, with which 2,711 units had been built. A 1939 draft VHA report estimated that slightly over half of all residential construction and about three-quarters of all house-building mortgages in the city had been financed under the DHA and NHA between January 1938 and May 1939.[53] Under the HIP to 31 May 1939, Vancouver banks made 2,985 loans valued in total at $833,113.

As local critics realized, however, the federal market housing program encountered serious difficulties on the West Coast. First, as the 1937 report of the city's special housing committee pointed out, the program favoured middle-income households in west-side districts.[54] In May 1938, only about 10 per cent of ninety-eight homes financed by one lending institution were located east of Ontario Street. At a time when relief tenants faced eviction due to rising rents, when homeless unemployed men occupied downtown buildings to protest their predicament, and when Better Housing Scheme families struggled to keep their homes, the average cost of forty-two DHA houses being built in May and June 1938 around the city was $3,705. Only four of these units were situated in east-side neighbourhoods such as East Hastings and Mount Pleasant; the remainder could be found in west-side districts such as Point Grey, Kitsilano, Little Mountain, and Shaughnessy. As well, although business licence records for contractors and realtors reveal that the federal programs injected some energy into the local construction industry, they certainly did not engender a complete recovery (see Chapter 2, Table 4). Despite the HIP and DHA, high unemployment continued to plague construction workers into the late 1930s.[55]

Furthermore, the supervision of building standards emerged as a controversial issue with the DHA/NHA programs, as it had with the Better Housing Scheme. A builder who took out a loan for the construction of more than one unit often teamed up with a realtor to market the houses, offering a commission that was hidden to the buyer.[56] The builders occasionally cut corners in construction standards and supplies in order to keep within a budget reduced by commission. Unfortunately, cutbacks in the civic building department resulted in insufficient staff to inspect new housing thoroughly, and neither lending institutions nor home owners were sufficiently watchful to catch problems.[57] The press made frequent charges of racketeering and jerry-building, but only two cases ever received public scrutiny. F.W. Nicolls of the National Housing Administration visited Vancouver in January 1939 to investigate the charges. In a week of 'plainspeaking,' he sternly lectured the city council, the builders, and the owners about the problem, threatened to cut off loans, and warned that his office in Ottawa would consult a 'white list' of reputable contractors when it screened applications.[58] For their part, builders formed the BC Building Contractors' Association in order to promote higher ethical standards and to advance the industry.[59] As a public relations gesture, the association built two demonstration houses on West 39th and West 29th avenues, and displayed sketches, plans, and models at the May 1939 home-builders' show.[60]

Finally, the DHA/NHA house styles did not immediately suit West Coast tastes. Vancouver's builders and owners found the plans and drawings submitted to DHA competitions and others issued by the National Housing Administration too 'down east' or 'Ontario' in style.[61] They preferred their long-established Tudor Revival and California bungalow styles to a 'square box, two stories high' (Figures 10 and 11). While somewhat reduced in size and complexity, the familiar styles, with some exceptions, continued to appear under the federal programs.[62] They also contrasted strikingly with the first prewar examples of the important West Coast modern tradition, including the B.C. Binning house, which went up despite a struggle with a lending institution over its progressive design (Figure 12).[63]

Yet questions of design and style and of home ownership itself under the NHA mattered little to those Vancouverites who did without affordable, adequate housing. The federal market programs simply did not meet their needs. Not surprisingly, by the late 1930s, community activist groups had determined to solve the problem by launching a campaign for social housing.

Both outside influences and local relief activism moulded the emergence of Vancouver's social housing movement. Direction came externally from Canadian and non-Canadian traditions of and developments in reform, from the LSR, the CCF, and the CPC, and from the introduction of a federal low-cost housing program. As well, local agitation to improve the maintenance and shelter of the unemployed and the relief recipient gave a militant edge to housing activism. By 1937, both local and outside forces had shaped a vigorous drive for social housing.

Figure 10 In 1936, Vancouver's first DHA house was built in Kitsilano in the California bungalow style. The contractor was Thomas R. Smalley.

Vancouver's housing activists were well aware of international developments in their field. The Bruce report, among other Canadian publications, described advances in Europe beginning in the 1850s and in the United States starting in the early 1900s.[64] Activists took special interest in post-First World War British legislation to subsidize low-rental projects and slum clearance programs undertaken by local authorities. As well, they recognized the achievements of the American New Deal, particularly the construction of low-rental complexes as public works projects under the 1933 National Industrial Recovery Act, and public housing schemes under the 1937 Wagner Steagall Act. Some activists had emigrated from England and were familiar with twentieth-

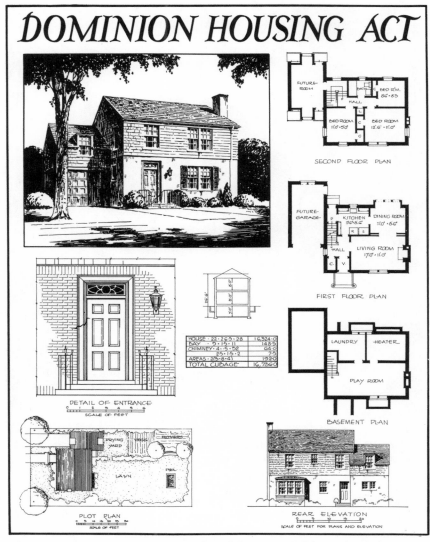

Figure 11 Many Vancouverites preferred their own California bungalow or Tudor Revival styles to the 'down east' two-storey 'squarebox' designs advertised by the National Housing Administration in Ottawa. [Canada, Department of Finance, *Dominion Housing Act: Architectural Competition; Low-Cost House Designs* (Ottawa 1936), 34]

century solutions of European housing problems.[65] P.R.U. Stratton, who authored the VHA draft report, was one of these. Moreover, distinguished figures in the housing and planning world visited Vancouver,

Figure 12 The West Vancouver house designed in the late 1930s by British Columbia artist B.C. Binning for himself and his wife Jessie is one of the first and best examples of West Coast modern domestic architecture. It, too, contrasted sharply with the first DHA houses.

spoke at public meetings, and commented upon the city's environment: Sir Raymond Unwin, for example.[66] Finally, Stratton and others read and valued the work of such authorities as Catherine Bauer.[67]

An international trend in the housing field toward social scientific surveying and reporting also came to be felt in Vancouver in an indirect way. By the mid-1930s, Leonard C. Marsh, who had trained as an economist at the London School of Economics under Sir William Beveridge, had become director of social research at McGill University. There he prepared studies on unemployment and contributed to reports on Montreal's housing problem.[68] Another welfare economist, Harry M. Cassidy, was a faculty member of the University of Toronto School of Social Work and acted as secretary of the committee responsible for the Bruce report. He later assumed the position of director of social welfare for the BC government, wrote a major report on the transient single unemployed, and attempted to introduce a provincial health insurance plan. A third social scientist, Coral W. Topping, taught in the Department of Economics, Political Science, and Sociology at UBC and administered the social work program between 1929 and 1943. Topping's students carried out surveys for Vancouver's 1937 housing report. He became acquainted with the work of Marsh and Cassidy not only through scholarship but also through connections to the United Church and the LSR.

The lingering tradition of the Canadian social gospel also affected West Coast housing issues in the 1930s. Although the social gospel had long since gone into decline, its 'moderate' form still existed in the United Church in the person of Hugh Dobson, the associate secretary of evangelism and social service, who moved from Regina to Vancouver in 1926.[69] Dobson continued to see Christianity as a social religion. In Vancouver during the Depression, he spearheaded the Church's social thrust. This took a range of forms, from welfare services performed by individual congregations to reports on urban conditions. The members of First United Church at Hastings Street and Gore Avenue, 'the Church of the Open Door,' furnished clothing to thousands hard hit by the Depression and took a soup kitchen to the men in the Prior Street jungle. Their minister, the Reverend Andrew Roddan, dealt, however ineptly, with the subject of homelessness in sermons, radio broadcasts, newspaper articles, and books.[70] At the same time, members of various congregations participated in a national study undertaken in 1932 by the general council of the United Church to assess the impact of the Depression and to make recommendations about the Church's role in establishing a new social order.[71] Harry Cassidy helped to prepare the report in Toronto, and the Vancouver committee included Dobson, Roddan, and Topping (an active member of the Canadian Memorial and West Point Grey United churches). In 1931, Dobson chaired a BC committee on unemployment and relief established by the local general ministerial association, and Topping served as a member. Five years later, Dobson became chair of a Vancouver presbytery committee to assist the Unemployed and Part-time Workers' Organization in an investigation of the city's high rents and evictions problem.

Activists during the 1930s in Vancouver were directly influenced by the Canadian housing reform tradition. This reached back to the work of the Commission of Conservation (1909-21), to the celebrated planner Thomas Adams (1914-20s), and to the TPIC (1919).[72] With the termination of the commission and the subsequent loss of energy of the TPIC, however, no effective national planning organization existed to lobby the federal government. Thus, in 1937, George S. Mooney led a new generation of planners and some older TPIC members in the organization of the National Housing and Planning Association (NHPA). (Mooney was the executive director of the Canadian Federation of Mayors and Municipalities (CFMM) as well as a member of the LSR and the CCF.) He regarded this new group as a replacement for both the commission and the TPIC.[73] He approached Alexander Walker, the secretary-engineer of Vancouver's town planning commission, to help create a local branch. The VHA, the group that guided the city's social housing movement for many years, was established in January 1938.

Many Vancouver women shared a commitment to solving housing problems. They had for precedents Octavia Hill's charitable work in London, American maternal feminists' work in domestic architectural design, the participation of working-class women in the Glasgow rent strikes, and the efforts of middle-class women in the Toronto Housing Company's development.[74] The work of the national and local councils of women had been instrumental in articulating housing concerns across Canada and in Vancouver in the pre-Depression years.[75] During the 1930s, the Vancouver council argued for adequate relief and shelter for single unemployed women (as well as for single transient men) and for a moratorium on mortgage payments.[76] By then, however, other individuals and women's organizations – especially working-class ones – had independently taken up the housing cause. Indeed, their work helped to redefine the role of local women in the housing field from a philanthropic to a political one.[77]

Contemporary intellectual and political solutions to Depression-era economic and social dislocation lay behind much of the agitation about Vancouver's housing problem, whether democratic socialist, communist, or liberal in nature. Of prime importance was the 1931 formation in central Canada of the LSR.[78] A group of democratic socialist intellectuals who were deeply concerned about the breakdown of the capitalist order during the Depression came together to develop solutions for a new, more just social order. Many, like Harry Cassidy, Leonard Marsh, and George Mooney, were academics or professionals motivated by social conscience and the desire for public recognition of their skills. Still, the members of the Vancouver LSR branch (formed by early summer 1932) tended to fit neither the academic nor the professional model.[79] Rather, for every C.W. Topping, there were several political figures who blended a sense of social justice with political ambitions for the CCF and for themselves, like Grace and Angus MacInnis or Dorothy Steeves.

The league's achievements included the publication in 1935 of its blueprint for the new social order, *Social Planning for Canada*. One chapter was written by Humphrey Carver, an architect with expertise in planning and housing, and presented the LSR's solution to the national shelter problem.[80] In response to unrestrained speculative development on the urban fringe and decay in the downtown core, a socialist government would initiate planning based on surveys and compulsory powers and establish a federal housing and planning authority to provide low-paid wage earners with accommodation. The dwellings would be owned by a federal, provincial, or municipal government or its agent. The benefits of this 'large-scale housing programme' would include a healthier, more appropriately designed social environment for wage-earning families. Another chapter suggested that non-profit or limited dividend housing corporations could also play a part in a government program.

The LSR gave 'quiet assistance' to the newly formed CCF.[81] It decided against formal affiliation with the party in order to preserve its educational objectives. Still, two league members, Frank Scott and Frank Underhill, helped to draft the Regina Manifesto, which in many ways expanded the LSR's own policy statement adopted eighteen months previously. In British Columbia, the LSR clubs decided to join the CCF as a group in 1933. By the mid-1930s, the league cooperated closely with the CCF at the national level, and members who did not view themselves as socialists left the organization. The league died out in British Columbia in the late 1930s, and its last national convention occurred in June 1941.

The CCF established a BC wing in 1933.[82] The provincial party was a federation of the Socialist Party of Canada, LSR branches, and CCF clubs. Many CCF members had participated in the province's lengthy socialist tradition. Of these, Angus MacInnis, Ernest E. Winch, and Dorothy Steeves became particularly prominent in the social housing movement of the 1930s and 1940s.

The CPC was also active in the housing movement. It had formed in 1921 in Ontario within the Comintern affiliation. Although it was initially an underground organization, it soon invented a legal party called the Workers' Party of Canada and in 1924 renamed itself the Communist Party of Canada. With a small but militant membership, the CPC attempted to exert influence over trade union activities through the Workers' Unity League.[83] Early in the Depression, party members organized unemployed workers' associations affiliated with the league across Canada and on the West Coast. Later, these associations set up branch and block organizations led by CPC members to represent the unemployed and the relief recipients in Vancouver on issues such as shelter allowances, rising rents, and evictions.

Not only left-wing intellectuals and politicians but also 'the government generation' was bent on refashioning Canada of the 1930s into the modern welfare state.[84] This 'new reform elite,' characteristically well-educated, middle or upper-class anglophone males, sought to bring order from the chaos of the Depression by using lobbying techniques, governmental process, and civil service appointments rather than by following the voluntarist and philanthropic example of the previous reform generation. As neither LSR advocates nor 'non-partisans,' they tended to work from within the Liberal party. A 'brain trust' among Liberal intellectuals had emerged by 1932-3 under the influence of Vincent Massey and Norman Rogers, and attempted to separate the party (and Mackenzie King) from its laissez-faire tradition and to accept a more interventionist stance.

Once in positions of power, this new generation of Liberal politicians was able to make substantial, although not radical, changes. Norman Rogers, for example, succeeded as minister of labour in founding the National Employment Commission, which not only created the HIP but also prepared the way for an unemployment insurance scheme. As well, the Department of Finance accepted its idea of extending federal housing legislation to include provisions for moderately priced dwellings. Nevertheless, the commission's proposal for low-rental projects and slum clearance as a means of stimulating increased construction and employment met with failure.[85] The Department of Finance and, in particular, Deputy Minister W.C. Clark, opposed a draft bill submitted by Rogers because it was a 'radical innovation' requiring federal, provincial, and municipal subsidization of low-income accommodation.[86]

Although Department of Finance officials objected to the NEC scheme, they later drew up their own low-rental housing plan under Part II of the 1938 NHA. The act provided local housing authorities with federal loans of up to 90 per cent of the construction cost, repayable at an annual interest rate of 1.75 to 2 per cent. The sponsoring municipality had to forego all but 1 per cent of taxes on the project, and the province had to agree to cover any losses. The act also placed limits on maximum rentals and family incomes. Unlike the NEC scheme, the NHA plan supplied no subsidy for reduced rents to make possible the inclusion of low-income households. In July 1938, when the legislation received royal assent, the federal structure for a low-rental housing program was in place. However flawed, the new plan animated Vancouver's housing activists.

By the late 1930s, external forces had combined to shape a local housing movement that was oriented towards social scientific methodology, social justice, state intervention, and older reform traditions. The movement's major goal was to achieve low-rental housing under federal legislation.

Social agitation on behalf of those on relief or unemployed also played a part in the development of Vancouver's social housing campaign. It focused on specific grievances and took a variety of directions, with few substantial results. Still, in the late 1930s, many of those who had fought for better conditions in relief accommodation began to work towards the achievement of a low-rental project. Moreover, the social housing movement absorbed some of the peaceable and militant strategies of relief activism.

Relief activists belonged mainly to labour, unemployed, left-wing, and women's organizations. They came from groups such as the Unemployed Workers' Association, the Single Unemployed Protective Association, British Columbia's joint committee on unemployment, and the Unemployed Women's Protective Association, formed to assist the jobless. They also represented the labour movement through the Vancouver, New Westminster, and District Trades and Labour Council, the Brotherhood of Railway Carmen of America, the Seafarers' Industrial Union, the Amalgamated Building Workers of Canada, and the Marine Workers' and Boilermakers' Union. Members of the CCF played forceful roles through the party and membership in other organizations. Many communists worked through unemployed groups, trade unions, and Finnish and Ukrainian associations. Progressive women's organizations such as the New Era League, the women's sections of the CCF and the Independent Labour Party, the Mothers' Council, the women's labour leagues, the joint committee between CCF and CPC Women, and the Women's International League for Peace and Freedom were spirited participants.[87] The desire for social change demonstrated by these radical groups stemmed from both personal experience of the Depression's impact and an ideological commitment to reconstruct society on a socialist model.

The issue of proper accommodation for the unemployed and the relief recipient also aroused the concern of other, non-political organizations, such as the VCSA, the United Church, and the Vancouver Council of Women.[88] As well, representatives of the building industry linked the issue of relief shelter to the federal market housing promotion. The motivation of organizations and individuals alike was complex. The desire for social control expressed in the report of the VCSA committee on homeless men undoubtedly lay behind the work of some groups. Yet the question of support for the unemployed also attracted public sympathy. Many Vancouverites had experienced the personal destructiveness of the Depression; they believed that the economic and social disorder of the decade was a national problem and 'no fault' of its victims.[89]

Activist groups pressed not only for work or improved maintenance but also for better accommodation for the unemployed and the relief recipient. Many of the activists' grievances reflected contemporary housing conditions. Protests about the treatment of reliefers usually involved the poor living arrangements in the 'pogies,' the necessity for many transient jobless men to live in jungles, or the lack of bed tickets for homeless single men, especially the relief camp strikers.[90] Complaints about maintenance assistance for the married unemployed encompassed rent relief cuts, landlords' rejection of lower shelter allowances, rising rents, evictions of relief recipients, and withholding of personal belongings following eviction.[91] By the mid-1930s, many organizations also objected to the insanitary and overcrowded housing occupied by relief and low-income households, the lack of decent accommodation for single women on relief, and the discrimination of the relief system against Asians.[92]

Agitators employed lobbying and individual advocacy to direct their protests and demands at the civic, provincial, and federal governments.[93] They telephoned the mayor or wrote to elected officials. Many went as delegates to city council to represent the interests of individuals and to argue for changes in policy. Organizations for the unemployed regularly sent delegations straight to the relief officer to challenge particular cases. The protesters tried briefs, memos, surveys, reports, resolutions, and petitions to government as well.[94] In its 1934 report to city council and to Premier Duff Pattullo, for example, the VCSA committee on homeless men recommended improved conditions in relief camps, better provisions for single men over age twenty-one living at home, supervised institutional care for single men who were physically unfit for camp life, and (demonstrating their concerns about social stability) a 'detention camp' in Vancouver for those expelled from the camps. A 1934 CCF unemployment council resolution to Mayor Louis D. Taylor specified the nature of the minimum needs of the unemployed, including an increased rent allowance paid in cash and administered by Victoria throughout the province. A BC joint committee on unemployment, representing sixty-five organizations and 30,665 persons, sent a memo in 1934 to Pattullo urging increases in direct relief and rent allowances, freedom for single people to sleep in places of their own choice, and alleviation of overcrowded accommodation. Several locals of the Workers' Alliance of British Columbia presented a 1937 brief to city council's social services committee about the rising rents, evictions, overcrowding, and insanitary conditions commonly experienced by Vancouver's unemployed. In addition, the Unemployed Workers' Association conducted a survey of the rental situation faced by relief recipients.

The protesters did not shrink from more militant but disciplined tactics.[95] The Single Unemployed Protective Association picketed the homes of families to stop their eviction. They frequently held mass meetings downtown that drew enormous crowds. In December 1930, about 1,000 men led by Workers' Unity League leader Tom McEwen met the civic relief officer on the Cambie Street grounds and demanded bed and meal tickets for single men and adequate support, including rent allowances, for married men. By April and May 1935, when the relief camp strike was in full swing, enormous rallies of thousands of people deplored, among other things, the living conditions in the camps and the lack of food and shelter for the strikers. Indeed, between 1935 and 1938, the 'snake' parades, distribution of leaflets, tin-canning, tag days, occupations of the city museum, the Georgia Hotel, the main post office, and the Vancouver Art Gallery, and even the On-to-Ottawa Trek may be seen in part as demonstrations about insufficient shelter for the single unemployed. This militancy aroused tremendous public sympathy for the strikers, and hundreds of citizens provided food and shelter, attended rallies, congregated outside occupied buildings, or waved farewell to delegations sailing off to Victoria to meet the premier.

Elected (and sometimes unelected) officials in the civic, provincial, or federal governments were the targets of this protest. Repeatedly, the mayor and city council requested financial assistance from the government in Victoria or in Ottawa, which in turn would attribute responsibility to the other senior government.[96] The federal government regarded relief as a provincial matter, and the province viewed the economic breakdown that necessitated relief as a national problem.

Achievements were thus few. If the social threat became too great, however, the senior governments would react by creating or closing camps, establishing a commission to investigate camp conditions, or providing funds for direct relief or public works. Even the city's welfare and relief department responded to the advocacy of the unemployed organizations to relieve the distress of their members.[97]

Associations of east-side property owners and lodging-house operators also went before city council to represent the interests of their members. They sometimes opposed the grievances of groups acting for the unemployed and the relief recipient, much as they later resisted the low-rental project advocated by social housing campaigners. Using letters, resolutions, and delegations, ratepayers and electors' associations for east-side wards, the Vancouver Federated Ratepayers' Association, the Italian Home Owners' and Electors' Association, and the Windermere District Improvement Association approached the city with demands for a moratorium on the mortgage payments of unemployed citizens, for 'work for taxes' schemes, for suspension of tax sales, for improvement in regulations leading to the sales, for shelter allowances for ratepayers on relief, and for alleviation of evictions.[98] By contrast, the Lodging and Restaurant Keepers' Association and the House Owners' Association wanted changes in the rent relief system that would benefit landlords rather than tenants: higher shelter allowances; free water; staggered licence fee payments; and assurances of rental payment before tenants received more relief work.[99]

Ratepayers succeeded in winning concessions from the city government but the lodging-house keepers failed altogether. In May 1936, with prior provincial approval and under pressure from property owners, the city extended to home owners on relief shelter allowances to be used for mortgage or tax payments.[100] In addition, it suspended tax sales for a time and introduced 'work for taxes' schemes.

The protests about relief shelter in the early 1930s in Vancouver greatly influenced the development of a local social housing movement. By mid-decade, relief and unemployment activism had merged with larger external forces to create a serious drive for low-rental housing. The movement itself was a loose collection of activist organizations with overlapping memberships and spokespeople representing the various groups. The activist who stood out the most was Helena Gutteridge, a fiery socialist with affiliations to the CCF, labour, feminism, and relief activism.

Indeed, in March 1937, the movement seized the opportunity offered by Gutteridge's election as city alderman to press for social housing. Born in England, this 'persistent lady' trained in London at the Regent Street Polytechnic and the Royal Sanitary Institute in hygiene and sanitary science, receiving an education that may have stimulated her interest in housing.[101] She participated in the British woman suffrage movement, and, following her emigration to Canada in 1911, she was active in the Pioneer Political Equality League, the British Columbia Woman's Suffrage League, the United Suffrage Societies of Vancouver, and the Vancouver City Central Woman's Suffrage Campaign Association. As a strong trade unionist as well as a feminist, she belonged to the Women's Minimum Wage League and the Women's Employment League, contributed to the *Labour Gazette* and *The B.C. Federationist*, and worked on the mothers' pension, workers' compensation, and peace issues. In the 1930s, as corresponding secretary for the CCF unemployment council, she joined the struggle to assist the jobless and homeless.[102] A member of the CCF, she ran for city council twice before her 1937 victory.

The housing issue began to simmer as soon as Helena Gutteridge became a council member. Within a week of the by-election, the first annual congress of the Greater Vancouver and New Westminster Youth Council passed a resolution urging the city to set up a special committee to investigate slum conditions in the city, publicize information on the issue, and press senior governments to take immediate action to remedy those conditions.[103]

On 28 June 1937, city council did establish a special housing committee to survey and report upon the residential situation.[104] Its members included Gutteridge as chair, A.J. Harrison, the civic secretary of zoning matters, as secretary, and Frank Buck, a UBC horticulture professor, as the representative of Vancouver's town planning commission. This special committee made social housing an issue of public debate in the city.

The special housing committee held its first meeting within two weeks and initiated the process of collecting housing data for the business district between Burrard and Beatty streets, in the east end between Cordova, Main, Prior, and Gore streets, and in the waterfront shacks and houseboats of Burrard Inlet and False Creek.[105] The committee assembled information about the living quarters of mothers' pension recipients, the shortage of rental housing, the relation of home building to population growth, and various British and American schemes. Assistance came from the town planning commission, the workers' alliance, the youth council, the VCSA, the LCW, and the Vancouver, New Westminster, and District Trades and Labour Council. C.W. Topping, some sociology department students, city hall employees, and clergymen such as Hugh Dobson, Andrew Roddan, and the Reverend Father Cooper also helped with the report. That winter, many of the energetic individuals who participated in the committee's meetings and surveys joined tours of the city's poorest residential areas.[106]

The committee presented an interim report to city council in November 1937, and continued with its data collection until early 1938. On 14 February, council adopted the final survey, which revealed 'a deplorable shortage of housing accommodation' and 'many persons living in what are generally described as "slum conditions" of the worst kind.'[107] The study focused particularly upon overcrowding, dilapidation, illegal suites, waterfront conditions, and the lag in construction behind a steady population increase. Clearly, the DHA program had not met the city's problem. The committee asked council to urge Ottawa to make funds available for a housing scheme.

By October 1937, activists drawn from the special housing committee and various interested organizations had inaugurated a 'campaign to secure a low-rent housing program for Vancouver.'[108] The campaign represented a coming together of groups such as the CCF, the Workers' Alliance of British Columbia, the youth council, the Trades and Labour Council, the VCSA, the LCW, and elements in the civic bureaucracy, the professions, the churches, and the university. The goal of these activists, as stated by Helena Gutteridge, was to obtain a national 'building programme to relieve overcrowding rather than slum clearance.'[109] In their view, 'the housing problem [was] a Dominion-wide question, and its solution rested with the federal government.' The campaigners applied indirect pressure on the federal government through city council. They directly approached the local MP Ian MacKenzie and Prime Minister Mackenzie King for a low-rental scheme.[110] The housing committee forwarded copies of its interim report to many members of the Legislative Assembly and Parliament, to contributing organizations, to the Social Services Council of Canada, and to other city governments. It also sent a copy to W.C. Clark, who politely replied that he had read it 'with very much interest indeed' and then apparently filed it for posterity![111] Despite emphasis on a federal solution, some campaigners lobbied Premier Duff Pattullo, the provincial Cabinet, and the Legislative Assembly for 'an adequate housing program.'[112]

The formation of the VHA in 1937-8 gave organizational energy and definition to the housing campaign. Early in 1937, George Mooney apprised Alexander Walker of plans to create the NHPA, and asked him to sit on the initiating committee as the BC representative.[113] In March, the Ottawa conference of the Union of Canadian Municipalities decided to proceed with founding the national organization. Much later in the year, Mooney visited Vancouver and encouraged the establishment of a local group. In December, Gutteridge, Dobson, and others attended an initiating meeting, and, in January 1938, a branch called the Vancouver Housing Association came into existence with a full constitution and an executive consisting of chair W.S. Owen (a lawyer) vice-chair Hugh Dobson, secretary John Jopson (a youth council activist), treasurer P.R.U. Stratton, committee members Helena Gutteridge, R.J. Lecky, A.J. Harrison, and ex-officio member Alexander Walker. Since the branch's major interest was housing, it dropped the word 'planning' from its name.

At the initial meeting, discussion already centred on an NHPA resolution for the creation of a national low-income housing scheme. The work of the VHA and the civic housing committee soon merged. The association decided to continue with the committee's survey, and members like Dobson attempted to educate the public about the housing problem through lectures and radio broadcasts.[114] As well, the VHA reinforced the civic committee's attempt to force the federal government to bring in a low-rental program under a public or semi-public body.

In the spring of 1938, such a program appeared imminent. The NHPA resolved to lobby Parliament about the implementation of the proposal contained in the NEC's final report.[115] The North Vancouver CCF member of parliament (and former reliefer), Grant MacNeil, informed Helena Gutteridge of the likelihood of a scheme in February, and suggested that she and her committee prepare to inaugurate such a program. By May, the federal Department of Finance was drafting the NHA. It quickly became clear, however, that the legislation would not fulfil the campaigners' expectations. Speaking to the Architectural Institute of British Columbia, F.W. Nicolls of Finance warned, 'It is not social legislation. We expect to get back every dollar put up.'[116]

When Parliament passed the new legislation in the summer of 1938, the campaigners concentrated on the acquisition of a low-rental scheme under Part II of the act. In August, the housing committee began to explain the salient points of the legislation to city council and to the building, civic planning, and parks committee. From the beginning, the

1 per cent tax exemption clause in NHA Part II presented a major obstacle in implementing its provisions in Vancouver. Helena Gutteridge believed that the clause would 'likely kill the whole scheme across the Dominion, because municipalities won't agree to it.'[117] A majority of city council members objected to the clause because it would diminish badly needed tax revenues, discriminate against citizens paying full taxes, and create a 'preferred class of property owners.'[118]

Many council members also opposed the federal program because the City of Vancouver had 'lost heavily' in the Better Housing Scheme 'spree.'[119] By the late 1930s, the city fully understood the scheme's financial failings. Indeed, in 1935 and again in 1937, it sought relief from both the provincial and the federal governments, but each time its requests were resisted. Helena Gutteridge remarked that the city had been 'badly stung' by the scheme and probably would not undertake another similar plan.[120]

Still, the drive to improve conditions in accommodation continued. The VHA survey was almost complete by December 1938.[121] As well, P.R.U. Stratton developed a VHA plan to build fifty low-cost, four-room cottages at Trout Lake to be rented at under $15 per month.[122] He argued that the city could still collect sufficient revenue under the 1 per cent tax clause to pay for the project's services, and he encouraged council to experiment with his plan before committing itself to the NHA program. In addition, the housing committee supported a move to rid the waterfront of shacks and houseboats, especially when the possibility of violence between 'shackers' and tugboat captains arose on the Fraser River.[123] The committee also initiated discussion of a housing standard bylaw to consolidate clauses relating to dwellings contained in several civic bylaws.[124] Housing conditions and schemes became a topic for heated debate in the municipal election that December.[125]

In January 1939, city council decided not to take up the NHA Part II low-rental plan.[126] Not even the attendance of F.W. Nicolls at a council meeting convinced it to try the plan; it did not accept his argument that the city should be prepared to shoulder some of the financial burden of a social housing program. In February, an attempt to use the national housing conference to make the federal government change the objectionable tax clause failed. Grace MacInnis, the VHA delegate at the Toronto meeting, suggested that local attempts to employ the act were necessary before the government would budge on the issue.[127] She recommended that the city approach the provincial government for enabling legislation. Yet Premier Duff Pattullo followed the advice of his finance minister, John Hart, who feared that the province might have to assist in loan repayment. Pattullo refused to take on 'guarantees of so uncertain character,'[128] despite an introduction to the Bruce report through Harry Cassidy and despite the personal endorsement of low-rental housing by Dr. G.M. Weir, British Columbia's minister of education, and Dr. H.E. Young, secretary of the provincial board of health.

Under the 'political generalship' of Helena Gutteridge, activists started an educational campaign in January 1939. At a public meeting at the Elks Hall,[129] about 300 people listened to Gutteridge explain the Trout Lake plan. Dobson, Owen, Jopson, Conservative party MP Howard Green, and Anglican archdeacon Sir Francis Heathcote expressed support. The audience also watched films showing Vancouver's slum conditions 'in black and white.' In March, the report of an assize jury of the BC supreme court turned public attention to the 'filth' and the 'crime' of cabins in Hogan's Alley in Strathcona.[130] Thereafter, at two or three meetings a week, Gutteridge used the assize jury's findings to make her point about the need for low-rental housing. Warning city council that 'when women's social concern is aroused, they always see things through to their logical conclusion,' Gutteridge also discussed the housing issue at a meeting of about fifty women's clubs held under the auspices of the LCW.[131] The contributions of MLA Dorothy Steeves and R.J. Lecky added strength to her address.

The 'vigorous campaign' continued in April, when Sir Raymond Unwin visited Vancouver at the VHA's invitation and largely through Stratton's efforts.[132] Unwin spoke to a Quadra Club luncheon sponsored by the BC committee for NHA and HIP, to city council, and to a women's meeting at the Georgia Medical-Dental Building auditorium. He argued that council should accept the tax exemption clause in NHA Part II because it resembled the subsidy principle used in Britain. In May, Mayor Lyle Telford, a former CCF member, publicly endorsed the scheme and the clause when he opened the home-building exhibition at the Hotel Vancouver.[133] As one onlooker mused, the low-rental housing proposal with 'more lives, apparently, than a cat' refused to become a dead issue.[134]

Gutteridge and other campaigners also took the plan back to the 'battleground' of the city council and its building, city planning, and parks committee.[135] Several indecisive meetings occurred; delegations representing the opposing sides appeared, and the pros and the cons of the issue came out.

Support for the scheme and for the NHA Part II came from a variety of local organizations. The building trades council, the Vancouver, New Westminster, and District Trades and Labour Council, the youth council, the Relief Projects Workers' Union, and the British Columbia Federation on Unemployment joined with the Building Exchange, the Greater Vancouver Health League, the Goodwill Activities Association, the BC division of the Canadian Federation of the Blind, the VCSA, the parent-teachers' association, and the BC committee for NHA and HIP.[136] A great many women's groups united with them: the Vancouver Council of Women; the Mount Pleasant Women's Christian Temperance Union; the Canadian Daughters' League; the Progressive Women's Federation; the New Era League; the women's auxiliaries of Shaughnessy and Chown Memorial United churches; the local section of the National Council of Jewish Women; the junior division of the Catholic Women's League of Canada; and the Civilian Pensions Mother's Organization.[137]

Representatives of these groups gave many reasons for their support of the low-rental housing plan. Some recognized the poor housing conditions disclosed in the local surveys, the social costs of these conditions as revealed in the assize jury's report, and the need for new low-priced dwellings. Others pointed to the desirability of stimulating business recovery and employment in the building industry, the example of public housing programs in other countries, and the federal offer to assist construction. No one overtly expressed the objective of preserving social stability among the unemployed or low-income groups as clearly as did the VCSA. Still, influenced by the assize jury's report, many campaigners associated social disorder with tenements and social stability with low-rental housing and slum clearance.

Opposition came from elements of the property industry such as the real estate exchange, the property owners' association, the ratepayers' association, and the board of trade.[138] The reasons for their resistance lay in the taxation clause of NHA Part II, which they believed gave an unfair advantage to public-housing occupants and discriminated against other taxpayers in the city. Moreover, they feared that low-rental projects would attract tenants away from 'decent housing' and leave independent landlords with relief recipients and the type of bitter management experience encountered earlier in the decade.

On 17 July 1939, the city council, the VHA, and the housing committee met to work out a solution to the dilemma.[139] The meeting resolved that the committee, the association, and those council members who wished should confer on a scheme to submit with council's approval to the voters during that fall's civic election. Unfortunately, the outbreak of the Second World War made further progress impossible. The city never held a plebiscite on the housing project. As well, Helena Gutteridge was defeated in the 1939 civic election. Despite attempts to have it extended, the NHA Part II deadline of 31 March 1940 passed without the initiation of a local scheme. The campaign for a low-rental project had failed, and Vancouver's housing problem was still unresolved.

The social housing movement of the 1930s was thus a vital but frustrated drive for change. Nevertheless, by the end of the decade, its voice in the public debate over housing in Vancouver was one to be reckoned with. On the one hand, business interests had obtained federal market housing programs to stimulate local construction, provide employment, and increase home ownership. On the other, the housing activist movement – composed of labour, unemployed workers', leftist, women's, and community organizations – had made social housing an issue of popular discussion. Activist groups defined the problem of residential conditions in Vancouver and established the goal of a local, federally funded, low-rental project. The injection of militancy and radicalism from the left gave the movement strategies, ideas, organizational support, and energy. By 1940, the social housing movement in Vancouver was ready to meet head-on the crisis in housing conditions during and after the Second World War.

4

'A Camp Existence': The Housing Problem in the 1940s

Housing shortages in wartime and postwar Vancouver intensified a long-standing need for adequate, affordable accommodation in the downtown area and its surrounding neighbourhoods. As contemporary observers realized, scarcities in building materials and labour, changes in demography, and some federal policies reduced the supply of housing. In turn, the accommodation shortages of the 1940s 'greatly aggravated' the serious problem created by the construction slowdown during the Depression, by the insufficient supplies of low-priced rental dwellings, and by the deterioration of housing stock built before the First World War.[1] The availability, affordability, and adequacy of dwellings are factors of equal importance in analyzing the housing problem of the 1940s.[2]

According to the 1941 and 1951 aggregated census figures collected by the Dominion Bureau of Statistics, the general picture of housing remained satisfactory, but a year-by-year examination of the decade reveals both a short-term crisis in homes for middle-income families and a continuing scarcity in affordable shelter for low-income households. After 1941, the housing situation gradually worsened until it reached a critical point in 1945-6 and then levelled off at the end of the decade. For many war workers, servicemen, and veterans, as well as their families, the housing problem was a temporary one. By the 1950s, they had moved to new homes in the suburbs or in adjacent municipalities. Yet for low-income households, chronic deficiencies in satisfactory, inexpensive rental accommodation persisted into and beyond the 1950s.

During the 1940s, lack of living space forced Vancouver's residents to crowd into apartments, rooms, cheap hotels, cabins, and waterfront shacks. 'One-room gypsies' trekked from lodging to lodging seeking permanent homes.[3] Others found more desperate solutions to their predicament. Unable to find accommodation for themselves and seven children, one couple lived in tents along the Capilano River. In another case, a mother with seven children occupied a shack in the bush near Burnaby Lake while her husband, a longshoreman, took a Cordova Street cabin. A few Vancouverites dealt with the housing problem in innovative, even eccentric, ways. After spending months in temporary quarters, for example, a serviceman and his wife turned a Spanish-style filling station near Locarno Beach into a comfortable bungalow, with a victory garden in the parking lot. One former Saskatchewan resident who wanted to bring his mother, brother, and sister to the West Coast built a house on a truck costing $190. A First World War veteran proclaimed that discarded British Columbia Electric trolleys 'in every backyard' were the answer to the lack of housing.[4] Frustrated by an unproductive job search after the war, a middle-aged ex-serviceman lived in caves near Siwash Rock in Stanley Park. No one, however, chose to protest shortages in quite the same manner as a Revere, Massachusetts, woman, whom Vancouverites read about in the *Vancouver Sun*. Faced with a similar postwar housing crisis, she sat on a fifty-foot pole proclaiming that it was 'as good a place to stay as lots of places we've lived.'[5]

Vancouver's housing shortage derived partly from the backlog of deferred construction that accumulated in the 1930s despite federal market housing programs. By 1937, this backlog amounted to about 6,000 units, and, four years later, it had climbed to an estimated 10,000 units.[6] By the outbreak of war, vacancies in rental accommodation had dropped to 'the dangerously low figure of two-thirds of 1 per cent.'[7] Vancouver therefore entered the wartime decade with a short housing supply.

The backlog increased with the slowdown in the local house-building industry arising from diversion of materials and labour to the war effort, postwar reconversion, and a rise in construction costs. Both skilled and unskilled workers enlisted in the armed forces or entered wartime shipbuilding or aircraft manufacturing industries. As well, many commodities required by builders were scarce.[8] By October 1944, deficiencies in building materials and labour had delayed the completion of 2,500 dwellings.[9]

Costs rose somewhere between 47 and 62 per cent from 1939 to 1945 and continued to mount after the war.[10] The shift from wartime to peacetime production continued to restrict the supply of construction workers and materials. In September 1945, shortages presented obstacles to the completion of 726 of 1,824 projects.[11] Even after the peacetime reconversion of war industry, building materials were still so scarce that a black market in plumbing supplies, bathtubs, electrical fittings, lumber, and flooring did a lively business. Supplies became more plentiful by 1949.[12] In addition, rising prices and wages and diminishing efficiency brought on by the demand for materials and workers increased construction costs and slowed house building.

In 1944, the report of the housing and community planning subcommittee of the federal government's advisory committee on reconstruction, known as the Curtis report, calculated the immediate accumulated building need for major Canadian cities as 230,000 units, based mainly upon wartime shortages, overcrowded households, and substandard replacement.[13] The estimated building need for Vancouver was 17,731 units.[14] Within the next two or three years, rough estimates of this requirement climbed to over 25,000 units.

Even as building efforts lagged, family formation and housing demand swelled. In contrast to the 1930s, marriages and births in Vancouver increased dramatically in the 1940s, while deaths continued to inch upwards as the population expanded (Table 14). In 1946, the marriage, birth, and death rates per 1,000 were 11.9, 22, and 9.8 respectively, as compared to 7.4, 14.5, and 9.6 per 1,000 between 1934 and 1938.[15] The volume of estimated house completions in Canada following the outbreak of war did not exceed net family formation until 1947.

An influx of war workers, servicemen's families, Prairie migrants, and European immigrants to Vancouver in the 1940s intensified the need for housing. Between September 1939 and June 1942, Greater Vancouver experienced an 80.5 per cent expansion in the employment of salaried and wage workers, especially in shipbuilding in North Vancouver and aircraft manufacturing in Vancouver and Richmond. The growth was smaller than in Halifax (108.9 per cent) or Windsor (121.1 per cent), but greater than in Toronto (56.6 per cent) or Winnipeg (30.2 per cent).[16] Observers expected these workers to stay in the area once the war ended. An unknown number of families accompanied servicemen stationed on the West Coast. In addition, the city continued to attract a steady flow of migrants from other parts of Canada, particularly the Prairie provinces. Between 1939 and 1946, British Columbia received 163,000 interprovincial migrants.[17] According to family allow-

Table 14

	Population*	Births**	Deaths	Marriages
1930	242,629	4,003	2,281	2,250
1931	246,593	3,730	2,300	1,767
1932	247,251	3,450	2,301	1,633
1933	243,711	3,188	2,239	1,776
1934	244,329	3,179	2,211	2,137
1935	247,558		2,466	2,227
1936	253,363	3,410	2,707	2,441
1937	259,987	3,780	2,782	2,783
1938	263,974	4,095	2,795	2,761
1939	269,454	4,107	2,798	3,496
1940	272,352	4,804	3,126	4,559
1941	275,304	5,303	3,266	4,578
1942	288,541	6,339	3,408	5,405
1943	299,460	7,180	3,808	4,548
1944	311,799	5,827	3,434	4,225
1945	323,850	5,711	3,560	4,516
1946	331,500	6,979	3,641	5,631
1947	347,870	7,811	3,768	5,471
1948	358,135	7,195	3,984	5,490
1949	369,040	7,522	3,980	5,155
1950	380,175	7,329	4,143	4,881

Vital Statistics for the City of Vancouver, 1930-50

* Assessor's estimate at close of year and census figures for 1931, 1941, and 1951.
**Exclusive of stillbirths.
Sources: British Columbia, Department of Health and Welfare, *Vital Statistics of the Province of British Columbia*, 1930-50; City of Vancouver, *Financial Statements and Annual Reports*, 1930-50.

ance figures, about 5,000 families settled in British Columbia in 1947, about half of them in Greater Vancouver. Moreover, then as now, many Prairie people wintered on the coast and returned home in the spring.[18] Finally, postwar immigration added substantially to population growth. Of 47,860 immigrant household heads in Vancouver in 1951, 2,270 arrived after 1946, compared to 1,460 between 1931 and 1945.[19]

Demobilization augmented the demand for accommodation following the Second World War. Although about 35,000 servicemen from Greater Vancouver and about 27,800 from Vancouver itself had enlisted in the forces, local observers expected twice as many to return to the area after the war's end.[20] Furthermore, about half of the discharged men were married, or would be married, within one year. By September 1946, 34,090 returned men (who had not necessarily enlisted in Greater Vancouver) already lived in Vancouver, 20,543 men still overseas would soon return, and about 1,800 war brides had arrived.[21] As well, all veterans receiving university or vocational training in British Columbia resided in Vancouver; single and married ex-servicemen made up about half of the UBC student enrollment immediately after the war.[22] By the 1951 census, about 24,000 of the over 101,000 household heads in Vancouver had seen service in the Second World War.[23]

As a consequence of family formation, migration, immigration, and demobilization, Vancouver's population rose by over 110,000 between 1939 and 1950. By contrast, between 1930 and 1938, it had increased by less than 22,000 (Table 14). Expansion in the number of available dwellings did not keep pace with this population growth. In September 1946, 93,200 families benefited from 80,750 existing dwellings, 2,843 under construction, and a minimum of 1,000 condemned places.[24] Between the summers of 1946 and 1947, when a population enlargement of 14,800 required an additional 4,600 units, the actual number of new dwellings amounted to 2,669 units. The sizable depression and wartime shortage was therefore enlarged by an annual deficit of about 2,000 units.

The curtailment of the 1938 NHA program and of the HIP reduced construction at the beginning of the war. As well, federal wartime programs applying to house construction sometimes reduced the availability of accommodation. In 1941, the government set up a construction control division within the Department of Munitions and Supply, eventually appointing a controller to restrict civilian building across Canada in order to divert materials to war industry.[25] The impact of construction controls on Vancouver's housing situation was extensive. The number of civic building permits issued dropped noticeably in 1942 and 1943 after the imposition of controls, whereas increases in 1944 and 1945 may be attributed to federal initiatives designed to relieve accommodation shortages (see Chapter 2, Table 3).

Controls also delayed house completions. Required to apply for both civic and federal building permits under wartime controls, builders and owners often started construction under a civic licence while waiting for a federal one and stopped when they reached the $500 or $1,500 limit, thereby increasing the number of incomplete units.[26] To the city building inspector's dismay, controls resulted in jerry-built housing when some owners circumvented value and size restrictions by putting up tiny dwellings known locally as 'Tom Thumb' or 'Peewee' houses. As the inspector commented, 'We welcome Tom Thumb houses, but not those that stick out like sore thumbs.'[27]

Regulations imposed by other controllers and branches within the Department of Munitions and Supply also discouraged and delayed civilian house construction.[28] The priorities branch, for example, gave preference in building supplies to federal housing programs for war workers, servicemen's families, and veterans over civilian home owners and contractors, thus curtailing private dwelling completions. After the war, the department's timber control inhibited construction by directing lumber away from the domestic market to the more lucrative export one until a policy change in 1947 rectified the situation.[29]

Despite their many benefits, rent controls implemented in Vancouver and North Vancouver under a 1940 Wartime Prices and Trade Board (WPTB) order-in-council affected housing availability during the war.[30] The controls applied to evictions as well as to rent levels, and defined the conditions under which a landlord could regain possession of a residence. In 1943, a WPTB order made eviction easier, with the result that a large number of notices to vacate became effective between 1 May and 1 October 1944; 704 notices matured in Vancouver between July and September alone. In the following year, 1,100 notices came due between June and October. Although repossession did not occur in all cases, the evictions carried out in Vancouver coincided with a growing housing shortage, and many tenants and their families could not find suitable accommodation. In July 1945, a freeze finally ended evictions under controls.

National housing registries had been set up under the WPTB to assist tenants in finding homes, and a postwar decision to terminate them only aggravated shortages. Vancouver's registry successfully placed thousands of families in accommodation and skilfully monitored the local situation for about five years. In 1946, the registry closed down, although over 6,000 still waited for a place to live.[31]

House conversion under the National Housing Administration of the Department of Finance had both negative and positive results. In Vancouver, the administration divided older apartment blocks and larger houses into smaller units for single people and couples involved in the war effort. Still, 'non-essential' former tenants and their families could not return to these premises, a predicament that created additional hardship during the shortages.[32] Moreover, the community at large perceived that these conversion projects absorbed building materials, labour, and government funds to shelter only a few people.

As the various factors of supply and demand came into play, shortages intensified, climaxed, and levelled off through the 1940s. They began to emerge in the first two years of the decade. In July 1940, a Vancouver Real Estate Exchange survey established vacancy rates of 0.7 per cent for houses and 4.2 per cent for suites.[33] By November, rental housing in the $20-a-month range was in heavy demand. During the following summer, Wartime Housing Limited (WHL), the federal crown corporation charged with providing war workers' accommodation, surveyed Vancouver's rental situation, found it deficient, and started to build homes for the employees of Burrard Drydock Company Limited and North Van Ship Repairs Limited in North Vancouver. More severe shortages developed with a rush between April and December 1942 as wartime employment mushroomed. WHL decided to construct more workers' units in North Vancouver.[34] A real estate exchange survey in June revealed a vacancy rate of 0.8 per cent for houses and 1.2 per cent for apartments. The WPTB housing registry opened its doors on Dunsmuir Street, and its staff began to assist despairing prospective tenants in their search for accommodation.

By 1943, Vancouver ranked second behind Halifax in housing congestion in Canada.[35] The vacancy rate declined even further, and a national housing registry survey uncovered only fifteen vacant houses in the city. Local newspapers offered pitifully few dwellings for rent. The maximum housing level occurred that summer, as 1,000 women from elsewhere in Canada arrived to work at Boeing aircraft plants at the same time that 156 eviction notices came due. Shortages halted the city's campaign to demolish waterfront shacks and frustrated the attempts of 300 out-of-town university students to find places to live. The housing registry was 'really beginning to roll.'[36] Between April and October, it received 4,685 applications for housing from servicemen's families, 2,316 from war workers, and 3,393 from civilians.[37] It placed only about 9,000 of 19,700 applications that year.

In 1944, 5,000 houses remained unfinished owing to scarcities of materials and labour.[38] Over 2,000 households, of which about one-third belonged to ex-servicemen, faced eviction that summer as landlords repossessed their properties. Once again, the registry filled only about half of its requests for housing.

The situation became acute in 1945, as the war ended and service personnel returned home. The registry settled 10,000 people between January and October; by December, an all-time high of 4,143 families – the majority of them including veterans – sought housing in the city.[39] The vacancy rate reached 0 per cent. Over 1,000 families encountered the threat of eviction between June and October. Scarcities in supplies and labour continued to tie up new house construction.

By May 1946, the situation remained 'terribly acute,' 'showing no sign of improvement,' and 'compressing more and more people into the same cubic space of living accommodation, at the cost of widespread inconvenience and distress.'[40] Although the armed forces had demobilized thousands of veterans in Vancouver by May, they expected to send 8,000 more, many with wives and children, back to the city from overseas. Federal government housing programs for veterans in Greater Vancouver were slow to start and to complete units. About 500 married university student veterans could not locate suitable housing for the fall. A total of 4,400 applicants sought accommodation in WHL units. Although more civic building permits were being issued, delayed construction and rising costs hindered production.

The housing shortage persisted and then levelled off in the last three years of the decade. Although the national housing registry no longer existed, WHL had 6,600 applications for houses on file by the end of 1947.[41] Several government-initiated subdivisions for veterans opened, but high building costs still impeded new construction. In October 1948, the waiting list for rental housing built directly by the federal government amounted to over 7,500 applications. Finally, in May 1949, the numbers on the list fell to about 3,300.[42] By then, housing shortages had troubled many Vancouverites for fully a decade.

In the 1940s, affordability was as much a problem as availability for many Vancouver renters. Although the majority of tenants wished to own their own homes, some did not. In June 1944, about 60 per cent of 1,028 tenants sampled in the city wanted to own a house, and 48 per cent of all tenants could have made a 10 per cent downpayment at that time.[43] Yet fewer than one-third of them had any definite idea of owning in the next few years because employment was uncertain and prices were high. House prices went up by 173 per cent on average for four-, five-, and six-room dwellings between 1939 and 1946, and the east side was particularly affected. Forty per cent of the sampled tenants planned to continue renting. Incomes of less than $1,200 or $1,500 played 'a major part' in framing their expectations. According to another survey made in 1949, the situation had not changed significantly; 46 per cent, compared to 48 per cent in 1944, could buy, and 54 per cent could rent. The deciding factor again appears to have been income.[44]

In fact, many Vancouverites realized their expectations of owning a home by 1951. The proportion of owner-occupied dwellings rose to 63 per cent, from 51 per cent in 1931 and 50.1 per cent in 1941 (see Chapter 2, Table 8). The trend towards ownership started early in the 1940s among those who benefited from wartime industrial expansion. In 1940-1, the City of Vancouver finally sold to war workers and others many of the Better Housing Scheme bungalows that had reverted to it during the Depression.[45] Two years later, the local mortgage company branches had disposed of all the houses that they had foreclosed in the 1930s, and owners held the only houses for sale.[46] In addition, many Vancouverites had accumulated wartime savings, and the federal government's postwar market housing programs encouraged the building and purchase of new units. In 1951, 68.5 per cent of dwellings in Greater Vancouver were occupied by owners.[47] Nevertheless, the rise in home ownership did not occur without considerable frustration for builders and owners, brought on by labour and materials shortages and rising costs.

The major instrument used to foster ownership was the 1944 NHA. Part I of the act reaffirmed the joint loan method initiated under the 1935 and 1938 legislation, but made mortgage money more widely available.[48] More significantly, a later amendment to the act introduced the Integrated Housing Plan (IHP), under which the federal government provided joint loans for veterans' dwellings and assumed the risk for any unsold units. The 1944 NHA Part I fostered a large amount of construction in Vancouver. Between 1946 and 1950, federal officials approved 7,030 loans for homes in the city, and between 1947 and 1950, work started on 5,916. Building under the IHP began rather slowly in 1946. By November, 280 units for Vancouver had been approved, fifty-eight started, and two finished. Fifty were going up in the Little Mountain area.[49] Builders subsequently erected more integrated housing in the Grandview Highway area between Nanaimo and Renfrew streets, in East Hastings, and in South Vancouver. The largest thrust of the plan, however, occurred on large land tracts in surrounding municipalities: Willingdon Heights in Burnaby, Victory Heights in New Westminster, Capilano Properties in the District of North Vancouver, and a development near Lion's Gate Hospital in the City of North Vancouver.

In the early 1950s, families continued to move into new homes built under the 1944 NHA in suburban Vancouver and in North Shore and Burnaby subdivisions such as the British Properties, Norgate, Boulevard Heights, Suncrest, and Southern View.[50] Construction slowed down when the Korean War increased costs for erecting and selling units, and by July 1951, houses priced at under $10,000 were fast disappearing.

Heavy emphasis upon home ownership in federal programs meant that builders put up very little housing for the 37 to 50 per cent of Vancouverites who lived as tenants. In 1947, the production of new rental units in Canada amounted to only about 30 per cent of all residential construction.[51] This trend was attributable partly to intensified postwar demand for owner occupancy and partly to wartime rent controls. Builders also found investment in the rental market unattractive because both construction costs and rents were high in the late 1940s.[52]

Despite rising expectations about home ownership after the war, it appeared 'evident' to federal officials 'that many purchasers of new houses would have preferred to rent rather than to purchase.'[53] Moreover, many low- and moderate-income tenants could not afford the uncontrolled rents commanded by new units built in the late 1940s, and the accommodation shortage was so great that no units 'filtered down' to those in need of inexpensive housing.

In 1944, the Curtis report determined that large percentages of low- and moderate-income tenants in Canada spent more than one-fifth of their earnings on rents.[54] In Vancouver, where the average monthly rent was $26, 88.5 per cent of the lowest third of 35,513 tenant households – who earned under $1,200 a year and had an annual average family income of $574 – paid disproportionate rent. On average, they could afford monthly rents of $9.57, but they actually paid $18.[55] Half of the middle third of tenants, who had incomes between $1,200 and $1,800 and average annual family earnings of $1,287, spent slightly more on rent than they could afford; they had average actual rents of $22 when one-fifth of income would amount to $21.45. Home ownership was a possibility for this middle group through Part I of the 1944 NHA, under which house payments ranged between $20 and $26 a month. However, renting remained a reality for those paying disproportionate rents in Vancouver. According to a federal survey of the city's tenants in 1944, two-fifths planned to remain renters.[56] Forty-two per cent of them reported 1943 incomes of under $1,200 and claimed maximum affordable rents of $20 a month.

Tenants of the lower third income grouping tended to live downtown, where rental housing was concentrated. In the lodging-house area west of Burrard, rents amounted to $16 to $28 per month for a room and $24 to $40 for a two-room suite.[57] East of Burrard, rents typically cost $14 to $30 per month for a room and $16 to $32 for a two-room suite. Monthly rates were still lower in the Strathcona area.[58] On average, a single house rented for about $16, an apartment for between about $16.50 and $23.50, a rooming house or cabin for $17, an unfurnished room for $6, and a furnished one for $9.50. Board and room cost $10 per month if unfurnished and $13 if furnished.

Controls imposed under the WPTB kept rents down.[59] Superseding provincial law, they applied to all dwelling places, including lodging and boardinghouses, and fixed charges at 2 January 1940 levels. Lifting of controls began in 1947, when accommodation built after 1 January of that year was freed from rental and eviction regulation. Starting in 1947, the WPTB also permitted rental increases of 10 per cent for self-contained housing completed before 1 January 1944.[60] Postwar inflation thus put the price of new rental units out of competition with that of older ones. Controls remained in effect in varying degrees throughout the 1940s.

If the controls program protected the interests of many tenants, the decision to sell off rental housing built directly by federal crown companies did not. Between 1941 and 1949, WHL and the Central Mortgage and Housing Corporation (CMHC) (later called the Canada Mortgage and Housing Corporation) completed over 2,800 homes for war workers, servicemen's families, and veterans in Vancouver, North Vancouver, and Richmond.[61] These companies began selling units to tenants in 1947, offering 1,953 in five years and disposing of 1,872 in four.[62] In April 1951, about 2,000 veterans' families still waited for housing after six years.[63] At a time when Vancouver desperately needed moderately priced rental accommodation, the federal government actually depleted stock through its own initiatives.

The government also attempted to encourage the construction of low- or moderate-cost rental dwellings under the NHA through a limited dividend corporation, Housing Enterprises of Canada (HEC) Limited. However, the company 'could not produce a desirable type of housing at the cost levels originally contemplated.'[64] Monthly rentals of between $45 and $65 for one- to three-bedroom apartments were too high for many veterans and others. In 1947, several projects across the country, including the row and apartment houses erected along Fourth and Broadway avenues, were transferred to the recently created CMHC.

Federal emphasis upon the construction of owned rather than rented units and the sale of government-built rental dwellings aggravated the difficulties faced by many tenants in finding accommodation in a satisfactory condition. Not surprisingly, households with the lowest incomes experienced the greatest hardship during the wartime and postwar housing shortages, and all too often they found themselves trapped in poor quality housing. Social assistance families experienced the worst housing conditions and paid rents in excess of their shelter allowances.[65] In east Kitsilano, 60 per cent of households surveyed by a committee of the Henry Hudson School parent-teacher association resided in substandard accommodation. Ten per cent of these, however, could afford more suitable housing but could not locate any.[66]

Several VHA studies also reported a shortage of less expensive accommodation. In 1954, the VHA surveyed 138 families with children occupying dwellings with shared bathroom and kitchen facilities in the area bounded by Burrard Avenue, Commercial Drive, Broadway Avenue, and Burrard Inlet; it did not include families with children inhabiting self-contained rental housing.[67] The survey concluded that 'a marked reduction' in the number of families occupying shared accommodation had occurred since the acute postwar housing shortage. While some households had moved into subdivisions created by CMHC or private builders, however, 'a large number of families [had] moved to substandard housing in the outer districts, where cheap accommodation in the shape of basement suites and housekeeping rooms [had] become available through the spread of multiple occupancy uses and the illegal conversion of single family homes.' Of the 138 households, 27 per cent were single-parent families, 16 per cent received social assistance allowances, and 40 per cent lived at or near subsistence levels. Skilled and unskilled wage earners represented the majority of male family heads; they and their families had been 'forced' to accept their lodgings 'simply because there was no other accommodation where children were accepted at rents they could afford to pay.' As well, the VHA found in a 1951 study that single working women had the choice of paying unaffordable rates to obtain better housing distant from their work or lower rents to secure inferior rooms closer to their jobs.[68] Similarly, many senior citizens with low income, some on pensions, continued to occupy downtown rooms and suites.[69]

Searching for the cheapest quarters, low-income households often competed with moderate-income families for the city's oldest, least satisfactory housing. Although in general the quality of housing in Vancouver was favourable, overcrowding, disrepair, and deficient basic facilities afflicted certain types of rental accommodation concentrated in the downtown area, much as they had before and during the depression. According to the 1941 census, for example, 13.2 per cent of Vancouver households experienced overcrowding.[70] The figure compares very favourably with the average of 18.5 per cent for twenty-seven Canadian cities. Nevertheless, the crowding situation first deteriorated and then improved in the next few years, as the availability of accommodation contracted after 1941 and expanded again at the end of the decade. By 1951, only 9.9 per cent of households in the city were overcrowded, although population growth had provoked a 6.7 per cent increase in the actual number of people living in crowded conditions.[71]

In 1941, the conditions of overcrowding for the 9,387 affected households were serious.[72] In contrast to those in uncrowded residences, their premises were more likely to need external repairs, to have shared toilet and bathing facilities, to lack proper food storage, and to shelter lodgers. Crowded households were less likely to possess telephones, electric vacuums, or even radios. Of these households, 83.5 per cent earned wages of under $1,500 per year, and rented their accommodation.

As in the prewar years, overcrowded households were concentrated in Vancouver's downtown core and surrounding neighbourhoods, coinciding with the highest population density. Strathcona experienced worsening overcrowding between 1944 and 1950.[73] Of 1,000 families surveyed in the area in the late 1940s, 48 per cent lived in crowded circumstances. More specifically, 38.6 per cent of those in single houses, 71.5 per cent in apartments, 63.9 per cent in rooming houses, and 57.3 per cent in cabins encountered congestion. Overcrowding was also high among the elderly and the seasonally employed living in boardinghouses in Chinatown, in the downtown area north of Hastings Street, and in east Kitsilano near False Creek. In 1947, the VHA estimated that crowding affected 40 per cent of the city's rooming population.[74]

Congestion apparently eased as the shortages declined at the decade's end. A 1948 Vancouver health department study of 600 lodging houses in the West End and elsewhere in the city expected more overcrowding than it found, and a later expanded survey of 1,000 lodging houses confirmed the results.[75] In 1951, a study of West End rooming houses found little overcrowding except among families.[76] By 1957, the overcrowding rate in the east end had decreased to 15 per cent.[77] In all probability, many families residing in downtown lodgings in the mid-1940s later moved into veterans' rental housing in Renfrew Heights and Fraserview, or into multiple occupancy units or illegal suites in outlying suburbs.

In 1941, 18.2 per cent of Vancouver's occupied dwellings needed external repairs, compared to an average of 16.5 per cent for twenty-seven major Canadian cities.[78] During the 1930s, many owners and landlords lacked sufficient cash to renovate or repair their buildings. Despite construction and rental controls and shortages of labour and building supplies, fuller employment and higher, steadier earnings made more exterior repairs possible in the 1940s. The total number of dwellings in disrepair fell from 12,943 to 5,495 over the decade.[79] Yet such a substantial drop may have reflected different measurement standards in the 1941 and 1951 census takings. In addition, intensive house building in the late 1940s drove the proportion of dwellings needing renovation down to 5.4 per cent by 1951.

While the exterior conditions of housing improved outside the downtown area, gradual deterioration continued in the city's core, and surrounding areas, where Vancouver's oldest accommodation – most of it wooden – was located (Figure 13). In 1948-9, lodging-house studies of the West End and elsewhere in the city demonstrated the lack of satisfactory exterior or structural maintenance in about one-third of the surveyed buildings.[80] A 1951 report of the rooming-house district east of Burrard Street between Dunsmuir Street and False Creek concluded that the small, poorly built residences were approaching the end of their useful lives and that 'not a few have already passed it.'[81] Nearly half of the 800 houses surveyed displayed poor structural condition. Landlords held their property on speculation and refused to spend 'a cent more than they have to on upkeep.' In east Kitsilano, 18 per cent of houses were in very bad repair, and some required demolition.[82] Health inspectors' reports of the downtown area routinely noted dilapidation in cheap hotels and cabins.[83] The city had declared many of these places unfit for human habitation, but in some cases people continued to live in them. A 1950 study described the state of deterioration in Strathcona with respect to exterior and interior walls, roofs, foundations, ceilings, floorings, and stairs as 'a menace.'[84] It rated only 0.6 per cent of residential properties as good, while 11.5 per cent were fair, 60 per cent poor, and 27.9 per cent bad. Time and again, health inspectors indicated that little could be done to stop the decay of downtown residential buildings as long as the housing shortages lasted. As late as 1957, major defects in housing remained in the east end, 32 per cent of 1,852 residential structures, or 4,612 units, were in a poor or very poor state of repair, and 16 per cent had damp walls and floors.[85]

The facilities and conveniences found in Vancouver's housing gener-

Figure 13 Today's historical preservationists cherish wooden houses built in Strathcona around the turn of the century. Yet in 1950, a housing report recommended gradual clearance and redevelopment of the area in order to preserve the healthy but declining community.

ally improved between 1941 and 1951 (Table 15). Residents enjoyed more furnaces, refrigerators, electric or gas ranges, bathtubs, and showers. Exclusive use of flush toilets declined slightly owing to wartime house conversions. Like owners, tenants benefited from more mechanical refrigeration. They were less likely, however, to have individual use of toilet and bathing facilities and did not possess significantly more conveniences such as radios, telephones, or electric vacuums in 1951 than in 1941.

Not unexpectedly, the downtown area was most seriously deficient in basic facilities (Table 15). In the West End, 40 per cent of all housekeeping rooms lacked the sink required by civic bylaw.[86] Few sleeping rooms supplied a washbasin. Moreover, half of the surveyed lodging houses failed to conform to a bylaw requiring the provision of a bath or shower, a toilet, and a washbasin for every three housekeeping rooms. Although

Table 15

Facilities, conveniences, disrepair, and overcrowding in Vancouver (1941 and 1951) and Strathcona (ca. 1950), by percentage

	Vancouver		Strathcona
Dwellings with	(1941)	(1951)	(ca. 1950)
Furnace	75.2	80.2	42.4
Electric/gas range	51.7	62.5	16.8
Mechanical refrigeration	28.7	54.0	46.5
Flush toilet	90.3*	89.7*	78.2**
Tub/shower	86.5*	87.9*	67.5**
Telephone	71.1	77.4	38.6
Radio	91.5	93.9	76.6
Exterior disrepair	18.2	05.4	27.9 (bad)
			60.0 (poor)
Overcrowding	13.2	09.9	48.2

*Exclusive use.
**Defective facilities (either no facilities or some shared by too many people; dirty or otherwise inadequate).
Sources: Canada, Dominion Bureau of Statistics, *Eighth Census of Canada, 1941* (Ottawa: King's Printer 1949), vol. 3, *Housing*, 11, table 3a, 33, table 10a, 53, table 10a, 62, table 12a, 71, table 15a, 75, table 16a, 79, table 17a, and 83, table 18a; idem, *Ninth Census of Canada, 1951* (Ottawa: Queen's Printer 1953), vol. 3, *Housing and Families*, table 18-6; ibid., vol. 3, *Housing, Principal Heating Equipment and Fuel*, Bulletin 3-7, table 22-6; ibid., vol. 3, *Housing, Household Living Conveniences*, Bulletin 3-8, table 42-6; ibid., vol. 3, *Housing, Plumbing, Lighting, Cooking, and Refrigeration Facilities*, Bulletin 3-10, tables 34-6, 38-6; ibid., vol. 3, *Housing, Crowded and Uncrowded Households*, Bulletin 3-13, tables 86-1; Leonard C. Marsh, *Rebuilding a Neighbourhood* (Vancouver: University of British Columbia 1950), 3, 18, tables 8, 9, 11, and 73, table 28.

West End lodging houses had central heating, they frequently did without adequate lighting in hallways and stairwells. The 'traditional soapbox' on the window ledge, rather than a properly screened and ventilated cupboard, continued to be the most common form of food storage. East of Burrard, lodging houses were deficient in housekeeping sinks, bathing and toilet conveniences, and central heating. Heat came from a gas ring or a hallway stove. Similarly, east Kitsilano tenements offered wood and coal cooking and heating appliances and insufficient numbers of toilets and bathrooms. In Strathcona, limited access to plumbing facilities was customary in apartments, rooming houses, and cabins.[87] Here, cupboards, coolers, or window boxes provided food storage as commonly as refrigerators did, and stoves or heaters afforded warmth as much as did furnaces. The use of wood or coal stoves exceeded that of any other form of cooking facility; the entire area boasted only nine electric ranges.

In the VHA's 1954 study of 138 households that shared accommodation, 63 per cent had suites with wood or coal stoves for heating, and 47 per cent shared a bath and 30 per cent a toilet with nine or more people.[88] In the east end in 1957, 18 per cent of residential structures offered toilets shared by over six persons, and 14 per cent provided a bath in an outside structure or no bath whatsoever. Indeed, the inspections in 1954 revealed that 60 per cent of dwellings surveyed were inadequate when 'all aspects of accommodation affecting its livability' were evaluated, despite a lowered rate of overcrowding.

Housing in the downtown area was often deficient in other aspects of physical condition and facilities. City health department officials and VHA activists raised concerns about basement and attic lodgings east and west of Burrard Street. Civic bylaws called for 7' 6" ceilings in these rooms and for no more than 400 square feet of living space in basements.[89] Of 1,000 lodging houses surveyed in 1949, 14.7 per cent of all occupied rooms were in basements or attics; more than half of the basement rooms and about one-quarter of the attic ones had insufficient head space.[90] Too frequently, basements and attics lacked adequate light and ventilation and convenient access to toilet and bathing facilities.[91] As well, basements were often plagued with vermin and dampness, and attics with excessive heat. In a 1952 study of Kitsilano's housekeeping rooms and suites within the boundaries of Alma Road, Trafalgar Street, Point Grey Road, and Fourth Avenue, 67 per cent of basement suites – which the city had banned in November 1950 – had ceilings lower than the permitted height of 7' 6".[92]

Another problem had emerged by the late 1940s, when civic officials expressed apprehension about the use of domestically produced gas for cooking purposes. In the early days of the British Columbia Electric Company, gas had been manufactured in such a way that the carbon monoxide content was limited to about 6 per cent, and death by gas, except in suicide cases, was not common. In 1947, however, the company changed its technology and produced a gas with a carbon monoxide content of about 30 per cent.[93] The gas supplied rings and stoves in the West End, the business district, Chinatown, and Strathcona, and increasingly in suburban neighbourhoods, including new ones such as Renfrew Heights.[94] At the same time, in Kitsilano, 22 to 31 per cent of dwellings furnished with gas cooking facilities that had been installed in the 1930s and 1940s were in contravention of civic bylaws by 1952. In 1951, gas plates and stoves represented 92 per cent of all cooking facilities in West End lodging houses.[95] Fixtures in older dwellings were frequently installed in sleeping areas with little or no ventilation, inadequate pressure, and rubber connections. Although the availability of electrical appliances had increased, landlords often resisted switching to electricity because gas was used for heating as well as cooking and rewiring was costly.

Between 1942 and 1949, gas poisoning incidents grew significantly. Over those years, there was an average increase of 3.7 accidental deaths by coal gas, with a sudden rise in 1947-9.[96] Suicides by coal gas showed an average increase of 4.1 deaths per 100,000 population. Finally, in the early 1950s, the problem of rising rates of death owing to domestic gas poisonings became of intense public concern. Fatalities increased from thirty-six in 1947 to eighty-eight in 1953, and forty-two deaths and sixty-eight recoveries from accidents and suicides occurred in the first half of 1954. Cooking and heating with manufactured gas represented a greater hazard in cheaper rental accommodation, where installation and maintenance were often inadequate and illegal.

The 'deadly domestic gas' situation resulted in several investigations and in a special committee of city council.[97] It remained a major concern of Vancouver's medical health officer, Dr. Stewart Murray. Late in 1953, after much discussion and despite opposition from apartment and rooming-house operators and owners, council brought in a bylaw requiring installation of safety devices on all gas appliances.[98] During the following August, the provincial government implemented legislation that overrode the Vancouver bylaw and required gas appliance inspection.[99] Nevertheless, local and provincial efforts did not prove effective. Only the arrival of natural gas from Alberta later in the decade solved the problem.

Civic officials and housing activists noted other problems in the downtown area's accommodation, such as deficient environments, vermin infestations, and unsatisfactory fire protection. In the West End, for example, despite their proximity to English Bay and Stanley Park, senior citizens and small children lacked green space immediately adjacent to their lodging houses.[100] In the VHA's 1954 shared accommodation study, 22 per cent of households had no access to play space for small children. The 'degrading' surroundings of the South False Creek industrial site interfered with a wholesome family life for east Kitsilano residents.[101] Although Strathcona had many 'good features,' it was surrounded by the British Columbia Electric Company gasworks on the west, a slaughterhouse on the north, and a city dump on the flats to the south. Furthermore, rodents and bedbugs infested downtown housing from Strathcona to the West End.[102] Serious fire hazards remained in the boardinghouses of Chinatown with their partitions, wood and coal stoves, coal oil lamps, and inadequate fire escapes, and in the tenements of east Kitsilano and east of Burrard with their exposed wiring, defective stovepipes, and tinder-dry wooden interiors.[103] In the east end in 1957, 10 per cent of residential buildings lacked sufficient fire exits.

Some areas offered better quality rental housing than others. The high-rent apartment block areas of South Granville, Cambie, and Oak almost never appear in health inspectors' reports and surveys. Inspectors often described houses in Kitsilano and Fairview as 'well run' and 'very clean.'[104] They also generally viewed as soundly built and appropriately maintained the 70 per cent of West End lodging places that were operated by their owners. For instance, Helena Gutteridge, who had been active in the housing campaign in the late 1930s, later retired to a top floor housekeeping room in a well-kept West End lodging house.[105] Nonetheless, lodging houses east of Burrard (80 per cent of which were speculative properties) and rooming houses in Strathcona usually suffered from bad management and poor structural condition.

As in the past, inadequate living conditions tended to occur in certain types of accommodation: cabins, Chinese boardinghouses, cheap hotels, and waterfront shacks. Forty cabins, 'the City's poorest type of accommodation,' still remained in Strathcona in 1950, while a few others survived in east Kitsilano and east of Burrard (see Chapter 1, Figure 2).[106] Usually dilapidated, dirty, and infested with vermin, cabins ordinarily used wood or coal stoves and coal oil lamps rather than electricity. Most had no bathtubs or hot water supply, and all provided 'common cast [cast-iron] toilets' and outside taps. The Chinese residents of boardinghouses located on or around East Pender Street continued to experience overcrowding, insufficient light and ventilation, fire danger, disease risks, vermin, deficient sanitary facilities, structural disrepair, and poor maintenance. Under civic pressure in 1947-8, a landlord successfully relocated 300 men who had been living in Marshall Wells Limited warehouses on Shanghai Alley, but hundreds of other men continued to dwell in unhealthy conditions.[107] Accommodation in downtown east-side hotels represented virtually no improvement over cabins or boardinghouses.[108] As well, the long-standing problem of foreshore shacks persisted throughout the 1940s. In 1949, 107 shacks on land, 234 floathouses, and about 525 fishing boats bordering Burrard Inlet, False Creek, and the Fraser River served as homes.[109] Water supply and waste disposal for the shacks remained matters of grave concern to civic officials.

Not everyone regarded cabins, hotels, or shacks as inadequate. The mother of historian Rolf Knight referred to 'coolie cabins' as 'the black hole of Calcutta,' but Knight himself saw these places in a better light.[110] His friend Pat Fitzpatrick, a bachelor on a pension, lived contentedly in a 'roomy enough' cabin partitioned off into bedroom and kitchen/living room areas. The low-income tenants of the Davenport Rooms on West Pender Street praised their clean, pest-free premises for good lighting, adequate sanitary facilities, and 'a nice lobby on the ground floor with chesterfield and chairs, with plenty of reading material, where [they] could read or talk.'[111] Along Burrard Inlet, eight 'boathouses' on Commissioner Drive 'ranged from one-room shacks to large solidly built houses' with flowers in window boxes or barrels and terraced gardens on the adjacent embankment.[112] If well maintained, these bungalows on rock and timber piers could last a couple of generations. Over in North Vancouver at Dollarton, authors Malcolm Lowry and Margerie Bonner were deeply attached to their rustic but comfortable waterfront home. Threatened by eviction between 1947 and 1954, 'they were heartbroken about the possibility of losing their beloved shack.'[113] When the eviction finally came and they left for overseas, Lowry's despondency and sense of loss intensified his alcoholism, and in 1957 he died by misadventure.

During the shortages of the 1940s, the city felt obliged to tolerate many cases of poor housing accommodation for moderate- or low-income families unable to find shelter elsewhere.[114] Inspections and warnings to operators and owners might or might not result in superficial improvements. Many places placarded as unfit for human habitation were demolished only after the shortage ended. In addition, landlords used rent controls and high building costs as excuses not to make improvements.

According to the VHA, the chief victim of the absence of decent, inexpensive homes was the serviceman or veteran and his family, whose plight was, 'to put it mildly, a crying scandal.'[115] As well, wounded Seaforth Highlanders returning from Italy, 'practically all of them in a highly nervous condition,' desperately needed, and frequently could not find, good homes for convalescence. 'After living a camp existence for 6 years, the veteran continue[d] to camp – in other peoples' homes, in basements, garages, or under any roof he ... [could] find.' Not infrequently, the wives and children of overseas men lived in filthy rooms in the downtown area.[116] Indeed, until shortages declined at the decade's end, many ex-servicemen and their families occupied rooms or suites in the lodging houses and cabins of the West End, business district, and east Kitsilano or moved into waterfront shacks.[117]

Groups other than veterans inhabited unsuitable housing. War workers, some of whom travelled long distances from downtown to the Boeing plant on Sea Island, rented damp basements, hotel rooms, or 'disreputable and filthy' houses.[118] Many families with young children lived in cramped, unwholesome lodgings in the downtown core.[119] Relief households commonly ended up 'huddled in hovels' because their shelter allowances of $6 per month for a family of three or $8 for six or more fell short of market rents.[120] Single working women found few respectable self-contained suites at moderate prices east and west of Burrard, and often had to spend more of their modest salaries than they could afford for better quarters.[121] The few hostels such as the Blue Triangle Residential Club, the YWCA, and the Sisters of Service Residential Club offered only a limited amount of space. The situation improved somewhat in the early 1950s, as multiple occupancy spread into one- and two-family zones in outlying districts. Single men, especially the elderly and the seasonally employed, crowded into cabins, lodging houses, and cheap hotels in the downtown east side, east Kitsilano, Chinatown, and Strathcona, or into waterfront shacks.[122]

Some of those hardest hit by the shortages were impoverished single elderly women and men. In 1949, about 14,000 persons over sixty-five resided in the City of Vancouver, and about half had incomes of under $60 per month.[123] Only 43 per cent of those over seventy drew the $40 old age pension, which was not universal until 1951.[124] Some had veterans' or war widows' allowances. Many 'helpless or indifferent' pensioners lived in one-room cabins with stoves, coal lamps, and minimal plumbing facilities.[125] All too often, they lived alone in basement or attic rooms or suites with inadequate sanitary, cooking, and heating facilities. Insensitive landlords discriminated as much against them as against families with children when it came to letting rooms or responding to their needs. Not infrequently, landlords intimidated older residents, especially women, by turning off the heat in order to force them to vacate their rooms and to make way for younger tenants. One old-timer of eighty-one lived an appalling existence in his Keefer Street room. Without family or friends to care for him in his 'physically and mentally ailing' state, he relied upon missions and civic social services for aid.[126] Finally, he was found dead 'nesting in a mound of refuse' after almost a week.

Still, in contrast to this 'picture to which only Dickens could do justice,' some elderly people found refuge with caring managers.[127] A woman who operated cabins called 'Little Haven' for about twenty-eight individuals on Glen Drive tried 'to give to each the shelter, privacy, and decency of their own little place.'[128] Moreover, landlords could not cope with older tenants who were no longer able to care for themselves. Few services and facilities existed in the community to assist and accommodate the infirm. Institutional options in the early 1940s included the Old People's Home, later called Taylor Manor, on Boundary Road, the Riverview mental hospital, and the thirty-three boarding homes for about 600 aged residents licensed under provincial welfare legislation.[129]

Vancouver's housing problem of the 1940s thus consisted in part of a lack of adequate housing for low-income households in the downtown area. This shortage had troubled many Vancouverites during and even before the 1930s. By 1950, it had become chronic. The problem also included a temporary shortage, throughout east- and west-side neighbourhoods, of owned and rented units that middle-income families could afford. A similar predicament had occurred during the Depression and after the First World War. In sum, the housing problem in wartime and postwar Vancouver consisted, on the one hand, of a continuing scarcity of satisfactory, low-income rental accommodation and, on the other hand, of occasional crises in middle-income residential supply. The intensity of the problem challenged activist groups to initiate a new, this time more successful, campaign for better housing.

5
Responding to the Housing Problem in the 1940s: The War on Canada's 'Number One Emergency'

Throughout the 1940s, the federal government prescribed a variety of remedies intended to ease the severity of the housing problem in Canada. In order to expedite the war effort and reconstruction, it first initiated temporary relief for the immediate emergency and later provided permanent market housing programs to fuel the postwar economy and increase housing supply. Still, Ottawa's unilateral action did not sufficiently ameliorate the deteriorating residential conditions in Vancouver.

Dissatisfied with the federal reaction, social activists increasingly responded through a wide range of organizations to Vancouver's worsening housing situation. Some activist groups attempted to eliminate the crisis faced by homeless veterans. Other organizations, many of which had participated in the social housing campaign of the 1930s, worked to correct both the chronic need for low-income dwellings and the temporary shortage in accommodation. Relatively quiet at first, the activists collectively gained strength as a movement by 1944 and commanded wide public support by 1946. Despite opposition from a vocal element of real estate interests, lenders, and builders, they effectively urged governments at all levels to make improvements in housing conditions. They attributed the major responsibility for resolving the housing problem to the federal government, but they also pressed the civic and provincial governments for change. They achieved an evictions freeze, emergency shelters, continuation of rent controls, and the construction of some rental units for veterans. In the end, local activists joined with national forces to obtain amendments to the NHA that made possible Little Mountain, the first public housing development in Vancouver.

The accomplishments of these activist groups were too often temporary and limited in scope. The federal government eventually sold off rental dwellings built for veterans and war workers, closed emergency shelter units, and conveyed responsibility for rent controls to the province, which soon terminated them. Little Mountain and other public housing complexes constructed between 1957 and 1970 barely touched the long-term problem of adequately accommodating low-income households. Yet despite these limitations, the story of the housing campaign demonstrates that activism secured concrete improvements in living conditions for many Vancouverites.

Between 1940 and 1946, the federal government imposed a number of programs intended to further the war effort and then facilitate recon-struction of the postwar economy by relieving the housing problem. Early in the war, it introduced controls over rents, evictions, construc-tion, and supplies, and built war workers' homes under WHL. At the same time, it limited operations under the 1938 NHA and replaced the HIP with the Home Extension and Home Conversion plans. Later, in anticipation of postwar readjustment, the government created a sub-committee on housing and town planning of its advisory committee on reconstruction, passed the 1944 NHA, and established the CMHC. Federal initiatives such as the IHP, the Housing Enterprises of Canada (HEC) scheme, and the Department of Veterans Affairs (DVA) housing program were responsible for the construction of thousands of new dwellings. Unfortunately, however beneficial in some respects, these federal efforts did not resolve the housing situation either at the national level or in Vancouver.

In 1939, Cabinet set up the WPTB under the War Measures Act to stop price inflation of 'any necessary of life' and to ensure supply.[1] A year later, it extended the board's regulatory powers to residential accommo-dation as a 'necessary of life' and appointed a rentals administrator. A subsequent board order applied controls to fifteen localities, including Vancouver and North Vancouver, and fixed maximum rental at 2 January 1940 levels. Voluntary committees in all controlled areas inves-tigated complaints, devised procedures, examined records, and obtained information respecting rentals. Vancouver's committee consisted of J.N. Ellis, a county court judge, J.G. Walker, a real estate executive, and W.J. Bartlett, a past president of Vancouver's trades and labour council.

As housing congestion spread across the country, the board gradually extended controls. By 1 December 1941, they applied nation wide, with rentals frozen at an 11 October 1941 level. A more decentralized, complicated system, with full-time appraisers, regional offices, and consolidated procedures slowly developed. In 1943, J.G. Walker became Vancouver's rentals appraiser; he heard disputes, and appeals on his decisions went to a special appeal court.

The WPTB rentals administration allowed changes in maximum rents and tenant evictions. It permitted rent increases if the landlord's costs rose, for example, or if repairs or improvements were necessary.[2] At first, tenants could be evicted for reasons such as non-payment of rent, broken lease conditions, inadequate care, repossession by the landlord for personal or family use, or sale of the dwelling with the condition of vacancy included. Later, in 1943, the WPTB limited eviction conditions to occupation by the landlord for personal or family use for a one-year period or to subdivision of the unit to accommodate more residents. It demanded a minimum six-month notice for repossession and a three-month notice for conversion. As well, landlords could not terminate leases between 30 September and 30 April for monthly or weekly tenure.

By 1942, the WPTB had committed itself to making full use of existing accommodation as well as to regulating rentals and evictions through the creation of a real property administration. Public pressure encouraged the board to go beyond imposing controls to providing housing in acutely congested areas.[3] Upon Minister of Finance J.L. Ilsley's advice, it increasingly exercised some responsibility in allocating, requisitioning, and rationing housing. In October, it issued Order No. 200, under which it could carry out compulsory surveys and permit every householder to let portions of a home regardless of local bylaws or legal agreements. In Vancouver, Order No. 200 took precedence over the city's zoning bylaws and the province's Shaughnessy Heights Restriction Act. As a result, many larger houses in older, one-family dwelling zones and in Shaughnessy Heights became multiple-family units. Although pressed by associations of property owners and lending institutions, the city government and the town planning commission had no power to stop the conversions.

The WPTB also attempted to utilize fully existing rental accommodation by establishing registries in congested areas and conducting compulsory surveys of residential space. These activities were carried out through the board's consumer branch, run by Byrne Hope Sanders and the women's regional advisory committees.[4] Thirty registries supervised by Mrs. Harvey Agnew, president of the YWCA's national council, were in full operation within months. Two dozen committees stood ready to swing into action when necessary. A committee was set up in Vancouver, chaired by Mrs. Laura Selman of the United Services Bureau, to create a registry and to organize a survey. The registry opened in December 1942 at 771 Dunsmuir Street under Millicent Fleming's office management. It took over the work of the bureau and the YWCA in finding rooms for home seekers, and soon attracted the services of about 100 volunteers. It placed advertisements in the local newspapers that called on the patriotism of Vancouverites to help the war effort by renting spare rooms. In April, the real property administration and the registry carried out a compulsory survey of Vancouver, Burnaby, and North Vancouver that revealed 2,097 vacant rooms and prompted 1,830 householders to volunteer space. The registry staff inspected premises, listed them, accepted applications, and placed home seekers throughout the four worst years of Vancouver's housing shortages.

Early in 1941, the federal government moved to restrict civilian building in order to divert valuable materials and labour to the war effort.[5] In April 1940, to manage war production, it replaced the War Supply Board with the Department of Munitions and Supply under C.D. Howe. The new department's priorities section and later its priorities branch met wartime industrial requirements, and individual controllers regulated the supply of materials such as timber, rubber, and steel. Initially, the priorities branch created a construction control division and appointed a priorities officer. Later, Cabinet named a controller of construction and separated the construction control division from the priorities branch.

In British Columbia, an advisory committee screened local applications for permits and advised the Ottawa control division on allocation. Construction control gradually limited residential building activity by requiring federal permits for houses costing over $5,000. In April 1943, it allowed house construction valued up to $500 to proceed without licence. It gave priority to builders erecting 100 or more new units, but by midsummer had placed curbs on the size of dwellings. In February 1944, the control division allowed houses costing up to $1,500 to be built without licences, although about a year later the limit was back to $500. The federal government discontinued construction controls in December 1945.

Late in 1940, upon the recommendation of its economic advisory committee, the federal Cabinet recognized that housing shortages in industrial areas impeded production, that private industry could not meet the need for accommodation, and that the government itself would have to build temporary housing for war workers.[6] Under the

War Measures Act and the Department of Munitions and Supply Act, Privy Council ordered the formation of a crown corporation reporting to C.D. Howe to erect war workers' housing. Wartime Housing Limited was incorporated on 28 February 1941.

The new company behaved as an independent developer in the private sector rather than as a national housing agency. Howe enlisted the successful Hamilton contractor, Joseph M. Pigott, as president, and appointed representatives of the professions, business, and labour as directors of the board.[7] WHL itself operated in a decentralized, business-like manner. Howe's position made him the impresario of a 'circus' of thirty wartime crown corporations spread across 3,000 miles. Although Pigott reported directly to him, he therefore only wanted to hear about major problems, rather than day-to-day operations.[8] By 1945, WHL maintained a headquarters in Toronto and fifty-one branch offices supervising work in seventy-three municipalities.

Intervening directly in the housing industry, WHL constructed and managed rental units for war workers and their families.[9] It first surveyed production areas to determine housing requirements. If it uncovered a serious shortage in a specific locality, it then undertook one or more building projects. The company assembled land through legal agreements with municipal authorities, expropriation from private owners, or use of federal property. It produced its own standard residential designs and specifications. It was given preference over private contractors on supplies of building materials. Up to 1945, when the last war worker's home was finished, WHL rented and managed 16,869 houses across Canada in addition to several staff houses. As well, it was responsible for schools, firehalls, pumphouses, garages, community centres, and office buildings necessary for the completion of its task.

WHL carried out two war workers' developments in Greater Vancouver, where private industry had failed to meet the wartime demand for housing. In June 1941, it surveyed the City of Vancouver and the District and City of North Vancouver and concluded that the employees of Burrard Drydock Company Limited and North Van Ship Repairs Limited desperately needed additional accommodation.[10] It subsequently built nearly 300 temporary single-family units and two staff houses in the Lonsdale area of the City of North Vancouver. In 1942, it erected 450 other single dwellings near Fell Avenue on the flats of the City and District of North Vancouver (see Chapter 1, Figure 1). Agreements with both the city and the district resolved the details of land transfer, payments in lieu of taxes, services, and postwar disposal of the units.

Later, WHL assisted the city in building one school and extending another. McCarter and Nairne, a prominent Vancouver architectural firm, supervised the North Vancouver project, as well as other ones in Esquimalt, Prince Rupert, and Nanaimo. Smith Brothers and Wilson, a well-known local contractor, built the housing. A WHL regional official, Norman B. Robinson, opened an office in North Vancouver to direct the construction and management of the BC program.

In December 1942, using the same architects and contractor, WHL provided 300 temporary houses in Richmond for Boeing Aircraft of Canada Limited workers employed at a Sea Island plant.[11] It expropriated land from farmers in Richmond, negotiated an agreement with the municipality for water supply, and gave the new subdivision of Burkeville a firehall and a community centre.

On the whole, WHL performed well in housing a limited number of workers employed in war industry. Officials such as Howe and Pigott argued in reports, speeches, articles, and films that the crown corporation performed an excellent, efficient job as a 'well-established' and 'smoothly operating' agency.[12] Contented tenants made their homes comfortable, planted victory gardens, and participated in community activities.

Moreover, in supplying thousands of badly needed rental units, WHL made significant contributions to Canadian housing in construction, design, and site planning. Its usual construction method of rapidly assembled semi-prefabrication or 'demountable' technology was innovative, although the North Vancouver and Richmond housing employed more traditional building techniques.[13] A plain but distinctive standard design simplified the 1930s 'Cape Cod' style, offering two, three, or four bedrooms and limited assortments of exterior wall finishes and colour combinations. It made the houses as easily recognizable to Canadians as the grain elevator or the chateau-style hotel (Figures 14, 15, and 16). The site planning of war workers' housing along crescents and cul-de-sacs in Burkeville, parts of North Vancouver, and elsewhere represented a notable departure from customary grid patterns (Figure 17).

WHL also contributed to the evolution of Canadian housing management techniques. Its management was based on a combination of paid personnel and local advisory committees, which permitted defrayed costs, smooth entry into a given neighbourhood, and the assistance of community organizations.[14] The tenant relations department, which its contemporaries generally held in high regard, consciously exercised a

Figure 14 In 1942, WHL laid out a subdivision with 450 rental houses on the flats of the North Vancouver shoreline. The war workers and their families who lived here were employed at nearby shipyards.

subtle but systematic strategy of social control under Lionel Scott's direction. The tenants and their families were guided by community counsellors and local organizations such as the VCSA, and supplied by WHL with buildings, equipment, and even a monthly magazine, *Home Life*. Under this direction, they initiated social, health, recreational, and athletic programs that improved the quality of life in their developments and also reduced the possibility of industrial disputes, maintained WHL property, curtailed juvenile delinquency, and diminished discord among neighbourhoods. This form of social engineering emerged from the European and North American traditions of welfare capitalism in planned workers' communities.[15] WHL was less heavily paternalistic, but used social control theory and wartime rhetoric to encourage community organization in its projects. Its goal was to develop and protect the democratic values for which the nation was fighting a world war.

Finally, the WHL program introduced the principle of joint responsibility between governments in rental housing projects.[16] Although it

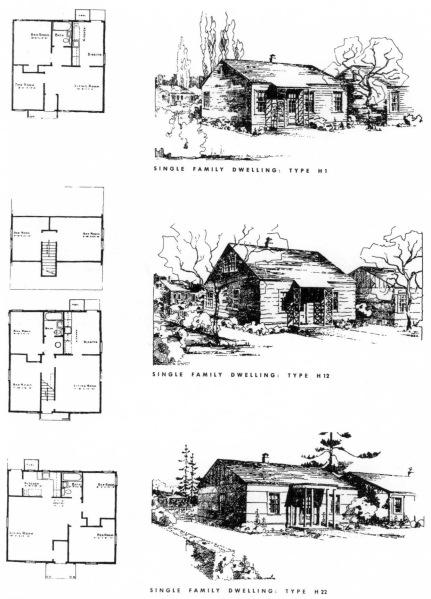

SINGLE FAMILY DWELLING: TYPE H1

SINGLE FAMILY DWELLING: TYPE H12

SINGLE FAMILY DWELLING: TYPE H22

Figure 15 From Nova Scotia to Vancouver Island, WHL used standard designs and a limited assortment of exterior finishes and colours for its two-, three-, and four-bedroom houses. Owing to the scarcity of plywood on the West Coast, wood-frame construction replaced the semi-prefabrication employed elsewhere in the country. [Burwell Coon, 'Wartime Housing,' Royal Architectural Institute of Canada *Journal* 19 (January 1942):7]

Figure 16 Some critics of WHL called this North Vancouver house an 'eyesore,' but the war worker's family living here was sufficiently content to plant a victory garden and hang curtains in the windows.

carried the burden of building and managing the houses, the company cooperated with municipalities over land assembly, services, payments in lieu of taxes, and final disposal of the property. The provincial governments provided enabling legislation to make the projects possible.

WHL operations did provoke criticism. Social activists protested that the houses provided accommodation for war workers with stable, modest incomes rather than offering widely available low-rental housing.[17] Rents, which the government did not subsidize, amounted to between $22 and $30 per month; low-income households paid up to $20 per month at that time, and could afford possibly $12.[18] Since 44 per cent of WHL tenants had previously paid rents under $20, war industry had obviously improved their financial situation. In fact, WHL rents, calculated to recoup construction costs over ten years, were slightly higher than NHA monthly payments covering a twenty-year mortgage and taxes.

Figure 17 In 1942-3, in a farmer's field in Richmond, WHL created Burkeville, a subdivision with crescents and cul-de-sacs for war workers at a nearby Boeing Aircraft of Canada plant. Critics called the 300 houses a 'big improvement' over the company's North Vancouver houses.

Criticism of WHL came from other sources as well. Bureaucratic rivalry and fears of socialism prompted federal Finance officials to feel highly suspicious of WHL, particularly those in the National Housing Administration and the WPTB rentals administration.[19] They suspected that WHL would overstep its mandate, build permanent houses in major centres, and compete with the National Housing Administration and private industry.

Furthermore, although in most cases WHL relations with municipal governments became smoother, initially they were 'very troublesome.'[20] Concerns centred around the quality of housing, the division of responsibility over services, and the loss of tax revenue. In Greater Vancouver, civic officials referred to the North Vancouver houses as an 'eyesore' and 'packing cases,' but afterwards called the units at Burkeville a 'big improvement.'[21] Although most municipalities came to accept the standard WHL agreement, one in particular never did. Richmond fought WHL for several years over responsibility for the costs of school facilities and services such as the sewage system.[22]

Lending institutions, builders, suppliers, and property owners opposed WHL operations for several reasons. They feared that the crown company would become involved in building permanent housing, that its projects would reduce property values in surrounding neighbourhoods, and that the units would deteriorate into slum housing if not removed after the war. They also resented that the corporation received supplies unavailable to private industry and therefore delayed construction under the NHA.

Opposition also came from the CCF at first. The corporation's work competed with the CCF drive for a planned public housing program undertaken jointly by federal, provincial, and municipal governments across Canada. As well, WHL, which had been created by order-in-council rather than legislation, remained largely unaccountable to Parliament. Although the CCF approved of the tenant relations department's activities, it feared that 'these miserable little wartime houses ... will become slums within a few years.'[23] It also worried that tax exemptions burdened local taxpayers and that the nature of the company's management was dictatorial, especially with respect to its customary three-day notice-to-vacate.

When the economic advisory committee of Cabinet recommended establishing WHL, it also debated the advantages and disadvantages of keeping the NHA program. In December 1939, the Department of Finance discontinued loans on individual houses costing over $4,000 and on all loans for apartment blocks and duplexes.[24] Almost a year later, under Deputy Minister of Finance W.C. Clark's influence, the economic advisory committee was inclined to terminate the NHA plan altogether. It wished to release labour and material resources for the war effort and to build up a backlog of housing demand that would require an infusion of government financial assistance in postwar house construction, thereby stimulating the economy, generating employment, and thwarting a postwar depression. Nevertheless, David Mansur of the Central Mortgage Bank and F.W. Nicolls of the National Housing Administration argued that the government should apply the NHA program to congested areas that were badly in need of permanent housing, such as Vancouver.[25] With Cabinet on the verge of ending NHA loans, the National Construction Council, lending institutions, suppliers, builders, civic leaders, members of parliament, architects, realtors, and economists came together to form a powerful lobby aimed at keeping the program alive.[26] In addition to reinforcing the argument of Mansur and Nicolls, the lobbyists pointed out that good quality permanent housing could be built under the NHA without draining government funds as WHL did. They also argued that older workers

would be unemployed if NHA were discontinued and that home ownership would discourage 'fifth column penetration into the ranks of
ordinary men and women.'[27] Officials connected with the Department
of Munitions and Supply, however (including the controller of construction and WHL senior management), recommended discontinuing NHA
loans during the wartime emergency.[28] They argued that the NHA
program could not meet the urgency of the housing situation in major
centres and that it diverted precious building supplies away from the
war effort and the construction of war workers' homes. In the end,
Cabinet compromised. It successfully sought Parliament's approval of
an appropriation to continue the government's share of the NHA joint
loan program, but with limited scope.[29]

Another dimension to the NHA's wartime history is found in the
response to an attempt by WHL to enter the permanent housing field.
On this issue, W.C. Clark was aligned with some of the forces that
pressed for the continuation of NHA loans, including Nicolls, the WBTB
rental administrator, the lumber suppliers, and the lending institutions.
They urged the restriction of WHL activities to constructing temporary
units in remote areas. In 1942, however, WHL negotiated an agreement
with Hamilton's civic government to build badly needed permanent
housing.[30] The crown company's opponents in Hamilton called the
proposal socialistic, and they condemned the extension of priorities on
building supplies to WHL to build permanent units that, in their
opinion, were high in cost and low in quality. Finally, a meeting of
officials in Munitions and Supply, WHL, and Finance, including both
C.D. Howe and J.L. Ilsley, resolved the controversy by restricting the
company's activities to the construction of temporary units in outlying
areas.

Indeed, after December 1942, a newly established housing coordination committee – consisting of representation from the departments of
Finance, Munitions and Supply, Labour, and WHL – acted as a regulatory
body to which WHL submitted its plans for approval before going to
Privy Council.[31] The committee coordinated all government activities
in housing. For the next year and a half, permanent and temporary
housing programs remained quite distinct. In Greater Vancouver, WHL
maintained its operations in areas of heavy wartime production such as
the North Shore and Sea Island, and the National Housing Administration remained active in the city of Vancouver itself.

Although the economic advisory committee continued NHA joint
loans, it terminated the HIP as of 31 October 1940.[32] Still, officials in

the Department of Finance and the WPTB recognized the value of a scheme like the HIP in expanding rental stock through conversions. A home extension plan set up by Finance in 1942 promoted conversions using HIP as a model.[33] Because the construction control division limited building activity and supplies were scarce, however, the plan had minimal impact.

Subsequently, real property administrator Russel Smart developed a plan under which Finance, acting through the National Housing Administration, leased large dwellings for five years and converted them into rental units. With the approval of the housing coordination committee and Cabinet, the Home Conversion Plan resulted in 36 conversions in 1943, 1,209 in 1944, 778 in 1945, and 76 in 1946. In Vancouver, Jocelyn Davidson of the National Housing Administration introduced the plan in June 1943 despite the reservations of the city council, the town planning commission, and the ratepayers' associations about federal power to override civic bylaws.[34] In addition, critics noted that the plan displaced tenants, sheltered too few extra occupants, commanded high rents, catered to single people or couples rather than families, accommodated some non-essential workers, and consumed government funds, labour, and materials in a non-productive manner. Still, it did provide suites for 500 families between September 1943 and January 1945, at which time 125 more suites were under construction.

The federal government also turned to the problem of accommodating Canadians during reconstruction. In 1941, it assigned housing as a subject of inquiry to its advisory committee on reconstruction, which in turn entrusted it to a subcommittee on postwar construction projects. In 1943, the advisory committee established a full subcommittee on housing and community planning, chaired by economist C.A. Curtis of Queen's University. Members included federal officials such as Piggott and Nicolls, architects, planners, sociologists, economists, and representatives of municipal interest groups. The subcommittee benefited from the expertise of its research adviser, Leonard Marsh, Dominion statistician H.F. Greenway, and Department of Finance economist O.J. Firestone. The subcommittee's mandate was to review existing legislation and administrative organization relating to housing and planning, and to report upon changes in that legislation and organization 'to ensure the most effective implementation of ... an adequate housing program for Canada' in the postwar years.[35]

When the subcommittee submitted the Curtis report to Parliament in March 1944, it recommended a comprehensive national housing strategy to provide better accommodation, stimulate the economy, furnish employment for those released from the forces and war industry, and deal with shelter 'as a matter of welfare and social concern.'[36] The Curtis report called for 'an equitable and comprehensive plan' to cover town planning, home ownership, renovation, slum clearance, low-rental projects, and rural and cooperative housing. The plan was to involve public, private, and cooperative financing and operation of schemes, and would rely mainly on the private construction industry.[37] Town planning involving all three governmental levels was to form the basis of housing developments. As well, housing programs were to distribute financial responsibility and decentralize administration among three governments. More specifically, the report promoted the extension of the 1938 NHA Part I to include prospective home owners of moderate income and the revision of Part II to introduce a federally subsidized low-rental program run through local housing authorities.

The NHA passed by Parliament in the summer of 1944 did not adopt the Curtis report's recommendations. Rather, in shaping the legislation, Deputy Minister W.C. Clark followed the recommendations of a Dominion Mortgage and Investments Association brief and, without doubt, his own strong inclinations. Although it attempted to foster 'pride of possession' among Canadians, the terms of Part I did not sufficiently expand accessibility to home ownership beyond the 1938 NHA.[38] The reduction in the borrowers' interest rate was 'less than most members of the Sub-committee had in mind.'[39] Moreover, while the subcommittee proposed a 10 per cent downpayment on all loans valued up to $6,000, the 1944 NHA brought in a scale of downpayments rising from about 10 per cent on a $4,000 home to about 17 per cent on a $6,000 one. In addition, the act permitted the thirty-year amortization period recommended by the subcommittee only in areas with appropriate planning and zoning provisions. Part II of the new legislation retained the 1938 act's joint loan plan for the construction of rental units. Despite the Curtis report's proposal for low-rental schemes operated by local housing authorities, the 1944 NHA offered a rental housing program through the agency of limited dividend companies and life insurance institutions, with no federal subsidy for rent reduction. Even the Dominion Mortgage and Investments Association – which believed that favourable lending conditions for private industry, full employment, and adequate social services reduced the need for subsidized shelter – could envisage the careful creation of public housing projects. Clark could not.[40]

The federal government attempted to ease postwar accommodation shortages by implementing the section of the 1944 NHA that guaranteed life insurance companies a 2.5 per cent return on funds invested in low- or moderate-cost rental projects. Although the insurance companies, Department of Finance officials, and the Dominion Mortgage and Investments Association worked out an agreement for this initiative following extensive discussions, it was only under pressure from the government that the companies formed HEC as a holding company.[41] Eventually, however, HEC parented several subsidiaries, which undertook projects in Montreal, Toronto, and other cities across the country using long-term federal loans at a 3 per cent interest rate. In October 1945, HEC organized a West Coast subsidiary, Housing Enterprises of Vancouver Limited (HEV), the officials of which represented regional offices of the major life insurance companies. In 1946, the City of Vancouver and HEV closed a land deal involving city-owned lots on Fourth Avenue and Broadway. HEV commenced construction of 349 moderate-cost apartment and terraced housing units mainly for veterans' households (see Chapter 1, Figure 1). The local architectural firm of Sharp and Thompson, Berwick, Pratt simplified and modernized the more traditional terrace style that had been used in the 1930s by their own firm and by Garden City, London County Council, and 'homes for heroes' designers between 1900 and 1930 (Figure 18).[42] Bennett and White Construction Company built the housing. HEV erected additional units in New Westminster and planned more for Vancouver. Nevertheless, despite federal priorities on building materials, HEC was unable to handle rising building costs and to maintain moderate rentals. It finally abandoned its program in 1947 after completing a handful of projects across the country.

In 1945-6, the federal Department of Finance devised the IHP in consultation with representatives of the chartered banks and the National House Builders' Association and added it to the 1944 NHA.[43] The plan allowed for agreements between the government and builders. A builder would construct veterans' housing conforming to NHA standards on a substantial area of subdivided land, at an approved sales price and with priority assistance on materials. If the builder failed to sell a house after six months, the government would purchase it at slightly below the agreed-upon price. The plan's objective was 'to promote the building of moderate- and low-cost housing units of modest quality.'[44]

In Greater Vancouver, the IHP was wholly or partly responsible for

Figure 18 In 1945-6, housing shortages led HEV to construct 349 apartments and townhouses for veterans' families along Broadway and West Fourth avenues. Today, the CMHC is razing the original buildings and housing many of the same families in new apartments on the same sites.

several large subdivisions in New Westminster, Burnaby, and North Vancouver.[45] In Vancouver itself, J.G. James and Son built a large integrated housing development between 45th and 49th avenues near Knight Road; Little, Maddock, and Meirte Limited undertook another sizable project between 42nd and 44th avenues and Manitoba and Columbia streets; and Sinclair Homesites Limited with Harry Ablowitz Realty Limited erected 'Dalkeith Place,' near Grandview Highway and Renfrew Street.[46]

In May 1945, the federal government replaced its housing coordination committee with an interdepartmental housing committee to initiate and coordinate its many projects and programs.[47] Late that year, it created another crown corporation, the CMHC, which reported first to Minister of Finance J.L. Ilsley and later to Minister of Reconstruction and Supply C.D. Howe. The CMHC consolidated most government housing programs and administered the operations of the 1944 NHA.[48] Modelled on the Central Mortgage Bank, the CMHC came into existence on 1 January 1946. Subsequently, it took over WHL, the Home Conversion Plan, and the HEC projects. In the fall of 1946, the CMHC appointed J.A. Jones as BC regional supervisor located in Vancouver and began to centralize its various activities in the local WHL office.[49]

Under the 1942 Veterans' Land Act, the federal government also assisted veterans in buying housing near major cities such as Vancouver. The DVA initiated a subdivision plan under which it bought land and erected housing for sale to ex-servicemen.[50] In 1945-6, the DVA implemented its plan in the Greater Vancouver area, with subdivisions of over 300 veterans' houses, including projects in Queensborough, New Westminster, and on Lulu Island, Richmond.

Although Ottawa's efforts to control rents and evictions and to increase supply proved beneficial, its unilateral efforts to resolve the need for 17,000 to 25,000 units in the mid-1940s did not succeed in Vancouver. First, the NHA did not furnish sufficient units of owned housing quickly enough. Officials approved loans for about 8,500 units between 1946 and 1950 under the 1944 act,[51] but rising costs and scarcity of supplies delayed completion and added to congestion. Second, the federal programs did not produce sufficient numbers of rental units. WHL built 1,050 units in North Vancouver and Richmond; the National Housing Administration's conversions resulted in over 600 suites; and HEV erected 349 apartments and terraced units. Yet private industry remained uninterested in building rental housing under the 1944 NHA. As a result, congestion worsened in the downtown area and its adjacent neighbourhoods. Little temporary shelter was available for stays by the day, week, or month until households could move into more permanent accommodation. Finally, the wartime shortages heightened the chronic need for low-income housing.

As conditions deteriorated in the 1940s, groups of activists undertook to solve Vancouver's housing problem. Many groups, including the VHA, the CCF, and the Communist party, had participated in the social housing campaign of the 1930s, but some, like the veterans' organizations, had not. No single formal structure united all the groups, although their memberships frequently overlapped. At least two of them, the CCF and the Labor Progressive Party (LPP), as the Communist party was known in the 1940s, bitterly opposed each other in the wider political context. No major figure emerged to lead the drive for improved housing. While a few individuals were more prominent than others, they all acted as representatives of organizations. As they had in the

1930s, women in particular continued to play important roles in the housing movement.

The objectives of the various activist groups differentiated them. Some, like the veterans' organizations and the Citizens' Rehabilitation Council of Greater Vancouver (CRCGV), tended to seek remedies for the immediate emergency created by the war and reconstruction. Others, including the CCF, the LPP, and the VHA, wanted a program to solve both the long- and short-range aspects of the housing problem.

Pressing Ottawa for social innovations much as they had following the First World War, veterans' organizations, such as the provincial command and the local branches of the Canadian Legion, the Army and Navy Veterans of Canada, the Canadian Corps Association, the War Amputations Association, and the coordinating Vancouver Veterans' Council, called for a quick resolution of the housing emergency. They were supported in their efforts by women's auxiliaries to the various regiments and services. In 1944, veterans' groups recommended imposition of an evictions freeze for servicemen's families, use of vacant dwellings for temporary accommodation, provision of WHL houses for soldiers' dependents, construction of government-assisted housing projects by limited dividend companies, and conversion of the old Hotel Vancouver to a veterans' hostel.[52] Within two years, as the 'rosy pictures painted to our boys overseas ... [had] become nightmares,' these organizations adopted other, often more far-reaching demands.[53] They wanted a federal housing ministry, a low-rental housing program, a low-cost homes scheme under the DVA in urban rather than rural areas, a ceiling on real estate prices, a series of new controls and priorities on building materials, a training scheme for skilled tradesmen, a plan for non-profit accommodation for low-income First World War veterans, and a continuation of the national housing registry.

According to the veterans, the federal government was morally responsible for helping to rehabilitate demobilized service personnel by providing housing as well as employment, health care, and education. Canadians, including elected members of government and bureaucrats, generally shared this view. To some extent, the leaders of veterans' groups used the issue of moral responsibility to animate those they represented on the housing question.[54] Once aroused, veterans who had recently returned from active service overseas were a social threat to some members of the Vancouver community, particularly after the widely reported V-E Day riots in Halifax.[55] As well, some veterans took advantage of the housing controversy for their own political purposes.

Jack Henderson, a president of the Canadian Legion's provincial command in the mid-1940s, was endorsed by the Non-Partisan Association (NPA) to run for school board in the 1944 civic elections, and also ran as a Liberal candidate in Vancouver East in the 1945 federal general election.[56] James Sinclair was known as the Liberal 'soldier MP' for North Vancouver. Many LPP members also participated in veterans' organizations to pursue their party's political objectives.

The CRCGV also concerned itself with the immediate problem of re-establishing demobilized armed forces personnel. It represented a diversity of groups: business, professional, social welfare, labour, government, veterans, and church.[57] Not surprisingly, its membership overlapped with that of other groups, such as veterans' organizations and the VHA.[58] In June 1944, Mrs. Laura Selman of the national housing registry described the veterans' problems with shelter to the rehabilitation council, which then set up a housing committee chaired by a former Conservative Cabinet minister, H.H. Stevens.[59] The council endorsed rehabilitation not only out of 'a sense of gratitu[de]' to veterans but 'because Canada's future stability and progress depend[ed] upon the combined effort of government and people in removing causes of dissatisfaction and unrest.'[60] The council not only warned the prime minister and the public of the potential danger for social unrest in the city's grim housing situation but also assisted Vancouver city council and the federal government in settling their differences over solutions to the short-term housing problem. Their anxiety about social disorder led council members to think largely in terms of temporary remedies.

At its provincial and national conventions, in its election manifestos, and in its publications, the CCF committed itself to a long-range, comprehensive, planned, and need-oriented national housing program, much as it had in the 1930s.[61] Its program was very much like the one recommended by the Curtis report. The party also drew upon a report put out by the British Columbia Post-War Rehabilitation Council. The report contained a section dedicated to planning and housing which called for a provincial authority responsible for these matters, enabling legislation for municipal authorities, federal subsidies or loans for local housing schemes, and adjustments to the NHA to subsidize low-rental projects. The CCF's program entailed federal, provincial, and municipal housing authorities, federal funding, low-rental housing, and slum clearance, and it recognized the relationship between housing and planning. The CCF also supported private home ownership, cooperative housing, and home improvement. It recommended priorities on building supplies for low wage earners, and proposed research into new materials and methods of construction. Moreover, the party typically advanced its program with boldness; at its thirteenth provincial convention meeting in Vancouver, it delivered a 'slashing attack' on the laxness of all three governments in failing to grapple with Canada's 'number one emergency,' the housing 'famine.'[62]

In the 1940s, the CCF in Vancouver relied upon elected members at all three governmental levels to advance its housing program: Dorothy Steeves, Laura Jamieson, Grace MacInnis, Ernest Winch, Harold Winch, and Grant MacNeil in Victoria; and Angus MacInnis in Ottawa. MacNeil, who had lived penniless in a waterfront shack in the early 1930s, argued for low-rental housing and appeared at eviction rallies. Angus MacInnis lobbied in Ottawa in aid of veterans' and public housing. Ernest Winch promoted seniors' projects before many other individuals and groups did so.[63]

Carrying on the fight for social housing initiated by Helena Gutteridge, CCF women in particular vigorously promoted improvements in residential conditions. Beginning before the war, Steeves continually raised the shelter issue in the provincial legislature and later served as a member of the British Columbia Post-War Rehabilitation Council.[64] Jamieson established cooperative houses for single working women during the war, and afterwards, as a city council member, she urged establishment of a local housing authority. Grace MacInnis presented the party's housing policy in her writings and in her speeches to public meetings and debates and to the legislature.

The LPP advocated policies on housing not very different from those of the CCF.[65] In particular, it supported low-rental housing projects assisted by federal funding, local housing authorities, slum clearance, and a national housing ministry. Nevertheless, the LPP employed more aggressive, militant tactics, especially at the civic level. In 1944 and 1945, party members such as John McPeake and Elgin Ruddell were instrumental in forming the '5000 Homes Now!' committee and the citizens' emergency housing committee. Ruddell was later an energetic member of the VHA. The LPP initiated public rallies and picket lines at scenes of eviction. As well, during the 1940s, its members gained positions of leadership in major BC unions and Vancouver's labour council.[66] All of these organizations agitated for improvements in housing conditions.[67] Some union leaders, such as McPeake of the International Union of Mine, Mill, and Smelter Workers and Harold Pritchett of the International Woodworkers of America, also led protests.

As well, party members who were veterans joined the New Veterans', East Hastings, and University branches of the Canadian Legion, although a movement to expel them began late in 1946 in British Columbia.

Despite the similarity of LPP and CCF answers to the housing problem, the two political parties could not act together on the issue. At the national level, the LPP wished to form a popular left-wing front with the CCF, but the democratic socialists rejected such a coalition. Hostility over this matter, as well as bitterness over struggles for control of the BC unions, extended into the local housing controversy. CCF member E.S. Scanlon withdrew from the '5000 Homes Now!' committee, for example, because the LPP had infiltrated the organization and made it into a 'political football.' McPeake denied Scanlon's charges and asserted that the group was 'broadly representative' of the public. In addition, Angus MacInnis refused to participate in the '5000 Homes Now!' meetings.[68]

Like the two left-wing political parties, the VHA directed its efforts towards resolving the long-term housing problem, although it certainly recommended immediate solutions for the postwar emergency. The group had disbanded during the war, but the return of P.R.U. Stratton from overseas service resulted in its quiet revival in October 1945.[69] By the following March, it hosted a conference for 100 delegates representing fifty-four local organizations. Thereafter, it maintained a constant, effective lobby with all levels of government and worked to develop a national organization to press Ottawa for a federal low-rental scheme.

Although influenced by the Curtis report, the VHA tended to emphasize public housing and slum clearance over the rest of the proposed comprehensive program.[70] It also demanded the consolidation of all housing and planning activities in one federal ministry, the creation of local authorities for the construction and the administration of low-income projects, and federal subsidy for rent on units in schemes undertaken by local housing authorities and limited dividend corporations. As well, it argued that the municipalities should ask provincial governments to request federal financial assistance if Ottawa refused to take the initiative. In March 1947, it launched a campaign for federal funding and legislation to create a local housing authority for a low-rental project. The VHA argued for appropriate accommodation for senior citizens and single working women as well as for low-income households in general.[71]

Although, on the whole, concerns about the need for low-cost housing motivated the VHA membership, some members also furthered their professional or political interests. For politicians like Grace MacInnis or Elgin Ruddell, the VHA complemented and reinforced CCF and LPP positions on housing. Members such as Jocelyn Davidson, a regional National Housing Administration and CMHC official, and Leonard Marsh, a UBC professor, were able to enhance their professional careers and interests by working with the VHA. Indeed, in the late 1940s, Marsh undertook a major housing survey, sponsored by the university, to further the VHA's objective of redeveloping Strathcona.[72]

A wide range of community groups and labour organizations supported the drive for action led by the veterans, the CRCGV, the CCF, the LPP, and the VHA. Many of these groups had sustained the 1930s social housing campaign. Labour organizations included the Vancouver and District Trades and Labour Council, the Vancouver Labour Council, and a long list of locals.[73] Broad community support came from church, service, professional, and welfare organizations. Women's associations were among the most committed advocates.[74] All these groups participated in the housing campaign by independently lobbying the three levels of government and by supporting the CRCGV or the VHA.

Reporting by local and national newspapers and journals brought the housing issue to public attention and cultivated a widespread sentiment for change. The press also demanded and offered solutions. The *Sun*, the *Daily Province*, and the *News-Herald* in Vancouver published stories, editorials, and articles on all aspects of the residential situation. Similarly, articles in popular national magazines such as *Maclean's* and *Saturday Night*, professional and business journals such as *Canadian Business* and the Royal Architectural Institute of Canada *Journal*, and political and labour publications such as the *CCF News*, the *Pacific Advocate (Tribune)*, and the Trades and Labour Congress of Canada *Journal* covered housing conditions and very often suggested solutions.[75] Some government officials blamed protests on inflammatory press coverage.[76] In fact, the local press and popular and serious journals increased public awareness of the shelter problem and generated constructive responses to it.

Protests about the housing question went to federal, provincial, and municipal governments.[77] The prime minister and the ministers of Finance, Munitions and Supply (later Reconstruction and Supply), National Defence, and Pensions and National Health (later Veterans Affairs), the WPTB chair, and the interdepartmental housing committee received letters, resolutions, telegrams, and delegations of officials from Vancouver organizations. The same groups also sent letters and delegations to the provincial government and the city council, which in turn exerted pressure upon the federal government. In addition, CCF members of the provincial legislative assembly made demands upon their government, and federal ministers requested action from each other. Moreover, internal reports went directly from local offices in Vancouver to top WPTB officials.[78] Finally, federal officials and ministers directly confronted the regional housing issue by reading critical editorials in Vancouver newspapers.[79] Calls for action ultimately reached federal Minister of Finance J.L. Ilsley and Minister of Munitions and Supply C.D. Howe. Prime Minister William Lyon Mackenzie King remained indifferent to the housing question and delegated responsibility to his two senior ministers.[80]

At the municipal level, city council felt pressure from within the civic bureaucracy to make changes in bylaws or policy affecting housing but often refused, either directly or indirectly because accommodation shortages made it difficult to solve longer-term problems. Despite a drive by a special committee, the medical officer, and industry to remove waterfront shacks, for example, the council imposed a moratorium on evictions because no other shelter was available.[81] Similarly, it decided to wait until postwar congestion subsided before introducing a housing standards bylaw recommended by a special committee.[82] In response to the urging of the town planning commission, building inspector, and chief fire warden, however, council rejected a request from apartment owners and builders to make a bylaw change that would augment the allowable amount of suite space in basements. The existence of WPTB Order No. 200, which superseded all civic bylaws, made conversion possible in any case.[83] Moreover, in 1943, on the town planning commission's recommendation, the city followed the provincial and federal example and set up a postwar housing committee to advise on reconstruction matters such as low-cost accommodation, urban rehabilitation, new suburbs, housing standards, and construction. The committee was composed of civic officials and community representatives.[84]

Having experienced the full impact of controls on building materials, rents, and evictions and of competition from government in supplying houses, the housing industry frequently opposed the efforts of local activists and advocated increased private sector construction. National organizations such as the Canadian Construction Association, the National House Builders' Association, and the Dominion Mortgage and Investments Association, and regional ones such as the British Columbia Building Contractors' Association, the Mortgage and Trust Companies Association of British Columbia, the Associated Property Owners of Vancouver, and the Apartment and Rooming House Operators' Association directed delegations, briefs, and resolutions to all three governments.[85] Individual companies such as Quality Homes Corporation and Vancouver Titles Limited petitioned the city and federal governments for assistance with respect to tax sale lots, services, and preference in building low-cost housing similar to that given to WHL. Their lack of success only heightened their hostility towards the crown company.[86]

Vancouver's housing movement was a continuation of the previous decade's campaign. Activism faded between 1940 and 1943 but never actually died. The December 1939 civic election resulted in Helena Gutteridge's defeat and in a resounding NPA victory. Despite the efforts of A.J. Harrison, the civic secretary of zoning matters, to explain the special housing committee's function, the new, right-wing council decided in January 1941 not to re-appoint what it perceived to be a troublesome body. The activist forces, including Gutteridge and Harrison, regrouped in the town planning commission's office in mid-April that year to continue the struggle for social housing as a committee of the Welfare Council of Greater Vancouver (previously the VCSA).[87] Helena Gutteridge soon departed for the BC interior, where she worked as a welfare manager among the Japanese Canadians at the Lemon Creek relocation project.[88] The Housewives' League and Consumers' Research Council, both communist organizations, continued to send delegations and letters to city council about low-rental schemes and other issues.[89] City council ignored the housing problem in its committee structure until 1943, when it created a postwar housing committee which for a while remained the focus of its efforts to deal with declining residential conditions.

Beginning in 1944, several other local committees and organizations emerged to press for action on the housing question.[90] In March, the Consumers' Research Council sponsored the '5000 Homes Now!' committee, which involved about fifty Vancouver organizations. Dominated by LPP members like the chair, John McPeake, the committee injected energy into the new housing campaign by holding conferences and presenting briefs to Victoria and Ottawa until its disbandment in September. As the war ended in May 1945, the welfare council formed a citizens' emergency housing committee to coordinate the efforts of several community organizations. The CRCGV embraced the housing cause in 1944, and took up the cry for the construction of 5,000 units. Finally, when the VHA regrouped late in 1945, it merged with the emergency housing committee to secure a strong social housing movement.

Between 1944 and 1949, Vancouver's housing activists initiated a series of protests, hoping to obtain federal government suspension of evictions, construction of additional affordable veterans' dwelling units by WHL and the CMHC, provision of temporary shelter for homeless ex-servicemen, and continuation of rent controls. They also supported independently devised veterans' and seniors' schemes, and many actively pursued a public housing project. Their struggles had an unmistakable impact on the civic and senior governments, in particular Ottawa, and achieved many concrete results.

Although expulsions actually started before 1944, the threat of mass evictions under WPTB regulations ignited agitation about the local housing situation early that year. Because the board had banned winter evictions, huge numbers of notices-to-vacate on 1 May 1944 or after accumulated in Vancouver and in other major cities.[91] More than half of the notices involved servicemen's families. Tenants faced with eviction could find little alternative shelter. MPs in the House of Commons brought the problem to the government's attention but to no avail. The WPTB, especially, believed that the press and the politicians of opposition parties had inflamed and distorted the situation.[92]

In Vancouver (and elsewhere), a militant campaign for an evictions suspension commenced in the summer of 1944.[93] At first, the CRCGV, labour and veterans' organizations, and city council sent resolutions requesting an evictions freeze to the federal government. As the number of evictions grew and the government failed to react to representations, the LPP and the veterans adopted more aggressive tactics. In mid-July, the LPP organized a street rally outside the home of an evicted serviceman's wife. Shortly afterwards, picketing Legion members halted the eviction of a widow whose son was serving overseas. An LPP delegation visited the BC attorney general, R.L. Maitland, in Victoria to protest the situation of an evicted Vancouver family forced to live in a tent. Despite Maitland's subsequent demands for action, the WPTB refused to respond beyond suggesting amendments to provincial legislation to give tenants greater security of tenure.[94]

As congestion increased and tension began to build over expected 1945 evictions, the WPTB considered ways of defusing a potentially disorderly situation. In December 1944 and February 1945, two orders-in-council extended the board's powers and imposed emergency shelter regulations previously used for Halifax on congested areas like Vancouver, New Westminster, Victoria, Ottawa, Toronto, Hull, and Hamilton.[95] Under the regulations, the board set up the Emergency Shelter Administration and appointed an administrator with sweeping powers to take possession of residential premises for use as emergency shelter, to forbid the unnecessary migration of servicemen's families, to centralize the work of national housing registries in the administrator's office, to prohibit demolitions of dwellings, to carry out surveys of local housing conditions, to launch publicity campaigns to locate additional housing, and to issue permits to rent within congested areas. The CMHC absorbed the Emergency Shelter Administration in January 1946, and Ottawa revoked the regulations late in 1948.

In Vancouver, the WPTB appointed retired Air Vice Marshal Leigh F. Stevenson as emergency housing 'czar.'[96] City council reluctantly supported the imposition of regulations. Owners of large houses who were unwilling to share them complained, while the civic housing committee approved and disheartened house hunters 'cheered' the new controls.[97] In mid-February 1945, the Emergency Shelter Administration opened its doors in downtown Vancouver. A 'happy appointment to a difficult position,' Stevenson immediately began to press for conversion of unoccupied army barracks and the old Hotel Vancouver into temporary shelter for service personnel families, but the Emergency Shelter Administration in Ottawa initially refused to accept his recommendations.[98] Stevenson succeeded in taking over Sea Island Camp No. 1, however, which WHL and the Pacific Command had transformed into housing for servicemen's families. Stevenson remained as administrator until November 1945, when his aide, J.G. Walker, replaced him.

Despite emergency shelter regulations, the evictions increased. When about 2,000 Vancouver households received notices-to-vacate between May and October 1945, protesters used the street rally and the picket line with greater effectiveness.[99] Both the LPP and the CCF organized rallies, frequently attended by two or three hundred neighbours and activists. MLAs such as Grace MacInnis and Grant MacNeil sometimes attended. For two weeks in July 1945, an anti-evictions committee stopped all expulsions by posting eight picketers at five houses for nine or twelve hours a day.

As social tension mounted in Vancouver and in other cities faced with the same problem, the WPTB held an emergency meeting.[100] On 25 July 1945, it issued Order No. 537, applicable to congested areas across

Canada. The order suspended notices-to-vacate in self-contained dwell-ings, stayed eviction proceedings, and prevented the issue of further notices. Although evictions seriously affected other cities, such as Toronto, Winnipeg, Montreal, and Hamilton, information appended to the order noted that the board took protest wires from Vancouver into special consideration before implementing the freeze. Unfortunately, the suspension order was flawed. It kept some property owners with large families in congested quarters, for example, because they could not reoccupy homes let to tenants.[101] Some evictions followed success-ful appeals by landlords, and the LPP, the groups and unions that it dominated, and some veterans' organizations continued to disrupt or prevent expulsions.

In May 1944, the federal government initially responded to the evictions situation and the protests not by altering the rental regulations but by expanding WHL's operations to furnish housing for soldiers' families. It directed the crown company to build additional, permanent, better quality houses. Acting Prime Minister J.L. Ralston, the Minister of National Defence, hinted at the new program on 27 April in the House of Commons. At a 2 May meeting, representatives of WHL, Finance, and Munitions and Supply finally decided to initiate a program of perma-nent housing for servicemen.

Between 1944 and 1946, WHL completed 10,144 additional units. Later, after the January 1947 integration of WHL and the CMHC, a fully developed program continued to build houses across Canada. By 1949, the total number of veterans' dwellings completed by the CMHC amounted to 20,159 units. According to historian John Bacher, the impact of agitation over evictions also contributed to the creation of the CMHC, the initiation of HEC projects, the stimulation of the production of house building supplies, and the extension in August 1945 of the Emergency Shelter Administration to the whole country.[102]

In Vancouver in 1944-5, protests over evictions procured 1,200 WHL houses. Fearful of social unrest, CRCGV representatives attended nego-tiations between city council and WHL for the construction of 200 permanent dwellings on solid foundations. They convinced the city to conclude two separate agreements with the crown company despite unfavourable financial terms for the eventual sale of the houses, the loss of tax revenue, and the transfer of lots to the crown for a nominal price. According to one council member, the WHL project was a 'Santa Claus scheme from which the city would get nothing back.'[103] The city argued that it was losing thousands of dollars in tax revenue on WHL housing;

it received $24 to $30 a year for each unit in lieu of taxes. In addition, it held that inadequate compensation for the future sale of lots and houses would jeopardize its sinking-fund. The BC Building Contractors' Association also opposed the scheme. It later called the WHL operation a 'shack-town rehabilitation scheme' with top priorities in building supplies providing rental houses without basements to ex-servicemen who did not want them. Nevertheless, labour and veterans' organizations, church representatives, and community groups exerted pressure on city council to adopt the agreement.[104]

Agreeably surprised with the construction standard and general appearance of the new WHL houses, the CRCGV subsequently pressed city council and Ottawa for more units.[105] Impelled by increasingly militant eviction protests, Minister of Munitions and Supply C.D. Howe offered an additional 1,000 WHL units to Vancouver's mayor on the very day of the WPTB's freeze announcement, and city council had little choice but to agree to the offer.[106] WHL architects McCarter and Nairne supervised the construction of these Burkeville-like houses, built on solid foundations and situated on serviced lots scattered within the area bounded by Main and Fraser streets, Broadway Avenue, and Marine Drive (Figure 19).[107] On 22 May 1945, a veteran's family moved into the first completed home of WHL's permanent housing program at 5149 Elgin Street.

In addition, the federal government eventually introduced temporary accommodation for households threatened with eviction to Vancouver and other Canadian cities. Following its establishment in 1945, the Emergency Shelter Administration took over Sea Island Camp No. 1 from the Canadian forces.[108] In July, the gravity of the evictions situation caused the administration to request Vancouver city council to operate Camp No. 2.[109] Under pressure, council reluctantly took over the camp in August and administered it for evicted families through the social services committee and social services administrator J. Chambers. The conversion and operation of the camp was a financial and managerial headache for the city. The camp needed expensive renovations, commanded low rents, required the provision of services, and constantly presented landlord-tenant problems such as rental arrears. Moreover, arrangements relating to services, schools, and social allowance payments had to be worked out with a testy Richmond municipal government. The city finally hired a realty company, Boultbee, Sweet, and Company Limited, to look after the camp's management. It attempted to extricate itself from the Sea Island operation in the fall of

Figure 19 As the housing shortage and evictions crisis worsened in 1944-5, C.D. Howe ordered WHL to build 1,200 permanent rental houses on serviced lots across Vancouver's east side.

1946, but did not succeed in doing so for another year. It finally returned the camp to the Emergency Shelter Administration (by then a division of the CMHC), which operated Camp No. 2 until early in 1949. Its unhappy experience discouraged the city from buying all Sea Island camps offered to it by the administration.

In 1945-6, agitation centred around the use of the old Hotel Vancouver as a temporary shelter for homeless Vancouverites.[110] Protesters realized that the elegant building that graced the corner of Georgia and Granville streets would soon stand empty after wartime use by the Department of National Defence. The present Hotel Vancouver at Georgia and Burrard had replaced the original building in 1939, and the owners, the CNR and CPR, contemplated selling and demolishing the old hotel. In March 1945, Leigh Stevenson officially recommended the hostel plan to the WPTB.[111] Thereafter, discussions about the fate of the hotel involved the Department of Finance and the Emergency Shelter Administration in Ottawa, Victoria MP R.H. Mayhew, Mayor J.W. Cornett, the special civic committee set up to consider the issue, the

CRCGV, and the president of the CPR. Issues in the debate included how to allocate responsibility for leasing, refurbishing, financing, and managing the hotel, the municipal property tax revenue, and the building's suitability as family accommodation. After endless negotiations, no solution had been found.[112] Neither the city nor Ottawa wanted the burden of the proposed hostel, and local organizations, WHL, and the army did not offer their services.

As the termination date of the federal government's lease for the old hotel approached, public agitation mushroomed. Representations to the government from community groups, veterans' organizations, trade unions, several BC members of parliament, and the CRCGV met with no success, and finally the LPP began to adopt the more militant tactics of a veterans' picket around the old hotel at New Year's (Figure 20) and a campsite and information picket on the nearby courthouse lawn.[113] At last, on 26 January 1946, LPP member and veteran Bob McEwen led an 'occupying force' from the Canadian Legion's New Veterans' Branch into the lobby of the old hotel.[114] Over the next few days, about 1,400 people 'registered' at the hotel, although the majority did not stay there. A committee, the members of which came from all political persuasions, maintained a military-style discipline.[115] According to the *Vancouver Sun*, 'Vancouver [had] seen nothing like the veterans' occupation since the famous sit-down strike in the post office during the depression era. But this time there was no violence, no cracked heads.'[116] As Vancouver MP and Minister of Veterans Affairs Ian Mackenzie pointed out to Minister of Finance J.L. Ilsley, public opinion sided with the veterans, and federal officials made no attempt to eject them.[117]

The occupation forced a quick resolution of the issue. Mackenzie travelled to Vancouver to negotiate with the veterans, the city council, the CRCGV, and the CPR. By 31 January, the CPR and the CRCGV had signed an agreement endorsed by all parties under which contributions from the city and the federal government, as well as the release of civil defence money, made possible the financial operation of the old hotel as a temporary hostel.[118] With the financial risk minimized, the CRCGV agreed to lease the building and operate the hostel. The veterans vacated the premises on 1 February. The council opened the shelter two weeks later and managed it for between 1,000 and 1,200 members of veterans' families until 1948.[119] By then, the railway companies had sold the property to the T. Eaton Company Limited. In 1949, Eaton's demolished the old hotel despite a campaign by some of the city's architects to preserve the heritage building.

Figure 20 In January 1946, veterans threw up a picket line around the old Hotel Vancouver at Granville and Georgia streets. Their objective was to have the hotel converted into a hostel. After their protests escalated to a full occupation of the building, the hotel became an emergency shelter for 1,200 families over the next two years. [*Pacific Advocate*, 4 January 1946]

In the fall of 1946, the CRCGV followed up its move to operate the old Hotel Vancouver by indicating to Ottawa its willingness to run the Dunsmuir Hotel on the same basis.[120] The Dunsmuir provided fifty-two family units and fifty-seven single ones for about 212 people. It remained a veterans' hostel until 1949, when the Salvation Army bought the building to shelter hard-up men.

The militancy of the occupation of the old Hotel Vancouver never completely deserted its tenants.[121] Whenever the lease expiry date approached, they and the New Veterans' Branch resisted attempts to close the hostel. Furthermore, as early as May and June 1946, the tenants, supported by the New Veterans' Branch, protested to the CRCGV's management about rent increases of $2.50 per room per month. A year later, when another 10 per cent raise occurred, some tenants staged a rent strike.

Thus, pressure to construct permanent housing for the old hotel's veterans developed quickly. In June 1947, their representatives insisted that they should not be thrown on to the streets of Vancouver when the council's lease finally expired in April 1948. They pressed city council for more WHL housing, and, standing on downtown sidewalks, they circulated petitions demanding homes.[122] Warning civic and federal authorities that eviction of the veterans from the old hotel would be impossible, the CRCGV, backed by the VHA and a variety of community, veterans, and labour organizations, interceded on behalf of the tenants and urged city council and C.D. Howe to build additional WHL housing.[123]

In fact, given the volatile social situation in Vancouver, both the city and Howe were prepared to enter into another agreement. In the first half of 1947, however, a deadlock developed between the two parties over the terms of the agreement. Knowing that the federal government planned to sell WHL units to their occupants, city council desired a new, more favourable arrangement.[124] At first, Howe and the CMHC insisted on retaining the standard agreement used for other Canadian cities. In April, three Vancouver MPs, Angus MacInnis (CCF), James Sinclair (Liberal), and Cecil Merritt (Conservative), met Howe and CMHC president David Mansur in Ottawa.[125] Howe intimated at that time that he would consider a low-cost housing scheme for the old hotel veterans, to be worked out following the 1 June deadline. Howe and Mansur also had discussions in Ottawa with Vancouver's ailing mayor, Gerry McGeer, and later with city council member George Miller.[126] Miller communicated a concrete proposal from the CMHC to city council, which set up a special committee to negotiate with federal officials in Vancouver. Rejecting a city counterproposal, David Mansur and the CMHC suggested a revised agreement for building veterans' rental housing projects that gave the city a purchase price of $92 per forty-foot lot or $77 per thirty-three-foot lot and an annual payment of $70 to $80 per unit in lieu of taxes. If the property were sold, the city could tax it at the normal rate, and unsold lots would return to it. The city was to hold a vested share of up to $600 in each sold house and a half of any accrued profit. As well, the city would provide services to the project's limits, and the CMHC would supply on-site services. Rents were to range from $27 to $37 per month for four- to six-room units. Encouraged by the CRCGV, city council approved the development in principle in October, and the CMHC received authority to enter the site on 1 December.[127] The agreement worked out between Vancouver and the CMHC, for what was to be the Renfrew Heights housing project, later became the model for revised agreements with other municipalities across the country.

At the same time that this agreement was being worked out, two local promoters proposed a private scheme to accommodate the veterans lodged in the old Hotel Vancouver and the Dunsmuir Hotel.[128] G.K. Gosling and E.J. Barrie, both Royal Canadian Air Force veterans, offered to purchase some hutments from Bremerton, Washington State, that the United States government had put up for sale to non-profit organizations, transport them, and situate them as permanent rental housing on city land near Boundary Road. They asked city council for a property lease at a rental sufficient to cover taxes, and they approached C.D. Howe for federal financial aid and assistance with custom duties. The plan also required a loan from a lending institution and advance payments from tenants.

Despite support from the old Hotel Vancouver veterans, the dominion and provincial commands of the Canadian Legion, the LPP, a city council member, CCF provincial leader Harold Winch, and three Vancouver MPs, the promoters of the Bremerton plan met with a negative response from Howe. Mayor Gerry McGeer and other council members pointed out that the Vancouver charter gave the city no power to import and rent houses, and they reminded the public of the financial misadventures of the Better Housing Scheme.[129] Howe and CMHC president David Mansur unsuccessfully offered Emergency Shelter funds if the city or the CRCGV agreed to operate the housing project. In reality, Howe believed that WHL/CMHC could build better temporary housing for a lower price. He was also waiting to negotiate the Renfrew Heights agreement with the city. Although Howe turned 'thumbs down' on the Bremerton scheme, some hutments eventually arrived in British Columbia under other sponsorship.[130] A few huts went by barge to Port Alberni, to H.R. Macmillan's logging interests on Vancouver Island, and to a senior citizens' project in Vancouver at East 5th Avenue and Cassiar Street.

The project that eventually emerged from the agreement worked out between the city and the CMHC, Renfrew Heights, was located south and east of Grandview Highway and Renfrew Street on a site envisioned by city council since 1945 as suitable for veterans' rental housing (see Chapter 1, Figure 1).[131] The new subdivision consisted of about 600 one- or one-and-a-half-storey houses of eight standard types of two-, three-, and four-bedrooms, designed under the direction of CMHC chief architect, Sam Gitterman (Figure 21). Although the houses bore a strong resemblance to earlier war workers' and veterans' housing, in fact their high standard of design showed a marked improvement. The units

Figure 21 In 1948, veterans' families moved from the old Hotel Vancouver and another emergency shelter, Seaforth Village, into about 600 rental houses in Renfrew Heights located on Vancouver's eastern boundary. The CMHC was responsible for the design and planning of the subdivision.

rented for between $33 and $45. Most of the old hotel veterans moved directly into their new homes in the summer of 1948.

In September 1946, a squatting tactic borrowed from communist-led housing campaigns in Britain spread to Vancouver.[132] About 1,500 people – mostly war veterans and their families – had moved into empty buildings in Kensington in London, and about 12,000 squatters had taken over army camps around the country. When Vancouver city council refused to shoulder the responsibility for making the Little Mountain barracks available as veterans' emergency shelter, a council member warned that ex-servicemen might squat in the camp much as they had occupied the old Hotel Vancouver. In response, the New Veterans' Branch claimed that it would take no direct action until all options were exhausted and until the buildings were threatened by demolition. At the same time, the CRCGV offered to operate Little Mountain as a temporary shelter. In mid-September, the *Vancouver Sun* carried a story and a photograph of a protest march in London's Oxford Street by squatters demanding the authorized seizure of empty flats for living space. The next day, two families who had been living in cheap lodgings on Cordova Street followed the example of the British squatters and occupied the Little Mountain huts without opposition from the army and with considerable public sympathy. A *Sun* editorial writer reflected that 'the corporal who told Little Mountain squatters that he was glad to see them will not, we trust, be confined to barracks for saying what a lot of other Vancouver people had in mind.'[133] Additional support came from the Canadian Legion and the Fairview LPP club, although the South Little Mountain Community Association worried that the squatters might 'change the outlook of this residential district.'[134]

Nevertheless, the federal government turned the Little Mountain huts over to UBC for married veterans' student housing.[135] Still, as squatters in Ottawa moved into empty barracks at Lansdowne Park (others later occupied vacant buildings in Montreal), the number of occupying Little Mountain families increased to eight and then to thirteen. The army cut off services and unsuccessfully banned further squatter households. When, by the end of September, the university took possession of the huts, it also reached an agreement with the squatters for sharing the premises until they found accommodation elsewhere. Despite disputes between the camp council and the city over rent increases due to higher assessments and the cost of improved services, the university operated the camp until the crisis in veterans' student housing had passed.

By September 1946, UBC had taken advantage of federal funds available through the Emergency Shelter Administration to develop other camps as student veterans' housing.[136] Acadia Camp, a former forestry training and military camp located on the university campus, accommodated 1,000 veterans and their families in three-room suites at $30 per month. Other sections of Acadia also provided for over 200 single students in dormitories, for many faculty families, including President Larry MacKenzie's, and for a group of seven households in trailers. Lulu Island Camp sheltered thirty-two married veterans, and 350 single men lived at Fort Camp on the university campus.

In May 1947, the CRCGV approached city council with an offer to operate the hutments lying behind Seaforth Armories as emergency shelter for veterans and their families.[137] It received two $15,000 grants from the civic and federal governments to convert the huts into living space renting at about $25 per month per unit. With additional funding, the CRCGV gradually renovated more huts and increased the number of suites to ninety-seven. The CMHC took over active management of Seaforth Village in June 1948.

Although they fulfilled a real need for housing, suites in the hutments were not well built. Late in 1948, poor wiring and inadequate fire precautions resulted in a series of fires.[138] A tenants' union, supported by the New Veterans' Branch, submitted demands to the CMHC for repairs and for the allocation of Renfrew Heights homes to Seaforth households.[139] When a young mother from the village attempted to drown her two children, many observers, including the CCF's MP Rod Young and its civic candidate Grace MacInnis, publicly attributed the tragedy partly to the living conditions in the huts and generally to the housing shortages. Consequently, by January 1949, the CMHC started to move the village's households with children into Renfrew Heights. It also fireproofed the huts.

In May 1948, still under pressure to provide more housing, city council approached the CMHC for another agreement to build more veterans' units, similar to the ones in Renfrew Heights.[140] It was prepared to furnish city-owned land near Fraserview Golf Course in the area bounded by Marine Drive, 54th Avenue, and Argyle Drive. Development of the new subdivision, known as Fraserview, proceeded smoothly in the fall of 1948 with a cooperative planning process involving CMHC representatives and city officials and a favourable agreement in place. All parties approved in principle a plan that owed much to the work of an architect/planner originally from Britain, Alan Crossley, and signed the agreement in November. The CMHC paid the city $175,000 for the property, made up of tax sale land, part of the golf course, and purchased or expropriated privately held lots. Eventually, this 'workingman's Shaughnessy Heights' would supply 1,100 new rental units for veterans.[141]

Events took a turn for the worse, however, over the expropriation of property from owners who had not already sold to the city. Expropriation occurred with the understanding that property would revert back to most owners when the site was resurveyed. Unfortunately, the CMHC started work before the expropriation process had been completed.[142] Charges of high-handedness were both common and deserved. Some property owners fought expropriation by enlisting the support of five Vancouver MPs, by protesting through the Fraserview property owners' association, and by blocking the path of the bulldozers. The CMHC responded by sending out a representative from Ottawa to settle the issue. By June 1949, it had let a contract to Biltmore Construction Company for the first seventy-four dwellings.

As Fraserview took shape, some residents, a few members of city council, and several officials of the Architectural Institute of British Columbia and the building contractors' association complained bitterly about the construction of a 'future slum' and a 'chicken coop project,' about the 'waste of public money,' and about the strangulation of private enterprise.[143] Mayor Charles E. Thompson 'barked' a reminder of the acute need for housing. He warned them of the 'great injustice' that they did to the CMHC by using Fraserview as 'a cat's paw for the building trades to ... discredit' the crown corporation.

In January 1950, the first family moved in to their Fraserview bunga-low from a one-room walk-up at Gore and Hastings.[144] Many observers saw the landscaped, fully serviced project, with its view south to the Fraser River, as the largest and finest veterans' rental project in Canada (see Chapter 1, Figure 1). With a wide selection of exterior finishing, roof materials, and plans, the housing offered 238 variations on thirty-four bungalow types, designed once again under CMHC direction (Figure 22). Almost two-thirds of the units had basements. Houses rented for between $33 and $45 a month.

The city and the CMHC initiated a second phase of development in 1950, but work on the additional houses came to a halt early in 1951 when building costs rose 20 to 30 per cent in response to the Korean War.[145] With only half of the projected 1,100 units built, city council, the VHA (supported by labour and veterans' organizations), the Van-couver Council of Women, and members of parliament Donald Fleming and Arthur Laing pressured Ottawa to complete Fraserview. The minister responsible for housing, Robert Winters, asserted that the project would be finished. Beginning in late 1951 and continuing into 1952, the CMHC called tenders and let contracts for blocks of the remaining houses. The 'no vacancy' sign for the 'largest veterans' housing subdi-vision in Canada' finally went up in October 1953, when the last five families moved into their homes.[146]

By the end of the war, many housing activists recognized the plight of senior citizens in finding affordable, adequate accommodation. In 1944, Burnaby's CCF MLA, E.E. Winch, suggested two types of resi-dences: cottage units for those caring for themselves and community living for others requiring some degree of non-institutional care.[147] Winch's ideas were not immediately put into practice. In 1947, the New Vista Society, an organization that sheltered women recently discharged from the provincial mental institution at Essondale and in which Winch played a major role, sold its halfway house to the BC government. It

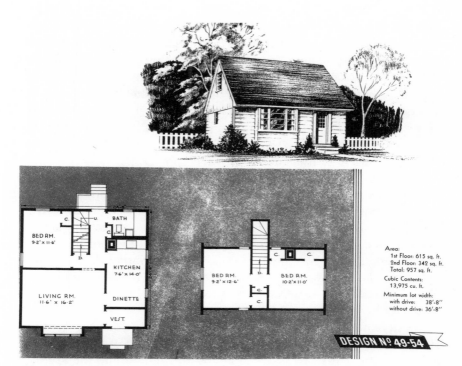

Figure 22 Still under pressure to provide more rental housing for veterans, the CMHC and the City of Vancouver worked together after 1949 to build the Fraserview subdivision, overlooking the Fraser River in South Vancouver. [CMHC, *Small House Designs* (Ottawa: King's Printer 1949), vol. 2, p. 19]

used the capital to inaugurate a seniors' housing scheme in Burnaby with the help of provincial grants, CMHC loans, and a municipal land grant.[148] Winch, a bricklayer and carpenter-builder, assisted in the construction of the New Vista cottage development, which opened in 1949. New Vista later added more bungalows and apartments. As well, in 1945, the Danish community opened Dania Home in North Burnaby with private funds and later extended the development using provincial grants and loans.[149] Under Hugh Dobson's influence, the BC conference of the United Church of Canada began in 1946 to wrestle with the seniors' housing problem and worked diligently to open its Fair Haven project in South Burnaby in 1951 with privately raised funds and provincial grants.[150] Finally, under the guidance of New Westminster city council, a seniors' scheme opened early in 1948 near Royal Columbian Hospital.[151]

Seniors themselves began to take action. Between 1945 and 1947, the

Old Age Pensioners' Organization Foundation Branch No. 1 formed a senior citizens' homes association to take advantage of low-rental provisions in the 1944 NHA, and requested assistance from city council, the BC government, the National Housing Administration, and the CMHC in implementing a project.[152] The city's coolness towards the proposal forced the association to turn for help to the Lions Club of Vancouver. The Lions raised money on tag days, purchased land in the Renfrew area for seniors' housing, and began construction in May 1947.

In 1949, the proposed removal of rent controls generated another strong public reaction. After the war, owing to acute shortages in rental accommodation, the federal government transferred controls from the jurisdiction of the War Measures Act to the Transitional Powers Act, and initiated a policy of 'gradual and orderly decontrol.'[153] Property owners pressed for and received increases in rents, but failed to obtain the withdrawal of controls.[154] Late in 1948, the federal government offered to keep controls for another year and then turn them over to individual provinces willing to assume responsibility for them.[155] As 1949 drew to a close, the CCF administration in Saskatchewan was the only provincial government eager to take over controls.[156]

When Ontario landlords took the issue of the constitutionality of federal controls to court, Ottawa decided to refer the question to the Supreme Court of Canada.[157] There, the federal and Ontario governments, the Canadian Congress of Labour, the Canadian Legion, and a counsel for tenants stated the case in favour of continued controls, and the Quebec government and the counsel for property owners argued in support of removal. Thereafter, a debate between tenant and landlord supporters broke out across the country. In British Columbia, landlords and realtors belonging to groups such as the Associated Property Owners of Vancouver, the Apartment and Rooming House Operators' Association, and the Vancouver Real Estate Board faced opposition from organizations such as the VHA, the Vancouver Council of Women, the Canadian Legion, the Salvation Army, the LPP, the CCF, and various labour, tenants', church, women's, and pensioners' groups.[158] Because the province would be able to take over controls, the premier was flooded with representations from individuals and organizations on both sides of the issue. Nonetheless, the BC government was not initially prepared to introduce rent control legislation. On 1 March 1950, a Supreme Court decision approved federal controls, and Ottawa announced that it would keep them until 30 April 1951.[159]

Still under pressure from the public, Premier Byron Johnson assumed responsibility for rent controls on 1 May 1951 under the Leasehold Regulations Act, and delegated their administration to the rentals control branch of the provincial Department of Labour.[160] The Social Credit government of W.A.C. Bennett finally terminated provincial controls on 31 March 1955. By the mid-1950s, although they expressed concern about tenants with low fixed incomes, the VHA and other groups no longer opposed their removal because 'in their present form controls are inequitable in their incidence.'[161] Instead, they unsuccessfully proposed a civic rent tribunal for appeals.

Throughout all the agitation over evictions, emergency shelter, veterans' and seniors' rental housing, and rent controls, the VHA, the CCF, and the LPP kept alive the goal of achieving a permanent low-income housing program fostered in the Depression years. The 1946 arrival in Vancouver of Leonard Marsh, 'Canada's most outstanding authority on housing problems,' reinforced the drive to correct the degenerating housing conditions in the downtown core.[162] Following his work with the federal government's advisory committee on reconstruction and the United Nations Relief and Rehabilitation Administration in Europe, Marsh joined the UBC Department of Architecture recently set up by Fred Lasserre. He later moved to the School of Social Work and the Faculty of Education. He was one of the bright, dynamic scholars brought to the university under Larry MacKenzie's able administration during postwar expansion. Marsh began speaking publicly on the housing issue, became active as a VHA director in the company of Grace MacInnis, P.R.U. Stratton, and others, and participated in the newly formed Community Planning Association of Canada with Lasserre, Stratton, and local architects N.E. Pratt and C.B.K. Van Norman.[163] His wife, Betty Marsh, a journalist, became the VHA's secretary.

In the summer of 1947, Marsh began a demonstration housing survey of Strathcona with the help of UBC students and the financial assistance of the CMHC and the city.[164] The survey, based on extensive questionnaire distribution and data assembly and analysis, represented the most scientific Vancouver housing study to date. UBC published the results and recommendations in a 1950 report. Marsh proposed gradually clearing the area lying between Gore and Campbell avenues and Hastings and Prior streets, and constructing public housing for displaced households. He believed that Strathcona was still a healthy community, not a slum, and that redevelopment at that time would preserve the neighbourhood. He suggested that the cheap hotels in the area north of Hastings were beyond improvement, and that the area should be made into an industrial zone. The tenants could be accommodated in the new public housing. Strathcona residents reacted angrily to distorted press coverage calling their neighbourhood a 'square mile of vice,' however, and firmly rejected any suggestion of wholesale redevelopment.[165] Eventually, public housing was built on city land on Campbell Avenue and on cleared land between Pender and Keefer streets.

More and more members of political parties other than the CCF and the LPP became advocates of public housing. Although it had refused to renew the special housing committee a few years earlier, by March 1945, the NPA-dominated city council had taken a different tack. It endorsed a CFMM proposal for low-rental housing built and operated by a local authority and subsidized by municipalities (20 per cent) and senior governments (80 per cent).[166] As long as the city did not have to carry a heavy financial burden, it was prepared to participate in social housing projects. Council members such as Halford D. Wilson and George C. Miller and mayors like Gerry McGeer and Charles E. Thompson, all NPA members, supported the notion of low-rental schemes if they had senior government assistance.[167] Furthermore, at the provincial level, the new Liberal party leader, Byron Johnson, once enthusiastic only about mortgage-assisted home ownership schemes, finally drew the province into a public housing program in 1949-50.[168]

The shift in thinking may be attributed to a recognition of the need for such housing during the acute wartime and postwar shortages and to the prospect of federal financial participation removing the risk for other governments. For Johnson, and possibly for the others, another, more overtly political reason existed. By dividing BC politics into two polarized camps – representing 'free enterprise' and 'individual freedom' on the part of the governing coalition of Liberals and Conservatives, and 'socialism with all its regimentation' on the part of the CCF – Johnson attempted to garner electoral support in the middle ground. He depicted himself as a social reformer in a free-market economy and threatened voters with a 'red scare.' He claimed that 'what is wanted in this province is free-enterprise with a high degree of social security rather than an experiment in socialism.'[169]

By 1947, pressure at the national level and in cities like Toronto and Vancouver for low-rental housing became more intense. The CFMM submitted a request for federally subsidized public housing to C.D. Howe, who asked the federation to draft a plan for such a program.[170] Howe later decided that the proper time to introduce such a plan still had not arrived. In Vancouver in 1948, at the urging of the VHA, the

town planning commission, a wide variety of community organizations, and the CCF member of city council, Laura Jamieson, the city
decided to establish a local housing authority if the senior governments
instituted a low-rental scheme as the CFMM proposed.[171] In December,
following discussions with the provincial Cabinet and the Union of
British Columbia Municipalities executive, city council began to consider the legal steps necessary to obtain a charter amendment to create
an authority. In 1949, despite the opposition of the BC Building
Contractors' Association and the Associated Property Owners of Vancouver but with provincial approval, city council appointed a temporary
local housing authority until Ottawa and Victoria devised a public
housing scheme.[172] Members of this authority included the CRCGV's
Major Oscar Erickson and the VHA's P.R.U. Stratton, as well as a city
council member as chair and two civic officials. The authority soon
recommended two sites for future developments, one of which was at
Ontario Street and 33rd Avenue.

Still under pressure from the CFMM in 1949, CMHC president Mansur
and the new minister responsible for housing, Robert H. Winters,
considered a variety of options for producing more low-cost housing. A
second mortgage scheme and a public housing program were two
possibilities,[173] and they finally opted for the latter. In September, they
introduced an amendment to the 1944 NHA for a federal-provincial
partnership – with costs to be divided 75 per cent to 25 per cent – to
subsidize the construction and deficits of public housing projects.[174] In
British Columbia, Premier Byron Johnson at first preferred a mortgage
reduction program to stimulate low-cost home ownership, but after
discussions with Winters and Mansur in Ottawa and Victoria, he
adopted the proposal. In mid-December, Johnson, Mansur, several
provincial Cabinet ministers and deputy ministers, and J.A. Jones, the
CMHC regional manager in Vancouver, conducted discussions about
housing conditions with delegations from various municipalities. The
Vancouver delegation was headed by Charles Thompson. On 12 December, as the wartime decade ended, the City of Vancouver and the
provincial government agreed in principle on a public housing
scheme.[175]

Thus by late 1949 Vancouver's social housing movement had finally
achieved the promise of a low-rental project. Early in 1950, the city
initiated such a scheme under the new federal legislation. It chose the
seven-acre Little Mountain site between 33rd and 37th avenues and
Main and Ontario streets, immediately east of Queen Elizabeth Park.[176]

It approached both the CMHC and Everett Brown, the recently appointed provincial housing commissioner reporting to the minister of finance in Victoria. The three parties involved in the federal-provincial partnership worked out plans and an agreement in the following months. A final agreement was ready by 1 November 1950.[177] It provided for land conveyance, provision of services by the city, CMHC payment for land and services, sharing of capital costs by Ottawa and British Columbia, creation of a local housing authority to manage the housing project, and a 75-12.5-12.5 per cent division on federal, provincial, and municipal contributions towards operating costs. Unfortunately, soaring prices owing to the Korean War delivered a death blow to these initial plans.[178]

Still, work on the Little Mountain project continued. The CMHC decided that maximum income levels allowable in the project and rents would have to be raised to meet capital and operating costs and that therefore households of lowest income would not be accepted.[179] Regional director T.B. Pickersgill also suggested that in order to cut costs the architects, Thompson, Berwick and Pratt (formerly Sharp and Thompson, Berwick, Pratt), should redesign the original masonry structures to resemble the HEV frame-and-stucco apartments and row houses on West Broadway and West Fourth avenues.[180]

The proposal for the project had the support of the VHA, labour, most city council members, the CMHC, the new BC premier, W.A.C. Bennett, and the provincial finance minister, Einar Gunderson.[181] Yet it met with vigorous opposition from developers C.B. Balfour and N.W. Hullah, builder J.S. Wood, a few city council members, the BC Building Contractors' Association, the Associated Property Owners of Vancouver, the Vancouver Real Estate Board, the Kitsilano Chamber of Commerce, the Suburban Property Owners' Association, and, in an about-face, the editors of the *Vancouver Sun* and the *Vancouver Daily Province*. They attacked Little Mountain in the building and town planning committee and in city council for several reasons: it represented 'socialized, subsidized housing'; it would not serve the lowest income households supported by social allowances or old age pensions; it asked citizens to subsidize the rents of other, moderately well-off citizens; it had not passed through the referendum process; and it would depreciate the value of surrounding properties.[182] Representatives of the housing industry also argued that private enterprise could provide low-rental housing under the NHA. The conflict continued well into 1953 even though a contract had already been let to Pyke and White Construction Limited.[183]

Figure 23 In the early 1950s, Vancouver's social housing movement achieved its objective when Little Mountain public housing was built with shared federal, provincial, and municipal responsibility. The apartments and townhouses accommodated 224 households.

When city council gave Little Mountain its final approval in June 1953, bulldozers moved onto the site, and construction of forty one-bedroom apartments, ninety-two two-bedroom apartments, forty-four three-bedroom apartments, and forty-eight three-bedroom row houses started in earnest (Figure 23).[184] After consultation with the city and the CMHC, the province appointed the members of the newly formed Vancouver Housing Authority. Three activists of the 1940s housing movement, Oscar Erickson, Laura Selman, and P.R.U. Stratton, sat on the public housing authority.[185] Sixteen families moved into Little Mountain on 1 April 1954, and the remainder had settled into their apartments and row houses by Hallowe'en. The anti-public housing forces continued to oppose all proposals for additional low-rental schemes.

In the end, Little Mountain started off its existence as a mixed-income project. Of its 224 households, about 10 per cent received under $150 a month, about 35 per cent ranged between $150 and $225, and about 55 per cent had incomes over $225.[186] The CMHC permitted minimum family incomes of $115 to $155 and maximum ones of $290 to $325. Indeed, the corporation and its president, Stewart Bates, who replaced David Mansur in 1954, approved of the mixed-income approach as it tended not to 'ghettoize' the project's poorest tenants.[187] Rents averaged $45 and spread from $25 to $80. When in the mid-1950s the city increased its social allowance for rentals, welfare recipients began to move into the housing.[188] Pensioners of the lowest income group lived in Little Mountain from the beginning.

Thus, by the early 1950s, a housing movement composed of activist groups had obtained an evictions freeze, emergency shelter, continuation of rent controls, construction of hundreds of veterans' rental units, and the Little Mountain public housing project. These initiatives came about by applying pressure on the federal government in conjunction with national lobby groups such as the CFMM and with similar campaigns in other major cities such as Montreal and Toronto.[189] Yet the force of protests in Vancouver over the local housing situation had a singular impact on Ottawa, which was particularly demonstrable in the imposition of an evictions freeze, the occupation of the old Hotel Vancouver, and the construction of hundreds of rental units.

Why were activists able to achieve these improvements in housing in Vancouver? First, the public felt an enormous, genuine sympathy for the problems with shelter faced by servicemen, veterans, and their families, particularly if the men had been stationed overseas. They tolerated and even supported incidents of occupation or squatting.

Second, the housing campaign came from a wide cross-section of organizations. Whatever their differences in other areas, and whether they cooperated with one another or not, activists from veterans', labour, women's, community, and political organizations endeavoured to rectify Vancouver's housing problem. Groups as diverse as the city's junior board of trade, the LPP, the International Woodworkers of America, the Canadian Legion, the Kinsmen Club, and the University Women's Club wanted better housing. Intense class struggle, such as that over rental housing in Glasgow in the early 1900s, did not occur in the 1940s in Vancouver.[190]

Third, some Vancouverites, especially the members of the CRCGV, saw the dissatisfaction about housing among returning servicemen as a possible threat to the social order. They remembered the general strikes following the First World War and the unrest among reliefers during the Depression. Despite the arguments of historians who explain housing reform using social control theory, however, attempts to defuse protests usually brought more agitation.[191] Squatting, rent strikes, and other tactics continued long after the old Hotel Vancouver had been converted into emergency shelter.

Fourth, the pressure on government from Vancouver's activists was highly political. It came in large part from left-wing parties that were stronger and better organized than in the 1930s. In addition, individuals in the NPA, Liberal, and Progressive Conservative parties eventually promoted the resolution of the housing question. Leigh Stevenson, a Progressive Conservative, became the first Emergency Shelter administrator and later sat in the provincial coalition government.[192] No doubt the shrewd electoral objective of outflanking the CCF was a major concern of Premier Byron Johnson and others; the CCF mounted a substantial threat to other parties in elections at all levels of government between 1944 and 1952.

Lastly, the pressure exerted to solve the immediate crisis of the 1940s also helped to relieve the long-term need for low-income housing. Public awareness of temporary wartime and postwar shortages soon embraced the chronic problem of low-rental accommodation. In other words, social housing finally came to Vancouver as part of the thrust to ameliorate the housing shortage brought on by the Second World War. Once the emergency passed, the urgency of the drive for permanent social housing programs diminished, but housing advocacy remained and led to the construction of other publicly assisted projects around the city.

The achievements of housing activism in the 1940s were sometimes short-lived. Not unexpectedly, the emergency shelter program was disbanded in 1949. Rent controls in British Columbia lasted as long as 1955 under both federal and provincial governments. Probably the biggest blow to the implementation of a massive national social housing program came with the CMHC's decision in 1946 to sell off war workers' and veterans' rental housing. The crown company started to dispose of the Sea Island houses in 1947 by offering them to tenants, and a year later began to make the Vancouver housing available.[193] Between 1947 and 1950, the CMHC sold over 1,000 units in the city.[194] In North Vancouver, tenants decided to buy their houses when faced with increased rent to meet higher taxes. The Renfrew Heights and Fraserview houses went on the block in the late 1950s. The last Fraserview and WHL units sold in 1966, and owners occupied the remaining Renfrew Heights houses by 1967.

The sale of the WHL/CMHC housing was controversial from the beginning. Arguably, tenants had the opportunity to become owners with a downpayment of 10 per cent of the selling price as calculated by the CMHC. If residents in Renfrew Heights and Fraserview had time to prepare financially for home ownership, however, tenants in the early WHL projects had less opportunity either to put together the necessary capital or (even when organized into an association) to alter the conditions of sale. According to the CMHC itself in 1947, tenants probably preferred to rent than to purchase the houses.

Social housing advocates, such as Humphrey Carver, have questioned the wisdom of divesting the 'all too successful' veterans' rental program.[195] A bureaucratic dispute between the departments of Finance and of Reconstruction and Supply (formerly Munitions and Supply), W.C. Clark's policy of preferring market over social housing programs, and a fear of and distaste for socialism among federal officials apparently frightened Ottawa into ridding itself of war workers' and veterans' houses.[196] In the end, whatever the assessment of Ottawa's decision to terminate the rental program, many of these homes shelter families to this day in Renfrew Heights, Fraserview, and east Vancouver.

If some of the advances made by housing activists were temporary, others were not. The veterans' apartments and townhouses built by HEV along Broadway and Fourth avenues are today either in use or in the process of being rebuilt by the CMHC. Little Mountain and other public housing projects such as Orchard Park and Raymur Place, which were constructed between 1957 and 1970, are still operational. They never provided enough units to satisfy the needs of all low-income households looking for a decent, affordable home. Still, Little Mountain is a benchmark in the history of housing in Vancouver. It was the first in a succession of social housing complexes that by the 1970s and 1980s included the cooperatives built under a 1973 amendment to the NHA. Furthermore, housing activism itself was a permanent phenomenon in Vancouver by 1950. The drive that produced Little Mountain became the movement that created other projects in later years. In this way, the activists of the 1940s made far-reaching, lasting contributions to social housing and housing advocacy in Vancouver.

6
Conclusion

A chronic housing problem of serious dimensions developed in Vancouver in the first half of this century. At the same time, a social housing movement emerged to ameliorate the problem. By 1950, this movement had achieved important but limited improvements. Do the definition of the problem and the story of this activism make any significant contributions to the history of housing, and are they at all helpful in finding some answers to our questions about housing in Vancouver today?[1]

By the early 1950s, despite Vancouver's generally satisfactory supply of housing for middle- and high-income households, the city suffered from a continuing, worsening scarcity of decent, low-income rental accommodation. At the same time, occasional crises in availability and affordability presented serious difficulties for many middle-income residents and increased hardships for the poor. Both aspects of the problem, which was not unique to Vancouver, had appeared before the Depression of the 1930s.

As in Canada as a whole, the housing statistics for Vancouver to 1951 reveal an overall good quality stock of urban residential space and rising rates of home ownership. Deryck Holdsworth has described a pre-1929 city of detached houses, widely accessible and largely occupied by owners, in middle- and working-class suburbs such as Point Grey and South Vancouver. By 1931, 51 per cent of dwellings across the entire, amalgamated city were owner-occupied. The proportion of owners remained about the same (50.1 per cent) in 1941 and climbed to 63 per cent in 1951. Moreover, the figures with respect to overcrowding, external disrepair, sanitary facilities, and basic conveniences compared favourably in 1931, 1941, and 1951 with those of other major Canadian cities.

Yet the decade-by-decade aggregated census statistics for Vancouver obscure the long-term need for good quality residential space for low-income individuals and families in the downtown area and parts of its immediately adjacent neighbourhoods. The statistics also hide periodic crises in the affordability and availability of housing. Before 1930, some Vancouverites of small income – the elderly, single working women, relief families, and seasonally or fully unemployed workers – could not afford the more expensive rent in apartment blocks or single houses, and lived in lodgings, cheap hotels, cabins, bachelor houses, or water-front shacks. Homelessness was common in times of depression. More-over, critical housing shortages after the First World War worsened living conditions in downtown lodgings.

In the 1930s, the 'chronic shortage of low rental housing' grew worse with high unemployment.[2] Overcrowding intensified as destitute households doubled up or occupied smaller units, and standards of rented accommodation fell as owners and operators failed to make improvements or circumvented civic building and zoning bylaws. Homelessness plagued single, transient, unemployed men in the city. As well, drastic reductions in new construction, foreclosures on mort-gages, and loss of property through inability to pay local taxes produced a severe housing crisis for ordinarily stable working- and middle-class families, heightening the persistent lack of inexpensive rental dwellings. Slow recovery later in the decade failed to bring substantial improve-ment in conditions.

In the 1940s, war and reconstruction generated housing shortages and expanded demand for homes for low- and middle-income groups, particularly for war workers, servicemen's families, and veterans. The temporary shortages put pressure on less costly rental units in the downtown area and in adjacent districts such as Kitsilano and Fairview. Increased crowding made living conditions worse. While more fortu-nate families moved into government-built subdivisions such as Fraserview and Renfrew Heights, or privately developed suburbs in North Vancouver and Burnaby, the elderly poor, single female workers, families on social assistance, and seasonal wage earners continued to live in cheap, substandard accommodation in the downtown core.

Although the housing situation had improved in many ways by the early 1950s, a continuing need for decent low-rental units and still unresolved postwar shortages of middle-income owned and rented accommodation afflicted Vancouver. Thus, the city's housing problem up to 1950 consisted of two elements: the long-standing, unfulfilled requirement for satisfactory low-rental dwellings; and the intermittent crises brought on by economic depression, war, and reconstruction.

What is the historiographical significance of this analysis of Vancouver's housing problem before 1950? Unlike Holdsworth's earlier studies, the first chapter of this book asserted that the problem developed long before the Depression. Before 1929, Vancouver was a city with cabins and cheap hotels as well as cottages and castles. In addition, the analysis is relevant to discussions among historians and historical geographers about living standards and tenure issues. Furthermore, it contributes to the newly emerging area of the social history of domestic architecture.

With its inception in early nineteenth-century Britain and renewal in the 1920s, the standard-of-living debate is a very old historiographical chestnut. Pessimists and optimists have been heatedly divided over whether industrial capitalism has improved workers' living standards and whether material factors, qualitative ones, or both should measure those standards.[3] Since 1963, under E.P. Thompson's influence, emphasis has shifted from statistical to impressionistic evidence and from economic to social history. Moreover, more recent studies have focused on local or regional conditions and issues such as housing, diet, and specific occupations. In the 1970s, the debate came to Canada with Terry Copp's *The Anatomy of Poverty* (1974) and Michael Piva's *The Condition of the Working Class in Toronto* (1979).[4] Both pessimists, Copp and Piva used housing as one of several qualitative factors in concluding that between 1900 and 1929 a capitalist economy deprived Montreal and Toronto workers of their fair share of the national income. Since then, other Canadian historians have used real wages and nutrition as bases of measurement. Employing a wide range of qualitative and quantitative factors, John Belshaw compared the earning power of Vancouver Island coal miners rather unfavourably to those of British miners, but argued more optimistically that West Coast accommodation and diet were 'in some ways undeniably superior to what had been left behind.'[5]

In the past, census figures for later decades and Holdsworth's account of pre-1929 housing offered an optimistic picture of workers' residential conditions in Vancouver. Although only the census manuscripts will be able to confirm the gravity of the housing problem up to 1950, the impressionistic and statistical evidence in this text suggests a gloomier side to that picture for those who, for whatever reason, had small incomes. The evidence also supports the assertions of Bettina Bradbury and others about the resourcefulness of poor households in contending with low living standards.[6] It reinforces the findings of Paul Yee and Kay Anderson about living conditions in Chinatown and Strathcona, and invites more research about the relationship between these conditions and the social behaviour and mobility of the residents.[7] The housing of native people in Vancouver (and Greater Vancouver) before 1950 is another possible subject for research. The sources used in this study reveal almost no information about their accommodation (see Chapter 1, Figure 3).

This investigation also contributes to Canadian work on tenure and class begun in the 1960s by Michael B. Katz and continued by Michael J. Doucet, Marc H. Choko, and Richard Harris.[8] At first, their time-consuming quantitative analyses linked tenure, class, and social mobility in cities such as Hamilton, Kingston, Toronto, and Montreal. More recently, following the publication of Kenneth T. Jackson's *Crabgrass Frontier*, Harris has come to focus more particularly upon working-class suburbs in North American cities, and he speculates that, by the 1910s and 1920s, these suburbs were widespread across the continent.[9] Holdsworth's portrayal of working-class South Vancouver, with his emphasis upon uniqueness removed, enhances Harris's hypothesis. This text also supports Harris's theory; it separates the downtown area, with its higher proportion of low-income rental accommodation for seasonal workers, from the skilled working- and middle-class suburbs, with their greater percentages of home ownership. As well, this analysis offers an impressionistic, partial answer to R.A.J. McDonald's recently posed question about 'the domestic circumstances of seasonal migrants and that of more stable urban workers.'[10]

Finally, this book looks at Vancouver's housing from the perspective of Canadian social architectural history rather than traditional architectural history.[11] It provides information about types of residence such as cabins, waterfront shacks, cheap hotels, lodgings, and Chinese bachelor houses, with which architectural historians ordinarily have not concerned themselves. In describing the homes of the transient or seasonal workers of British Columbia's resource industries, as well as the unemployed, the elderly, the poor, and single working women, the study deals with accommodation for social groups not normally examined by architectural historians. It shows the transformation over the decades of residential structures built in Vancouver's early years. The West End mansions of the city's elite and the Kitsilano bungalows of its middle class became the lodging houses written up in reports by civic health inspectors. As medical officers predicted before the First World War, the once-new cabins and hotels along Cordova or Powell streets declined into the blighted buildings disdained by redevelopment studies after the Second World War. Foreshore shacks appeared, disappeared, and reappeared throughout the first half of the century, and they remained a popular form of accommodation into the second half.

This description of Vancouver's residential problems before 1950 leads to several observations relevant to today's housing and heritage issues. First, the study chronicles the long history of certain types of accommodation not normally credited with much importance. Yet cabins, bachelor houses, lodgings, and shacks played significant roles in British Columbia's social history, and deserve greater consideration in our material history and in the preservation of our heritage buildings.

Second, despite its substandard character, the less expensive rental housing of the downtown district continues into the 1990s to shelter households that could not afford to live elsewhere. During the shortages of the 1940s, city building inspectors refused to permit demolition of structures unless unsafe and unsound, because they knew that the displaced occupants had no other place to go. Owing in part to that refusal, Vancouver today has a large stock of substandard housing on the east side of the downtown district. The existence of such accommodation has kept the level of absolute homelessness lower than that of other North American cities. Yet the need to renovate the old structures (many with heritage value) or replace them with social housing projects has now become an emergency.

Finally, today's observers may very well conclude that our own housing difficulties are in essence the same as earlier in the century. Although the factors leading to the present problem may be different, the chronic shortage of satisfactory low-rental dwellings and the occasional serious crisis in middle-income rented and owned housing remain with us.

Over the decades, both governments and local activist groups responded to Vancouver's pre-1950 housing problem. In reaction to nationwide crises in accommodation brought on by war and depression, the federal government developed strategies that applied to Vancouver and other Canadian urban centres. Although the province of British Columbia, the city, and housing activists usually played no formal part in initiating legislation and plans, they became instrumental in implementing and continuing them. Furthermore, the federal government encountered intense pressure for change from below. Activist groups directly addressed their demands to the city council, the province, and the federal government. Vancouver and Victoria in turn urged Ottawa to act, and other governments and organizations across the country similarly challenged federal politicians and bureaucrats. In response, Ottawa created additional programs to meet local and national emergencies. Thus, although unilateral decision-making in Ottawa produced many nationwide schemes, pressure from activists and governments across Canada and in Vancouver helped to introduce, implement, and continue federal programs.

Between 1919 and 1949, the national government developed several plans intended to stimulate or stabilize the economy and to generate employment across Canada and in Vancouver: the 1919 federal plan, known as the Better Housing Scheme in British Columbia; the DHA and NHA programs; the HIP; and wartime and reconstruction measures such as rent and construction controls, war workers' projects, home conversion, and DVA housing. In peacetime these programs relied heavily on private sector involvement, and in wartime the federal government intervened in a more direct manner. Although activist organizations, civic government, and sometimes local business leaders would later ask for particular programs to be implemented or continued, it was often the influence of powerful federal 'mandarins,' such as W.C. Clark, or energetic ministers, such as C.D. Howe, that prompted the measures initially.

Public pressure for improvements in Vancouver's housing conditions emerged in the 1910s and 1920s, mounted in the 1930s, and peaked in the 1940s. Initially, activists entreated federal authorities to make more funds available for the Better Housing Scheme. Their drive to obtain public housing began in earnest in the late 1930s, met with success in 1949 with an NHA amendment, and saw the completion of the Little Mountain project in 1954. During and after the war, activists called for evictions relief, additional rental housing built by federal crown corporations, emergency shelters, and continuation of rent controls. In the beginning, the movement towards socially-oriented housing programs consisted of representatives of women's, veterans', and labour organizations and of civic bureaucrats and professionals. In the 1930s and 1940s, the CCF and the LPP politicized the campaign when they joined forces with those organizations and other groups such as the VHA, CRCGV, and service clubs. The 'reform' of earlier years became the 'activism' of the Depression and wartime decades.

Although activist organizations applied pressure to the Vancouver city council and the BC government, both were reluctant to intervene in the housing issue. After the Better Housing Scheme experiment, neither the city nor the provincial government would become involved in any program with the potential for financial risk. Even though constitutional responsibility for housing lay with the province, both Vancouver and Victoria regarded the problem as national in scope and in remedy. In the 1940s and early 1950s, their perspectives on intervention began to alter as conditions deteriorated, activist pressure increased, the political threat of the CCF grew, the Liberal and Progressive Conservative parties became more committed to housing reforms, and the federal government offered to share responsibility for implementing and operating projects. In the end, a majority on city council supported large-scale schemes like Fraserview and Little Mountain, and the provincial governments of Byron Johnson and then W.A.C. Bennett approved public housing in Vancouver.

At the same time, opposition to the activist groups emerged and exerted pressure on all three governments. Beginning in the late 1930s, elements in the property, lending, and building industries enthusiastically promoted state initiatives to stimulate housing construction in the private sector, and increasingly rejected measures like subsidized public housing and rent controls. Opposition became most strident and forceful in the early and mid-1950s with the development of the Little Mountain public housing complex and proposals to build additional projects.

What is the historiographical significance of this story of the struggle for social housing in Vancouver? First, the analysis, which is based on the integration of national and local evidence, adds to the work of housing historians who have focused on federal decision-making, studied events in specific cities, or already begun to merge the national and local dimensions of housing issues.[12] In the future others are likely to broaden the context of this account by investigating housing problems and responses in other Canadian cities, researching the work of national organizations like the CFMM, and comparing housing activism in this country to that of other nations.

Furthermore, this text adds to recent literature on housing activism in Britain and the United States. Historians in those countries have described the impact of local activism in shaping government housing initiatives.[13] Although their writing varies in emphasis and scope, Martin J. Daunton, David Englander, Joseph Melling, and Sean Damer have connected the tension of landlord-tenant relations with the introduction of rent controls and council housing in early twentieth-century

Britain. In the United States, Peter Marcuse, Thomas S. Hines, Rosalie Genevro, Ann L. Buttenweiser, and Neil H. Lebowitz have examined the effect of competition among local interest groups for federal programs such as rent controls and public housing. Robert B. Fairbanks has reported on the growth and achievements of Cincinnati's low-cost housing movement. Robert Lawson, Joel Schwartz and others have revealed the success of New York's tenant activists in forcing concessions from landlords and government. This study of Vancouver differs from British and American work that portrays either a mass working-class movement or the interaction of interest groups. Instead, it has described a social housing movement composed of left-wing, labour, women's, community, and veterans' organizations. In its depiction of this broad-based movement, it is similar to the work of Englander and Lawson, both of whom acknowledge combined class support for successful housing drives.[14]

In contrast to the 'activist' theme of this book, writers in the 1970s such as Enid Gauldie, Anthony S. Wohl, John Burnett, and John N. Tarn took a liberal-progressive approach to housing history.[15] They described a natural progression in Britain from laissez-faire to state intervention in housing once authorities clearly perceived the problem of working-class shelter. Vancouver's experience, however, demonstrates no such natural progression. Instead, crises in shelter brought on by depression, war, and reconstruction precipitated direct or indirect state involvement to stabilize the economy or to generate employment, and local pressure compelled Ottawa to develop more socially oriented initiatives to meet the long- and short-term aspects of the accommodation problem.

The 'activist' approach to Vancouver's experience also differs from the 'social control' perspective found in both the American and British housing literature. In 1962, Roy Lubove regarded housing reform in New York City during the Progressive era as an instrument of social control.[16] Almost a decade later, Gareth Stedman Jones viewed both philanthropic and new suburban housing as upper- and middle-class strategies to control London's working class.[17] As has been seen, this analysis examines the role of a far more wide-ranging movement, although it does not completely discard social control theory.[18] Some activists apparently believed in introducing housing improvements to minimize social unrest after both world wars and during the Depression. Moreover, in bringing in a soldiers' housing program or an evictions freeze, the federal government also adhered to a goal of maintaining order during social crisis.

The historiographical perspective of this account reinforces other approaches to housing history. It is in general agreement, for example, with the many historians of Canadian housing who have argued that the reforms of the first half of the twentieth century have not fundamentally altered the inequalities of capitalist society.[19] Terry Copp and Michael Piva made this assertion about philanthropic and regulative reforms in Montreal and Toronto before 1921-9. Alan Moscovitch and Albert Rose have noted that government has attended to the residual residential construction that the private sector cannot profitably handle. John Bacher, David Hulchanski, Alvin Finkel, and the present author have remarked on two related phenomena: the interconnected role of government and business in housing reform; and federal emphasis upon the welfare of the housing market rather than the welfare of the disadvantaged in accommodation. As the aggregate census figures and information specific to the downtown area show, improvements in Vancouver housing under federal legislation benefited middle-income families more than low-income households.

In demonstrating the significant role played by local women's groups in the social housing movement, this 'activist' history also contributes to housing literature based on gender. The book has taken the story of women's involvement beyond philanthropical reform to social and political activism.[20] Although Vancouver women did not invent a 'grand domestic revolution in women's material conditions' or lead rent strikes, as their more militant counterparts in Glasgow did, they promoted the housing cause on city council and in the legislative assembly, attended and spoke at eviction rallies, organized demonstrations for shelter relief, set up and ran registries, and sat on the Vancouver Housing Authority. Initiatives made possible through their efforts, such as war workers' lodgings, veterans' projects, emergency shelter, and public housing, benefited other women and their families. As well, both the VHA study of single working women's accommodation and the cooperative houses established by Laura Jamieson assisted unmarried female workers. Nonetheless, this activism did not alter the unequal status of women in Canada's patriarchal society, and emerged from maternal, as well as socialist, feminism.[21]

Finally, this study adds a new dimension to current architectural historical writing about modern housing. The history of wartime housing in North Vancouver, Richmond, and Vancouver and the veterans' units in Renfrew Heights and Fraserview reveals the stylistic significance of this architect-designed housing in the development of Canadian domestic architecture. These small, plain dwellings reflected a gradual minimalization in traditional design, simplification in ornamentation and outline, reduction in size, and an opening up of early twentieth-century floor plans.[22] The first WHL houses, derived from the Cape Cod styles of the 1920s and 1930s through National Housing Administration 'Design No. 501,' displayed the greatest minimalization in interior and exterior design. After the early 1940s, veterans' dwellings began to offer a less simplified appearance and plan. Both the war workers' and the veterans' units played a part in bringing advanced building technology and modern kitchen, bathroom, laundry, and heating facilities to Canadian housing.

These war workers' and veterans' houses represent as historically important a type of domestic architecture as the examples of the West Coast modern style still extant on the west side of the city or on the north shore of Burrard Inlet.[23] Both types deserve consideration from preservationists, who are now beginning to fight to keep the first and the best examples of Vancouver's postwar architecture. Unfortunately, developers have already started to replace the Renfrew Heights and Fraserview housing.

What historical lessons may we learn from this account of Vancouver's early social housing movement? First, local activism worked in the past, and it can still work today. In the 1930s and 1940s, however, the housing problem was national in scope and in remedy, and Ottawa felt pressure from groups in major cities across the country. Now, for ideological, fiscal, and constitutional reasons, the federal government is less disposed to act. Thus, Vancouver's housing advocates increasingly have to look to the civic and the provincial governments for a response.

Second, many of the solutions proposed in the 1930s and 1940s by activist groups, the federal government, or both – including temporary and permanent programs for home ownership, rehabilitation, conversion, rent control, public housing, registries, cooperative projects, and privately and publicly owned rental accommodation – are still applicable today. In fact, the origins of some recent creative approaches to housing problems lie in the initial, fertile period of national policy development. The idea for the so-called 'third sector,' for example, in which community-based organizations build social housing, was present in the 1944 Curtis report.[24] Its author, Leonard Marsh, envisaged housing constructed by public, private, and cooperative sectors. Moreover, the wide range of approaches used in the 1940s met the dual nature of the accommodation problem. This experience suggests that a variety of solutions to meet both low- and middle-income needs is necessary even now.

A rupture in the collective memory of Vancouver's social housing movement probably occurred around 1970, when P.R.U. Stratton closed the office of the Vancouver Housing Association and retired.[25] This book has sought to reconstruct the story of the movement's actions and achievements in the first half of this century. Today's housing advocates may now reach into the past for inspiration in meeting the challenges of the 1990s. Clearly, the history of housing activism in Vancouver is one to remember and celebrate.

Notes

The following abbreviations appear in this section:

BCARS British Columbia Archives and Records Services
CC Office of the City Clerk
CCD City Clerk's Department
CHR *Canadian Historical Review*
CMHC Central Mortgage and Housing Corporation
CRA City of Richmond Archives
CS City Solicitor
CVA City of Vancouver Archives
DBS Dominion Bureau of Statistics
FD Finance Department
HD Health Department
JUH *Journal of Urban History*
MHO Medical Health Officer's
MO Mayor's Office
NAC National Archives of Canada
PDS Public Documents
PLD Permits and Licenses Department
SSD Social Service Department
TPC Town Planning Commission
UCA United Church Archives
UHR *Urban History Review/Revue d'histoire urbaine*
VHA Vancouver Housing Association
WPTB Wartime Prices and Trade Board

Introduction
1 Sheila Baxter, *Under the Viaduct: Homeless in Beautiful B.C.* (Vancouver: New Star Books 1991).
2 A significant exception is Jim Green, formerly of the Downtown Eastside Residents' Association. The Canadian women's movement also experienced this 'rupture in historical memory' and temporarily lost the history of socialist feminism in this country. For its restoration we must thank Joan Sangster,

Dreams of Equality: Women on the Canadian Left, 1920-1950 (Toronto: McClelland and Stewart 1989), 224. An example of ruptured memory among housing activists of the 1960s may be found in Richard Harris's *Democracy in Kingston: A Social Movement in Urban Politics, 1965-1970* (Montreal and Kingston: McGill-Queen's University Press 1988).

3 Deryck W. Holdsworth, 'House and Home in Vancouver: The Emergence of a West Coast Urban Landscape, 1886-1929' (Ph.D. diss., University of British Columbia 1981); idem, 'House and Home in Vancouver: Images of West Coast Urbanism, 1886-1929,' in *The Canadian City*, ed. Gilbert A. Stelter and Alan F.J. Artibise, Carleton Library no. 109 (Toronto: Macmillan of Canada with the Institute of Canadian Studies, Carleton University 1979), 186-211; idem, 'Cottages and Castles for Vancouver Home-Seekers,' in *Vancouver Past: Essays in Social History*, ed. R.A.J. McDonald and Jean Barman (Vancouver: University of British Columbia Press 1986), 11-32.

4 Michael Doucet and John Weaver, *Housing the North American City* (Montreal and Kingston, London, Buffalo: McGill-Queen's University Press 1991), 298.

5 For work on national policy-making, see John C. Bacher, *Keeping to the Marketplace: The Evolution of Canadian Housing Policy* (Montreal and Kingston, London, Buffalo: McGill-Queen's University Press 1993); idem, 'Canadian Housing "Policy" in Perspective,' *Urban History Review/Revue d'histoire urbaine* (hereafter cited as *UHR*) 15, 1 (June 1986):3-18; idem, 'Too Good to Last? The Social Service Innovations of Wartime Housing,' *Women and Environments* 10, 2 (Winter 1988):10-13; J. David Hulchanski, 'The 1935 Dominion Housing Act: Setting the Stage for a Permanent Federal Presence in Canada's Housing Sector,' *UHR* 15, 1 (June 1986):19-39; John C. Bacher and J. David Hulchanski, 'Keeping Warm and Dry: The Policy Response to the Struggle for Shelter among Canada's Homeless, 1900-1960,' *UHR* 16, 2 (October 1987):147-63; Jill Wade, 'Wartime Housing Limited, 1941-1947: Canadian Housing Policy at the Crossroads,' *UHR* 15, 1 (June 1986):41-59; Alvin Finkel, *Business and Social Reform in the Thirties* (Toronto: James Lorimer 1979), 100-16; Robert G. Bryce, *Maturing in Hard Times: Canada's Department of Finance through the Great Depression* (Montreal and Kingston: McGill-Queen's University Press with the Institute of Public Administration of Canada 1986), 159-71; John T. Saywell, ed., *Housing Canadians: Essays on the History of Residential Construction in Canada*, Discussion Paper no. 24 (Ottawa: Economic Council of Canada 1975), 150-216; Albert Rose, *Canadian Housing Policies (1935-1980)* (Toronto: Butterworths 1980); and Allan Moscovitch and Glenn Drover, eds., *Inequality: Essays on the Political Economy of Social Welfare* (Toronto: University of Toronto Press 1981). For the role of a provincial government, see Beverly J. Grieve, 'Continuity and Change: Provincial Housing Policy in British Columbia, 1945-1985' (M.A. thesis, University of British Columbia 1985). For the local perspective, in addition to Holdsworth's work, see Shirley Campbell Spragge, 'A Confluence of Interests: Housing Reform in Toronto, 1900-1920,' in *The Usable Urban Past: Planning and Politics in the Modern Canadian City*, ed. Gilbert A. Stelter and Alan F.J. Artibise, Carleton Library no. 119 (Toronto: Macmillan of Canada with the Institute of Canadian Studies, Carleton University 1979), 247-67; Lorna F. Hurl, 'The Toronto Housing Company, 1912-1923: The Pitfalls of Painless Philanthropy,' *Canadian Historical Review*

(hereafter cited as *CHR*) 65, 1 (March 1984):28-53; and Kaye Staniforth Melliship, 'The Contribution of Theories of the State in Analyzing Local Government Housing Initiatives: The City of Vancouver's Housing Actions, 1900-1973' (M.A. thesis, University of British Columbia 1985). For studies that integrate local and national developments, see Doucet and Weaver's *Housing the North American City*; John Weaver, 'Reconstruction of the Richmond District in Halifax: A Canadian Episode in Public Housing and Town Planning, 1918-1921,' *Plan Canada* 16, 1 (March 1976):36-47; Jane Lewis and Mark Shrimpton, 'Policy-Making in Newfoundland during the 1940s: The Case of the St. John's Housing Corporation,' *CHR* 65, 2 (June 1984):209-39; Marc H. Choko, Jean-Pierre Collin, and Annick Germain, 'Le logement et les enjeux de la transformation de l'espace urbain: Montréal, 1940-1960 [première et deuxième parties],' *UHR* 15, 2 (October 1986):127-36, and 15, 3 (February 1987):243-53; Jill Delaney, 'The Garden Suburb of Lindenlea, Ottawa: A Model Project for the First Federal Housing Policy, 1918-24,' *UHR* 9, 3 (February 1991):151-65; and Jill Wade, 'The "Sting" of Vancouver's Better Housing Spree,' 1919-1949,' *UHR* 20, 2 (March 1993):92-103.

6 See note 5 for the articles appearing in the June 1986 issue of *UHR*. For the 'new social history,' see Viv Nelles, 'Rewriting History,' *Saturday Night* 96 (February 1981):11-12, 14, 16; and Gregory S. Kealey, 'The Writing of Social History in English Canada, 1970-1984,' *Social History* 10, 3 (October 1985):347-65.

7 J.L. Granatstein, Irving M. Abella, T.W. Acheson, David J. Bercuson, R. Craig Brown, and H. Blair Neatby, *Nation: Canada since Confederation*, 3rd ed., formerly published as *Twentieth Century Canada* (Toronto: McGraw-Hill Ryerson 1990), 399; Robert Bothwell, Ian Drummond, and John English, *Canada since 1945: Power, Politics, and Provincialism* (Toronto: University of Toronto Press 1981), 82-3.

8 For the British literature, see Joseph Melling, *Rent Strikes: People's Struggle for Housing in West Scotland, 1890-1916* (Edinburgh: Polygon 1983); idem, 'Clydeside Housing and the Evolution of State Rent Control,' in *Housing, Social Policy and the State*, ed. Joseph Melling (London: Croom Helm 1980), 139-67; Sean Damer, 'State, Class and Housing: Glasgow, 1885-1919,' in *Housing, Social Policy and the State*, 73-112; David Englander, *Landlord and Tenant in Urban Britain, 1838-1918* (Oxford: Clarendon Press 1983); Martin J. Daunton, ed., *Councillors and Tenants: Local Authority Housing in English Cities, 1919-1939* (Leicester: Leicester University Press 1984); and Manuel Castells, 'The Industrial City and the Working Class: The Glasgow Rent Strike of 1915,' in *The City and the Grassroots: A Cross-Cultural Theory of Urban Social Movements* (Berkeley and Los Angeles: University of California Press 1983), 27-37. Castells offers a far-ranging study of worldwide urban movements in the remainder of his book. For the American literature, see Ronald Lawson, 'The Rent Strike in New York City, 1904-1980: The Evolution of a Social Movement Strategy,' *Journal of Urban History* (hereafter cited as *JUH*) 10, 3 (May 1984):235-58; Ronald Lawson and Mark Naison, eds., *The Tenant Movement in New York City, 1904-1984* (New Brunswick, NJ: Rutgers University Press 1986); Thomas S. Hines, 'Housing, Baseball, and Creeping Socialism: The Battle of Chavez Ravine, Los Angeles, 1949-1959,' *JUH* 8, 2 (February 1982):123-43; Neil H. Lebowitz, '"Above Party, Class, or Creed":

Rent Control in the United States, 1940-1947,' *JUH* 7, 4 (August 1981):439-70; Rosalie Genevro, 'Site Selection and the New York City Housing Authority, 1934-1939,' *JUH* 12, 4 (August 1986):334-52; Joel Schwartz, 'Tenant Unions in New York City's Low-Rent Housing, 1933-1949,' *JUH* 12, 4 (August 1986):414-43; Peter Marcuse, 'The Beginnings of Public Housing in New York,' *JUH* 12, 4 (August 1986):353-90; Ann L. Buttenwieser, 'Shelter for What and for Whom? On the Route toward Vladeck Houses, 1930 to 1940,' *JUH* 12, 4 (August 1986):391-413; and Robert B. Fairbanks, *Making Better Citizens: Housing Reform and the Community Development Strategy in Cincinnati, 1890-1960* (Urbana and Chicago: University of Illinois Press 1988). For the Canadian literature, see Marc H. Choko, 'Le mouvement des squatters à Montréal, 1946-1947,' *Cahiers d'histoire* 2 (Printemps 1982):27-39; idem, *Crises du logement à Montréal (1860-1939)* (Montréal: Éditions coopératives Albert Saint-Martin 1980); Albert Rose, *Regent Park: A Study in Slum Clearance* (Toronto: University of Toronto Press 1958); and Jill Wade, '"A Palace for the Public": Housing Reform and the 1946 Occupation of the Old Hotel Vancouver,' in *Vancouver Past*, ed. McDonald and Barman, 288-310.

9 'Citizens in Action' is the title of ch. 5 of Albert Rose's *Regent Park*, 46-60.

10 For literature on housing conditions, see Terry Copp, *The Anatomy of Poverty: The Condition of the Working Class in Montreal, 1897-1929* (Toronto: McClelland and Stewart 1974), 70-87; Michael J. Piva, *The Condition of the Working Class in Toronto, 1900-1921*, Cahiers d'histoire no. 9 (Ottawa: University of Ottawa Press 1979), 125-42; Jay White, 'The Homes Front: The Accommodation Crisis in Halifax, 1941-1951,' *UHR* 20, 3 (February 1992):117-27; and Jennifer Dunkerson, 'Wartime Housing and Boarding: A Case Study of the Catherine Street North Area of Hamilton, Ontario,' *UHR* 20, 3 (February 1992):109-16. For literature based on the social control thesis, see Gareth Stedman Jones, *Outcast London: A Study in the Relationship between Classes in Victorian Society* (Oxford: Clarendon Press 1971); Roy Lubove, *The Progressives and the Slums: Tenement House Reform in New York, 1890-1917* (Pittsburgh: University of Pittsburgh Press 1962); and Sean Purdy, '"This Is Not a Company: It Is a Cause": Class, Gender, and the Toronto Housing Company, 1912-1920,' *UHR* 21, 2 (March 1993):75-91. For literature explaining state intervention, see Martin J. Daunton, *House and Home in the Victorian City: Working-Class Housing, 1850-1914* (London: Edward Arnold 1983); Anthony S. Wohl, *The Eternal Slum: Housing and Social Policy in Victorian London* (Montreal: McGill-Queen's University Press 1977); John Burnett, *A Social History of Housing, 1815-1985*, 2nd ed. (London and New York: Methuen 1986); Enid Gauldie, *Cruel Habitations: A History of Working Class Housing, 1780-1918* (London: George Allen and Unwin 1974); and John Nelson Tarn, *Five Per Cent Philanthropy: An Account of Housing in Urban Areas between 1840 and 1914* (Cambridge: Cambridge University Press 1973). For the role of housing finance and the real estate and property management business, see Ross Paterson, 'Housing Finance in Early 20th Century Suburban Toronto,' *UHR* 20, 2 (October 1991):63-71; Doucet and Weaver's *Housing the North American City*; and Michael Doucet and John Weaver, 'The North American Shelter Business, 1860-1920: A Study of a Canadian Real Estate and Property Management Agency,' *Business History Review* 58 (Summer 1984):234-62.

11 For literature on women, family, and design in relation to housing, see Dolores Hayden, *The Grand Domestic Revolution: A History of Feminist Designs in American Homes, Neighbourhoods, and Cities* (Cambridge, MA, and London: MIT Press 1981); Gwendolyn Wright, *Building the Dream: A Social History of Housing in America* (New York: Pantheon 1981); idem, *Moralism and the Model Home: Domestic Architecture and Cultural Conflict in Chicago, 1873-1913* (Chicago: University of Chicago Press 1980); Veronica Strong-Boag, *The New Day Recalled: Lives of Girls and Women in English Canada, 1919-1939* (Toronto: Copp Clark Pitman 1988), 113-44; John C. Bacher, 'Under the Threat of Expulsion: Women Were Blamed for the Housing Shortage during World War II,' *Women and Environments* 10, 2 (Winter 1988):14-15; Clifford Edward Clark, *The American Family Home, 1800-1960* (Chapel Hill and London: University of North Carolina Press 1986); Melling, *Rent Strikes*, passim; Damer, 'State, Class and Housing,' passim; and David P. Handlin, *The American Home: Architecture and Society, 1815-1915* (Boston and Toronto: Little, Brown 1979). For literature on ethnicity and race, see Thomas Lee Philpott, *The Slum and the Ghetto: Neighbourhood Deterioration and Middle-Class Reform, Chicago, 1880-1930* (New York: Oxford University Press 1978); Carolyn Tyirin Kirk and Gordon W. Kirk, 'The Impact of the City on Home Ownership: A Comparison of Immigrants and Native Whites at the Turn of the Century,' *JUH* 7, 4 (August 1981):471-98; Kenneth T. Jackson, 'Race, Ethnicity, and Real Estate Appraisal: The Home Owners Loan Corporation and the Federal Housing Administration,' *JUH* 6, 4 (August 1980):419-52; idem, 'The Spatial Dimensions of Social Control: Race, Ethnicity, and Government Housing Policy in the United States, 1918-1968,' in *Modern Industrial Cities: History, Policy, and Survival*, ed. Bruce M. Stave (Beverly Hills and London: Sage 1981), 79-128; Roger D. Simon, 'Housing and Services in an Immigrant Neighbourhood: Milwaukee's Ward 14,' *JUH* 2, 4 (August 1976):435-58; and Donna R. Gabaccia, *From Sicily to Elizabeth Street: Housing and Social Change among Italian Immigrants, 1880-1930* (Albany: State University of New York Press 1984). For literature on tenure, class, and social mobility, see Michael J. Doucet, 'Working Class Housing in a Small Nineteenth-Century Canadian City: Hamilton, Ontario, 1852-1881,' in *Essays in Canadian Working Class History*, ed. Gregory S. Kealey and Peter Warrian (Toronto: McClelland and Stewart 1976), 83-105; R. Harris, G. Levine, and B.S. Osborne, 'Housing Tenure and Social Classes in Kingston, Ontario, 1881-1901,' *Journal of Historical Geography* 7 (July 1981):271-89; A. Gordon Darroch, 'Occupational Structure, Assessed Wealth and Homeowning during Toronto's Early Industrialization, 1861-1899,' *Histoire sociale/Social History* 16 (November 1983):381-410; Michael B. Katz, Michael J. Doucet, and Mark J. Stern, 'Property: Use Value and Exchange Value,' in *The Social Organization of Early Industrial Capitalism* (Cambridge, MA: Harvard University Press 1982), 131-57; Michael B. Katz, *The People of Hamilton, Canada West: Family and Class in a Mid-Nineteenth-Century City* (Cambridge, MA: Harvard University Press 1975); Marc H. Choko, *The Characteristics of Housing Tenure in Montreal*, Research Paper no. 164 (Toronto: Centre for Urban and Community Studies, University of Toronto, 1987); Richard Harris, *Class and Housing Tenure in Modern Canada*, Research Paper no. 153 (Toronto: Centre for Urban and Community Studies, University of Toronto, 1984); idem, *The Growth of Home Ownership in Toronto, 1899-1913*, Research Paper

no. 163 (Toronto: Centre for Urban and Community Studies, University of Toronto, 1987); Richard Harris and Marc H. Choko, *The Evolution of Housing Tenure in Montreal and Toronto since the Mid-Nineteenth Century*, Research Paper no. 166 (Toronto: Centre for Urban and Community Studies, University of Toronto 1988); and Matthew Edel, Elliott D. Sclar, and Daniel Luria, *Shaky Palaces: Homeownership and Social Mobility in Boston's Suburbanization* (New York: Columbia University Press 1984). For literature on suburbanization, see ibid.; Kenneth T. Jackson, *Crabgrass Frontier: The Suburbanization of the United States* (New York and Oxford: Oxford University Press 1985); and Veronica Strong-Boag, 'Home Dreams: Women and the Suburban Experiment in Canada, 1945-60,' *CHR* 72, 4 (December 1991):471-504.

Chapter 1: Housing and Reform in Pre-Depression Vancouver

1 Deryck W. Holdsworth, 'House and Home in Vancouver: The Emergence of a West Coast Urban Landscape, 1886-1929' (Ph.D. diss., University of British Columbia 1981), 33, 113, 135, 137, 160-1, 248, 261, 263, 267, 271, 276; idem, 'Cottages and Castles for Vancouver Home-Seekers,' in *Vancouver Past: Essays in Social History*, ed. R.A.J. McDonald and Jean Barman (Vancouver: University of British Columbia Press 1986), 11-32.
2 Donna McCririck, 'Opportunity and the Workingman: A Study of Land Accessibility and the Growth of Blue Collar Suburbs in Early Vancouver' (M.A. thesis, University of British Columbia 1981), 117-27.
3 John Weaver, review of *Vancouver Past*, ed. McDonald and Barman, *CHR* 68, 4 (December 1987):644.
4 R.A.J. McDonald, 'Working Class Vancouver, 1886-1914: Urbanism and Class in British Columbia,' in *Vancouver Past*, ed. McDonald and Barman, 67-8; Margaret Andrews, 'Medical Services in Vancouver, 1886-1920: A Study in the Interplay of Attitudes, Medical Knowledge, and Administrative Structures' (Ph.D. diss., University of British Columbia 1979).
5 Jean Barman, 'Neighbourhood and Community in Inter-war Vancouver: Residential Differentiation and Civic Voting Behaviour,' in *Vancouver Past*, ed. McDonald and Barman, 98-120; idem, *The West beyond the West: A History of British Columbia* (Toronto, Buffalo, and London: University of Toronto Press 1991), 191-2.
6 Vancouver, Town Planning Commission, *A Plan for the City of Vancouver, British Columbia, Including Point Grey and South Vancouver, and a General Plan of the Region, 1929*, prepared by Harland Bartholomew and Associates (Vancouver 1929) (hereafter cited as Bartholomew plan), 234.
7 Percentages were calculated from Canada, Dominion Bureau of Statistics (hereafter cited as DBS), *Sixth Census of Canada, 1921* (Ottawa: King's Printer 1927), vol. 3, *Population*, 39, table 11. The type for the remaining 0.7 per cent of dwellings was not given.
8 DBS, *Seventh Census of Canada, 1931: Census Monograph no. 8, Housing in Canada*, prepared by Harold F. Greenway (Ottawa: King's Printer 1941), 147, table 6. Apartment houses, semi-detacheds, row and terraced housing, hotels and rooming houses, and other types of dwellings represented 11.8, 1.6, 0.7, 5.9, and 0.2 per cent, respectively, of total dwellings. For one-room dwellings, see DBS, *Sixth*

Census of Canada, 1921 (Ottawa: King's Printer 1923), Bulletin XIII, 13, table 10.
9 DBS, *Sixth Census of Canada, 1921*, vol. 3, 66-7, table 21. The average monthly rent in Vancouver was $34.77, compared to $35.21 in Toronto. Eight hundred and eighteen families paid a monthly rent of under $9 in Vancouver, 703 in Toronto.
10 DBS, *Census Monograph no. 8*, 51, 58-9. For type of construction, see ibid., 144, table 3. However imperfect, the accepted standard for overcrowding is one room per person; a dwelling with less than one room per person is crowded. See Michael Doucet and John Weaver, *Housing the North American City* (Montreal and Kingston, London, Buffalo: McGill-Queen's University Press 1991), 423-4; and John R. Miron, *Housing in Postwar Canada: Demographic Change, Household Formation, and Housing Demand* (Montreal and Kingston: McGill-Queen's University Press 1988), 178.
11 M. Allerdale Grainger, *Woodsmen of the West* (Toronto: McClelland and Stewart 1964), 15; Robert M. Galois, 'Social Structure in Space: The Making of Vancouver, 1886-1901' (Ph.D. diss., Simon Fraser University 1979), 281-3; Margaret W. Andrews, 'The Emergence of Bureaucracy: The Vancouver Health Department, 1886-1914,' *JUH* 12, 2 (February 1986):135.
12 City of Vancouver Archives (hereafter cited as CVA), Public Documents (hereafter cited as PDS) #11, Medical Health Officer's (hereafter cited as MHO) Reports, 1911-1913.
13 CVA, Records of the Health Department (hereafter cited as HD records), 145-C-1, Archival file re Housing, Lodging Houses, 'Report of Housing Conditions Existing in the West End of Vancouver, B.C. [and List nos. 1 and 2],' 30 September 1920, 'Elaboration of Sheet No. 1,' November 1920, 'Elaboration of List No. 2,' n.d., M.S.P. Ellis to F.T. Underhill, 28 April 1922, and Ellis to Underhill, 5 July 1927.
14 CVA, Records of the Permits and Licenses Department (hereafter cited as PLD records), 126-B-11, Business License Register, 1929.
15 DBS, *Sixth Census of Canada, 1921*, vol. 3, 61-3, table 19.
16 Canada, Board of Inquiry into the Cost of Living, *Report* (Ottawa: King's Printer 1915), vol. 1, 474, 476, 478, 480-1, 490.
17 CVA, PDS #11, MHO Report, 1911, 11, 1912, 4, 14, and 1913, vii-viii.
18 CVA, PLD records, 126-B-11, Business License Register, 1929.
19 CVA, HD records, 145-C-1, Archival file re Housing, Lodging Houses, J.A. Hynes to Underhill, 13 March 1925.
20 CVA, PDS #11, MHO Report, 1911, 5, 1912, 14, 21, and 1913, vii-viii.
21 Some cabins still exist on Keefer and Union streets in Strathcona and on West 7th Avenue in Fairview; see Michael Kluckner and John Atkin, *Heritage Walks around Vancouver* (Vancouver and Toronto: Whitecap Books 1992), 19, 20.
22 Data for calculating the percentage for 1921 came from DBS, *Sixth Census of Canada, 1921*, vol. 3, 39, table 11. See also DBS, *Census Monograph no. 8*, 147, table 6.
23 CVA, PDS #11, MHO Report, 1913, vii.
24 CVA, Records of the Town Planning Commission (hereafter cited as TPC records), 61-B-4, file 7, 'Apartments; City License Inspector's Figures, May 1928.' Between 1922 and 1927, the annual numbers were 408, 444, 485, 501, 549, and 579.
25 CVA, PLD records, 126-B-11, Business License Register, 1929.

26 CVA, Records of the Board of Parks and Recreation, 50-F-1, file 1, Album of Newsclippings and Photographs, 1925-1931, 2, 7 July 1925. For more about this early social environment, see R.A.J. McDonald, 'Lumber Society on the Industrial Frontier: Burrard Inlet, 1863-1886,' forthcoming in *Labour/Le Travail*, passim.

27 CVA, PDS #11, MHO Report, 1911, 9-10.

28 *Vancouver News-Advertiser*, 19 and 27 August 1894, cited in Galois, 'Social Structure in Space,' 428, note 102.

29 CVA, HD records, 103-B-1, Health Inspectors, c. 1895-1911 file, Essay by J. Hynes, 3-4.

30 CVA, PDS #11, MHO Report, 1912, 15, and 1913, vii; *Vancouver News-Advertiser*, 21 July 1896 and 3 August 1899, cited in Galois, 'Social Structure in Space,' 458, note 106.

31 CVA, PDS #11, MHO Report, 1911, 10, and 1912, 14. For more on the location and conditions of Chinese residences, see Kay J. Anderson, *Vancouver's China-town: Racial Discourse in Canada, 1875-1980* (Montreal and Kingston, London, Buffalo: McGill-Queen's University Press 1991), passim.

32 Daphne Marlatt and Carole Itter, comps. and eds., 'Opening Doors: Vancouver's East End,' *Sound Heritage* 8, 1 and 2 (1979):118.

33 CVA, PLD records, 126-B-11, Business License Register, 1929.

34 Marlatt and Itter, 'Opening Doors,' 41.

35 Canada, Royal Commission on Chinese and Japanese Immigration, Session 1902, *Report*, Sessional Paper no. 54 (Ottawa: King's Printer 1902; reprint ed., New York: Arno Press 1978), 14.

36 Ibid., 15; CVA, HD records, 145-C-1, Archival file re Housing, Lodging Houses, 'Report of Housing Conditions [List no. 2],' 7.

37 CVA, PDS #11, MHO Report, 1911, 4, 10, and 1912, 15.

38 Marlatt and Itter, 'Opening Doors,' 33, 42, 144, 148-49.

39 Diane L. [Indiana] Matters, 'Public Welfare, Vancouver Style, 1910-1920,' *Revue d'études canadiennes/Journal of Canadian Studies* 14, 1 (Spring 1979):4. Missions included the Metropole Hostel (Salvation Army) with 94 beds, the Vancouver City Rescue Mission with 300 beds, the Central City Mission with 250 beds, the Strathcona Institute for Sailors and Loggers (British and Foreign Sailors Society) with 40 beds, the Seamen's Institute (Anglican Church) with 30 beds, the Canadian Camp Brotherhood, and St. Luke's Home.

40 For a description of Hastings Park camp, see Elizabeth Lees, '"1914 Popularity and Flags – 1922 Misery and Rags",' in *Working Lives*, comp. Working Lives Collective (Vancouver: New Star Books 1985), 171. See also Patricia E. Roy, 'Vancouver: "The Mecca of the Unemployed," 1907-1929,' in *Town and City: Aspects of Western Canadian Urban Development*, ed. A.F.J. Artibise, Canadian Plains Studies no. 10 (Regina: Canadian Plains Research Center, University of Regina 1981), 393-413. The Metropole Hostel of the Salvation Army and the Central City Mission received provincial as well as municipal grants; see Matters, 'Public Welfare,' 4. In the 1890s and in 1907, the city utilized space in the first public library and the old city jail to shelter the transient single unemployed.

41 CVA, PDS #11, HD Annual Report, 1910.

42 CVA, Records of the Social Services Department, 106-F-1, file 4, T.T. Hill to G. Sutton-Brown, 22 December 1960. In 1936, the relief and welfare department

took over the operation of Taylor Manor.

43 McCririck, 'Opportunity and the Workingman,' 117-27; Marlatt and Itter, 'Opening Doors,' 7, 34, 68, 80, 105-7.

44 Holdsworth, 'House and Home,' 197; James R. Conley, 'Class Conflict and Collective Action in the Working Class of Vancouver, British Columbia, 1900-1919' (Ph.D. diss., Carleton University 1986), 574-5; Dorothy G. Steeves, *The Compassionate Rebel: Ernest Winch and the Growth of Socialism in Western Canada* (Vancouver: J.J. Douglas 1977), 26.

45 Calculated from data found in CVA, Records of the Finance Department (hereafter cited as FD records), 97-D-3, Better Housing Scheme Ledger Account, 1924-1925, 113-A-15, Better Housing Scheme Ledger Account, 1920-1923, and 115-E-2, Soldiers' Housing Accounts, 1920.

46 Canada, House of Commons, Special Committee on Housing, *Minutes of Proceedings and Evidence*, no. 4, 12 March 1935, 101.

47 Anthony S. Wohl, *The Eternal Slum: Housing and Social Policy in Victorian London* (Montreal: McGill-Queen's University Press 1977); John Burnett, *A Social History of Housing, 1815-1985*, 2nd ed. (London and New York: Methuen 1986); Enid Gauldie, *Cruel Habitations: A History of Working Class Housing, 1780-1918* (London: George Allen and Unwin 1974); Roy Lubove, *The Progressives and the Slums: Tenement House Reform in New York, 1890-1917* (Pittsburgh: University of Pittsburgh Press 1962); Anthony Jackson, *A Place Called Home: A History of Low-Cost Housing in Manhattan* (Cambridge, MA and London: MIT Press 1976); Thomas Lee Philpott, *The Slum and the Ghetto: Neighbourhood Deterioration and Middle-Class Reform, Chicago, 1880-1930* (New York: Oxford University Press 1978); Terry Copp, *The Anatomy of Poverty: The Condition of the Working Class in Montreal, 1897-1929* (Toronto: McClelland and Stewart 1974), 70-87; and Piva, *Condition of the Working Class*, 125-42.

48 Andrews, 'The Emergence of Bureaucracy,' 135.

49 CVA, PDS #11, MHO Report, 1913, vii-viii.

50 CVA, HD records, 145-C-1, Archival file re Housing, Lodging Houses, Young to Underhill, 11 December 1913, and Underhill to Young, 23 December 1913.

51 John Bottomley, 'Ideology, Planning and the Landscape: The Business Community, Urban Reform and the Establishment of Town Planning in Vancouver, British Columbia, 1900-1940' (Ph.D. diss., University of British Columbia 1977).

52 Bartholomew plan, 247. See also John C. Weaver, 'The Property Industry and Land Use Controls: The Vancouver Experience, 1910-1945,' in *British Columbia: Historical Readings*, ed. W. Peter Ward and R.A.J. McDonald (Vancouver: Douglas and McIntyre 1981), 426-48.

53 Susan Walsh, 'The Peacock and the Guinea Hen: Political Profiles of Dorothy Gretchen Steeves and Grace MacInnis,' in *Not Just Pin Money: Selected Essays on the History of Women's Work in British Columbia*, ed. Barbara K. Latham and Roberta J. Pazdro (Victoria: Camosun College 1984), 365-79; Joan Sangster, *Dreams of Equality: Women on the Canadian Left, 1920-1950* (Toronto: McClelland and Stewart 1989), passim.

54 Minutes, 6 January 1913, 70, 3 February 1913, 90, 6 February 1913, 105-6, and 2 February 1914, 16-18, Papers of Vancouver Council of Women, M657, box 6, Special Collections Division, University of British Columbia Library.

55 CVA, Records of the Office of the City Clerk (hereafter cited as CC records), 13-F-4, City Comptroller, 1921 file, W. Butterworth to [City of Vancouver], 14 May 1921; ibid., 14-A-1, Soldiers, 1921 file, W.H. Roberts to mayor, 14 July 1921, Reg A. Webb to W.R. Owen, 14 July 1921 [representation from Amputation Club of B.C.], 14 July 1921, and numerous letters from individual veterans to the city, 15-16 July 1921; *Vancouver Sun*, 4 September 1919, 2, and 4 November 1919, 4.

56 Andrew E. Jones, *The Beginnings of Canadian Government Housing Policy, 1918-1924*, Occasional Paper no. 1/78 (Ottawa: Centre for Social Welfare Studies, Carleton University, [1978]), 56, note 95.

57 CVA, PDS #11, MHO Report, 1912, 6, 20; CVA, HD records, 145-C-1, Archival file re Housing, Lodging Houses, Underhill's notes for a draft model bylaw.

58 Michael Simpson, *Thomas Adams and the Modern Planning Movement: Britain, Canada and the United States, 1900-1940* (London and New York: Mansell 1985), 71-117.

59 Veronica J. Strong-Boag, *The Parliament of Women: The National Council of Women of Canada*, History Division Paper no. 18 (Ottawa: National Museums of Canada 1976), 207-8, 256-7, 315, 367-8; Desmond Morton and Glenn Wright, *Winning the Second Battle: Canadian Veterans and the Return to Civilian Life, 1915-1930* (Toronto, Buffalo, and London: University of Toronto Press 1987).

60 Keith Ralston, 'Organizing,' in *Working Lives*, comp. Working Lives Collective, 147-53; Robert James Gordon Mitchell, 'The Family Welfare Bureau of Greater Vancouver: Its Origins and Development, 1927 to 1952' (M.S.W. thesis, University of British Columbia 1952); A.E. Roberts, '"When He Saw the Multitude He Had Compassion on Them",' *The Western Recorder* 7, 6 (December 1931):3-4; Andrew Roddan, 'The Interesting Story of First United Church in Vancouver,' *Christian Citizen*, September 1934, 8-9; Henry MacFarlane Morrow, 'The Community Services of First United Church' (M.S.W. thesis, University of British Columbia 1948); Gillian Weiss, 'The Brightest Women of Our Land: Vancouver Clubwomen, 1910-1928,' in *Not Just Pin Money*, ed. Latham and Pazdro, 199-209; idem, '"As Women and as Citizens": Clubwomen in Vancouver, 1910-1928' (Ph.D. diss., University of British Columbia 1983).

61 For more information on Gutteridge and Jamieson, see Irene Howard, *The Struggle for Social Justice in British Columbia: Helena Gutteridge, the Unknown Reformer* (Vancouver: UBC Press 1992); and Sangster, *Dreams of Equality*, passim.

62 Conley, 'Class Conflict and Collective Action,' 576, 588, 591; R.A.J. McDonald, 'Business Leaders in Early Vancouver, 1886-1914' (Ph.D. diss., University of British Columbia 1977), 302-3; Dominion Mortgage and Investments Association, 'The Dominion Mortgage and Investments Association, Proceedings of the Fourteenth Annual Meeting ... Held at ... Vancouver ... September 8th and 9th, 1930,' and 'The Mortgage and Trust Companies Association of British Columbia, Proceedings of Annual Meetings for the Years 1929 and 1930,' *The Dominion Mortgage & Investments Year Book* 14 (1930):11-64a, 65a-8a; Bottomley, 'Ideology, Planning and the Landscape,' 116; Holdsworth, 'House and Home,' 91-2; and Adriane Janice Carr, 'The Development of Neighbourhood in Kitsilano: Ideas, Actors and the Landscape' (M.A. thesis, University of British Columbia 1980).

63 In *The Beginnings of Canadian Government Housing Policy*, Jones offers the best analysis of the federal program's origins, nature, abandonment, and achieve-

ments.
64 Canada, 'Proceedings of the Conference between the Government of Canada and the Provincial Governments at Ottawa, November, 1918,' in *Dominion Provincial and Interprovincial Conferences from 1887 to 1926* (Ottawa: King's Printer 1951), 101, 103.
65 National Archives of Canada (hereafter cited as NAC), Records of the Department of Finance, RG 19, vol. 705, file 203-1, P.C. 2997, 3 December 1918. See also Canada, Privy Council, *Housing Project of Federal Government: Orders in Council* (Ottawa: King's Printer 1919), for national orders-in-council mentioned in this and subsequent notes.
66 NAC, RG 19, vol. 705, file 203-1, P.C. 3067, 12 December 1918; ibid., P.C. 374, 20 February 1919.
67 Jones, *Beginnings of Canadian Government Housing Policy*, 12-14.
68 Canada, Royal Commission on Industrial Relations [T.G. Mathers, Chairman], *Report of Commission*, printed as supplement to *Labour Gazette* 19, 7 (July 1919):6, 13, 19.
69 Mark Swenarton, *Homes Fit for Heroes: The Politics and Architecture of Early State Housing in Britain* (London: Heinemann Educational Books 1981), 189-96.
70 DBS, *Census Monograph no. 8*, 23.
71 Swenarton, *Homes Fit for Heroes*, 192; Jones, *Beginnings of Canadian Government Housing Policy*, 40-1.
72 British Columbia, Better Housing Act, *Statutes of British Columbia*, 1919, 9 Geo. 5, c. 8.
73 NAC, RG 19, vol. 712, file 203-3, J.D. MacLean to T. Adams, 29 April 1919; 'General Housing Scheme of the Province of British Columbia'; P.C. 907, 1 May 1919; telegram from John Hart to minister of finance, 27 May 1919; Executive Council Order 810, 19 June 1919. See also NAC, RG 19, vol. 705, file 203-1, 'Advances to Provinces under Housing Act, Dec. 12, 1923,' 15 December 1923.
74 Jones, *Beginnings of Canadian Government Housing Policy*, 23.
75 NAC, Records of the Royal Commission on Industrial Relations [Mathers Commission], 1919, RG 33/95, M-1980, 260, 535-6; *Vancouver Sun*, 9 November 1919, 3; CVA, CC records, 13-E-4, Housing Committee, 1919 file, J.E. Elkins to Mayor Gale, 21 March 1919; ibid., 13-E-5, Soldiers, 1919 file, 'Memorandum of Agreement,' [22 May 1919]; Jill Wade, 'The "Sting" of Vancouver's Better Housing "Spree," 1919-1949,' *UHR* 21, 2 (March 1993):92-103.
76 CVA, CC records, 13-E-4, Housing Committee, 1919 file, Elkins to Gale, and G.D. Ireland to Elkins, 21 March 1919; *Vancouver Sun*, 15 March 1919, 13, and 25 March 1919, 1, 9.
77 CVA, CC records, 13-E-5, Soldiers, 1919 file, 'Rules and Regulations Governing the Acquiring of Land and the Building of [Dwellings] for Returned Soldiers'; ibid., for the indenture entered into between the mortgagor and the City of Vancouver; ibid., 13-F-4, City Comptroller, 1921 file, for examples of applications for allotment under the Better Housing Scheme. The civic officials were the city's solicitor (or assistant), accountant, and building inspector.
78 British Columbia, Legislative Assembly, *Sessional Papers*, 1920, 'Report of the Superintendent of British Columbia Soldier Settlement,' G13; ibid., 1921, 'Report of the Superintendent of British Columbia Soldier Settlement,' G12. The adjacent

municipalities of Burnaby, New Westminster, North Vancouver City and District, West Vancouver, and Port Coquitlam also participated.

79 British Columbia, Legislative Assembly, *Sessional Papers*, 1920, G12-15; ibid., 1919-20, 'Report of the Supervising Architect,' D22.

80 CVA, FD records, 93-C-5, file 13, F. Jones to C.A. Dunning, 25 March 1937.

81 Canada, House of Commons, Special Committee on Housing, *Minutes*, 57-71, 331-4; John Bacher, *Keeping to the Marketplace: The Evolution of Canadian Housing Policy* (Montreal and Kingston, London, Buffalo: McGill-Queen's University Press 1993), 61-2.

82 DBS, *Census Monograph no. 8*, 33; Canada, Advisory Committee on Reconstruction, Subcommittee on Housing and Community Planning [chaired by C.A. Curtis], *Final Report of the Subcommittee, March 24, 1944* (hereafter cited as Curtis report) (Ottawa: King's Printer 1944), 25; A.E. Grauer, *Housing: A Study Prepared for the Royal Commission on Dominion-Provincial Relations* (Ottawa: King's Printer 1939), 35-8.

83 Jones, *Beginnings of Canadian Government Housing Policy*, 41-3.

84 Simpson, *Thomas Adams and the Modern Planning Movement*, 105-8.

85 Doucet and Weaver, *Housing the North American City*, 291-2.

86 About fifty-nine others were erected in Burnaby, New Westminster, North Vancouver, Port Coquitlam, and West Vancouver; see British Columbia, Legislative Assembly, *Sessional Papers*, 1921, 'Report of the Superintendent of British Columbia Soldier Settlement,' G12.

87 CVA, CC records, 13-E-2, Building Inspector, 1919 file, A.J. Bird to mayor and council, 29 December 1919.

88 The data in this paragraph were collected from the sources provided in note 45.

89 Using Ontario Street as the dividing line, east-side houses numbered eighty-seven and west-side ones sixty-five.

90 Government employees included clerks at the post office, customs, and Soldier Civil Re-establishment Board, a veterinary surgeon with the BC government, an accountant with the provincial liquor warehouse, and clerks, police officers, labourers, firefighters, janitors, and a school nurse with all three municipalities.

91 Canadian Reconstruction Association, Women's Department, *Better Houses for Canadians* (Toronto 1919).

92 *Vancouver Sun*, 20 February 1919, 4.

93 CVA, CC records, 13-E-2, Building Inspector, 1919 file, A.J. Bird to chairman, building committee, 3 November 1919; ibid., 13-E-6, City Comptroller (2), 1920 file, Bird to A.J. Pilkington, 22 September 1920; ibid., 13-E-6, Council Minutes (1), 1920 file, Minutes, 9 February 1920; ibid., 13-F-3, Building Inspector, 1921 file, Bird to Pilkington, 25 November 1921. Andrew J. Haggart, a veteran who later became building inspector and who owned a Better Housing Scheme home, joined the building department at this time.

94 CVA, CC records, 13-E-2, City Comptroller, 1919 file, G.F. Baldwin to finance committee, 29 October 1919; ibid., 13-E-5, Soldiers, 1919 file, 'Memorandum of Changes in the Rules and Regulations under the Better Housing Scheme Requested by Allotment Committee.'

95 See note 45 for the sources of data about the scheme.

Chapter 2: The Housing Problem in the 1930s

1 J. David Hulchanski, 'The 1935 Dominion Housing Act: Setting the Stage for a Permanent Federal Presence in Canada's Housing Sector,' *UHR* 15, 1 (June 1986):25.

2 Ontario, Lieutenant Governor's Committee on Housing Conditions in Toronto, *Report* (Toronto 1934), 64; DBS, *Seventh Census of Canada, 1931: Census Monograph no. 8, Housing in Canada*, prepared by Harold F. Greenway (Ottawa: King's Printer 1941), 34-6.

3 United Church Archives, Vancouver School of Theology (hereafter cited as UCA), Papers of Hugh Dobson, B7, file S, 'Housing Vancouver: A Survey of the Housing Position in Vancouver by the Vancouver Housing Association,' August 1939.

4 *Vancouver Sun*, 2 January 1930, 1, and 19 April 1930, 27.

5 NAC, Records of the Department of Finance, RG 19, vol. 709, file 203-1A, 'The Operation of the National Housing Act,' appendix 8, 10; DBS, *Census Monograph no. 8*, 157, table 17; DBS, *Eighth Census of Canada, 1941* (Ottawa: King's Printer 1949), vol. 9, *Housing*, 5, table 1a.

6 CVA, TPC records, 61-C-6, file 14, 'Housing – The Great Challenge,' 1941, 1. According to the TPC, the total housing stock in Vancouver in 1936 consisted of 52,001 dwellings: 49,322 single houses, 570 apartment houses, 75 hotels, 352 duplexes, 404 converted residences, 295 cabins, tenements, and rooming houses, and 983 apartments in store buildings; see CVA, J. Alexander Walker Papers, 77-B-5, file 4, 'Total Number of Buildings – 1936.'

7 [Graph Revealing a 'Startling Housing Need' in Vancouver], *B.C. Journal of Commerce and Building Record*, 51, 55 (16 November 1937):1.

8 M.C. Urquhart and K.A.H. Buckley, eds., *Historical Statistics of Canada*, 1st ed. (Cambridge: Cambridge University Press; Toronto: Macmillan of Canada 1965), ser. A233-43, 22.

9 City of Vancouver, *Financial Statements and Annual Reports* (1939), 67.

10 *Vancouver Sun*, 21 August 1935, 5, 29 August 1935, 7, 18 March 1936, 18, and 20 November 1937, 2.

11 F.H. Leacy, ed., *Historical Statistics of Canada*, 2nd ed. (Ottawa: Statistics Canada and Social Science Federation of Canada 1983), ser. S246.

12 UCA, Dobson papers, B7, file S, 'Housing Vancouver,' 1939; and a series of Vancouver Real Estate Exchange Limited surveys of buildings and vacancies in Vancouver, 1937-40, in CVA, TPC records, 77-B-5, files 4, 6, and 7.

13 CVA, CC records, 15-B-4, Relief Officer, July-December 1930 file, H.W. Cooper to W.C. Atherton, 24 November 1930.

14 CVA, Records of the Mayor's Office (hereafter cited as MO records), 33-A-5, Unemployment, 1930 file, Cooper to Atherton, 3 July 1930.

15 DBS, *Seventh Census of Canada, 1931* (Ottawa: King's Printer 1934), vol. 6, *Unemployment*, 1268, table 2.

16 In 1932 and 1933, the average annual unemployment rates in Canada were 26 and 26.6 per cent. Between 1934 and 1939, the rate fell from 20.6 per cent to 14.1 per cent. See James Struthers, *No Fault of Their Own: Unemployment and the Canadian Welfare State, 1914-1941* (Toronto: University of Toronto Press 1983), appendix 1, 215.

17 In 1931, the unemployment rate in Canada was 17.4 per cent, while in Vancou-

ver it was 30.2 per cent. See DBS, *Seventh Census of Canada, 1931*, vol. 6, *Unemployment*, 1268, table 2.

18 Ibid., 358-9, table 20. See also CVA, CC records, 15-B-4, Relief Officer, July-December 1930 file, 'Married Applications to October 25th, 1930 – 12 o'clock Noon'; and CVA, MO records, 33-D-5, Vancouver Board of Trade file, 'Record of Trades among Married City Relief Cases Reporting for Work at Employment Service,' 1937.

19 British Columbia, Legislative Assembly, *Sessional Papers*, 1933, 'Annual Report of the Department of Labour for the Year Ended December 31st, 1931,' E12. The Employment Service of Canada was provincially operated but federally funded.

20 The 22,515 individuals included 9,472 single men, 11,634 married men, 1,147 women, 146 Chinese, and 116 Japanese, and the total with dependants was 50,688 persons; see CVA, CC records, 15-F-1, file 1, 'Statement of Registrations for Unemployment Relief Taken at Hamilton Hall, 1 August 1931 to 30 June 1932.' For the location of relief cases in May 1934, see CVA, Photograph Collection, CV P RE 11.

21 DBS, *Census Monograph no. 8*, 103-4.

22 CVA, CC records, 16-E-7, file 17, M.H. Blackley to W.R. Bone, 9 June 1936.

23 CVA, MO records, 33-A-5, Unemployment, 1930 file, 'Memorandum Relative to Unemployment and Relief in the City of Vancouver,' August 1930.

24 CVA, FD records, 93-A-4, file 3, 'Relief Act, 1932,' 19 November 1932. Other western Canadian civic governments followed similar procedures, while in central Canada, charitable agencies with private and public funding carried the responsibility; see CVA, MO records, 33-B-2, Relief (1), 1932 file, Cooper to the Mayor, 27 April 1932, reporting a tour of Ottawa, Toronto, and Winnipeg by relief officer Cooper and alderman John Bennett in which they examined unemployment methods.

25 Ronald Liversedge, *Recollections of the On to Ottawa Trek*, ed. Victor Hoar, Carleton Library no. 66 (Toronto: McClelland and Stewart 1973), 15-34. See also Marion Elizabeth Lane, 'Unemployment during the Depression: The Problem of the Single Unemployed Transient in British Columbia, 1930-1938' (B.A. honours graduating essay, University of British Columbia 1966); and John Douglas Belshaw, 'The Administration of Relief to the Unemployed in Vancouver during the Great Depression' (M.A. thesis, Simon Fraser University 1982).

26 CVA, CC records, 15-D-1, MHO, January to June 1931 file, Cooper to Atherton, 3 September 1931; ibid., 15-D-4, Relief Officer, January to June 1931 file, J.W. McIntosh to the mayor and council, 24 June 1931. For a visual record of the jungles, see Bruce Macdonald, *Vancouver: A Visual History* (Vancouver: Talon Books 1992), 43.

27 CVA, MO records, 33-B-2, Relief (1), 1932 file, 'Report of the Committee on Homeless Men,' July 1932.

28 CVA, FD records, 93-A-4, file 3, 'Relief Act 1932'; British Columbia, Legislative Assembly, *Sessional Papers*, 1933, E10; A.E. Grauer, *Public Assistance and Social Insurance: A Study Prepared for the Royal Commission on Dominion-Provincial Relations* (Ottawa: King's Printer 1939), 18.

29 For the numbers of men in provincial and federal camps, see the Department of Labour annual reports in the British Columbia, Legislative Assembly, *Sessional*

Papers, 1934-6. See also 'The Report of the Macdonald Commission' in Liversedge, *Recollections of the On to Ottawa Trek*, 137; and Macdonald, *Vancouver*, 42.

30 CVA, FD records, 93-A-4, file 3, 'Council Minutes,' 9 June 1933; Laurel Kimbley, comp. and Jo-Ann Canning-Dew, ed., *Hastings and Main: Stories from an Inner City Neighbourhood* (Vancouver: New Star Books 1987), 73. Each government contributed one-third of the costs until 1934, when monthly grants-in-aid from Ottawa to the province, coupled with a municipal contribution on a 40-60 per cent basis, replaced them; see Grauer, *Public Assistance and Social Insurance*, 19.

31 Liversedge, *Recollections of the On to Ottawa Trek*, 82; Kimbley and Canning-Dew, comp. and ed., *Hastings and Main*, 69.

32 CVA, MO records, 33-F-1, Relief, 1939 file, Bone to H.L. Corey, 30 December 1938; CVA, Records of the Social Service Department (hereafter cited as SSD records), 106-A-7, file 5A, 'Chronological Survey of Social Legislation, 1871-1943.'

33 CVA, CC records, 16-F-6, file 14, Bone to the mayor and council, 16 December 1937.

34 DBS, *Census Monograph no. 8*, 109, 173-4, table 33; DBS, *Eighth Census of Canada, 1941*, vol. 9, 98, tables 20a-21a, 104, table 21c.

35 CVA, FD records, 93-A-4, file 3, Cooper to L.D. Taylor, 20 June 1932, and 'Memorandum Re Relief,' 12 October 1932. See CVA, MO records, 33-B-2, Relief (2), 1932 file, Bone to Taylor, 12 September 1932 and 24 October 1932, Bone to Mrs. S. Docherty, 9 December 1932, and 'Summary of Vancouver's Relief Situation,' 16 December 1932. Finally, see CVA, CC records, 15-F-1, file 2, '[Report on] Allsopp ... Re: Disconnection of Water Pipes,' [1932]; ibid., file 3, [Correspondence about the case of landlord Richmond and tenant Merry, August-September 1931]; ibid., 15-F-3, file 8, J.M. McKenzie to city relief committee, 21 November 1932; ibid., 16-A-4, file 14, Bone to Taylor, 17 January 1933; ibid., 16-A-5, file 2, Bone to Taylor, 24 August 1933; ibid., 16-D-3, file 7, Bone to the relief and employment committee, 23 April 1935; ibid., 16-F-3, file 11, P.R. Bengough to F. Howlett, 26 April 1936. In October 1933, 1,496 of 4,025 cases were from one to thirty-seven months in arrears.

36 CVA, CC records, 16-D-3, files 8 and 9, [Correspondence about the cases of Mrs. A.H. Evans and the striking longshoremen], August-November 1935; ibid., 16-D-5, file 4, Mrs. L.N. Stoneman to relief committee, 17 September 1935.

37 Between 1930 and 1935, the three governments shared costs equally; in 1934, federal grants-in-aid went monthly to each province, which then supplemented civic expenditures on a 60-40 per cent basis. See CVA, CC records, 15-F-1, file 4, Bone to Taylor, 21 September 1932; ibid., 16-A-5, file 1, Bone to Mrs. J.A. McIntyre, 6 June 1933; ibid., 16-B-7, file 5, W.W. Smith to mayor and council, 27 August 1934; ibid., 16-B-7, file 7, Bone to Taylor, 17 October 1934; ibid., 16-D-3, file 6, 'British Columbia, Department of Labour, Unemployment Relief Branch, Serial No. 55, Regulations Governing Administration of Relief in Municipalities,' 1 February 1935; ibid., 16-E-7, file 16, Bone to C.E. Tisdall, 11 January 1936; and ibid., 16-F-6, file 11, Bone to R.P. Pettipiece, 20 March 1937. See also CVA, MO records, 33-B-2, Relief (1), 1932 file, 'Rental Policies,' 1932; ibid., Relief (2), 1932 file, 'Summary of Vancouver's Relief Situation,' 16 December 1932, and

Bone to Mrs. Best, 30 December 1932; ibid., 33-C-6, Relief Dept., 1936 file, Bone to A. Davison, 17 January 1936; and ibid., 33-F-1, Relief, 1939 file, Bone to Corey, 16 February 1939. As well, see CVA, TPC records, 77-B-5, file 6, A.J. Harrison to Bone, 21 January 1939.

38 CVA, SSD records, 106-D-2, file 6, Bone to Taylor, 8 June 1933; CVA, MO records, 33-C-6, Relief Dept., 1936 file, 'Relief Report,' 1-15 January 1935.

39 CVA, CC records, 16-A-4, file 11, E. Cooper to Taylor, 30 June 1933; ibid., 16-D-3, file 7, E. Pearce to Bone, 18 April 1935; CVA, MO records, 33-B-2, Relief (2), 1932 file, Taylor to council on unemployment relief, 13 December 1932; CVA, TPC records, 77-B-5, file 3, Bone to Harrison, 27 September 1937.

40 *Vancouver Sun*, 2 April 1931, 10.

41 CVA, CC records, 15-F-1, file 1, 'Statement of Registrations for Unemployment Relief Taken at Hamilton Hall,' 1 August 1931 to 30 June 1932; ibid., 15-F-1, file 2, Cooper to A.G. Harvey, 6 June 1932; ibid., 16-D-5, file 3, '[Petition] for the Unity of Chinese and White Workers,' [1935]; ibid., 17-B-5, file 14, Bone to Corey, 1 April 1938. See also CVA, Records of the City Solicitor (hereafter cited as CS records), 115-C-2, file 11, CS to special committee on sale of properties, 31 March 1939. In the last half of 1932, 146 Chinese and 116 Japanese received unemployment relief. For more on the residential conditions of Chinese men, see Kay J. Anderson, *Vancouver's Chinatown: Racial Discourse in Canada, 1875-1980* (Montreal and Kingston, London, Buffalo: McGill-Queen's University Press 1991), passim.

42 DBS, *Census Monograph no. 8*, 160-1, table 21.

43 CVA, TPC records, 61-C-6, file 14, [Report of the special committee on housing], 15 November 1937, 2; ibid., 61-E-5, file 7, Harrison to TPC zoning committee, 26 October 1938, map, and R.C. Singleton to A. Haggart, 20 January 1939.

44 CVA, TPC records, 61-E-5, file 7, M. Travis-Barker to Harrison, 9 October 1938.

45 CVA, MO records, 34-A-2, Housing Act, 1940 file, Haggart to building, civic planning, and parks committee, 20 November 1940; CVA, TPC records, 61-C-6, file 14, [Report of the special committee on housing], 15 November 1937, 2; City of Vancouver, *Financial Statements and Annual Reports* (1931), 112; *Vancouver Sun*, 4 June 1931, 18.

46 The number of registered licences also rose when a temporary employee in the health department was appointed to carry out a lodging-house survey in 1931; see CVA, CC records, 15-D-1, MHO, October-December 1931 file, J.W. McIntosh to personnel committee, 21 May 1931 and 6 October 1931; and *Vancouver Sun*, 4 June 1931, 18.

47 CVA, TPC records, 61-E-5, file 7, License Inspector, Corporation Counsel, MHO, Building Inspector, and Secretary, Zoning Matters, to building, civic planning, and parks committee, 26 July 1938, [Information sheets and recommendations respecting rooming houses and 1928 zoning bylaw], n.d., 'Definitions of Building, Lodging, Rooming, Boarding, and Apartment House,' n.d., and Harrison to TPC zoning committee, 28 September 1938.

48 Ibid., 62-A-1, file 3, 'Zoning Survey of Ward One,' 31 December 1934; ibid., file 4, 'Ward One: Synopsis of Survey,' [1934]; ibid., 61-E-5, file 7, Harrison to TPC zoning committee, 26 October 1938; CVA, MO records, 34-B-4, West End Survey, 1941 file, 'The West End Survey,' May 1941.

49 In 1925, several descendants of the original Stanley Park squatters took their claims to the Supreme Court of Canada. Only one of them, a descendant of Aunt Sally, could prove sixty years of occupancy. The other five lost their claims to the city and became its tenants in their own shacks. See *Vancouver Sun*, 21 May 1931, 4; and CVA, Records of the Board of Parks and Recreation, 50-F-1, file 1, Album of Newsclippings and Photographs, 1925-31, 2, 7 July 1925, and 189, 28 May 1931. In 1955, one shacker still occupied a cottage near Brockton Point; see CVA, Newsclippings, M8839, 10 May 1955.

50 CVA, TPC records, 61-C-6, file 14, [Report of the special committee on housing], 15 November 1937, 1; ibid., 77-B-5, file 4, 'Special Committee Reporting on the Sanitary Conditions of False Creek to Social Services Committee, 22 January 1938'; ibid., file 6, Harrison to Bone, 21 January 1939; CVA, Newspaper Clippings, M4289-1, 14 July 1939; CVA, MO records, 33-D-3, Kitsilano Indian Reserve, 1937 file, A. Grundy to J.W. Cornett, 15 June 1937; CVA, CC records, 27-C-4, file 11, R.R. Holland to J.J. McRae, 2 September 1936; ibid., 27-D-7, file 28, [Minutes of special committee re foreshore shacks], 26 March 1940; ibid., 16-A-1, file 14, E.L. Slevin to J.W. McIntosh, 18 August 1933; ibid., 16-E-2, file 9, C.F. Andrews, Mrs. F.W. Field, K.A. Mikkila, G.M. Irish, and C. Villman to the mayor and council, 3 November 1936; ibid., 16-E-4, file 4, Slevin to McIntosh, 11 June 1936.

51 CVA, CC records, 27-D-7, file 28, '[Report of] Special Committee Re Foreshore Shacks,' 23 January 1940; CVA, TPC records, 61-C-6, file 14, [Report of the special committee on housing], 15 November 1937; ibid., 77-B-5, file 4, 'Survey of Living Quarters on False Creek, Sept. 21-23, 1937'; ibid., 77-B-6, file 3, Harrison to special committee re Fraser River shacks and waterfront area, 10 July 1939. For a visual record of the shacks, see Macdonald, *Vancouver*, 42-3.

52 CVA, Records of the Board of Police Commissioners, 75-D-4, file 17, H.S. Wood to acting chief constable, 27 June 1936; CVA, CS records, 115-C-1, file 30, [Correspondence re removal of Kitsilano Indian Reserve squatters in June 1937]; CVA, CC records, Minutes of the building, civic planning, and parks committee, 26A, vol. 9, 7 November 1938, 82.

53 CVA, MO records, 33-B-2, Relief (2), 1932 file, Bone to Taylor, 15 November 1932; ibid., 33-C-6, Relief Department, 1936 file, F. Howlett to W.W. Smith, 14 May 1936; CVA, CC records, 16-A-7, file 3, E. Habenicht to city relief department, 6 May 1933; ibid., file 17, Bone to Smith, 1 April 1936; ibid., 16-E-7, file 17, Bone to Smith, 29 April 1936, and 4 June 1936.

54 CVA, CC records, 16-C-2, file 8, [Petitions submitted to city council re the Evans family eviction], April 1934. See also Jean Evans Shiels and Ben Swankey, '*Work and Wages!' Semi-Documentary Account of the Life and Times of Arthur H. (Slim) Evans* (Vancouver: Trade Union Research Bureau 1977), 69-75.

55 DBS, *Census Monograph no. 8*, 157, table 17. The difficulties experienced by Vancouver's wage earners in keeping their homes during the Depression reinforces the argument about the precariousness of working-class homeownership advanced by Matthew Edel, Elliott D. Sclar, and Daniel Luria in *Shaky Palaces: Homeownership and Social Mobility in Boston's Suburbanization* (New York: Columbia University Press 1984).

56 DBS, *Eighth Census of Canada, 1941*, vol. 9, 116, table 24a, 117, table 25a, 123,

table 26a, 128, table 27a.
57 CVA, FD records, 93-F-7, file 1, W.L. Woodford to A. Wells Gray, 7 January 1937.
58 CVA, CS records, 115-C-2, file 17, Woodford to A.E. Lord, 9 March 1940.
59 CVA, FD records, 93-A-5, file 1, T. Prinn to finance committee, 25 October 1932; *Vancouver Daily Province*, 27 November 1936, 14, and 9 August 1939, 4.
60 CVA, CC records, 27-C-2, file 5, 'Help Vancouver Grow; Pay Your Taxes Now!' [1935]. This plan provided for the consolidation of arrears and interest accrued to 31 December 1934, with payment extended over a six-year period in annual installments. Interest at 5 per cent per annum was paid on the total balance of the consolidated sum. Total taxes for the current year had to be paid at the same time as the annual installment or before the passing of the tax sale bylaw for the current year.
61 CVA, FD records, 93-A-5, file 1, Prinn to A.J. Pilkington, 16 September 1932.
62 British Columbia Archives and Records Services (hereafter cited as BCARS), Records of the Premier of British Columbia, GR 1222, box 12, file 5, Mrs. J.B. Mitchell to D. Pattullo, 16 October 1936.
63 CVA, CC records, 27-D-2, file 35, F. Jones and C. Brakenridge to board of works committee, 10 May 1937; CVA, FD records, 100-A-4, file 4, [Documents on 'work for taxes' scheme, September-December 1937]; *Vancouver Daily Province*, 16 September 1938, 1; *Vancouver Sun*, 26 June 1939, 1, 12.
64 CVA, FD records, 100-A-4, files 5 and 6, [Applications approved under the 'work for taxes' scheme, 1937].
65 Ibid., 93-A-4, file 3, Pilkington to J.B. Williams, 16 June 1933, and Williams to Pilkington, 27 June 1933; CVA, CC records, 16-E-17, file 17, Bone to Smith, 6 June 1936, and Smith to relief and employment committee, 9 June 1936; ibid., 16-D-3, file 6, 'Regulations Governing Administration of Relief in Municipalities,' 1 February 1935.
66 DBS, *Census Monograph no. 8*, 55, 76, 85, 150, table 9, 166-7, table 24.
67 Canada, Advisory Committee on Reconstruction, Subcommittee on Housing and Community Planning [chaired by C.A. Curtis], *Final Report of the Subcommittee, March 24, 1944* (Curtis report) (Ottawa: King's Printer 1944), 94, table 18.
68 DBS, *Census Monograph no. 8*, 183, table 37.
69 UCA, Dobson papers, B7, file S, 'Housing Vancouver,' 1939.
70 CVA, MO records, 34-A-2, Housing Act, 1940 file, 'City of Vancouver ... Partial Housing Survey; Inspections by R. Startup,' 1940.
71 DBS, *Eighth Census of Canada, 1941*, vol. 9, 71-2, table 15a, 75-6, table 16a; 'Housing Conditions in Canada, 1941,' *Sanford Evans Statistical Service*, Index No. 3-99, 3.
72 'Housing Conditions in Canada,' 2; DBS, *Eighth Census of Canada, 1941*, vol. 9, 9, table 2A.
73 Curtis report, 102, table 23; 16.7 per cent of rented homes required repairs, compared to 19.8 per cent of owned homes.
74 UCA, Dobson papers, B7, file S, 'Housing in Vancouver,' 1939; CVA, TPC records, 77-B-5, file 5, 'Report on Housing Problems,' 5 July 1939; ibid., 77-B-6, file 3, 'A Report of Housing Conditions in Certain Sections of the City,' 20 November 1940.
75 CVA, TPC records, 77-B-6, file 3, 'A Report of Housing Conditions in Certain

Sections of the City,' 20 November 1940.

76 DBS, *Eighth Census of Canada, 1941*, vol. 9, 79, table 17a.

77 *Vancouver Sun*, 30 November 1938, 1.

78 CVA, CC records, 27-D-7, file 28, A.H. Horsell to L. Telford, 5 May 1940.

79 Ibid., 27-D-5, file 17, 'Slums of the Water Front,' 1939.

80 CVA, TPC records, 77-B-6, file 3, Harrison to special committee re Fraser River shacks and waterfront area, 10 July 1939.

81 Ibid., 61-C-6, file 14, [Report of the special committee on housing], 15 November 1937. At the time, the bridge had the name 'Connaught' and a position slightly east of the present structure.

82 CVA, CC records, 27-D-4, file 2, S. Murray to building, civic planning, and parks committee, 16 November 1938.

83 Ibid., Murray to Howlett, 29 November 1938; ibid., 27-D-7, file 28, [Survey of foreshore shacks along Fraser River east of Nanaimo], 1940, and [Report of special committee re foreshore shacks], 23 January 1940; CVA, TPC records, 77-B-5, file 4, 'Survey of Living Quarters on False Creek, September 21-23, 1937.'

84 CVA, TPC records, 77-B-5, file 4, [Report of special committee on the sanitary conditions of False Creek to social services committee], 22 January 1938.

85 CVA, CC records, 15-D-1, MHO, January-June 1931 file, J.W. McIntosh to finance committee, 1 April 1931; ibid., 15-E-4, file 15, J.H. Hynes to McIntosh, 13 April 1932 and 1 November 1932.

86 CVA, CC records, 16-C-2, file 9, A.E. Burton to city clerk, 24 August 1934.

87 Liversedge, *Recollections of the On to Ottawa Trek*, 16; *Vancouver Sun*, 15 May 1931, 32.

88 CVA, CC records, 16-B-7, file 4, Bone to the mayor and council, 1 May 1934; Liversedge, *Recollections of the On to Ottawa Trek*, 16.

89 'The Report of the Macdonald Commission,' in Liversedge, *Recollections of the On to Ottawa Trek*, 137.

90 CVA, CC records, 15-D-1, MHO, January to June 1931 file, McIntosh to mayor and council, 24 June 1931; ibid., 15-D-4, Relief Officer, July-September 1931 file, Cooper to Atherton, 3 September 1931.

91 *Vancouver Sun*, 25 July 1931, 2.

92 CVA, CC records, 15-D-4, Relief Officer, July-September 1931 file, Cooper to Atherton, 3 September 1931.

93 Ibid., Dr. H.A. McDonald, Relief Medical Officer, quoted in certificate attached to document.

94 Ibid., Cooper to Atherton, 8 September 1931, and Cooper to W.J. Bingham, 21 September 1931. See also *Vancouver Sun*, 5 September 1931, 1.

95 CVA, TPC records, 77-B-5, file 6, 'Sir Raymond Unwin's Impressions of Vancouver,' 1939.

Chapter 3: Responding to the Housing Problem in the 1930s

1 John C. Bacher, *Keeping to the Marketplace: The Evolution of Canadian Housing Policy* (Montreal and Kingston, London, Buffalo: McGill-Queen's University Press 1993), 66-93; J. David Hulchanski, 'The 1935 Dominion Housing Act: Setting the Stage for a Permanent Federal Presence in Canada's Housing Sector,' *UHR* 15, 1 (June 1986):19-39.

2 Ontario, Lieutenant Governor's Committee on Housing Conditions in Toronto, *Report* (hereafter cited as Bruce report) (Toronto 1934), 117.
3 Joint Committee of the Montreal Board of Trade and the City Improvement League, *A Report on Housing and Slum Clearance for Montreal* (Montreal 1935); Montreal Council of Social Agencies, Committee on Housing, *Housing for the Low Wage Earner* (Montreal 1936); City Improvement League, Montreal, Committee on Housing, *A Survey of the Location of the Present Housing of the Unemployed in Montreal*, prepared with the help of the Montreal Junior Board of Trade (Montreal 1936); DBS, *Seventh Census of Canada, 1931: Census Monograph no. 8, Housing in Canada*, prepared by Harold F. Greenway (Ottawa: King's Printer 1941), 34-6.
4 *Labour Gazette* 30 (October 1930):1166; 31 (February 1931):189; 31 (March 1931):311; 34 (March 1934):245, 247; 34 (December 1934):1102; and 35 (February 1935):165.
5 Canada, House of Commons, Special Committee on Housing, *Report to the House* (Ottawa: King's Printer 1935), 3.
6 Canada, House of Commons, Special Committee on Housing, *Minutes of Proceedings and Evidence, nos. 1-11* (Ottawa: King's Printer 1935), no. 10, 334-58; Hulchanski, 'The 1935 Dominion Housing Act,' 23-6.
7 NAC, Records of the Department of Finance, RG 19, vol. 705, file 203-1A.
8 Ibid., vol. 704, file 203-1A, W.C. Clark to A. Meighen, 2 July 1935; ibid., vol. 705, file 203-1A, T.D. Leonard to Clark, 29 June 1935.
9 Ibid., vol. 706, file 203-1A, 'Form of Agreement between Lending Institutions and the Minister of Finance under the Dominion Housing Act, 1935, as Approved by Order-in-Council, P.C. 2388, Dated August 10, 1935'; ibid., vol. 705, file 203-1A, vol. 1, [Press Release], 20 December 1935.
10 Canada, Act to Assist the Construction of Houses [Dominion Housing Act], *Statutes of Canada*, 1935, 25 & 26 Geo. 5, c. 58; Robert B. Bryce, *Maturing in Hard Times: Canada's Department of Finance through the Great Depression* (Montreal and Kingston: McGill-Queen's University Press 1986), 165-6.
11 NAC, RG 19, vol. 706, file 203-1A, Clark to C.A. Dunning, 20 January 1936; Bryce, *Maturing in Hard Times*, 166; Canada, Department of Finance, *Dominion Housing Act: Architectural Competition; Low-Cost House Designs* (Ottawa: King's Printer 1936).
12 Canada, House of Commons, *Debates*, 1935, vol. 4, 3910-65.
13 J.R.H. Wilbur, ed., *The Bennett New Deal: Fraud or Portent?* (Toronto: Copp Clark 1968), 81.
14 James Struthers, *No Fault of Their Own; Unemployment and the Canadian Welfare State, 1914-1941* (Toronto: University of Toronto Press 1983), 127.
15 NAC, RG 19, vol. 710, file 203-1A, 1-25, 'Critique of the Dominion Housing Act, 1935,' by Percy Nobbs (October 1935); ibid., vol. 711, file 203-2-L, D.B. Mansur to Clark, 6 August 1936; A.E. Grauer, *Housing; A Study Prepared for the Royal Commission on Dominion-Provincial Relations* (Ottawa: King's Printer 1939), 39-41; Canada, Advisory Committee on Reconstruction, Subcommittee on Housing and Community Planning [chaired by C.A. Curtis], *Final Report of the Subcommittee, March 24, 1944* (Curtis report) (Ottawa: King's Printer 1944), 26-7; Bacher, *Keeping to the Marketplace*, 87-93, 111-16; Hulchanski, 'The 1935 Dominion Housing Act,' 35-8; NAC, Records of the Wartime Prices and Trade Board, RG 64,

vol. 89, file 106, 'Preliminary Report on the Housing Situation in Canada and Suggestions for Its Improvement,' prepared by Lesslie R. Thomson (Ottawa: Department of Munitions and Supply 1942), 100-5; Bryce, *Maturing in Hard Times*, 166.

16 NAC, RG 19, vol. 706, file 203-1A, 'Press Release,' 23 September 1936, Clark to Dunning, 15 September 1936, and Clark to Dunning, 16 September 1936, with 'Suggested Programme for Low-Cost Housing' attached.

17 Ibid., vol. 711, file 203-2-L, Mansur to Clark, 6 August 1936, 5.

18 Hulchanski, 'The 1935 Dominion Housing Act,' 36, table 3, 38.

19 NAC, Records of the Department of Labour, RG 27, vol. 3347, file 1, 'House Renovation Scheme [Press Release],' 17 October 1936; ibid., vol. 3358, file 10; ibid., file 4, 'Preliminary Report on Housing.' W.A. Mackintosh, the Queen's University economist, recommended the plan to the NEC.

20 Canada, An Act to Increase Employment by Encouraging the Repair of Rural and Urban Homes [Home Improvement Loans Guarantee Act], *Statutes of Canada*, 1937, 1 Geo. 6, c. 11; NAC, RG 19, vol. 712, file 203-6A, S.H. Logan to Dunning, 28 September 1936; NAC, RG 27, vol. 3347, file 1, 'Home Renovation Scheme [Press Release for 17 October 1936].'

21 NAC, RG 19, vol. 706, file 203-1A, A.B. Purvis to Clark, 16 February 1938.

22 NAC, RG 27, vol. 3376, file 2, and vol. 3347, file 1; NAC, RG 19, vol. 706, file 203-1A-3. See also NAC, RG 19, vol. 706, file 203-1A-3, [Radio Broadcast, 3 December 1936]; NAC, RG 27, vol. 3354, file 10; ibid., vol. 3357, file 3, for records of the HIP committees, and file 20, Purvis to F.G. Rutley, 16 September 1936.

23 NAC, RG 27, vol. 3354, file 10, Press Release, no. 30, vol. 3347, file 4, Press Release, no. 11, and vol. 3356, file 4, 'Women and the Home Improvement Plan.' Press releases relating to the modernization and decoration of the home were particularly directed to women; see ibid., vol. 3347, file 5.

24 Grauer, *Housing*, 42-3; Curtis report, 27; NAC (Thomson), 'Preliminary Report on the Housing Situation,' 106-8; NAC, RG 19, vol. 705, file 203-1A, vol. 1, Press Release, no. 107, 13 February 1940; ibid., vol. 709, file 203-1A, 'The Operation of the National Housing Act up to December 31, 1941, and the Home Improvement Loans Guarantee Act up to Its Termination October 30, 1940.' Ontario received 60,000 loans worth over $24 million, while British Columbia had under 13,000 loans, valued at over $4 million.

25 Canada, An Act to Assist in the Construction of Houses [National Housing Act], *Statutes of Canada*, 1938, 2 Geo. 6, c. 49.

26 Grauer, *Housing*, 43-4, 75a; Curtis report, 27-8, 327-8, tables 90a, 90b, and 90c, 329; NAC (Thomson), 'Preliminary Report on the Housing Situation,' 109-25; DBS, *Canada Year Book*, 1941, 342, table 23; NAC, RG 19, vol. 705, file 203-1A, vol. 1, Press Release, no. 107, 13 February 1940; ibid., vol. 709, file 203-1A, 'The Operation of the National Housing Act,' 26 January 1942.

27 CVA, Newspaper Clippings, M4289-1, 15 May 1936. This first DHA house is located at 3424 West 6th Avenue in Kitsilano. Canada Permanent Mortgage Corporation financed a loan of between $3,500 and $4,000. Thomas R. Smalley was the contractor.

28 *Vancouver Sun*, 3 November 1936, 3.

29 Designated lenders in Vancouver included Canada Permanent Mortgage Corpo-

ration, Sun Life Assurance Company, Confederation Life Association, Mutual Life Assurance Company, and Manufacturers' Life Assurance Company; see NAC, RG 19, vol. 706, file 203-1A, 'Districts in Which Loans Will Be Considered by the Approved Lending Institutions under the Dominion Housing Act.'

30 *Vancouver Sun*, 6 March 1936, 21.

31 Ibid., 24 September 1936, 1, 3, 5. John Weaver suggested to me the powerful influence of a 'dead' market on the lending institutions.

32 Ibid., 16 October 1935, 14, 7 February 1936, 14, and 24 March 1936, 5.

33 Ibid., 23 May 1936, 19.

34 Ibid., 16 May 1936, 19, and 24 September 1936, 1, 3, 5.

35 *Who's Who in British Columbia, 1940-41* (Vancouver: S. Maurice Carter 1941), 118; *Vancouver Sun*, 6 March 1936, 21, and 28 January 1937, 4.

36 CVA, CC records, 15-F-1, filé 3, R.J. Lecky to W.R. Bone, 27 July 1932; *Vancouver Sun*, 30 November 1931, 1.

37 CVA, MO records, 33-B-2, Relief (1), 1932 file, 'Report of the Committee on Homeless Men, July 1932.'

38 Ibid.

39 *Vancouver Sun*, 20 January 1937, 1, and 17 March 1937, 18. Here again, I thank John Weaver for pointing out the impact of the inactive market on lenders.

40 Ibid., 17 October 1936, 1, 7.

41 Ibid., 2 December 1936, 21, 28 January 1937, 4, 11 February 1937, 7, and 23 February 1937, 3; CVA, Newspaper Clippings, M4289-1, 19 February 1937; CVA, CC records, Minutes of the building, town planning, and parks committee, 26A, vol. 9, 22 February 1937, 12.

42 *Vancouver Sun*, 17 April 1937, 22.

43 Ibid., 22 January 1937, 4.

44 For examples see ibid., 27 March 1937, 23, 10 April 1937, 23, and 17 April 1937, 22-3.

45 Ibid., 25 February 1937, 11. Mary Sutherland made this assertion.

46 Ibid., 27 February 1937, 23-5, 17 April 1937, 22, and 28 January 1937, 4.

47 Ibid., 16 April 1937, 7, 20 May 1937, 2, and 4 August 1937, 12.

48 Ibid., 8 January 1938, 21, and 24 February 1938, 5.

49 For examples see ibid., 19 February 1938, 22, 12 March 1938, 23, 5 April 1938, 4, 23 April 1938, 27, 30 April 1938, 26, and 28 May 1938, 25. The National Housing Administration in Ottawa made available blueprints and specifications for a $10 fee.

50 Ibid., 26 January 1939, 3, and 17 February 1938, 1.

51 Ibid., 6 May 1939, 28.

52 Ibid., 14 May 1938, 25, 21 May 1938, 25, and 3 September 1938, 23; NAC, RG 19, vol. 709, file 203-1A, 'Operation of the National Housing Act,' [Schedule H], 10.

53 UCA, Papers of Hugh Dobson, B7, file S, 'Housing Vancouver: A Survey of the Housing Position in Vancouver by the Vancouver Housing Association,' August 1939. The report also asserted that the NHA established a sounder mortgage system. See also VHA, *Housing Vancouver: A Survey of the Housing Position in Vancouver* (Vancouver 1946), 24-5.

54 CVA, TPC records, 61-C-6, file 14 [Report of the special committee on housing],

15 November 1937, table showing the inequalities of the DHA in Vancouver; CVA, CC records, 26D, vol. 69, 6 May 1938, 91; *Vancouver Sun*, 25 June 1938, 23.

55 CVA, MO records, 33-D-5, Vancouver Board of Trade file, W.E. Payne to the Board, 30 June 1937, including 'Record of Trades among Married City Relief Cases Reporting for Work at Employment Service.' See also the applications for the 1937 'Work for Taxes' scheme in CVA, FD records, 100-A-4, file 4.

56 CVA, Newspaper Clippings, M4289-1, 1 February 1939. The *Vancouver Sun* unreservedly referred to these builders and realtors as 'building sharks' and 'the "gyp" variety'; see 23 January 1939, 20, and 24 January 1939, 5.

57 Ibid.; *Vancouver Sun*, 26 January 1939, 18, 10 February 1939, 6, and 4 March 1939, 29.

58 *Vancouver Sun*, 21 January 1939, 26, 24 January 1939, 5, and 27 January 1939, 4.

59 Ibid., 17 September 1938, 25, 10 February 1939, 6, and 4 March 1939, 29.

60 Ibid., 6 May 1939, 28, 8 July 1939, 24, and 22 July 1939, 23.

61 Ibid., 28 May, 1938, 25, and 4 February 1939, 23; Canada, Department of Finance, *Dominion Housing Act: Architectural Competition*, passim.

62 Deryck W. Holdsworth, 'Cottages and Castles for Vancouver Home-Seekers,' in *Vancouver Past: Essays in Social History*, ed. R.A.J. McDonald and Jean Barman (Vancouver: University of British Columbia Press 1986), 11-32; *Vancouver Sun*, 14 May 1938, 25, and 21 May 1938, 25. Some DHA-type housing was built. Vancouver architect C.B.K. Van Norman designed Cape Cod cottages under the federal program; see ibid., 10 October 1936, 7.

63 Nicholas Tuele, *B.C. Binning: A Classical Spirit* (Victoria: Art Gallery of Greater Victoria 1985); Dennis Sexsmith, 'B.C. Binning, cet inconnu,' *Vie des Arts* 32, 127 (Juin-été 1987):32-5, 78-9.

64 Bruce report, 78-91.

65 UCA, Dobson papers, B7, file S, 'Housing Vancouver,' 1939, ch. 6.

66 *Vancouver Sun*, 8 April 1939, 27, 11 April 1939, 12, 13 April 1939, 6, 15 April 1939, 27, and 20 May 1939, 26; CVA, TPC records, 77-B-5, file 6, 'Sir Raymond Unwin's Impressions of Vancouver'; UCA, Dobson papers, B13, file 6, [Notes on Sir Raymond Unwin]. Another visitor was Mrs. Harold J. Laski, vice-chair, Fulham Borough Council's housing committee; see *Vancouver Sun*, 27 February 1939, 24.

67 Catherine Bauer, *Modern Housing* (Boston and New York: Houghton Mifflin 1934); UCA, Dobson papers, B13, file 6, 'Vancouver Housing Association ... A Short Housing Bibliography,' [1938]. The bibliography, which Stratton sent to Dobson, includes references to Bauer and many contemporary American publications and cites locations in the TPC library or the Vancouver Public Library.

68 Joint Committee, *Report on Housing and Slum Clearance*, 3; Montreal Council of Social Agencies, *Housing for the Low Wage Earner*, 1; and City Improvement League, *Survey of the Location of the Present Housing of the Unemployed*, 1. For Cassidy, see Bruce report, 6; and Allan Irving, 'The Doctors versus the Expert: Harry Morris Cassidy and the British Columbia Health Insurance Dispute of the 1930s,' *BC Studies*, 78 (Summer 1988):53-79. For Topping, see CVA, TPC records, 61-C-6, file 14, [Report of the Special Committee on Housing], 15 November 1937. See also CVA, CC records, 27-C-6, file 24.

69 Richard Allen, *The Social Passion: Religion and Social Reform in Canada, 1914-28* (Toronto: University of Toronto Press 1971), 52.

70 Andrew Roddan, *God in the Jungles: The Story of the Man without a Home* (Vancouver, [1931]); idem, *Canada's Untouchables: The Story of the Man without a Home* (Vancouver: Clarke and Stuart 1932); UCA, Records of First United Church (Institutional Mission), Vancouver, I-33, B7, file 13, 'The Interesting Story of First United Church in Vancouver,' by Andrew Roddan (September 1934); *Vancouver Sun*, 4 July 1931, 8, 18 July 1931, 10, 1 August 1931, 21, 12 September 1931, 10, 17 October 1931, 20, 24 October 1931, 10, and 31 October 1931, 22.

71 Marilyn Joan Harrison, 'The Social Influence of the United Church of Canada in British Columbia, 1930-1948' (M.A. thesis, University of British Columbia 1975), 71-2, 99-101.

72 Michael Simpson, *Thomas Adams and the Modern Planning Movement: Britain, Canada, and the United States, 1900-1940* (London and New York: Mansell 1985), 71-117.

73 CVA, TPC records, 61-C-6, file 14, G.S. Mooney to A. Walker, 16 January 1937, and Walker to Mooney, 17 January 1938.

74 E. Moberly Bell, *Octavia Hill: A Biography* (London: Constable 1942); Dolores Hayden, *The Grand Domestic Revolution: A History of Feminist Designs for American Homes, Neighborhoods, and Cities* (Cambridge, MA, and London: MIT Press 1981); Sean Damer, 'State, Class and Housing: Glasgow, 1885-1919,' in *Housing, Social Policy and the State*, ed. Joseph Melling (London: Croom Helm 1980), 73-112; Shirley C. Sprague, 'A Confluence of Interests: Housing Reform in Toronto, 1900-1920,' in *The Usable Urban Past: Planning and Politics in the Modern Canadian City*, ed. Gilbert A. Stelter and Alan F.J. Artibise, Carleton Library no. 119 (Toronto: Macmillan of Canada with the Institute of Canadian Studies, Carleton University 1979), 247-67.

75 Veronica J. Strong-Boag, *The Parliament of Women: The National Council of Women in Canada*, History Division Paper no. 18 (Ottawa: National Museums of Canada 1976), 207-8, 256-7, 315, 367-8.

76 Papers of the Vancouver Council of Women, M657, box 7, file 3, 1930-1, 88-9, 99, file 4, 1931-2, 147, file 6, 1933-4, 71-2, 181, 200, and file 7, 1934-5, 88, 91, Special Collections Division, University of British Columbia Library.

77 Eugenie Ladner Birch and Deborah S. Gardner described the redefinition of gender roles in the housing field from philanthropic to professional and/or bureaucratic in 'The Seven Percent Solution: A Review of Philanthropic Housing, 1870-1910,' in *JUH* 7, 4 (August 1981):429-31.

78 Michiel Horn, *The League for Social Reconstruction: Intellectual Origins of the Democratic Left in Canada, 1930-1942* (Toronto: University of Toronto Press, 1980).

79 Dorothy June Roberts, 'Doctrine and Disunity in the British Columbia Section of the CCF, 1932-1956' (M.A. thesis, University of Victoria 1972), 24, 26; Horn, *League for Social Reconstruction*, 68, 84, 187; Barbara K. Latham and Roberta J. Pazdro, eds., *Not Just Pin Money: Selected Essays on the History of Women's Work in British Columbia* (Victoria: Camosun College 1984), 368.

80 League for Social Reconstruction, Research Committee, *Social Planning for Canada* (Toronto: Thomas Nelson and Sons 1935), 246-7, 451-63; Humphrey Carver, *Compassionate Landscape* (Toronto: University of Toronto Press 1975), 51.

81 Horn, *League for Social Reconstruction*, 37-8.

82 Roberts, 'Doctrine and Disunity,' 6-29; Elaine Bernard, 'The Rod Young Affair in the British Columbia Co-operative Commonwealth Federation' (M.A. thesis, University of British Columbia 1979), 9-24.

83 Ivan Avakumovic, *The Communist Party in Canada: A History* (Toronto: McClelland and Stewart 1975), 67.

84 Doug Owram, *The Government Generation: Canadian Intellectuals and the State, 1900-1945* (Toronto, Buffalo, and London: University of Toronto Press 1986).

85 NAC, RG27, vol. 3347, file 4, [Press Release], 9 September 1936; Canada, National Employment Commission, *Final Report* (Ottawa: King's Printer 1938), appendix E, 101-3.

86 NAC, RG 27, vol. 3388, file 1, Purvis to N. Rogers, 25 March 1937; NAC, RG 19, vol. 705, file 203-1A, Clark to Dunning, 9 March 1937, with 'A Low Rental Housing Program: Summary of Criticisms'; J.L. Granatstein, *The Ottawa Men: The Civil Service Mandarins, 1935-1957* (Toronto: Oxford University Press 1982), passim.

87 The names of oganizations listed in this paragraph have been taken from sources in notes 90, 91, and 92. For more on local activism in the 1930s involving women, see Irene Howard, 'The Mothers' Council of Vancouver: Holding the Fort for the Unemployed, 1935-1938,' in *Vancouver Past*, ed. McDonald and Barman, 249-87.

88 Mary Patricia Powell, 'A Response to the Depression: The Local Council of Women of Vancouver,' in *In Her Own Right: Selected Essays on Women's History in B.C.*, ed. Barbara Latham and Cathy Kess (Victoria: Camosun College 1980), 255-78.

89 Marion Elizabeth Lane, 'Unemployment during the Depression: The Problem of the Single Unemployed Transient in British Columbia, 1930-1938' (B.A. honours graduating essay, University of British Columbia 1966), 97.

90 CVA, CC records, 15-B-4, Relief Officer, July-December 1930 file, H.W. Cooper to W.C. Atherton, 18 December 1930; ibid., 15-D-6, file 9, J.D. Vulliamy to C. Jones, 29 December 1931, J. Todd to city clerk, 26 June 1931, and C. Robinson to city clerk, 24 July 1931; ibid., 16-F-3, file 11, W. Page to mayor and council, 30 March 1936, G.H. Henry to acting mayor and council, 6 October 1936; ibid., 16-C-2, file 9, A.E. Burton to city clerk, 24 August 1934; BCARS, Records of the Premier of British Columbia, GR 1222, box 127, file 10, Burton to D. Pattullo, ca. 27 August 1934; Ronald Liversedge, *Recollections of the On To Ottawa Trek*, ed. Victor Hoar, Carleton Library no. 66 (Toronto: McClelland and Stewart 1973), 15-16; Lorne Brown, *When Freedom Was Lost: The Unemployed, the Agitator, and the State* (Montreal and Buffalo: Black Rose Books 1987).

91 CVA, CC records, 15-F-3, file 8, J. McKenzie to city relief committee, 21 November 1932; ibid., 16-A-7, file 3, E. Habenicht to city relief department, 6 May 1933, and A. Falconer to city clerk, 28 April 1933; ibid., 16-F-3, file 10, M. McLellan to finance committee, 7 July 1936, J. Beynon to finance committee, 7 July 1936 and 3 September 1936, and J. Offer to city clerk, 18 December 1936; ibid., 16-F-3, file 11, P.R. Bengough to F. Howlett, 26 April 1936, Ukrainian Labour Temple Association to city council, 26 April 1936, Vancouver and District Waterfront Workers Association to city council, 8 July 1936, M. McLellan to finance committee, 22 September 1936, and C. Doherty to city council, 11 November

1936; ibid., 16-F-4, file 8, 'Report on Conditions Prevailing among Vancouver's Unemployed [by the Workers' Alliance of British Columbia, June 1937]'; ibid., file 9, Workers' Alliance, 'Resolution for the Creation of Useful, Productive Work' and 'Resolution Re High Rentals & Evictions'; Liversedge, *Recollections of the On to Ottawa Trek*, 17-18.

92 CVA, CC records, 16-A-4, file 11, E. Cowper to L.D. Taylor, 30 June 1933; ibid., 16-D-3, file 7, E. Pearce to Bone, 18 April 1935; ibid., 16-D-5, file 3, '[Petition] for the Unity of Chinese and White Workers,' 1935; ibid., 16-E-7, file 17, M.H. Blackley to Bone, 9 June 1936; ibid., 16-F-4, file 8, 'Report on Conditions Prevailing among Vancouver's Unemployed'; ibid., 17-A-2, file 2, E. Grey to city clerk, 15 March 1937; BCARS, Records of the Premier of British Columbia, GR 1222, box 127, file 9, 'Memorandum on Relief and Other Matters Presented by British Columbia Joint Committee on Unemployment,' 7 December 1934.

93 Liversedge, *Recollections of the On To Ottawa Trek*, 23, 32-3; CVA, CC records, 16-C-2, file 8, [Protests over the Evans family's eviction].

94 See notes 90, 91, and 92. See also CVA, MO records, 33-B-2, Relief (1), 1932 file, 'Report of the Committee on Homeless Men, July 1932'; CVA, CC records, 16-C-2, file 9, [CCF Unemployment Council resolution to endorse the minimum needs of the unemployed, November 1934]; ibid., 16-F-3, file 10, J. Beynon to city clerk, 30 June 1936; ibid., 16-F-4, file 8, 'Report on Conditions Prevailing among Vancouver's Unemployed'; and BCARS, Records of the Premier of British Columbia, GR 1222, box 127, file 9, 'Memorandum on Relief and Other Matters.'

95 Jean Evans Shiels and Ben Swankey, *'Work and Wages!' Semi-Documentary Account of the Life and Times of Arthur H. (Slim) Evans* (Vancouver: Trade Union Research Bureau, 1977), 69-75; CVA, CC records, 15-B-4, Relief Officer, July-December 1930 file, Cooper to Atherton, 18 December 1930; Liversedge, *Recollections of the On To Ottawa Trek*, 23, 58-84; Lane, 'Unemployment during the Depression,' 82-122; Howard, 'The Mothers' Council of Vancouver,' 249-87.

96 CVA, MO records, 33-A-5, Unemployment, 1930 file, W.H. Malkin to W.L.M. King, 22 May 1930, and H. Baldwin to Malkin, 31 May 1930.

97 Liversedge, *Recollections of the On To Ottawa Trek*, 23.

98 CVA, CC records, 15-E-7, file 12, M. Marchant and S.E. Johnston to mayor and council, 9 August 1932, Ward 7 Ratepayers' Association to mayor and council, 23 July 1932, H. Reid to C. Jones, 9 August 1932, and A. Rowan to Jones, 22 August 1932 and 24 August 1932; ibid., 16-A-4, file 12, H. Reid to Jones, 8 July 1933, and H.D. Wilson to Jones, 14 July 1933; ibid., 16-A-4, file 13, D.G. Cameron to mayor and council, 10 November 1933; ibid., 16-B-7, file 2, A. Tremblay to Jones, 23 August 1934, Wilson to mayor and council, 8 October 1934, and Rowan to Jones, 15 November 1934; ibid., 16-D-3, file 4, [Petitions from Italian Home Owners' and Electors' Association and Windermere District Improvement Association to mayor and council, 3 August 1935]; ibid., 16-E-7, file 12, Ward 3 Ratepayers' Association to city clerk, 18 February 1936; ibid., 16-E-7, file 13, H. Reid to F. Howlett, 11 April 1936 and Reid to Howlett, 9 May 1936, and Rowan to Howlett, 16 May 1936; *Vancouver Sun*, 11 July 1935, 18.

99 CVA, CC records, 16-A-4, file 14, Bone to Taylor, 14 March 1933; ibid., 16-B-7, file 1, Mrs. B. Winstone to city clerk, 9 May 1934; ibid., 16-B-7, file 3, Winstone to council, 22 October 1934; ibid., 16-B-7, file 4, Bone to W.W. Smith, 22

February 1934; ibid., 16-D-3, file 4, A.O. Matthews to C.E. Tisdall, 26 March 1935, and Winstone to city clerk, 10 April 1935. Ratepayers' associations sometimes made demands for landlords as well; see ibid., 16-E-7, file 16, Bone to Tisdall, 15 January 1936.

100 CVA, CC records, 16-E-7, file 17, Bone to Smith, 6 June 1936, and Smith to relief and employment committee, 9 June 1936.

101 CVA, Newspaper Clippings, M3818, 'Persistent Lady Who Strove and Arrived,' n.d. For an eloquent, definitive biography of Gutteridge, see Irene Howard, *The Struggle for Social Justice in British Columbia: Helena Gutteridge, the Unknown Reformer* (Vancouver: UBC Press 1992). See also Susan Wade, 'Helena Gutteridge: Votes for Women and Trade Unions,' in *In Her Own Right*, ed. Latham and Kess, 187-99; Linda Louise Hale, 'Appendix: Votes for Women; Profiles of Prominent British Columbia Suffragists and Social Reformers,' in *In Her Own Right*, ed. Latham and Kess, 292; and Susan Walsh, 'Equality, Emancipation, and a More Just World: Leading Women in the B.C.C.C.F.' (M.A. thesis, Simon Fraser University 1984), 87-122.

102 CVA, CC records, 16-C-2, file 9, [CCF Unemployment Council resolution].

103 Ibid., 16-F-4, file 8, 'Resolutions of the First Annual Greater Vancouver and New Westminster Youth Congress (Held in Vancouver, March 27-29, 1937).'

104 CVA, TPC records, 61-C-6, file 14, [Report of the special committee on housing, 15 November 1937]. For another treatment of the special committee's work from Gutteridge's perspective, see Howard, *Struggle for Social Justice*, 194-213.

105 CVA, TPC records, 77-B-6, file 1, [Minutes of the first meeting of the housing committee, 9 July, 29 September, 7 October, and 3 November 1937].

106 UCA, Dobson papers, B7, file S, 'Went around City to See Housing,' and 'Itinerary, 30th December 1937.'

107 CVA, TPC records, 77-B-5, file 3, Howlett to A.J. Harrison, 15 February 1938; ibid., 61-C-6, file 14, [Report of the special committee on housing].

108 *Vancouver Sun*, 9 October 1937, 14.

109 CVA, Newspaper Clippings, M4289-1, 8 January and 16 February 1938.

110 NAC, RG 19, vol. 710, file 203-1A, E.W. MacKay to King, 15 February 1938 and J. Jopson to King, 26 April 1938, with copy to I. Mackenzie; CVA, TPC records, 77-B-5, file 4, housing committee to mayor and council, 6 December 1937.

111 CVA, TPC records, 77-B-5, file 3. In particular, see Clark to Harrison, 8 December 1937.

112 CVA, CC records, 16-F-4, file 9, '[Workers' Alliance] Resolution for the Creation of Useful, Productive Work,' 1937.

113 CVA, TPC records, 61-C-6, file 14, Correspondence between Mooney and A. Walker, 16 January 1937 to 19 January 1938.

114 CVA, Newspaper Clippings, M4289-1, 20 December 1938; *Vancouver Daily Province*, 27 June 1938, 8; UCA, Dobson papers, B7, file S, 'The Housing Problem of Canada,' 8 March 1938; NAC, RG 19, vol. 710, file 203-1A, VHA secretary to Dunning, 14 May 1938.

115 CVA, TPC records, 61-C-6, file 14, '[Notice] to All Members of the Provisional Committee, the National Housing and Planning Association,' April 1938; ibid., 77-B-5, file 3, G. MacNeil to H. Gutteridge, 17 February 1938.

116 CVA, Newspaper Clippings, M4289-1, 27 May 1938.

117 CVA, TPC records, 77-B-6, file 1, housing committee to building, civic planning, and parks committee, 18 August 1938; CVA, Newspaper Clippings, M4289-1, 9 November 1938.

118 CVA, Newspaper Clippings M4289-1, 14 February 1939.

119 Ibid., 29 June 1937; *Vancouver Sun*, 12 January 1939, 1; CVA, CC records, 27-C-1, file 4, '[Brief] Re Better Housing,' 5 August 1935; CVA, FD records, 93-F-7, file 1, W.L. Woodford to A.W. Grey, 7 January 1937, and F. Jones and D.E. McTaggart to Dunning, 25 March 1937; NAC, RG 19, vol. 712, file 203-3, McTaggart to Dunning, 2 April 1937, A. MacInnis to Dunning, 9 April 1937, Dunning to McTaggart, 12 April 1937, and Dunning to MacInnis, 12 April 1937.

120 *Vancouver Sun*, 9 October 1937, 14.

121 CVA, Newspaper Clippings, M4289-1, 20 December 1938.

122 *Vancouver Sun*, 17 July 1939, 1-2; CVA, TPC records, 77-B-6, file 1, [Minutes of housing committee meeting, 29 December 1938 and 12 July 1939]; ibid., 77-B-5, file 2, Stratton to housing committee, 6 December 1938.

123 CVA, CC records, 27-D-4, file 2; *Vancouver Sun*, 19 October 1938, 15; *Vancouver Daily Province*, 12 October 1938, 7, and 28 October 1938, 34.

124 CVA, TPC records, 77-B-6, file 1, [Minutes of housing committee meeting, 14 January 1938]; ibid., 61-C-6, file 14, special committee on housing standard by-law to building, civic planning, and parks committee, 24 November 1939; CVA, MO records, 34-A-2, Housing Act, 1940 file, H.L. Corey to mayor and council, 21 March 1940; CVA, CC records, 27-E-3, file 18, [Draft standard of housing bylaw, 1940]. These discussions led to the city's 'Partial Housing Survey,' conducted by R. Startup in 1940, and to the formulation of a draft bylaw in 1941.

125 *Vancouver Daily Province*, 2 December 1938, 11, and 12 December 1938, 5.

126 *Vancouver Sun*, 17 January, 1, 2, and 21 January 1939, 1, 10; CVA, Newspaper Clippings, M4289-1, 20 January 1939.

127 CVA, TPC records, 77-B-5, file 6, Harrison to Mrs. G. MacInnis, 19 January 1939, G. MacInnis to Harrison, 14 March 1939, and 'Report of National Conference on Housing,' by G. MacInnis (1939). See also S.P. Lewis, *Grace: The Life of Grace MacInnis* (Madeira Park: Harbour Publishing 1993), 135.

128 BCARS, Records of the Premier of British Columbia, GR 1222, box 14, file 7, H. Cassidy to Pattullo, 27 November 1934; ibid., box 31, file 5, Harrison to Pattullo, 1 May 1939, 'Memorandum to the Honourable the Prime Minister,' 4 May 1939, and Pattullo to Harrison, 5 May 1939; *Vancouver Sun*, 22 June 1939, 1, and 23 June 1939, 22.

129 *Vancouver Sun*, 6 January 1939, 3, and 6 March 1939, 1, 5.

130 CVA, TPC records, 77-B-5, file 6, [Report by assize jury, supreme court of British Columbia], 22 March 1939; ibid., file 5, 'Extract from a Memorandum by the Assize Jury to the Chief Justice of the Supreme Court of B.C.,' 22 March 1939; CVA, Newspaper Clippings, M4289-1, 25 March 1939; *Vancouver Sun*, 29 March 1939, 11. Publicity was also given to civic discussions about fire-trap tenements on Triumph and Powell streets.

131 *Vancouver Sun*, 25 March 1939, 27, and 29 March 1939, 3.

132 Ibid., 4 March 1939, 29, 8 April 1939, 27, 11 April 1939, 12, 13 April 1939, 6, 15 April 1939, 27-8, and 20 May 1939, 26; CVA, TPC records, 61-C-6, file 14, Stratton

to Walker, 5 April 1939; ibid., 77-B-5, file 6, 'Sir Raymond Unwin's Impressions of Vancouver,' 1939.
133 *Vancouver Sun*, 11 May 1939, 12.
134 Ibid., 4 March 1939, 29.
135 Ibid., 4 February 1939, 1, 14, 6 March 1939, 1, 15, 9 May 1939, 5, 17 June 1939, 3, and 17 July 1939, 1-2.
136 CVA, TPC records, 61-C-6, file 14, [Notes by A. Walker on reverse of agenda of building, civic planning, and parks committee, 16 June 1939]; ibid., 77-B-5, file 5, Bengough to Telford, 28 June 1939, [Resolution of Greater Vancouver Health League], 14 June 1939, C. Pritchard to Howlett, 14 June 1939, R.J. Lecky to mayor and council, 15 June 1939, and R.H. Leadless to Harrison, 10 February 1939; ibid., file 6, [Minutes of special meeting of building, civic planning, and parks committee], 14 February 1939, Howlett to Harrison, 2 May 1939, 16 May 1939, and 31 May 1939, 'Memorandum and Resolution [in support of low-rental housing]' from the B.C. Old Age Pensioners Benevolent Association, Victoria Road Branch of the Communist Party, and Parent-Teacher Federation, J. Jopson to Harrison, 16 June 1939, and Leadless to Harrison, 14 February 1939; CVA, CC records, 27-D-5, file 17, [Letters and delegations endorsing and opposing a low-rental housing scheme under NHA Part II].
137 CVA, TPC records, 61-C-6, file 14, [Notes by Walker on reverse of agenda of building, civic planning, and parks committee]; ibid., 77-B-5, file 5, 'Memorandum and Resolution [from Shaughnessy Heights United Church Women's Guild, n.d.], Progressive Women's Federation to City Council,' 24 April 1939, and Mrs. J. Jackson to city council, 12 April 1939; ibid., file 6, Howlett to Harrison, 2 May 1939, 16 May 1939 and 31 May 1939; CVA, CC records, 27-D-5, file 17, [Letters and delegations endorsing and opposing a low-rental housing scheme].
138 CVA, TPC records, 61-C-6, file 14, [Notes by Walker on reverse of agenda of building, civic planning, and parks committee]; ibid., 77-B-5, file 5, F. Hoole to housing committee, 16 June 1939, A.L. Rowan to [city council], 2 May 1939, and [Minutes of meeting between city council and VHA]; ibid., file 6, Howlett to Harrison, 16 May 1939; CVA, CC records, 27-D-5, file 17, [Letters and delegations endorsing and opposing a low-rental scheme].
139 CVA, TPC records, 77-B-5, file 5, [Minutes of meeting of city council and VHA].

Chapter 4: The Housing Problem in the 1940s
1 NAC, Records of the Department of Finance, RG 19, vol. 716, file 203C-17, 'Submissions on Behalf of the "5000 Homes Now!" Committee,' 19 April 1944; VHA, *Housing Vancouver*, abridged ed. (Vancouver 1947), 2; *Vancouver Sun*, 12 February 1942, 26.
2 Leonard C. Marsh, *Rebuilding a Neighbourhood* (Vancouver: University of British Columbia 1950), iii.
3 *Vancouver Sun*, 28 April 1947, 2, 9 August 1946, 13, 10 July 1947, 11, 27 August 1943, 3, and 14 May 1947, 3; *Vancouver Daily Province*, 30 January 1947, 10.
4 *Vancouver Daily Province*, 4 September 1946, 26; *Vancouver Sun*, 4 September 1946, 13.
5 *Vancouver Sun*, 16 July 1949, 1.
6 CVA, TPC records, 61-C-6, file 14, 'Housing – The Great Challenge' [by Frank

Buck, 1943].

7 VHA, *Housing Vancouver* (1947), 2.
8 NAC, Records of the Department of Munitions and Supply, RG 28, ser. A, vol. 342, file 196-46-1-1, F.K. Ashbaugh to M. Sharp, 14 November 1945; ibid., file 196-46-5, vol. 2, '[Memorandum] Re: Material and Labour Shortages in British Columbia,' 8 August 1945.
9 NAC, RG 19, vol. 728, file 203-CP, D. Gordon to J.L. Ilsley, 20 November 1944, enclosing letter from M.G. Fleming, 27 October 1944.
10 O.J. Firestone, *Manpower and Material Requirements for a Housing Program in Canada* (Ottawa: King's Printer 1946), 34.
11 NAC, RG 19, vol. 4017, Interdepartmental housing committee document no. 86, 'Residential Construction Survey (Vancouver),' 14 September 1945.
12 *Vancouver Sun*, 29 April 1947, 9, and 9 March 1949, 13.
13 Curtis report, 11-13.
14 CVA, CC records, 18-D-2, file 5, 'Citizens' Rehabilitation Council of Greater Vancouver: Housing,' [ca. 16 May 1945]; VHA, *Housing Vancouver* (1947), 11.
15 VHA, *The Housing Situation in Vancouver* (Vancouver 1948), 2; Central Mortgage and Housing Corporation (hereafter cited as CMHC), *Annual Report* (1947), 17-18.
16 Curtis report, 132, 135; VHA, *Housing Vancouver: A Survey of the Housing Position in Vancouver* (Vancouver 1946), 42.
17 NAC, RG 28, ser. B, vol. 264, Canada, Department of Reconstruction and Supply, 'Canada's Industrial War Effort, 1939-1945,' (1947); VHA, *Housing Situation in Vancouver*, 2.
18 CVA, TPC records, 77-B-6, file 4, Welfare Council of Greater Vancouver, housing committee, Minutes, 3 May 1944.
19 DBS, *Ninth Census of Canada, 1951* (Ottawa: Queen's Printer 1953), vol. 3, *Housing and Families*, table 122-7.
20 CVA, CC records, 18-D-2, file 5, 'Citizens' Rehabilitation Council of Greater Vancouver: Housing'; NAC, Records of CMHC, RG 56, vol. 17, file 105-10, vol. 2, L.F. Stevenson to D. Gordon, 31 July 1945.
21 CVA, MO records, 34-C-7, Housing (1), 1947 file, 'CMHC Municipal Survey,' 14 September 1946.
22 CVA, CC records, 18-D-2, file 5, 'Citizens' Rehabilitation Council of Greater Vancouver: Housing'; BCARS, Records of the Premier of British Columbia, GR 1222, box 173, file 11, 'Brief Prepared by Housing Committee, U.B.C., Branch No. 72, Canadian Legion.'
23 DBS, *Ninth Census of Canada, 1951*, vol. 3, table 117-13.
24 CVA, MO records, 34-C-7, Housing (1), 1947 file, 'CMHC Municipal Survey'; VHA, *Housing Situation in Vancouver*, 2.
25 J. de N. Kennedy, *History of the Department of Munitions and Supply: Canada in the Second World War* (Ottawa: King's Printer 1950), vol. 2, 80-7.
26 *Vancouver Sun*, 9 July 1943, 8.
27 CVA, Newspaper Clippings, M4289-2, 24 March 1943 and 25 March 1943.
28 See Kennedy, *History of the Department of Munitions and Supply*, vol. 2, for descriptions of all the various controls.
29 *Vancouver Sun*, 1 May 1947, 1.

30 NAC, Records of the Wartime Prices and Trade Board (hereafter cited as WPTB records), RG 64, vol. 29, 'Canadian Rental and Eviction Controls: World War II and the Post War Years,' 1 December 1947, 49, 54, passim.

31 *Vancouver Sun*, 1 October 1946, 8.

32 NAC, RG 19, vol. 728, file 203CP, M. Fleming to O. Lobley, 27 October 1944.

33 CVA, TPC records, 77-B-5, file 7, 'The Vancouver Real Estate Exchange Lmtd: Vacant Houses and Business Premises in Letter Carrier Delivery Area,' 1 July 1940; *Vancouver Sun*, 8 November 1940, 26, 16 June 1941, 1, and 13 August 1941, 2.

34 *Vancouver Daily Province*, 27 July 1942, 22; CVA, TPC records, 77-B-5, file 7, 'Vancouver Real Estate Exchange Lmtd: Vacant Houses and Business Premises in Letter Carrier Delivery Area,' 1 June 1942; NAC, RG 64, vol. 215, file G-05-02, 'Weekly Statistical Report – Feb. 15 to 22nd [1943].'

35 *Vancouver Sun*, 2 December 1943, 15, as well as 4 February 1943, 14, 17 August 1943, 1, 20 August 1943, 1, and 3 September 1943, 17; *Vancouver Daily Province*, 6 January 1943, 5, and 21 January 1943, 1; CVA, TPC records, 77-B-5, file 8, 'Vancouver Real Estate Exchange Lmtd: Survey of Vancouver, Showing Number of Buildings and Vacancies,' 18 July 1944.

36 CVA, Newspaper Clippings, M4289-2, 6 March 1943.

37 *Vancouver Daily Province*, 12 November 1943, 1; NAC, RG 19, vol. 716, file 203-C-17, 'Submissions on Behalf of the "5000 Homes Now!" Committee.'

38 *Vancouver Sun*, 20 October 1944, 24, as well as 25 August 1944, 17; CVA, TPC records, 77-B-5, file 8, 'Monthly Report – May 1944.'

39 *Vancouver Daily Province*, 4 October 1945, 3; *Vancouver Sun*, 5 December 1945, 13; VHA, *Housing Vancouver* (1946), 3; NAC, RG 64, vol. 700, file 25-1-3, Minutes of special WPTB meeting, 23 July 1945.

40 NAC, RG64, vol. 1457, file A-10-9-13, vol. 1, 'Notes on Discussions with Rentals Officials in Western Canada,' 11 May 1946; *Vancouver Sun*, 7 March 1946, 2, 23 July 1946, 1, and 20 September 1946, 15; VHA, *Housing Vancouver* (1947), 13.

41 VHA, *Housing Situation in Vancouver*, 2-3, 5; *Vancouver Sun*, 19 March 1947, 13.

42 CVA, MO records, 34-F-2, Housing, 1949, file, 'Memorandum on the Housing Situation in Vancouver,' May, 1949; *Vancouver Sun*, 7 October 1948, 37.

43 NAC, RG 19, vol. 716, file 203C-17, 'Vancouver Housing Opinion Survey,' September 1944.

44 CVA, CC records, 34-F-2, Housing, 1949 file, 'City of Vancouver Housing Authority, Housing Survey,' [1949].

45 CVA, FD records, 113-A-15, Better Housing Scheme Ledger Account, 1920-3.

46 *Vancouver Daily Province*, 25 February 1943, 25.

47 DBS, *Ninth Census of Canada, 1951*, vol. 3, Bulletin 3-4, *Housing: Tenure and Type of Dwelling*, 11-1.

48 Canada, An Act to Promote the Construction of New Houses [National Housing Act], *Statutes of Canada*, 1944, 8 Geo. 6, c. 46; CMHC, *Annual Report* (1946), 5-6. Figures were calculated from ibid. (1946), 28, table 4, (1947), 28, table 2, (1948), 52, table 3, (1949), 55, table 3, and (1950), 53, table 3.

49 *Vancouver Sun*, 18 May 1946, 15, 4 September 1946, 1, 7 September 1946, 13, 26 September 1946, 7, 19 November 1946, 2, 3 December 1946, 9, 19 December 1946, 1, 19 March 1947, 13, 10 July 1947, 26, 6 March 1948, 6, 2 April 1948, 17, 1 May 1948, 23, 24, 25, 51, and 17 September 1948, 48; *Vancouver Daily Province*,

4 September 1946, 6, 7 September 1946, 31, and 28 February 1948, 1, 2.

50 *Vancouver Sun*, 4 March 1950, 29, 18 March 1950, 32-3, 1 April 1950, 25, 6 May 1950, 26, 13 May 1950, 33, 8 June 1950, 11, 10 June 1950, 26, 2 November 1951, 25, and 24 November 1951, 17. For prices, see ibid., 5 January 1951, 10, 4 April 1951, 9, and 20 July 1951, 21.

51 CMHC, *Annual Report* (1947), 19. This figure included WHL/CMHC housing.

52 Joan L. Selby, 'Urban Rental Housing in Canada, 1900-1985: A Critical Review of Problems and the Response of Governments' (M.A. thesis, University of British Columbia 1985), 90-3.

53 CMHC, *Annual Report* (1947), 19; see also Selby, 'Urban Rental Housing,' 91-3, and *Vancouver Sun*, 29 April 1950, 15.

54 Curtis report, 113. Leonard Marsh (and others) argued that the average tenant family should not allocate over one-fifth of its budget to rent. A rent falling within this limit was 'proportionate' rent: one that did not was 'disproportionate.'

55 Curtis report, 110-15, 119-20; DBS, *Eighth Census of Canada, 1941* (Ottawa: King's Printer 1949), vol. 9, *Housing*, 98, table 21a. Of 71,116 households in Vancouver in 1941, 35,513 were tenants and 35,603 owners; ibid., 182, table 36, and 6, table 1a. By 1951, Vancouver had 101,330 households, of which 63,885 were owners and 37,445 tenants; DBS, *Ninth Census of Canada, 1951*, vol. 3, 98-17.

56 NAC, RG 19, vol. 3567, file H-02, 'Housing Preferences of Vancouver Tenants,' conducted by DBS, Department of Trade and Commerce, [1944].

57 VHA, *A Survey of Rooming Houses in the West End and Downtown Districts of Vancouver* (Vancouver 1951), 1b-9.

58 Marsh, *Rebuilding a Neighbourhood*, 12-14.

59 For rent controls, see NAC, RG 64, vol. 29, 'Canadian Rental and Eviction Controls'; and Curtis report, 37-40, 255-61.

60 *Vancouver Sun*, 7 April 1947, 1.

61 In these years, Vancouver obtained about 1,800 units, North Vancouver 750, and Richmond 300 from WHL and CMHC. See Chapter 5, pp. 119-20, 141, 147. Vancouver's total does not include the Fraserview units built in 1949-50.

62 CMHC, *Annual Report* (1952), 76, table 15.

63 *Vancouver Sun*, 18 April 1951, 23.

64 CMHC, *Annual Report* (1947), 10; *Vancouver Daily Province*, 26 April 1947, 11. These rentals applied to the Vancouver projects.

65 Warren Andrew Wilson, 'Housing Conditions among Social Assistance Families: Implications for Rental Allowances in Social Assistance and Low-Rental Housing Needs' (M.S.W. thesis, University of British Columbia 1955).

66 CVA, CC records, 28-E-6, file 12, 'Kitsilano Survey (Demonstration Housing Survey), 1947.'

67 Papers of the Angus MacInnis Memorial Collection, M397, box 40B, file 9, 'Survey of Families with Children Living in Shared Accommodation,' May 1954, Special Collections Division, University of British Columbia. The VHA estimated that probably 200 families shared accommodation in the survey area. See also Michael Wheeler's 'Evaluating the Need for Low-Rental Housing: A Review of Conditions among Family Applications for the Little Mountain Low-Rental Housing Project, Vancouver, and Consideration of Criteria for Future Housing

Projects' (M.S.W. thesis, University of British Columbia 1955), based on the VHA survey and other sources.

68 VHA, *'We, Too, Need Housing!' A Survey of the Housing Needs of Single Girls Employed in Downtown Vancouver* (Vancouver 1951).

69 VHA, *Housing for Our Older Citizens* (Vancouver 1949); idem, *A Survey of Rooming Houses in the West End.*

70 Curtis report, 96.

71 DBS, *Ninth Census of Canada, 1951*, vol. 3, Bulletin 3-13, *Housing: Crowded and Uncrowded Households*, 86-1.

72 DBS, *Eighth Census of Canada, 1941*, vol. 9, 182, table 36, 183, table 37, 184-203, table 38.

73 Marsh, *Rebuilding a Neighbourhood*, 18, table 11, 19.

74 VHA, *Housing Vancouver* (1947), 2.

75 CVA, TPC records, 61-C-6, file 14, 'Lodging House Study,' August 1948; CVA, HD records, 146-B-3, file 8, 'Report on 1,000 Vancouver Lodging Houses,' 16 February 1949.

76 VHA, *Survey of Rooming Houses in the West End*, 3, 9.

77 Vancouver, Planning Department, *Vancouver Redevelopment Study*, prepared for the Housing Research Committee (Vancouver 1957), 7.

78 Curtis report, 102, table 23.

79 DBS, *Eighth Census of Canada, 1941*, vol. 9, 11, table 3a; idem, *Ninth Census of Canada, 1951*, vol. 3, 18-6.

80 CVA, TPC records, 61-C-6, file 14, 'Lodging House Study,' (1948); CVA, HD records, 146-B-3, file 8, 'Report on 1,000 Vancouver Lodging Houses,' (1949).

81 VHA, *Survey of Rooming Houses in the West End*, 9-10.

82 VHA, *Housing Vancouver* (1947), 2.

83 CVA, HD records, 145-C-4 to 145-D-4, Health inspectors' reports, ca. 1930-65. These reports, which are arranged by street address, are most useful for the late 1940s and early 1950s.

84 Marsh, *Rebuilding a Neighbourhood*, iii, 3.

85 Vancouver, Planning Department, *Vancouver Redevelopment Study*, 7.

86 VHA, *Survey of Rooming Houses in the West End*, 4,5, 10.

87 Marsh, *Rebuilding a Neighbourhood*, 17, 18, tables 8 and 9.

88 Papers of the Angus MacInnis Memorial Collection, M397, box 40B, file 9, 'Survey of Families with Children Living in Shared Accommodation,' May 1954, Special Collections Division, University of British Columbia; Vancouver, Planning Department, *Vancouver Redevelopment Study*, 7.

89 CVA, CC records, 28-C-7, file 8, 'Memo Re Basement Suites in Apartment Houses,' [1947].

90 CVA, HD records, 146-B-3, file 8, 'Report on 1,000 Vancouver Lodging Houses.'

91 CVA, TPC records, 61-C-6, file 14, 'Lodging House Study.'

92 CVA, PLD records, 124-A-5, file 3, '[Survey of use and occupancy of existing dwellings in the Area Bounded by Bayswater, Trafalgar, the Lane South of 4th Avenue and the Lane North of Broadway and in the Area Bounded by Alma, Bayswater, Point Grey Road, and the Lane North of 4th Avenue],' 3 July 1952.

93 CVA, CC records, 78-B-1, file 1, '[Brief to] Special Committee of Rooming House Owners and Operators of Vancouver to Mayor and Aldermen,' 16 March 1954.

94 *Vancouver Sun*, 2 December 1948, 13. For Kitsilano, see CVA, PLD records, 124-A-5, file 3, '[Survey of use and occupancy of existing dwellings].'
95 VHA, *Survey of Rooming Houses in the West End*, 3-4. For descriptions of specific cases in the downtown core, see CVA, HD records, 145-C-4 to 145-D-4.
96 CVA, CC records, 28-E-6, file 7, W. Bradshaw to S. Murray, 20 October 1950; ibid., 20-D-1, file 9, S. Murray to W. Orr, 22 April 1954, and Murray to chair and members, building and town planning committee, 14 June 1954.
97 CVA, CC records, 28-E-6, file 7, and 28-F-2, file 14; CVA, TPC records, 78-A-3, Gas Poisoning, 1953 file, and 78-B-1, file 1; *Vancouver Sun*, 1 February 1951, 15, and 16 February 1951, 1, 2.
98 CVA, CC records, 78-B-1, file 1, 'By-law No. 3406: A By-law to Amend By-law No. 2483, Being the "Gas Fitting By-law",' 19 October 1953; *Vancouver Sun*, 2 October 1953, 53, and 15 January 1954, 8.
99 *Vancouver Sun*, 3 April 1952, 1, 16 March 1954, 8, 15, 12 August 1954, 1, and 14 December 1954, 1.
100 VHA, *Survey of Rooming Houses in the West End*, 5; Vancouver, Planning Department, *Vancouver Redevelopment Study*, 7.
101 CVA, CC records, 28-E-6, file 12, 'Kitsilano Survey,' 1947; CVA, TPC records, 61-C-6, file 14, 'University of British Columbia Demonstration Housing Survey,' May 1947.
102 See CVA, HD records, 145-C-4 to 145-D-4 for specific cases at particular addresses. See also Marsh, *Rebuilding a Neighbourhood*, 16-17; CVA, TPC records, 61-C-6, file 14, 'Vancouver Health Department – City Hall – General Observations on Other Types of Housing in Vancouver,' August 1948, and 'Lodging House Study,' August 1948; and CVA, HD records, 146-B-3, file 8, 'Report on 1,000 Vancouver Lodging Houses,' February 1949.
103 CVA, HD records, 145-C-4 to 145-D-4, for individual cases; CVA, CC records, 28-E-6, file 12, 'Kitsilano Survey,' 1947; Vancouver, Planning Department, *Vancouver Redevelopment Study*, 7.
104 CVA, HD records, Inspection History Cards, MCR 25, Reels 1 to 8 (Microfilm copy); ibid., 145-C-5, [report on 761 Cardero Street, 1948-9], 145-C-6, [report on 1674 Davie Street, 1948-9], 145-C-7, [report on 1667 Harwood Street, 1948], and 145-D-2, [report on 1245 Nicola Street, 1948]; VHA, *Survey of Rooming Houses in the West End*, 2, 6-7, 9-10.
105 Irene Howard, *The Struggle for Social Justice in British Columbia: Helena Gutteridge, the Unknown Reformer* (Vancouver: UBC Press 1992), 240-2.
106 Marsh, *Rebuilding a Neighbourhood*, 9; CVA, TPC records, 61-C-6, file 14, 'Vancouver Health Department – City Hall – General Observations on Other Types of Housing in Vancouver'; CVA, CC records, 28-E-6, file 12, 'Kitsilano Survey,' 1947; CVA, HD records, 145-C-4 to 145-D-4, Health inspectors' reports, passim.
107 *Vancouver Sun*, 1 March 1947, 13, and 16 July 1948, 9; CVA, HD records, 145-C-4, [report on 1 to 25 Canton Alley, 1946-7]. For descriptive material on Chinese boardinghouses, see, for example, ibid., 145-C-4, [reports on Alexander Street], 145-C-5, [reports on Carrall Street], 145-C-6, [reports on East Georgia Street], and 145-D-2, [reports on East Pender Street], passim.
108 See, for example, CVA, HD records, 145-C-5, [reports on cheap hotels on West and East Cordova Street, including the Atlantic Hotel, the Marble Rooms, and

the Sterling Hotel at 77, 107, and 177 West Cordova, 1930s to 1950s]; and ibid., 145-D-3, [Reports on other cheap hotels on Powell Street, such as the Grand Trunk Rooms and Ohio Rooms at 55 and 245 Powell Street, 1940s to 1950s].

109 CVA, CC records, 28-E-2, file 20, S. Murray to housing committee, 22 August 1949, with attached report, 'Foreshore Survey,' February 1949.

110 Rolf Knight, *Along the No. 20 Line: Reminiscences of the Vancouver Waterfront* (Vancouver: New Star Books 1980), 51-3.

111 CVA, HD records, 145-D-3, [report for 1124 West Pender Street, including the petition from the tenants of the Davenport Rooms to the Metropolitan Health Committee, 25 February 1952].

112 Knight, *Along the No. 20 Line*, 75, 79.

113 Recollections of William McConnell, 1984-5, quoted in Sheryl Salloum, *Malcolm Lowry: Vancouver Days* (Madeira Park: Harbour Publishing 1987), 118, as well as 44, 128.

114 CVA, HD records, 145-C-5, [report on houseboats at foot of Cardero Street, 1946], 145-D-3, [report on cabins, 532 Prior Street, 1950], 145-D-1, [report on lodging house, 210 Keefer Street, 1948-54], 145-C-5, [report on Chinese boardinghouses, 517 Carrall Street, 1946-51, and 535-41 Carrall Street, 1946-50], and 145-C-4, [reports on cabins, 472 Alexander Street, 1947, and lodging house, 406 Alexander Street, 1945-52].

115 VHA, *Housing Vancouver* (1947), 3; NAC, RG 19, vol. 716, file 203-C-17, J. Clarke to I. Mackenzie, 21 September 1944.

116 CVA, TPC records, 77-B-6, file 4, Minutes, housing committee, Welfare Council of Greater Vancouver, 3 May 1944, with attached report from the national housing registry, April 1944.

117 CVA, HD records, 145-D-1, [reports on lodging house, 210 Keefer Street, 1948-54], 145-D-3, [report on cabins, 217½ Prior Street, 1949], 145-C-6, [report on lodging house, 1263 Davie Street, 1947-8], and 145-C-5, [report on houseboat, foot of Cardero Street, 1946]; CVA, TPC records, file 4, Welfare Council of Greater Vancouver, housing committee, 'Statement on Housing,' August 1944; *Vancouver Sun*, 31 July 1946, 3.

118 *Vancouver Daily Province*, 15 February 1943, 4; *Vancouver Sun*, 10 May 1943, 19; NAC, RG 19, vol. 716, file 203 C-17, J. McPeake to W.L.M. King, 19 April 1944, with brief, 'Submissions on Behalf of the "5000 Homes Now!" Committee.'

119 CVA, HD records, 145-C-4, [report on lodging houses at 437 Alexander Street, 1948, and 663 Cambie Street, 1945], 145-D-1, [report on lodging house at 210 Keefer Street, 1948-54], 145-D-2, [report on Cobalt Hotel, 917 Main Street, 1944-53], 145-D-3, [report on lodging house, 546 Prior Street, 1944], 145-C-4, [report on lodging house at 1357 Barclay Street, 1946-9, 809 Bidwell Street, 1951, and on a shack below Burrard Bridge, 1948], and 145-C-6, [report on lodging house, 1526 Davie Street, 1944-6].

120 CVA, CC records, 18-F-2, file 8, [Annual Report of the Social Services Department, 1946]; CVA, MO records, 34-B-1, Relief, 1940 file, 'City of Vancouver Monthly Relief Schedule,' [1940].

121 VHA, *'We, Too, Need Housing!'*

122 For example, see Marsh, *Rebuilding a Neighbourhood*, 12.

123 VHA, *Housing for Our Older Citizens*, 1-7; idem, *Survey of Rooming Houses in the*

West End, 8.

124 Dennis Guest, *The Emergence of Social Security in Canada* (Vancouver: University of British Columbia 1980), 145.

125 CVA, HD records, 145-C-4, [report on cabins at 343 Alexander Street, 1944-53]. Forty cabins at this address housed pensioners for the most part. After many inspections and repeated warnings, the cabins were demolished in 1953.

126 CVA, HD records, 145-D-1, [Health inspector's report for 750 Keefer Street], clipping for *Vancouver Daily Province*, 22 October 1948, 42.

127 VHA, *Survey of Rooming Houses in the West End*, 6.

128 CVA, HD records, 145-C-7, [report on cabins at 204 Glen Drive, 1945-52]. By 1952, St. James Anglican Church operated 'Little Haven.'

129 VHA, *Housing for Our Older Citizens*, 8-14. Not included here are the seniors' housing projects started by private groups later in the 1940s.

Chapter 5: Responding to the Housing Problem in the 1940s

1 Curtis report, 37-40, 255-61; NAC, WPTB records, RG 64, vol. 29, 'Canadian Rental and Eviction Controls, World War II and the Post War Years,' 1 December 1947; CVA, CC records, 17-E-3, file 6, Clipping from *Vancouver Daily Province*, 13 December 1940, and WPTB, Order no. 23, 'Order Respecting Vancouver Rentals Committee,' 13 December 1940; Vancouver Sun, 13 August 1943, 9, and 17 August 1943, 2.

2 Curtis report, 38, note 1, 256, 259-60.

3 NAC, RG 64, vol. 699, file 25-1, vol. 2, C. DeMara to D. Gordon, 4 July 1942, J.L. Ilsley to D. Gordon, 13 July 1942, and WPTB, Order no. 200, 'Respecting Housing Accommodation in Congested Areas,' 20 October 1942; CVA, Newspaper Clippings, M4289-2, 10 August 1943; CVA, TPC records, 61-F-5, file 1, Minutes of zoning committee, 17 November 1942 and 29 January 1943; *Vancouver Sun*, 5 November 1942, 17.

4 NAC, RG 64, vol. 215, file G.05.02, WPTB Press Releases no. 0228, 6 October 1942, and no. 0502, 14 May 1943; ibid., vol. 699, file 25-1, vol. 2, 'Report from Consumer Branch, WPTB, on Voluntary Housing Registries,' 30 November 1942, WPTB Press Release no. 0235, 14 October 1942, Weekly Statistical Report, 27 April 1943, and Press Release, 14 April 1943; *Vancouver Sun*, 7 October 1942, 17, 19 October 1942, 17, and 19 December 1942, 3; CVA, Newspaper Clippings, M4289-2, 29 January 1943, 6 March 1943, and 6 May 1943. Taken over by the Emergency Shelter Administration and CMHC, Vancouver's registry closed down by 30 September 1946; see *Vancouver Sun*, 1 October 1946, 8. For the registry's reports, see UCA, Papers of Hugh Dobson, B7, file R, 'Monthly Report, National Housing Registry,' April 1944; CVA, TPC records, 77-B-5, file 8, 'Monthly Report,' May 1944; and NAC, RG 64, vol. 215, file G.05.02, 'Weekly Statistical Report,' 24 June 1943.

5 J. de N. Kennedy, *History of the Department of Munitions and Supply: Canada in the Second World War* (Ottawa: King's Printer 1950), vol. 2, 80-7.

6 NAC, Records of the Department of Finance, RG 19, vol. 3980, file H-1-15, 'Report of the Economic Advisory Committee on Housing Policy,' 13 November 1940, and 'Minutes of a Meeting of the Economic Advisory Committee,' 15 October 1940; NAC, Records of the Privy Council Office, RG 2, ser. 4, P.C. 1286, 24

February 1941; Jill Wade, 'Wartime Housing Limited, 1941-1947: Canadian Housing Policy at the Crossroads,' *UHR* 15, 1 (June 1986):41-59; John C. Bacher, *Keeping to the Marketplace: The Evolution of Canadian Housing Policy* (Montreal and Kingston, London, Buffalo: McGill-Queen's University Press 1993), 129-63; idem, 'Too Good to Last? The Social Service Innovations of Wartime Housing,' *Women and Environments* 10, 2 (Winter 1988):10-13.

7 *The Canadian Who's Who*, vol. 5 (Toronto: Trans-Canada Press 1951), 806-7; Michael Doucet and John Weaver, *Housing the North American City* (Montreal and Kingston, London, Buffalo: McGill-Queen's University Press 1991), 300-1. WHL's first board of directors included: W.L. Somerville, architect, Toronto; Charles David, architect, Montreal; William E. Tibbs, administrator, Halifax Relief Commission; R.J. Gourley, president, Beaver Lumber Company, Winnipeg; H.C. Wilson, general manager and director, Maritime Trust Company, St. John; W.T. Gagnon, president, Aird and Son Limited, Montreal; and Ernest Ingles, vice-president, International Brotherhood of Electrical Workers, London; see NAC, Records of Defence Construction Limited, RG 83, vol. 70, Minutes, vol. 1, 'Wartime Housing Limited; Register of Directors,' and Minutes of WHL directors, 24 March 1941, 3; *The Canadian Who's Who*, vol. 4 (Toronto: Trans-Canada Press 1948), 346, 377-8, 880, 1002; and Ernest Ingles, 'Wartime Housing Limited,' *Canadian Congress Journal* 20, 6 (June 1941):15.

8 Robert Bothwell, 'Who's Paying for Anything These Days? War Production in Canada, 1939-45,' in *Mobilization for Total War: The Canadian, American, and British Experience, 1914-1918, 1939-1945*, ed. Nandor A.F. Dreiszieger (Waterloo: Wilfrid Laurier University Press 1981), 62; NAC, RG 83, vol. 70, Minutes, vol. 2, Minutes of WHL shareholders, 29 May 1945, 5.

9 Kennedy, *History of the Department of Munitions and Supply*, vol. 1, 480-9; O.J. Firestone, *Residential Real Estate in Canada* (Toronto: McClelland and Stewart 1974), 488, table 109.

10 *Vancouver Sun*, 16 June 1941, 22, 13 August 1941, 2, 12 January 1942, 18, 1 April 1942, 3, and 14 April 1942, 13; *Vancouver Daily Province*, 21 June 1941, 36, and 28 June 1941, 18; NAC, RG 83, vol. 70, Minutes, vol. 1, Minutes of WHL executive committee, 24 June 1941, 4, 7-8; NAC, RG 2, ser. 4, P.C. 7535, 25 September 1941; P.C. 9362, 2 December 1941; P.C. 3234, 23 April 1942; P.C. 8726, 25 September 1942. See the following in the city clerk's offices of the City and the District of North Vancouver: Agreement between the City and H.M. the King in right of Canada respecting the sale of land, 1 December 1941; Agreement between the City and WHL, 1 December 1941; Indenture between the City and H.M. the King in right of Canada respecting the lease of land, 1 December 1941; City By-law no. 1631, 1943 [WHL collateral agreement bylaw]; City By-law no. 1632, 1943 [WHL tax sale lands purchase bylaw]; District By-law no. 1241, 1943 [WHL collateral agreement bylaw]; District By-law no. 1242, 1943 [WHL tax sale lands purchase bylaw]; and Indenture between WHL, H.M. the King in right of Canada, and the Board of School Trustees, City of North Vancouver, 25 May 1943.

11 NAC, RG 2, ser. 4, P.C. 10862, 1 December 1942; *Vancouver Sun*, 10 May 1943, 19, and 28 May 1943, 1; *Vancouver Daily Province*, 27 March 1943, 5; City of Richmond Archives (hereafter cited as CRA), Records of the City Clerk's Depart-

ment (hereafter cited as CCD records), MR 13, file 2216, Agreement between H.M. the King in right of Canada and the Township respecting water supply, 1 December 1943. WHL named the subdivision after Stanley Burke, Sr., the president of Boeing Aircraft of Canada Limited.

12 NAC, RG 83, vol. 70, Minutes, vol. 2, Minutes of WHL shareholders, 29 May 1945, 6; NAC, RG 19, vol. 709, file 203-1A-1, C.D. Howe to J.L. Ilsley, 24 February 1945; Burwell R. Coon, 'Wartime Housing,' Royal Architectural Institute of Canada *Journal* 19, 1 (January 1942):3-8; Ingles, 'Wartime Housing Limited,' 15-16; Lionel Scott, 'Community Housing,' *Canadian Forum* 23, 267 (April 1943):8-10; idem, 'Some Facts about Community Centres,' RAIC *Journal* 22, 2 (February 1945):24-5; W.L. Somerville, 'Planned Homes for Our Munitions Workers,' *Canadian Homes and Gardens* 19, 1 (January 1942):11-13, 42; idem, 'Planning Wartime Communities,' *Canadian Homes and Gardens* 21, 1-2 (February 1944):38; idem, 'Site Planning for Wartime Housing,' RAIC *Journal* 19, 6 (June 1942):129-31; NAC, RG 64, vol. 89, file 106, 'Preliminary Report on the Housing Situation in Canada and Suggestions for Its Improvement,' prepared by Lesslie R. Thomson (Ottawa: Department of Munitions and Supply 1942), 222-67; NAC, National Film, TV, and Sound Archives, 'Wartime Housing,' a National Film Board of Canada documentary film directed by Stanley Jackson and narrated by Lionel Scott, 1941, 16 mm colour print; ibid., 'Community Organization,' a WHL documentary film directed by Tenant Relations Department, [1942], 16 mm colour print; Canada, House of Commons, *Debates*, 1942, vol. 3, 2570-2, and vol. 5, 4977-8; ibid., 1943, vol. 4, 3852-3; ibid., 1944, vol. 2, 1700; ibid., 1945, vol. 1, 2273; Canada, House of Commons, 'First Report of Subcommittee No. 1 [on WHL],' *Journals* 82 (1942-3):540-1; *Vancouver Sun*, 13 February 1942, 6; *Vancouver News-Herald*, 18 March 1942, 9.

13 In addition to the journals and films in note 12, see Leonard L. Knott, 'Prefabrication and the Post-War House,' *Canadian Business* 16, 9 (September 1943):46-51, 136, 138, 140, 144, 146; idem, 'War Housing Boom,' *Canadian Business* 14, 8 (August 1941):16-24, 68, 70; C. Stevenson, 'New Homes for Canada [Homes in Centres of War Industry],' *Canadian Home Journal* 38 (February 1942):12-13; *Vancouver Daily Province*, 14 August 1941, 23; Wade, 'Wartime Housing Limited,' 48; H. Peter Oberlander, 'Canada's Planning Experience in Housing Her War Veterans,' American Society of Planning Officials *Planning* (1949):198-201.

14 Kennedy, *History of the Department of Munitions and Supply*, vol. 1, 486-8; NAC (Thomson), 'Preliminary Report on the Housing Situation,' 232-4; NAC, National Film, TV, and Sound Archives, 'Community Organization'; Wade, 'Wartime Housing Limited,' 49-50.

15 Gwendolyn Wright, *Building the Dream: A Social History of Housing in America* (New York: Pantheon Books, 1981), 58-72, 177-92.

16 Kennedy, *History of the Department of Munitions and Supply*, vol. 1, 485-6; Curtis report, 36-7, 264-5; and NAC (Thomson), 'Preliminary Report on the Housing Situation,' 235-8. In *Canadian Housing Policies (1935-1980)* (Toronto: Butterworths 1980), 29-33, Albert Rose asserted that the 1949-64 federal-provincial partnership in public housing put this experience of intergovernmental cooperation to use in only a perfunctory way.

17 Leonard C. Marsh, 'Principles of Low Rent Housing,' *Public Affairs* 10, 4 (October

1947):234-8; Helen Marsh, 'From "Shacktown" to "My Town": Wartime Housing Community Projects,' *National Home Monthly* 45, 11 (November 1944):24.

18 Curtis report, 107, 113, 263, table 62; Canada, House of Commons, 'First Report of Subcommittee No. 1,' 540, 542; NAC, Records of the Department of Munitions and Supply, RG 28, ser. A, vol. 7, J. Pigott to J. de N. Kennedy, 3 January 1949; NAC, RG 83, vol. 70, Minutes, vol. 2, Minutes of WHL shareholders, 29 May 1945, 3-4.

19 Wade, 'Wartime Housing Limited,' 50-3.

20 NAC, RG 83, vol. 70, Minutes, vol. 2, Minutes of WHL shareholders, 29 May 1945, 5.

21 CVA, Newspaper Clippings, M8453, 14 April 1943, and M4289-2, 24 April 1943; CVA, CC records, 28-A-1, Wartime Housing, 1944 file, 'WHL: Agreement re Houses for Returned Men,' 12 September 1944.

22 CRA, CCD records, MR13, file 2216, Correspondence re Burkeville school issue; *Vancouver Sun*, 29 June 1945, 4; NAC, RG 83, vol. 70, Minutes, vol. 2, Minutes of WHL shareholders, 29 May 1945, 5.

23 *Vancouver Sun*, 12 February 1942, 26.

24 NAC, RG 19, vol. 704, file 203-1A, Press Release, 6 December 1939; ibid., vol. 3980, file H-1-15, 'Report of the Economic Advisory Committee on Housing Policy,' by W.C. Clark, 13 November 1940; John C. Bacher, 'W.C. Clark and the Politics of Canadian Housing Policy, 1935-1952,' *UHR* 27, 1 (June 1988):4-15.

25 NAC, RG 19, vol. 3980, file H-1-15, D.B. Mansur to W.C. Clark, 6 November 1940, with attached memorandum entitled 'Housing'; ibid., vol. 3540, Housing, 1935-45 file, F.W. Nicolls to Clark, 3 November 1941, and 'Memorandum ... Re: National Housing Act Operations in Winnipeg and Vancouver'; ibid., vol. 704, file 203-1A, Nicolls to J.L. Ilsley and Clark, 24 January 1942, with attached 'Memorandum ... Re: The Housing Situation in Canada and the National Housing Act.'

26 NAC, RG 19, vol. 709, file 203-1A, vol. 1, H.M. Moore to J.L. Ilsley, 9 January 1942, H. Boultbee to Ilsley, 31 January 1942, J.H. Stratton to Ilsley, 27 February 1942, W.J. LeClair to Ilsley, 18 March 1942 and 28 April 1942, 'Copy of Resolution Adopted by the Council of the City of Winnipeg at a Special Meeting Held on March 23rd, 1942,' A.S. Mathers to Ilsley, 24 March 1942, H. Cleaver to W.L.M. King, 25 March 1942, J.V. Desaulviers to Ilsley, 29 April 1942, G.M. Pitts to Ilsley, 9 May 1942, and W.H. Grisenthwaite to Ilsley, 11 May 1942. See also ibid., vol. 706, file 203-1A, C.A. Curtis to Ilsley, 28 July 1942, and G.M. Garton to Ilsley, 9 April 1942; and ibid., vol. 3540, Housing, 1935-45 file, J.W. Macdonald to Howe, 30 October 1942. These letters represented the interests of the Ontario Retail Lumber Dealers' Association, Sun Life Assurance Company of Canada, Quality Homes Corporation, Canadian Lumbermen's Association, City of Winnipeg, National Construction Council of Canada, a member of parliament, Montreal Real Estate Board, Garton and Hutchinson, Real Estate and Investments, Royal Architectural Institute of Canada, and Dominion Mortgage and Investments Association.

27 NAC, RG 19, vol. 709, file 203-1A, vol. 1, Moore to Ilsley, 9 January 1942.

28 NAC, RG 19, vol. 704, file 203-1A, 'Brief on Housing with Special Reference to the National Housing Act,' by C. Blake Jackson, 4 May 1942, and V.T. Goggin to

Howe, 2 May 1942, with attached memoranda by J. Pigott and W.L. Somerville, 'Re: Continuance of National Housing Act,' 1 May 1942.

29 Curtis report, 27; NAC, RG 19, vol. 705, file 203-1A, vol. 1, Press Release, 14 December 1942; Bacher, *Keeping to the Marketplace*, 121-5; idem, 'W.C. Clark and the Politics of Canadian Housing Policy'; Alvin Finkel, *Business and Social Reform in the Thirties* (Toronto: James Lorimer 1979), 112.

30 NAC, RG 19, vol. 3980, file H-1-15, and, in particular, G.K. Shiels to secretary, Treasury Board, 1 October 1942, and Clark to D. Gordon, 9 November 1942.

31 NAC, RG 2, ser. 4, P.C. 10797, 26 November 1942. According to Bacher, Clark had clearly gained the upper hand in the bureaucratic struggle between WHL and Department of Finance forces; see Bacher, 'W.C. Clark and the Politics of Canadian Housing Policy,' 9-10.

32 Curtis report, 27.

33 Firestone, *Residential Real Estate in Canada*, 487, 490, 491, table 112; NAC, RG 19, vol. 728, file 203 CP.

34 *Vancouver Sun*, 28 June 1943, 13, 9 July 1943, 1, 13 July 1943, 20, 23 July 1943, 4, 10 August 1943, 13, 8 October 1943, 4, and 27 January 1945, 2; CVA, Newspaper Clippings, M4289-2, 25 June 1943 and 28 September 1943.

35 Curtis report, 4.

36 Ibid., 9.

37 Ibid. For the growing perception in the 1940s of the importance of town planning, see NAC, National Film, TV, and Sound Archives, 'A Tale of New Cities,' a documentary film produced by Crawley Films Limited, 1947, 16 mm colour print, which revived the planner Hippodamus to explain the fundamentals of community planning in relation to ancient Greece and modern Stratford, Ontario. The cooperative housing movement had started in Canada by the late 1930s; for the Cape Breton example, see Mary Ellicott Arnold, *The Story of Tompkinsville* (New York: Cooperative League 1940).

38 NAC, RG 19, vol. 3447, Post-War Housing file, 'Housing in Relation to Post-War Reconstruction,' by the Dominion Mortgage and Investments Association, 24 February 1944; Bacher, 'W.C. Clark and the Politics of Canadian Housing Policy,' 10-11; NAC, National Film, TV, and Sound Archives, 'Pride of Possession,' a documentary film produced by Crawley Films Limited, directed by Peter Cook, and hosted by Kate Aitken, 1951, 16 mm colour print; Canada, An Act to Promote the Construction of New Houses [National Housing Act], *Statutes of Canada*, 1944, 8 Geo. 6, c. 46.

39 B.H. Higgins, 'Appraisals of the Canadian Housing Act,' *Public Affairs* 8, 3 (Spring 1945):168.

40 NAC, RG 19, vol. 3447, 'Housing in Relation to Post-War Reconstruction,' 8; Bacher, 'W.C. Clark and the Politics of Canadian Housing Policy,' 11.

41 NAC, RG 19, vol. 704, file 203-1A, 'Press statement by the Minister of Finance regarding amendments to National Housing Act, facilitating rental housing operations by life insurance companies,' 5 September 1945; ibid., vol. 709, file 203-1A-1, 'Memorandum for: Dr. W.A. Mackintosh Re: Life Insurance Companies,' 3 July 1945, J.E. Fortin to J.R. Tolmie, 8 August 1945, with attached memorandum, and 'Memorandum to Mr. Ilsley Re: Housing Enterprises of Canada, Limited,' 22 November 1945; ibid., vol. 2734, file 700-17, 'Memoran-

dum Re: Life Insurance Companies' Joint Effort in Rental Housing,' 6 November 1945; Humphrey Carver, *Compassionate Landscape* (Toronto: University of Toronto Press 1975), 80; *Vancouver Sun*, 6 October 1945, 17, 6 November 1945, 5, 26 February 1946, 11, 21 March 1946, 1, 10 May 1946, 4, 1 February 1947, 15, 4 February 1947, 9, 14 February 1947, 12, 17 March 1947, 1, 18 March 1947, 3, 19 April 1947, 17, 9 May 1947, 7, 14 May 1947, 1, 6, 15 May 1947, 2, and 5 August 1947, 2.

42 Canadian Architectural Archives, University of Calgary, Records of Thompson, Berwick, Pratt, Acc. No. 45A/78.35, 36T74, Drawings for proposed group houses, Trout Lake, 1936; Mark Swenarton, *Homes Fit for Heroes: The Politics and Architecture of Early State Housing in Britain* (London: Heinemann Educational Books 1981); John Nelson Tarn, *Five Per Cent Philanthropy: An Account of Housing in Urban Areas between 1840 and 1914* (Cambridge: The University Press 1973), 137-42, 165-74; Harold Kalman, *Exploring Vancouver 2: Ten Tours of the City and Its Buildings*, rev. ed. (Vancouver: University of British Columbia Press 1978), 159.

43 NAC, RG 19, vol. 3539, Housing, 1945 file, W.A. Mackintosh to [Builders from the National House Builders' Association], 13 July 1945, and A.W. Rogers to W.C. Clark, 14 May 1945, with attached note, 'Housing: Extracts from Replies of the Banks'; CMHC, *Annual Report* (1946), 5-6.

44 NAC, RG 28, ser. A, vol. 344, file 196-46-11, 'Memorandum #2 re Integrated Housing Developments'; NAC, National Film, TV, and Sound Archives, 'Operation Integrated,' a documentary film sponsored by CMHC, [1952?], 16 mm black and white print.

45 These subdivisions included Victory Heights in New Westminster, Willingdon Heights in Burnaby, and Capilano Properties in North Vancouver.

46 *Vancouver Sun*, 26 September 1946, 7, 19 November 1946, 2, 19 December 1946, 1, 19 March 1947, 13, and 6 March 1948, 6; *Vancouver Daily Province*, 7 September 1946, 31, and 28 February 1948, 1, 2.

47 NAC, RG 2, ser. 4, P.C. 3409, 10 May 1945, and P.C. 7484, 28 December 1945. Interdepartmental housing committee meetings commenced on 23 May 1945; see NAC, RG 28, ser. A, vol. 142, file 3-I-15. Later, when CMHC formed, the committee was reconstituted under P.C. 7484, 28 December 1945; see NAC, Reports of the Interdepartmental Committees, ser. 4, RG 35, vol. 1, file IHC-2.

48 Canada, An Act to Incorporate the Central Mortgage and Housing Corporation [The Central Mortgage and Housing Corporation Act], *Statutes of Canada*, 1945, 9 & 10 Geo. 6, c. 15; NAC, RG 64, box 700, file 25-1-4, Mansur to Mackintosh, 30 July 1945; NAC, RG 19, vol. 3539, 'Memorandum to the Cabinet Re: Central Mortgage and Housing Corporation Bill,' 2 October 1945; CMHC, *Annual Report* (1946), 5-7, and (1947), 10.

49 CVA, CC records, 18-D-7, file 4, Howe to O. Erickson, 30 October 1946.

50 Firestone, *Residential Real Estate in Canada*, 487; *Vancouver Sun*, 31 May 1945, 20, and 28 November 1946, 1.

51 CMHC, *Annual Report* (1946), 28, table 4, (1947), 28, table 2, (1948), 52, table 4, (1949), 55, table 3, and (1950), 53, table 3.

52 *Vancouver Sun*, 4 August 1944, 17. For agitation following the Great War, see Desmond Morton and Glenn Wright, *Winning the Second Battle: Canadian Veterans and the Return to Civilian Life, 1915-1930* (Toronto, Buffalo, and London:

University of Toronto Press 1987).
53 *Vancouver Sun*, 20 March 1946, 2, and 21 March 1946, 11.
54 CVA, Newspaper Clippings, M4289-3, 25 August 1944.
55 *Vancouver Sun*, 16 May 1945, 10, and 28 May 1945, 4.
56 Ibid., 22 November 1944, 10, 27 October 1944, 15, and 31 December 1945, 3; CVA, Newspaper Clippings, M4289-3, 28 July 1944.
57 Papers of Frank E. Buck, U87, box 11, file 13, Meeting of the Rehabilitation Section of the Coordinating Council for War Work and Civilian Services, 22 February 1944, Special Collections Division, University of British Columbia Library; ibid., file 15, 'The Citizens' Rehabilitation Council of Greater Vancouver: Summary of Activities, 1940-1948.'
58 For example, Jack Henderson of the Canadian Legion and Major O.L. Erickson and A.W. Cowley of the Rehabilitation Council belonged to the VHA. Moreover, organizations such as the Local Council of Women, Vancouver Labour Council, and town planning commission were represented in both the VHA and the CRCGV; see Papers of Frank E. Buck, U87, box 11, file 13, Meeting of the Rehabilitation Section of the Coordinating Council, Special Collections Division, University of British Columbia Library; and BCARS, Records of the Premier of British Columbia, GR 1222, box 205, file 7, 'Summary of Vancouver Housing Association Activities during 1948.'
59 Papers of Frank E. Buck, U87, box 11, file 15, 'Citizens' Rehabilitation Council: Summary of Activities,' 3, Special Collections Division, University of British Columbia Library; Richard Wilbur, *H.H. Stevens, 1878-1973* (Toronto: University of Toronto Press 1977), 213.
60 NAC, Records of the Privy Council, RG 2, vol. 9, file H-13, A.W. Cowley to W.L.M. King, 22 June 1945; CVA, Newspaper Clippings, M4289-3, 1 August 1944.
61 Papers of the Angus MacInnis Memorial Collection, M397, box 30B, file 8a, *Security with Victory: CCF Manifesto, Dominion General Election, 1945* (Ottawa: National Office of the CCF, 1945), 24-5, Special Collections Division, University of British Columbia Library; British Columbia Post-War Rehabilitation Council, *Reports of the Post-War Rehabilitation Council: The Interim Report (1943) and Supplementary Report (1944)* (Victoria: King's Printer 1945), 150; *Federationist*, 25 March 1943, 4, and 22 April 1943, 4; *CCF News*, 18 January 1945, 4, 16 May 1945, 3, 30 September 1945, 3, and 22 August 1946, 1.
62 *Vancouver Sun*, 27 August 1946, 15.
63 Morton and Wright, *Winning the Second Battle*, 201; *Vancouver Sun*, 11 March 1944, 5, and 11 July 1945, 13; CVA, TPC records, 61-C-6, file 14, E.E. Winch to F. Buck, 16 October 1944; CVA, MO records, 34-C-7, Housing (2), 1947 file, H. Green to G. Miller, 12 May 1947; Papers of the Angus MacInnis Memorial Collection, M397, box 40B, file 10, A. MacInnis to H.E. Winch, 2 December 1949, Special Collections Division, University of British Columbia Library.
64 For Steeves, see *Vancouver Daily Province*, 18 March 1936, 6; *Vancouver Sun*, 2 November 1938, 3; British Columbia Post-War Rehabilitation Council, *Reports*, 166, 199; Joan Sangster, *Dreams of Equality: Women on the Canadian Left, 1920-1950* (Toronto: McClelland and Stewart 1989), passim; and Susan Walsh, 'Equality, Emancipation, and a More Just World: Leading Women in the B.C.C.C.F.' (M.A. thesis, Simon Fraser University 1984), 153-95. For Jamieson,

see Laura E. Jamieson, 'Co-op Living in Vancouver,' *Canadian Forum* 23, 267 (April 1943):18-19; *Federationist*, 1 July 1943, 3; *Vancouver Sun*, 20 January 1948, 2; Sangster, *Dreams of Equality*, passim; Walsh, 'Equality, Emancipation, and a More Just World,' 122-52. For MacInnis, see *CCF News*, 17 February 1944, 1, 16 March 1944, 5, 22 February 1945, 1, 12 April 1945, 3, 7 February 1946, 6, 5 September 1946, 3, and 22 May 1947, 2; *Vancouver Sun*, 11 March 1944, 5, and 11 July 1945, 13; Sangster, *Dreams of Equality*, passim; and Walsh, 'Equality, Emancipation, and a More Just World,' 195-223; and S.P. Lewis, *Grace: The Life of Grace MacInnis* (Madeira Park, BC: Harbour Publishing 1993), passim.

65 Ivan Avakumovic, *The Communist Party in Canada: A History* (Toronto: McClelland and Stewart 1975), 103, 135, 176, 273; *Pacific Advocate*, 25 November 1944, 4, and 18 January 1946, 1, 3. After the Communist party was made illegal in 1940, it regrouped as the LPP.

66 Irving Martin Abella, *Nationalism, Communism, and Canadian Labour: The CIO, the Communist Party, and the Canadian Congress of Labour, 1935-1936* (Toronto: University of Toronto Press 1973), 80, 177-8.

67 *Vancouver Sun*, 26 July 1944, 13, 27 June 1945, 13, 18 September 1946, 6, 25 March 1947, 1, 14 May 1947, 8, 1 December 1947, 7, and 8 December 1947, 3; *Main Deck*, 11 August 1943, 4; *'756' Review*, November 1944, 1, February 1945, 4, and June 1945, 3; CVA, CC records, 26A, Minutes of the building, civic planning, and parks committee, vol. 9, 22 May 1944, 337, 5 June 1944, 339, and 9 April 1945, 382, and vol. 10, 9 July 1945, 3; NAC, RG 19, vol. 716, file 203-17, M.A. Knight to W.L.M. King, 13 June 1945, and telegram from E. Leary to King, 13 July 1945; ibid., vol. 4018, G.W. Caron to King, 6 July 1945; CVA, Newspaper Clippings, M4289-3, 19 August 1944.

68 *Vancouver Sun*, 31 March 1944, 15, and 13 April 1944, 11.

69 CVA, TPC records, 61-C-5, file 8, Minutes of citizens' emergency housing committee, 1 October 1945; *Vancouver Sun*, 2 March 1946, 15, and 25 March 1947, 9. During the war, Stratton, a Seaforth Highlander, had spent six years both in the active services and in the intelligence branch; see CVA, CC records, 19-A-3, file 12, A.T.R. Campbell to city clerk, 17 January 1947; and interview with Stratton, Vancouver, 14 January 1990.

70 VHA, *Housing Vancouver: A Survey of the Housing Position in Vancouver* (Vancouver 1946), 51-6.

71 VHA, *Housing for Our Older Citizens* (Vancouver 1949); idem, *'We, Too, Need Housing!' A Survey of the Housing Needs of Single Girls Employed in Downtown Vancouver* (Vancouver 1951).

72 *Vancouver Sun*, 29 June 1946, 5; Leonard Marsh, *Rebuilding a Neighbourhood* (Vancouver: University of British Columbia 1950).

73 These were the locals of the following: Marine Workers' and Boilermakers' Industrial Union; International Woodworkers of America; United Steelworkers of America; Aeronautical Mechanics' Lodge 756; Dock and Shipyard Workers' Union of Vancouver and District; Retail Clerks' Union; Hotel and Restaurant Employees' Union; Stenographers', Typists', Bookkeepers', and Assistants' Local Union; Sheet Metal Workers' International Association; Boilermakers' and Iron Shipbuilders' Union; and Amalgamated Association of Street and Electric Railway and Motor Coach Employees of America Pioneer Division. See BCARS, Records

of the Premier of British Columbia, GR 1222, box 205, file 7, 'Summary of Vancouver Housing Association Activities during 1948'; Papers of Frank E. Buck, U87, box 11, file 13, Minutes of meeting of the rehabilitation section of the Co-ordinating Council for War Work and Civilian Services in Greater Vancouver, Special Collections Division, University of British Columbia Library; CVA, CC records, 26A, vol. 10, 8 August 1945, 6, and 24 February 1947, 149; ibid., 18-D-3, file 17 [Representations re low-rental housing program]; ibid., file 18, C.W. Caron to C. Jones, 6 July 1945, G.M. Morrison to R. Thompson, 10 July 1945, and E. Tallmann to J.W. Cornett, 25 July 1945; ibid., 19-A-6, file 1, M. MacLeod to city clerk, 21 May 1947; and ibid., 19-A-7, file 14, Resolution from 11th Annual Convention of District Council no. 1, IWA-CIO, [March 1948].

74 These organizations included the following: First United Church; Vancouver Council of Women; University Women's Club of Vancouver; Women's Voluntary Services; Lions' Ladies Club; Women's Christian Temperance Union; Vancouver Council of Jewish Women; Canadian Daughters' League; B'nai B'rith Women; Vancouver Business and Professional Women's Club; Catholic Women's League of Canada; British Columbia Mainland Canadian Association of Social Workers; Family Welfare Bureau of Greater Vancouver; Kinsmen Club of Vancouver; Soroptimist Club; Architectural Institute of British Columbia; British Columbia Medical Association; Foster Day Care Association; Catholic Charities; Greater Vancouver Health League; Junior Chamber of Commerce; United Church Board of Evangelism and Social Service; Vancouver Elementary School Teachers' Association; Victorian Order of Nurses; New Era League; Vancouver Parent-Teacher Federation; Welfare Council of Greater Vancouver; West End Business Girls' Club; Children's Aid Society of Vancouver; Women's International League for Peace and Freedom; Overseas Nursing Sisters Association of Canada; Community Chest and Council of Greater Vancouver; Gordon Neighbourhood House; and Junior Board of Trade. See BCARS, Records of the Premier of British Columbia, GR 1222, box 205, file 7, 'Summary of Vancouver Housing Association Activities during 1948'; ibid., file 4, 'Organizations Represented on the Vancouver Housing Association (as of October 1949)'; CVA, CC records, 18-D-2, file 6, A.M. Morrison to city clerk, 2 July 1945; ibid., 18-E-7, file 1, [Resolutions from various groups supporting a low-rental housing program according to the Curtis report]; ibid., 26A, vol. 9, 6 March 1945, 375-6, vol. 10, 11 June 1946, 78, and 10 June 1947, 189; NAC, RG 19, vol. 716, file 203-17, [Representations from these groups]; and *Vancouver Sun*, 14 July 1943, 1, and 21 August 1943, 20.

75 See J. David Hulchanski, *Canadian Town Planning and Housing, 1940-1950: A Historical Bibliography* (Toronto: Centre for Urban and Community Studies, University of Toronto, 1979); and Allan Moscovitch with Theresa Jennison and Peter Findlay, *The Welfare State in Canada: A Selected Bibliography, 1840 to 1978* (Waterloo: Wilfrid Laurier University Press 1983).

76 NAC, RG 64, box 708, file 25-14-17-1, 'Responsibility for Shelter,' with memorandum from D. Gordon, 7 December 1944.

77 For representations to the federal government, see NAC, RG 19, vol. 716, file 203C-17, and vol. 2730, file 200-2; and *Vancouver Sun*, 29 July 1944, 7, 1 June 1945, 3, 13 June 1945, 1, and 25 June 1945, 10. For representations to the

province, see *Vancouver Sun*, 10 March 1944, 1, 27 June 1945, 1, 2 March 1946, 14, 19 March 1946, 5, and 10 April 1946, 2. For representations to the city, see CVA, CC records, 26A, vol. 9, 6 March 1945, 375-6; and *Vancouver Sun*, 10 March 1944, 1, 6 June 1944, 5, 4 August 1944, 17, and 1 December 1944, 1. For representations from the province to Ottawa, see *Vancouver Sun*, 26 July 1944, 13, and 10 July 1945, 7; and NAC, RG 64, box 701, file 25-2, vol. 1, R.L. Maitland to D. Gordon, 20 July 1944. See also *Vancouver Sun*, 18 July 1943, 1, and 11 March 1944, 5; and the 1944-6 correspondence between Ian Mackenzie, Minister of Veterans Affairs (Pensions and National Health), and J.L. Ilsley, Minister of Finance, in NAC, RG 19, vol. 716, file 203C-17.

78 NAC, RG 64, box 215, file G.05.02; NAC, RG 19, vol. 4017, 'Memorandum Respecting the Housing Situation in Vancouver.'

79 For Donald Gordon's encounter with a critical *Vancouver Sun* editorial, see NAC, RG 19, vol. 716, file 203C-17.

80 NAC, RG 64, box 700, file 25-1-3, Minutes of special meeting, 23 July 1945; *Vancouver Sun*, 27 July 1945, 1; John C. Bacher, 'Keeping to the Private Market: The Evolution of Canadian Housing Policy, 1900-1949' (Ph.D. diss., McMaster University 1985), 400.

81 CVA, CC records, 17-E-7, file 1, G. Buscombe to building, civic planning, and parks committee, 27 August 1941; ibid., 27-D-7, file 28; CVA, CS records, 115-C-3, file 13; *Vancouver Sun*, 29 June 1944, 15.

82 CVA, HD records, 146-B-3, file 8, Minutes of special committee on minimum of housing standards by-law, 26 October 1948; *Vancouver Sun*, 6 January 1948, 2, and 22 March 1949, 13.

83 CVA, CC records, 17-E-7, file 1, A. Haggart to building, civic planning, and parks committee, 5 November 1941; ibid., 28-B-7, file 6, Special committee re requested amendments respecting suites in apartment houses to building, civic planning, and parks committee, 15 February 1945; ibid., 28-C-2, file 10; *Vancouver Sun*, 25 February 1947, 3.

84 CVA, TPC records, 61-C-6, files 13, 14, and 16, and 77-B-5, files 8 and 9.

85 NAC, RG 19, vol. 3390, file 04747H-8, 'The Place of Private Industry in the Post-War Building Programme,' 20 January 1944, and National House Builders' Association Incorporated, *Canada's Stake in House Building* (Toronto [1952]); NAC, RG 19, vol. 3980, Canadian Construction Association brief to the special committee on reconstruction and re-establishment, House of Commons, 25 November 1943, and brief of the Dominion Mortgage and Investments Association, 24 February 1944; BCARS, Records of the Premier of British Columbia, GR 1222, box 201, file 2, BC Building Contractors' Association, 20 November 1948; ibid., box 205, file 5, Canadian Construction Association, 'A Statement on Lower Cost Housing for Canadians,' 29 July 1949; CVA, CC records, 28-D-3, file 6, Proposals from BC Building Contractors' Association housing committee, 16 June 1947; ibid., 26A, vol. 9, 19 April 1943, 288-9, [Resolutions from Mortgage and Trust Companies Association of BC and from 123 builders and contractors re WHL construction in Vancouver]; CVA, MO records, 34-C-3, Housing, 1946 file, telegram from BC Lumber Survey Limited to D.D. Rosenberry, [1946]; ibid., 34-C-7, Housing (1), 1947 file, 'Brief Presented February 5, 1947, by President G.L. Monahan'; ibid., 34-E-2, Housing, 1949 file, [Resolutions from BC Building

Contractors' Association, 1949]; CVA, TPC records, 61-C-5, file 5, 'Associated Property Owners of Vancouver, Incorporated, News Memo, No. 3,' December 1946; *Vancouver Sun*, 15 March 1944, 13, 20 October 1944, 24, 28 June 1945, 1, 18 March 1949, 14, and 2 May 1949, 12.

86 CVA, CS records, 115-C-3, file 9, 'A Plan to Build 1000 Low Cost Homes in Vancouver Annually,' [1942]; CVA, Photograph Collection, 163-1.

87 CVA, TPC records, 77-B-5, file 7, 'Memo re Housing Committee,' [January 1941], A.J. Harrison to G. Buscombe, 8 January 1941, and minutes of meeting to consider housing conditions, 15 April 1941; ibid., 77-B-6, file 4, Minutes of housing committee, Vancouver Council of Social Agencies, 25 September 1941.

88 Irene Howard, *The Struggle for Social Justice in British Columbia: Helena Gutteridge, the Unknown Reformer* (Vancouver: UBC Press 1992), 214-39.

89 CVA, CC records, 17-F-3, file 1, M. Jackson to city clerk, 9 April 1941; ibid., 18-A-4, file 16, B. Friesen to city council, 31 August 1942 and 2 November 1942; ibid., 77-B-6, file 4, F. Howlett to Harrison, 2 February 1942; Sangster, *Dreams of Equality*, 139, 173, 178-9, 185-8.

90 For the '5000 Homes Now!' committee, see CVA, CC records, 26A, vol. 9, 6 March 1944, 328, and 20 March 1944, 329; *Vancouver Sun*, 1 March 1944, 13, 6 March 1944, 11, 7 March 1944, 13, 16 March 1944, 13, 21 March 1944, 13, 24 March 1944, 17, 11 April 1944, 13, 13 April 1944, 11, and 20 September 1944, 15; Papers of the Angus MacInnis Memorial Collection, M397, box 40B, file 9, J. McPeake to [A. MacInnis], 13 March 1944, and minutes of '5000 Homes Now!' committee executive, 23 March 1944, Special Collections Division, University of British Columbia Library; and NAC, RG 19, vol. 716, file 203C-17, McPeake to W.L.M. King, 19 April 1944, with attached 'Submissions on behalf of the "5000 Homes Now!" Committee.' For the citizens' emergency housing committee, see *Vancouver Sun*, 9 December 1944, 15, 1 June 1945, 3, 15 June 1945, 26, 21 June 1945, 11, and 23 June 1945, 15; UCA, Dobson papers, B7, file R, Minutes of [Welfare Council of Greater Vancouver] housing committee, 3 May 1944; and CVA, TPC records, 61-C-5, file 8, Minutes [of Welfare Council], 30 May 1945, and minutes of citizens' emergency housing committee, 18 June 1945, 25 June 1945, 20 July 1945, 17 August 1945, and 1 October 1945.

91 By 1 May, about 300 notices had accumulated. Between July and October, there were 704; see NAC, RG 64, vol. 29, 'Canadian Rental and Eviction Controls, World War II and the Post-War Years,' 43, 49-50; UCA, Dobson papers, B7, file R, 'Monthly Report, National Housing Registry,' April 1944; and *Vancouver Sun*, 25 August 1944, 17.

92 NAC, RG 64, vol. 29, 'Canadian Rental and Eviction Controls, World War II and the Post-War Years,' 43, 45-6, 47.

93 *Vancouver Sun*, 26 July 1944, 13, 29 July 1944, 7, 4 August 1944, 17, 18 August 1944, 1, and 19 August 1944, 17; CVA, Newspaper Clippings, M4289-3, 25 and 28 August 1944.

94 NAC, RG 64, box 701, file 25-2, vol. 1, R.L. Maitland to D. Gordon, 20 July 1944; ibid., vol. 2, Maitland to J.L. Ilsley, 7 September 1944, and Ilsley to Maitland, 28 September 1944.

95 Firestone, *Residential Real Estate in Canada*, 498; NAC, RG 2, Ser. 4, P.C. 9439, 19 December 1944, and P.C. 1173, 22 February 1945; NAC, RG 64, vol. 708, file

25-14-18-1, WPTB Press Release no. 01026, 23 December 1944; ibid., file 25-14, D. Gordon to A.G.L. McNaughton, 26 December 1944; NAC, RG 19, vol. 363, file 101-102-1-1, J.L. Ilsley to J. Hart, 22 December 1944; ibid., vol. 3980, Housing file, Gordon to I. Mackenzie, 10 April 1945; *Vancouver Sun*, 23 December 1944, 9.

96 *Vancouver Sun*, 9 January 1945, 1.

97 CVA, Newspaper Clippings, M4289-3, 23 December 1944; ibid., M4289-4, 5 January 1945 and 15 February 1945; *Vancouver Sun*, 16 February 1945, 5.

98 CVA, Newspaper Clippings, M4289-4, 10 January 1945, and M8921, 28 September 1945; NAC, Records of CMHC, RG 56, vol. 17, file 105-10, vol. 2, L.F. Stevenson to D.G. Mackenzie, 7 April 1945, with attached letter, Stevenson to Air Officer Commanding, Western Air Command, 7 April 1945; *Vancouver Sun*, 26 August 1944, 15.

99 NAC, RG 19, vol. 4017, 'Memorandum Respecting the Housing Situation in Vancouver,' 1 May 1945; NAC, RG 64, vol. 700, file 25-1-3, Minutes of special WPTB meeting, 23 July 1945, appendix A, 2; *Vancouver Sun*, 25 August 1944, 17, and 23 July 1945, 1. For LPP rallies, see ibid., 5 June 1945, 13, 14 July 1945, 3, 17 July 1945, 8, and 18 July 1945, 13. For CCF rallies, see ibid., 10 July 1945, 3, 11 July 1945, 13, and 13 July 1945, 8.

100 NAC, RG 64, box 700, file 25-1-3, 'Minutes of special meeting of July 23, 1945'; Canada, WPTB, *Canadian War Orders and Regulations*, vol. 7 (1945), order no. 537.

101 *Vancouver Sun*, 13 August 1947, 6, 21 August 1947, 2, 14 February 1949, 1, 14 March 1946, 11, 20 March 1946, 3, 27 March 1946, 1, and 1 May 1946, 6.

102 Bacher, 'Keeping to the Private Market,' 457-8, 482-3; Canada, Houses of Commons, *Debates*, 1944, vol. 3, 2425; NAC, RG 83, vol. 70, Minutes, vol. 1, Minutes of WHL directors, 10 May 1944; NAC, RG 2, vol. 9, file H-13, 'Report for Interdepartmental Housing Committee by Mr. Jas. A. Hall Representing Wartime Housing Ltd.'; Firestone, *Residential Real Estate in Canada*, 488, table 109.

103 *Vancouver Sun*, 11 July 1944, 1, 1 August 1944, 13, 3 August 1944, 19, 4 August 1944, 17, 5 December 1944, 11, 20 March 1945, 9, and 8 June 1945, 1; Agreements between the City of Vancouver, H.M. the King in right of Canada, and WHL, 25 September 1944 and 1 July 1945, located in the city clerk's department, City of Vancouver; CVA, CC records, 28-A-1, file 52, Minutes of special committee for wartime housing, 2 August 1944; ibid., 28-B-7, file 42, city clerk to C.D. Howe, 18 August 1945.

104 CVA, CC records, 28-A-1, file 52, C.H. Thorn to special committee, 13 July 1944, E.D. Fletcher to special committee, 20 July 1944, and A. Darlington to city clerk, 17 July 1944; ibid., 24A, vol. 47, 14 August 1944, 358; CVA, Newspaper Clippings, M4289-3, 2 August 1944; *Vancouver Sun*, 17 July 1944, 9, 26 July 1944, 13, 3 August 1944, 2, 11 August 1944, 4, 15 August 1944, 13, and 14 December 1944, 1.

105 *Vancouver Sun*, 1 December 1944, 1, 5 December 1944, 11, 20 March 1945, 1, 29 May 1945, 9, and 1 June 1945, 3.

106 CVA, FD records, 98-C-6, file 3, telegram from C.D. Howe to W.L. Woodford, 26 July 1945; CVA, CC records, 24 A, vol. 48, 26 July 1945, 809; Agreement between the City, H.M. the King in right of Canada, and WHL, 1 September 1945, located

in the city clerk's department, City of Vancouver; *Vancouver Sun*, 25 July 1945, 1, 26 July 1945, 2, 7 August 1945, 11, and 14 August 1945, 9.

107 *Vancouver Sun*, 7 September 1944, 5; CVA, Newspaper Clippings, M4289-5, 22 May 1945; CVA, Photograph Collection, 150-1, CMHC's album of photographs and plans of WHL housing in Vancouver and Victoria, [1941].

108 CVA, CC records, 28-B-7, file 28, L. Stevenson to mayor, 20 June 1945.

109 Ibid., Stevenson to Mayor, 16 July 1945; NAC, RG 19, vol. 728, file 203-CMHC-1, 'Report on a Survey of Emergency Shelter Tenants (November 1946-February 1947)'; CVA, SSD records, 106-A-6, file 3, and, in particular, city clerk to J.I. Chambers, 9 August 1945; *Vancouver Sun*, 4 September 1946, 1-2, and 9 February 1949, 26.

110 Jill Wade, '"A Palace for the Public": Housing Reform and the 1946 Occupation of the Old Hotel Vancouver,' in *Vancouver Past: Essays in Social History*, ed. R.A.J. McDonald and Jean Barman (Vancouver: University of British Columbia Press 1986), 288-310.

111 NAC, RG 19, vol. 716, file 203C-17, vol. 1, L.F. Stevenson to D.G. Mackenzie, 16 March 1945, and memorandum re 'Vancouver Hotel' by Eric Gold, 14 February 1946.

112 Ibid., file 203C-17; CVA, CC records, 28-C-1, file 4, and 28-C-4, file 18.

113 NAC, RG 19, vol. 716, file 203C-17; *Vancouver Sun*, 31 December 1945, 3, and 5 January 1946, 1-2; see BCARS, Records of the Premier of British Columbia, GR 1222, box 113, file 17 for representations to the provincial government during the occupation of the old hotel.

114 For accounts of the occupation, see the *Vancouver Sun*, the *Vancouver Daily Province*, and the *News-Herald* from 28 January to 1 February 1946; *Pacific Advocate*, 1 February 1946; Paddy Sherman, *Bennett* (Toronto: McClelland and Stewart 1966), 51; and Barry Broadfoot, *The Veterans' Years: Coming Home from the War* (Vancouver and Toronto: Douglas and McIntyre 1985), 66-8.

115 *Vancouver Sun*, 28 January 1946, 1. The committee's members were aligned with the Liberals (2), the Conservatives (2), the CCF (2), the LPP (1), and the Social Credit (1).

116 Ibid., 1, 2.

117 NAC, RG 19, vol. 716, file 203C-17, vol. 1, Telegram from I. Mackenzie to J.L. Ilsley, 29 January 1946.

118 CVA, CC records, 28-C-3, file 14, Minutes of air raid precaution committee, 29 January 1946.

119 *Vancouver Sun*, 15 February 1946, 12, 18 February 1946, 1, 29 March 1946, 15, 30 April 1946, 7, 25 October 1946, 3, 29 May 1947, 1, 14 February 1948, 1, 24 December 1948, 15, and 1 February 1949, 13; CVA, MO records, 34-C-7, Housing (1), 1947 file, 'Occupation of Old Vancouver Hotel and Dunsmuir Hotel,' 2 July 1947; ibid., 34-D-5, Housing, 1948 file, H.H. Stevens to city council, 11 August 1948; NAC, RG 19, vol. 728, file 203-CMHC-1, 'Report on a Survey of Emergency Shelter Tenants (November 1946-February 1947).'

120 *Vancouver Sun*, 25 September 1946, 6, 2 October 1946, 2, 7 November 1946, 11, 24 August 1949, 21, 6 June 1950, 7, and 8 June 1950, 7; CVA, CC records, 18-E-7, file 2, A.W. Cowley to city clerk, 5 October 1946; CVA, MO records, 34-C-7, Housing (1), 1947 file, 'Occupation of Old Vancouver Hotel and Dunsmuir

Hotel,' 2 July 1947.

121 *Vancouver Sun*, 30 May 1946, 9, 31 May 1946, 9, 1 June 1946, 9, 7 November 1946, 1, 8 November 1946, 1, 30 May 1947, 6, 2 June 1947, 1, 21 June 1947, 2, 25 June 1947, 13, and 11 July 1947, 7. In July 1947, CRCGV officers estimated that twenty of 500 tenant households were on rent strike.

122 Ibid., 21 June 1947, 2, and 25 June 1947, 13.

123 Ibid., 9 November 1946, 3, and 25 February 1947, 8; Papers of Frank E. Buck, U87, box 11, file 15, 'The Citizens' Rehabilitation Council of Greater Vancouver: Summary of Activities, 1940-1948,' Special Collections Division, University of British Columbia Library.

124 *Vancouver Sun*, 7 May 1947, 26, 14 May 1947, 6; CVA, CC records, 28-C-6, file 16, Minutes of special council meeting, 18 September 1946; ibid., 28-D-4, file 44, J.A. Jones to G. McGeer, 8 April 1947. For the lengthy negotiations between the city, Howe, and CMHC over the construction of more veterans' rental units in Vancouver and for the final agreement, see CVA, MO records, 34-C-7, Housing, 1947 file.

125 *Vancouver Sun*, 19 April 1947, 1; CVA, MO records, 34-C-7, Housing (2), 1947 file, H. Green to G. Miller, 12 May 1947.

126 *Vancouver Sun*, 3 June 1947, 1; David Ricardo Williams, *Mayor Gerry: The Remarkable Gerald Grattan McGeer* (Vancouver and Toronto: Douglas and McIntyre 1986), 287.

127 *Vancouver Sun*, 9 October 1947, 1, 18 October 1947, 5, and 6 December 1947, 30.

128 Ibid., 14 February 1947, 1, 2, 10 March 1947, 1, and 27 May 1949, 9; CVA, CC records, 28-D-3, file 8, for negotiations over the Bremerton scheme.

129 CVA, MO records, 34-C-7, Housing (1), 1947 file, A.E. McKay to G. McGeer, 12 April 1947, H.W. Purcell to McGeer, 2 May 1947, McGeer to J. Price, 7 May 1947, telegram from J. Henderson to McGeer, 13 May 1947, and J.C.G. Herwig to mayor, 3 June 1947; ibid., Housing (2), 1947 file, H. Green to G. Miller, 12 May 1947; *Vancouver Sun*, 14 February 1947, 1, 2, 1 April 1947, 9, 2 April 1947, 4, 5 May 1947, 1, 2 May 1947, 32, 2 June 1947, 1, and 13 June 1947, 3; Jill Wade, 'The "Sting" of Vancouver's Better Housing "Spree," 1919-1949,' *UHR* 21 (March 1993):92-103.

130 *Vancouver Sun*, 4 September 1947, 3, 9 October 1947, 7, 13 February 1948, 17, and 21 July 1948, 3.

131 CVA, CC records, 28-D-3, file 6, city clerk to special committee re housing, 25 November 1947; CVA, Newspaper Clippings, M7913, 13 July 1948 and 2 October 1948; Carver, *Compassionate Landscape*, 110-1; S.A. Gitterman, 'An Old Challenge,' in Canada Mortgage and Housing Corporation, *Housing a Nation: 40 Years of Achievement/Un toit pour tous: quarante années de réalisations* (Ottawa: CMHC, [1986]), 81-8; *Vancouver Sun*, 12 July 1948, 9, and 21 July 1948, 17.

132 At the time, Bob McEwen, a leader in the old hotel occupation, asserted that Vancouver's veterans had set a pattern for squatters' movements around the world; see *Vancouver Sun*, 31 December 1946, 11. See also ibid., 9 September 1946, 1, 10 September 1946, 3, 11 September 1946, 12, 12 September 1946, 1, 13 September 1946, 3, 14 September 1946, 2, 18 September 1946, 1, and 19 September 1946, 1.

133 Ibid., 20 September 1946, 4.

134 CVA, CC records, 18-E-7, file 2, A. Morison to city council, 30 October 1946, H. Rush to city clerk, 27 September 1946, and R. McNicol to mayor and council, 14 September 1946.

135 *Vancouver Sun*, 21 September 1946, 1, 2, 23 September 1946, 3, 25 September 1946, 1, 28 September 1946, 30, 1 October 1946, 9, and 5 October 1946, 12; Marc H. Choko, *Crises du logement à Montréal (1860-1939)* (Montréal: Éditions coopératives Albert Saint-Martin 1980), appendix B, 167; CVA, CC records, 28-E-3, file 29, R. Young to city council, 15 March 1949, B. Marsh to R. Thompson, 3 May 1949, Minutes of special committee re taxes, Little Mountain Camp, 8 April 1949, and 'Increased Taxation at Little Mountain Camp,' 1949; NAC, RG 19, file 728, file 203-CMHC-1, 'Report on a Survey of Emergency Shelter Tenants (November 1946-February 1947).'

136 CMHC, *Annual Report* (1946), 7, and (1947), 57, table 17. The University of British Columbia had completed 301 units by 1947. See also *Vancouver Sun*, 5 February 1946, 2, and 20 September 1946, 15; P.B. Waite, *Lord of Point Grey: Larry MacKenzie of U.B.C.* (Vancouver: University of British Columbia Press 1987), 124-6; Augusta Margaret Thomasson, 'Acadia Camp: A Study of the Acadia Camp Residence at the University of British Columbia from September, 1945 to May, 1949' (M.S.W. thesis, University of British Columbia 1951); and Lee Stewart, *It's Up to You: Women at UBC in the Early Years* (Vancouver: University of British Columbia Press for the UBC Academic Women's Association 1990), 84-7.

137 CVA, CC records, 28-D-6, file 1, and 28-D-7, file 11, for records of the funding arrangements for Seaforth Village; CVA, MO records, 34-D-5, Housing, 1948 file, Minutes of finance committee meeting, 26 May 1948.

138 *Vancouver Sun*, 20 November 1948, 17, 22 November 1948, 15, 23 November 1948, 12, 1 December 1948, 2, and 11 December 1948, 26; Thomasson, 'Acadia Camp,' 3-4.

139 *Vancouver Sun*, 24 November 1948, 25, 25 November 1948, 12, 26 November 1948, 32, 30 November 1948, 26, 19 January 1949, 5, and 19 February 1949, 5.

140 Ibid., 7 May 1948, 1; CVA, FD records, 93-F-7, file 6.

141 CVA, Newspaper Clippings, M3335-1, 20 September 1948, and 16 November 1948.

142 *Vancouver Sun*, 11 February 1949, 1, 15 February 1949, 1, 18 February 1949, 9, 19 May 1949, 1, 3, 21 May 1949, 3, and 3 June 1949, 21; CVA, Newspaper Clippings, M3335-1, 11 February 1949, 15 February 1949, 18 February 1949, and 17 June 1949; CVA, FD records, 93-B-2, file 1, T. Flanagan to chair and members of personnel committee, 25 February 1949. Other companies subsequently received contracts; see CVA, Newspaper Clippings, M3335-1, 29 September 1950.

143 CVA, Newspaper Clippings, M3335-1, 17 December 1949, 19 December 1949, and 20 December 1949; *Vancouver Sun*, 19 December 1949, 27.

144 CVA Newspaper Clippings, M3335-1, 12 January 1950, and 29 September 1950; Canada, CMHC, *Small House Designs*, 3 vols. (Ottawa: King's Printer 1949); Harold Kalman, Ron Phillips, and Robin Ward, *Exploring Vancouver: The Essential Architectural Guide* (Vancouver: UBC Press 1993), 204, #435.

145 CVA, Newspaper Clippings, M3335-1, 4 April 1951; *Vancouver Sun*, 3 April 1951, 1, 4 April 1951, 2, 8 May 1951, 18, 8 June 1951, 16, 20 September 1951, 21, 29 October 1951, 17, 16 February 1952, 21, and 9 July 1952, 15.

146 CVA, Newspaper Clippings, M3335-1, 9 July 1952; *Vancouver Sun*, 10 October 1953, 11.

147 CVA, TPC records, 61-C-6, file 14, E.E. Winch to F. Buck, 16 October 1944.

148 CVA, CC records, 28-A-1, file 54, [records re New Vista Society's proposed boardinghouse], 1944; Papers of E.E. Winch, Angus MacInnis Memorial Collection, M397, box 55A, file 19, [speech on the New Vista Society], n.d., Special Collections Division, University of British Columbia Library; ibid., file 26, [Papers re New Vista Society's seniors' housing, ca. 1952-6], Special Collections Division, University of British Columbia Library; ibid., box 40B, file 9, 'E.E. Winch's "New Vista",' Special Collections Division, University of British Columbia Library; VHA, *Houses for All: Proceedings of the Housing Conference ... Sponsored by the Vancouver Housing Association* (Vancouver 1954), 28-31; Dorothy Jean Barberie, 'The "New Vista": A Housing Project, Burnaby, B.C.: A Review of Its Welfare and Administrative Experience, 1949-59,' (M.S.W. thesis, University of British Columbia 1959); *Vancouver Sun*, 2 June 1949, 19, 28 September 1950, 19, 18 January 1951, 19, 19 January 1951, 21, 23 July 1953, 19, 14 December 1953, 12, 14 July 1954, 16, 9 July 1955, 8, and 15 September 1955, 10.

149 Patricia Louise Sharp, 'Housing Projects for Old People: An Exploratory Review of Four Selected Housing Projects for Old People in the Greater Vancouver Area' (M.S.W. thesis, University of British Columbia 1957), 22-6.

150 UCA, Dobson papers, box 15, files 9 and 11B; Sharp, 'Housing Projects for Old People,' 14-17; *Vancouver Sun*, 14 January 1954, 15, and 21 January 1955, 15; CVA, TPC records, 61-C-6, file 15, 'The Fair Haven United Church Homes for Senior Citizens' (1951).

151 *Vancouver Sun*, 18 February 1947, 9, 20 May 1947, 9, and 9 January 1948, 17.

152 CVA, CC records, 18-D-2, file 6, G.V. Pelton to city council, 7 December 1945; ibid., 18-E-7, file 1, R. Knox to mayor and council, 25 February 1946, and J.V. Anderson to R. Thompson, 13 February 1946; ibid., 19-B-4, file 11, J. Davidson to chair, social services committee, 22 April 1948; ibid., 28-C-1, file 24, [Communications with Senior Citizens' Homes Association], 1945-7; *Vancouver Sun*, 29 May 1947, 26.

153 NAC, RG 64, vol. 29, 'Canadian Rental and Eviction Controls, World War II and the Post War Years,' 59-67; NAC, RG 19, vol. 3393, file W-2-3, 'Memorandum to the Cabinet: re: Rental Control,' 8 March 1950; BCARS, Records of the Premier of British Columbia, GR1222, box 114, file 6, D.C. Abbott to B. Johnson, 9 November 1949; British Columbia, Legislative Assembly, *Sessional Papers*, 1956, vol. 2, Department of Labour, '[Annual Report, 1954]; Report of the Activities of the Rentals Control Branch,' H156-57; *Vancouver Sun*, 1 March 1950, 1.

154 *Vancouver Sun*, 6 November 1946, 24.

155 BCARS, Records of the Premier of British Columbia, GR 1222, box 114, file 6, D.C. Abbott to premier, 23 October 1948.

156 *Vancouver Sun*, 25 November 1949, 1, and 9 December 1949, 27.

157 Ibid., 14 October 1949, 1, 26 January 1950, 10, and 1 March 1950, 1.

158 Ibid., 25 October 1949, 14, 4 November 1949, 1, 2, 6 December 1949, 8, 7 January 1950, 38, and 1 March 1950, 1; CVA, MO records, 34-F-1, Housing, 1950 file, H. Stevens to C. Thompson, 23 December 1949; CVA, TPC records, 61-C-5, file 5, Associated Property Owners of Vancouver, *News Memo*, no. 3 (December 1946);

BCARS, Records of the Premier of British Columbia, GR 1222, box 201, file 2, [Resolution from British Columbia Command, Canadian Legion], 25 January 1949; ibid., box 205, file 8, telegram from N. Morgan to B. Johnson, 17 November 1949, Mrs. M.I.F. Carver to G. Wismer, [November 1949], J. Morton to Johnson, 2 December 1945, J. Rockandel to Johnson, 28 November 1949, A.E. Craddock to Johnson, 26 November 1949, telegram from F. Collins to Johnson, 14 December 1949, D.A. Wade to Johnson, 20 December 1948, E.G. Reid to Johnson, 29 December 1949, and telegram from VHA to Johnson, 14 December 1949; ibid., box 223, file 3, Mrs. T.S. Paton to Johnson, 6 January 1950, G.H. Mitchell to Johnson, 3 February 1950. Many individual citizens wrote to the premier on the rent control issue as well, and their representations may be found in the premier's papers cited in this note.

159 *Vancouver Sun*, 24 March 1950, 1.

160 British Columbia, Legislative Assembly, '[Annual Report, 1954]; Report of the Activities of the Rentals Control Branch'; *Vancouver Sun*, 12 April 1954, 21.

161 Papers of the Angus MacInnis Memorial Collection, M397, box 55A, file 26, VHA *Bulletin*, no. 26 (March 1955), Special Collections Division, University of British Columbia Library.

162 *Vancouver Sun*, 21 May 1947, 9. See also Papers of Leonard Marsh, U184, Special Collections Division, University of British Columbia Library, for more on Marsh's life at this time.

163 *Vancouver Sun*, 15 February 1947, 13, 28 March 1947, 13, 17 September 1947, 19, 26 February 1948, 17, and 24 November 1948, 17.

164 Ibid., 21 May 1947, 9, and 23 September 1947, 28. See also CVA, TPC records, 61-C-6, file 14, 'University of British Columbia Demonstration Housing Survey, May 1947,' 'University of British Columbia Demonstration Housing Survey; Progress Report – 31 July 1947,' and 'University of British Columbia Demonstration Housing Survey; Interim Report, 30 July 1947.' The report that emerged from the survey is Marsh's *Rebuilding a Neighbourhood*.

165 UCA, Dobson papers, box 7, file S, Clipping from *Vancouver Daily Province*, 4 November 1948.

166 NAC, RG 19, vol. 716, file 203C-17, R. Thompson to J.L. Ilsley, 10 January 1946.

167 CVA, Papers of H.D. Wilson, Add. Mss. 362, vol. 33, file 9, Wilson to building, civic planning, and parks committee, 13 December 1948; Wilson chaired the civic housing committee after 1948. See also *Vancouver Sun*, 28 March 1947, 7, 20 September 1947, 1, 2, 20 January 1948, 2, 15 December 1948, 9, and 23 August 1949, 11.

168 CVA, Newspaper Clippings, M4289-1, 17 February 1938.

169 BCARS, Records of the Premier of British Columbia, GR 1222, box 259, file 2, Radio speech by Johnson on 'Provincial Affairs,' 16 February 1948.

170 CVA, MO records, 34-C-7, Housing (4), 1947 file, J.A. Allan to C. Jones, 18 July 1947 and 4 September 1947; ibid., 34-E-2, Housing, 1949 file, 'A Proposed Outline for National Low-Rent Housing Legislation Submitted by the Canadian Federation of Mayors and Municipalities to the Federal Government at the Request of the Rt. Hon. C.D. Howe, Minister of Reconstruction,' 17 September 1947; ibid., 34-D-5, Housing, 1948 file, VHA secretary to Howe, 18 May 1948; Albert Rose, *Regent Park: A Study in Slum Clearance* (Toronto: University of Toronto

Press 1958), 46-60; Carver, *Compassionate Landscape*, 82-4.

171 *Vancouver Sun*, 20 January 1948, 2, 28 January 1948, 17, 21 April 1948, 21, 24 November 1948, 17, and 15 December 1948, 9; CVA, Papers of H.D. Wilson, Add. Mss. 362, vol. 33, file 9, Wilson to building, civic planning, and parks committee, 13 December 1948.

172 *Vancouver Sun*, 23 March 1949, 4, 4 May 1949, 17, 18 May 1949, 1, 28 May 1949, 13, and 9 June 1949, 5. Oscar Erickson was the father of internationally renowned architect Arthur Erickson; for more on Oscar Erickson, see Edith Iglauer, *Seven Stones: A Portrait of Arthur Erickson, Architect* (Madeira Park, BC, and Seattle: Harbour Publishing and University of Washington Press 1981), 36-42.

173 NAC, RG 19, vol. 358, file 135-0-167, D.B. Mansur to R.H. Winters, 29 June 1949; ibid., vol. 3439, Housing file, M.W. Sharp to D.C. Abbott, 30 August 1949; BCARS, Records of the Premier of British Columbia, GR 1222, box 115, file 11, Winters to Johnson, 13 September 1949.

174 *Vancouver Sun*, 29 July 1949, 1, 2, 30 July 1949, 1, 1 August 1949, 10, 5 August 1949, 1, 6 August 1949, 2, 9 August 1949, 1, 2, 15 August 1949, 1, 27, 16 August 1949, 1, 30 August 1949, 1, 8 September 1949, 10, 9 September 1949, 30, 21 September 1949, 1, 23 September 1949, 47, 1 November 1949, 32, 22 November 1949, 1, 25 November 1949, 59, and 8 December 1949, 21; BCARS, Records of the Premier of British Columbia, GR 1222, box 205, file 4, 'Memorandum of Discussions at the Meetings with the British Columbia Municipalities, Victoria – December 12th and 13th, 1949,' 20 December 1949.

175 *Vancouver Sun*, 12 December 1949, 17; BCARS, Records of the Premier of British Columbia, GR 1222, box 264, file 1, 'Press Release,' 12 December 1949.

176 *Vancouver Sun*, 12 April 1950, 4, 14 April 1950, 1, 18 April 1950, 13, 17 May 1950, 1-2, and 25 May 1950, 19.

177 CVA, FD records, 93-F-7, file 5, [Agreement between the City of Vancouver, H.M. the King in right of British Columbia, and CMHC, 1 November 1950]; *Vancouver Sun*, 15 November 1950, 9, and 30 November 1950, 21.

178 *Vancouver Sun*, 8 August 1951, 17.

179 Ibid., 15 January 1952, 13, and 29 January 1952, 3; *Vancouver Daily Province*, 15 January 1952, 5, and 29 January 1952, 13.

180 CVA, CC records, 28-F-5, file 33, T.B. Pickersgill to A. Proctor, 4 June 1952, and minutes of the building and town planning committee, 13 November 1952. T.B. (Tom) Pickersgill was the brother of J.W. (Jack) Pickersgill, a Liberal Cabinet minister in the Louis St. Laurent and L.B. Pearson governments.

181 *Vancouver Sun*, 5 September 1952, 3, 26 September 1952, 25, 4 November 1952, 19, 21 November 1952, 17, 4 February 1953, 19, 17 February 1953, 8, 28 May 1953, 8, 24 June 1953, 13, and 22 July 1953, 9.

182 Ibid., 22 August 1951, 4, 16 January 1952, 14, 12 November 1952, 25, 15 November 1952, 4, 15, 10 February 1953, 15, 27 May 1953, 25, 28 May 1953, 23, 24 June 1953, 13, and 25 June 1953, 18; *Vancouver Province*, 15 November 1952, 1, 12 June 1953, 6, and 18 June 1953, 6.

183 *Vancouver Sun*, 15 May 1953, 1, 26 May 1953, 2, and 16 June 1953, 3.

184 Ibid., 29 July 1953, 6; Michael Wheeler, 'Evaluating the Need for Low-Rental Housing: A Review of Conditions among Family Applications for Little Mountain Low-Rental Housing Project, Vancouver, and Consideration of Criteria for Future

Housing Projects' (M.S.W. thesis, University of British Columbia 1955), appendix A.

185 *Vancouver Province*, 14 August 1953, 2; *Vancouver Sun*, 1 April 1954, 26, and 20 May 1955, 2; Papers of the Vancouver Council of Women, M657, box 4, file 11, Vancouver Housing Authority, *Report* (1954), Special Collections Division, University of British Columbia Library.

186 Wheeler, 'Evaluating the Need for Low-Rental Housing,' 81-3, 98, and appendix A.

187 CVA, TPC records, 78-B-5, Housing – Low Rental, 1955 file, W.A.C. Bennett to G. Sutton-Brown, 9 November 1955.

188 CVA, CC records, 20-D-6, file 11, J.I. Chambers to A. Sprott, 12 April 1954; BCARS, Records of the British Columbia Housing Commissioner, GR 1000, box 1, file 4, Vancouver Housing Authority, *Report* (1959), 3.

189 Choko, *Crises du logement à Montréal*, appendix B, 165-81; Merrily Weisbord, *The Strangest Dream: Canadian Communists, the Spy Trials, and the Cold War* (Toronto: Lester and Orpen Dennys 1983), 179-80.

190 See notes 73 and 74; Joseph Melling, *Rent Strikes: People's Struggle for Housing in West Scotland, 1890-1916* (Edinburgh: Polygon Books 1983); idem, 'Clydeside Housing and the Evolution of State Rent Control, 1900-1939,' in *Housing, Social Policy, and the State*, ed. Joseph Melling (London: Croom Helm 1980), 139-67; and Sean Damer, 'State, Class, and Housing: Glasgow, 1885-1919,' in *Housing*, ed. Melling, 73-112.

191 Roy Lubove, *The Progressives and the Slums: Tenement House Reform in New York, 1890-1917* (Pittsburgh: University of Pittsburgh Press 1962); Gareth Stedman Jones, *Outcast London: A Study in the Relationship between Classes in Victorian Society* (Oxford: Clarendon Press 1971).

192 CVA, Newspaper Clippings, M8921, passim.

193 CVA, CC records, 28-C-6, file 16, Minutes of special meeting of council, 18 September 1946; CVA, FD records, 113-A-11, WHL Journal, 1948-64; CMHC, *Annual Report* (1947), 15, 45, table 45; *Vancouver Sun*, 25 August 1948, 6.

194 CMHC, *Annual Report* (1947), 15-16, 19, and (1950), 72, table 14; *Vancouver Sun*, 26 April 1947, 1, 7 May 1947, 13, 11 June 1947, 13, 11 October 1947, 17, 17 October 1947, 17, 18 October 1947, 5, 17, 22 October 1947, 17, 24 October 1947, 17, 30 October 1947, 17, 1 November 1947, 15, 4 November 1947, 13, 18 November 1947, 15, 2 December 1947, 13, 12 December 1947, 1, 7 February 1948, 17, and 10 March 1948, 17; CVA, FD records, 98-C-6, file 2, R.S. Wells to T. Trent, 5 December 1968, and Wells to Trent, 6 July 1967; ibid., 113-A-11, WHL Journal, 1948-64.

195 Carver, *Compassionate Landscape*, 109-10.

196 Bacher, 'W.C. Clark and the Politics of Canadian Housing Policy, 1935-52,' 5-13; Wade, 'Wartime Housing Limited,' 53-6.

Chapter 6: Conclusion

1 Anthony Sutcliffe, 'Why Planning History?' *Built Environment* 7, 2 (1981):65. According to Sutcliffe, 'history allows the planner [and housing specialist] to take his [or her] bearings, to establish new objectives and to map out routes towards them.'

2 UCA, Papers of Hugh Dobson, B7, file S, 'Housing Vancouver: A Survey of the Housing Position in Vancouver by the Vancouver Housing Association,' August 1939.

3 For a summary of the debate, see Arthur J. Taylor, ed., *The Standard of Living in the Industrial Revolution* (London: Methuen 1975), xi-iv.

4 Terry Copp, *The Anatomy of Poverty: The Condition of the Working Class in Montreal, 1897-1929* (Toronto: McClelland and Stewart 1974), 70-87; Michael J. Piva, *The Condition of the Working Class in Toronto, 1900-1921*, Cahiers d'histoire no. 9 (Ottawa: University of Ottawa Press 1979), 125-42. See also Eleanor Bartlett, 'Real Wages and the Standard of Living in Vancouver, 1901-1929,' *BC Studies* 51 (Autumn 1981):8; and W. Peter Ward and Patricia C. Ward, 'Infant Birth Weight and Nutrition in Industrializing Montreal,' *American Historical Review* 89, 2 (April 1984):324-45.

5 John Douglas Belshaw, 'The Standard of Living of British Miners on Vancouver Island,' *BC Studies* 84 (Winter 1989-90):63.

6 Bettina Bradbury, 'Pigs, Cows, and Boarders: Non-Wage Forms of Survival among Montreal Families, 1861-91,' *Labour/Le Travail* 14 (Fall 1984):9-46; Jennifer Dunkerson, 'Wartime Housing and Boarding: A Case Study of the Catherine Street North Area of Hamilton, Ontario,' *UHR* 20, 3 (February 1992):109-16.

7 Paul Yee, *Saltwater City: An Illustrated History of the Chinese in Vancouver* (Vancouver and Toronto: Douglas and McIntyre; Seattle: University of Washington Press 1988); Kay J. Anderson, *Vancouver's Chinatown: Racial Discourse in Canada, 1875-1914* (Montreal and Kingston: McGill-Queen's University Press 1991). Donna R. Gabaccia, *From Sicily to Elizabeth Street: Housing and Social Change among Italian Immigrants, 1880-1930* (Albany: State University of New York Press 1984); Thomas Lee Philpott, *The Slum and the Ghetto: Neighbourhood Deterioration and Middle-Class Reform, Chicago, 1880-1930* (New York: Oxford University Press 1978).

8 Michael B. Katz, *The People of Hamilton, Canada West: Family and Class in a Mid-Nineteenth-Century City* (Cambridge, MA: Harvard University Press 1975); Michael B. Katz, Michael J. Doucet, and Mark J. Stern, *The Social Organization of Early Industrial Capitalism* (Cambridge, MA: Harvard University Press 1982). See also Marc H. Choko, *The Characteristics of Housing Tenure in Montreal*, Research Paper no. 164 (Toronto: Centre for Urban and Community Studies, University of Toronto, 1987); Richard Dennis, *Landlords and Rented Housing in Toronto, 1885-1914*, Research Paper no. 162 (Toronto: Centre for Urban and Community Studies, University of Toronto, 1987); Michael J. Doucet, 'Working Class Housing in a Small Nineteenth Century Canadian City: Hamilton, Ontario, 1852-1881,' in *Essays in Canadian Working Class History*, ed. Gregory S. Kealey and Peter Warrian (Toronto: McClelland and Stewart 1976), 83-105; Richard Harris, *Class and Housing Tenure in Modern Canada*, Research Paper no. 153 (Toronto: Centre for Urban and Community Studies, University of Toronto, 1984); idem, *The Growth of Home Ownership in Toronto, 1899-1913*, Research Paper no. 163 (Toronto: Centre for Urban and Community Studies, University of Toronto, 1987); Richard Harris and Marc H. Choko, *The Evolution of Housing Tenure in Montreal and Toronto since the Mid-Nineteenth Century*, Research Paper no. 166 (Toronto: Centre for Urban and Community Studies, University of Toronto,

1988); Richard Harris and Chris Hamnett, 'The Myth of the Promised Land: The Social Diffusion of Home Ownership in Britain and North America,' *Annals of the Association of American Geographers* 77, 2 (1987):173-90; Richard Harris, G. Levine, and B.S. Osborne, 'Housing Tenure and Social Classes in Kingston, Ontario, 1881-1901,' *Journal of Historical Geography* 7, 3 (July 1981):271-89; and A. Gordon Darroch, 'Occupational Structure, Assessed Wealth, and Homeowning during Toronto's Early Industrialization, 1861-1899,' *Histoire sociale/Social History* 16 (November 1983):381-410. As well, see Dunkerson, 'Wartime Housing and Boarding.'

9   Kenneth T. Jackson, *Crabgrass Frontier: The Suburbanization of the United States* (New York and Oxford: Oxford University Press 1985); Richard Harris, 'American Suburbs: A Sketch of a New Interpretation,' *JUH* 15, 1 (November 1988):98-103.

10 R.A.J. McDonald, 'Working Class Vancouver, 1886-1914: Urbanism and Class in British Columbia,' in *Vancouver Past: Essays in Social History*, ed. R.A.J. McDonald and Jean Barman (Vancouver: University of British Columbia Press 1986), 67-8.

11 For another example of the social history of housing, see Gwendolyn Wright, *Building the Dream: A Social History of Housing in America* (New York: Pantheon Books 1981).

12 For work on national policy-making, see John C. Bacher, *Keeping to the Marketplace: The Evolution of Canadian Housing Policy* (Montreal and Kingston, London, Buffalo: McGill-Queen's University Press 1993); idem, 'Canadian Housing "Policy" in Perspective,' *UHR* 15, 1 (June 1986):3-18; idem, 'Too Good to Last? The Social Service Innovations of Wartime Housing,' *Women and Environments* 10, 2 (Winter 1988):10-13; J. David Hulchanski, 'The 1935 Dominion Housing Act: Setting the Stage for a Permanent Federal Presence in Canada's Housing Sector,' *UHR* 15, 1 (June 1986):19-39; John C. Bacher and J. David Hulchanski, 'Keeping Warm and Dry: The Policy Response to the Struggle for Shelter among Canada's Homeless, 1900-1960,' *UHR* 16, 2 (October 1987):147-63; Jill Wade, 'Wartime Housing Limited, 1941-1947: Canadian Housing Policy at the Crossroads,' *UHR* 15, 1 (June 1986):41-59; Alvin Finkel, *Business and Social Reform in the Thirties* (Toronto: James Lorimer 1979), 100-16; Robert G. Bryce, *Maturing in Hard Times: Canada's Department of Finance through the Great Depression* (Montreal and Kingston: McGill-Queen's University Press with the Institute of Public Administration of Canada, 1986), 159-71; John T. Saywell, ed., *Housing Canadians: Essays on the History of Residential Construction in Canada*, Discussion Paper no. 24 (Ottawa: Economic Council of Canada 1975), 150-216; Albert Rose, *Canadian Housing Policies (1935-1980)* (Toronto: Butterworths 1980); and Allan Moscovitch and Glenn Drover, eds., *Inequality: Essays on the Political Economy of Social Welfare* (Toronto: University of Toronto Press 1981). For the role of a provincial government, see Beverly J. Grieve, 'Continuity and Change: Provincial Housing Policy in British Columbia, 1945-1985' (M.A. thesis, University of British Columbia 1985). For the local perspective, see Shirley Campbell Spragge, 'A Confluence of Interests: Housing Reform in Toronto, 1900-1920,' in *The Usable Urban Past: Planning and Politics in the Modern Canadian City*, ed. Gilbert A. Stelter and Alan F.J. Artibise, Carleton Library no. 119 (Toronto: Macmillan of Canada with the Institute of Canadian Studies, Carleton University, 1979), 247-67; Lorna F. Hurl, 'The Toronto Housing Company, 1912-1923: The Pitfalls

of Painless Philanthropy,' *CHR* 65, 1 (March 1984):28-53; and Kaye Staniforth Melliship, 'The Contribution of Theories of the State in Analyzing Local Government Housing Initiatives: The City of Vancouver's Housing Actions, 1900-1973' (M.A. thesis, University of British Columbia 1985). For studies that integrate local and national developments, see Michael Doucet and John Weaver, *Housing the North American City* (Montreal and Kingston, London, Buffalo: McGill-Queen's University Press 1991); John Weaver, 'Reconstruction of the Richmond District in Halifax: A Canadian Episode in Public Housing and Town Planning, 1918-1921,' *Plan Canada* 16, 1 (March 1976):36-47; Jane Lewis and Mark Shrimpton, 'Policy-Making in Newfoundland during the 1940s: The Case of the St. John's Housing Corporation,' *CHR* 65, 2 (June 1984):209-39; and Marc H. Choko, Jean-Pierre Collin, and Annick Germain, 'Le logement et les enjeux de la transformation de l'espace urbain: Montréal, 1940-1960 [première et deuxième parties],' *UHR* 15, 2 (October 1986):127-36 and 15, 3 (February 1987):243-53.

13 For the British literature, see Joseph Melling, *Rent Strikes: People's Struggle for Housing in West Scotland, 1890-1916* (Edinburgh: Polygon 1983); idem, 'Clydeside Housing and the Evolution of State Rent Control,' in *Housing, Social Policy and the State*, ed. Joseph Melling (London: Croom Helm 1980), 139-67; Sean Damer, 'State, Class and Housing: Glasgow, 1885-1919,' in *Housing*, ed. Melling, 73-112; David Englander, *Landlord and Tenant in Urban Britain, 1838-1918* (Oxford: Clarendon Press 1983); and Martin J. Daunton, ed., *Councillors and Tenants: Local Authority Housing in English Cities, 1919- 1939* (Leicester: Leicester University Press 1984). For the American literature, see Ronald Lawson, 'The Rent Strike in New York City, 1904-1980: The Evolution of a Social Movement Strategy,' *JUH* 10, 3 (May 1984):235-58; Ronald Lawson, ed., assisted by Mark Naison, *The Tenant Movement in New York City, 1904-1984* (New Brunswick, NJ: Rutgers University Press 1986); Thomas S. Hines, 'Housing, Baseball, and Creeping Socialism: The Battle of Chavez Ravine, Los Angeles, 1949-1959,' *JUH* 8, 2 (February 1982):123-43; Neil H. Lebowitz, '"Above Party, Class, or Creed": Rent Control in the United States, 1940-1947,' *JUH* 7, 4 (August 1981):439-70; Rosalie Genevro, 'Site Selection and the New York City Housing Authority, 1934-1939,' *JUH* 12, 4 (August 1986):334-52; Joel Schwartz, 'Tenant Unions in New York City's Low-Rent Housing, 1933-1949,' *JUH* 12, 4 (August 1986):414-43; and Peter Marcuse, 'The Beginnings of Public Housing in New York,' *JUH* 12, 4 (August 1986):353-90. For the Canadian literature, see Marc H. Choko, 'Le mouvement des squatters à Montréal, 1946-1947,' *Cahiers d'histoire* 2 (Printemps 1982):27-39; idem, *Crises du logement à Montréal, 1860-1939* (Montréal: Éditions coopératives Albert Saint-Martin 1980); and Jill Wade, "A Palace for the Public": Housing Reform and the 1946 Occupation of the Old Hotel Vancouver,' in *Vancouver Past*, ed. McDonald and Barman, 288-310. Melliship's thesis also acknowledges the impact of local activism; see 'Contribution of Theories of the State,' 167-8.

14 Englander, *Landlord and Tenant in Urban Britain*, 294; and Lawson, *Tenant Movement*, 6.

15 Enid Gauldie, *Cruel Habitations: A History of Working Class Housing, 1780-1918* (London: George Allen and Unwin 1974); Anthony S. Wohl, *The Eternal Slum: Housing and Social Policy in Victorian London* (Montreal and Kingston: McGill-

Queen's University Press 1977); John Burnett, *A Social History of Housing, 1815-1985*, 2nd ed. (London and New York: Methuen 1986); John Nelson Tarn, *Five Per Cent Philanthropy: An Account of Housing in Urban Areas between 1840 and 1914* (Cambridge: Cambridge University Press 1973).

16 Roy Lubove, *The Progressives and the Slums: Tenement House Reform in New York, 1890-1917* (Pittsburgh: University of Pittsburgh Press 1962).

17 Gareth Stedman Jones, *Outcast London: A Study in the Relationship between Classes in Victorian Society* (Oxford: Clarendon Press 1971).

18 This mid-ground approach to social control reflects the influence of Don S. Kirschner's 'The Ambiguous Legacy: Social Justice and Social Control in the Progressive Era,' *Historical Reflections* 2 (1975):69-88; and Walter I. Trattner, ed., *Social Welfare or Social Control? Some Historical Reflections on 'Regulating the Poor'* (Knoxville: University of Tennessee Press 1983), 3-14.

19 See the books by Copp and Piva mentioned in note 4. See also Moscovitch and Drover's *Inequality*, Rose's *Canadian Housing Policies*, Bacher's 'Canadian Housing "Policy" in Perspective,' Hulchanski's 'The 1935 Dominion Housing Act,' Wade's 'Wartime Housing Limited,' and Finkel's *Business and Social Reform in the Thirties*.

20 For the literature on gender and housing, see Dolores Hayden, *The Grand Domestic Revolution: A History of Feminist Designs in American Homes, Neighbourhoods, and Cities* (Cambridge, MA, and London: MIT Press 1981); Wright, *Building the Dream*; idem, *Moralism and the Model Home: Domestic Architecture and Cultural Conflict in Chicago, 1873-1913* (Chicago: University of Chicago Press 1980); Veronica Strong-Boag, *The New Day Recalled: Lives of Girls and Women in English Canada, 1919-1939* (Toronto: Copp Clark Pitman 1988), 113-44; idem, 'Home Dreams: Women and the Suburban Experiment in Canada, 1945-60,' *CHR* 72, 4 (December 1991):471-504; John C. Bacher, 'Under the Threat of Expulsion: Women Were Blamed for the Housing Shortage during World War II,' *Women and Environments* 10, 2 (Winter 1988):14-5; Melling, *Rent Strikes*, passim; Damer, 'State, Class and Housing,' passim; and Irene Howard, 'The Mothers' Council of Vancouver: Holding the Fort for the Unemployed, 1935-1938,' in *Vancouver Past*, ed. McDonald and Barman, 249-87.

21 See also Joan Sangster, *Dreams of Equality: Women on the Canadian Left, 1920-1950* (Toronto: McClelland and Stewart 1989).

22 Wright, *Moralism*, 234-5; 'The Modern Home [Model House No. 501 Sponsored by the Dominion Government],' *Canadian Home Journal* 36 (January 1940):27.

23 Sherry McKay, 'Western Living, Western Homes,' Society for the Study of Architecture in Canada, *Bulletin* 14, 3 (September 1989):65-73.

24 Peter Dreier and J. David Hulchanski, 'Affordable Housing: Lessons from Canada,' *The American Prospect* 1 (Spring 1990):120-1. Cooperative housing was built on Cape Breton Island before the Curtis report; see Mary Elliott Arnold, *The Story of Tompkinsville* (New York: Cooperative League 1940).

25 Interview with P.R.U. Stratton by the author, Vancouver, 14 January 1990.

Index

5th Avenue East, 147
13th Avenue West, 35
33rd Avenue, 156
37 Pender Street West, 59
37th Avenue, 156
42nd Avenue, 130
44th Avenue, 130
45th Avenue, 130
49th Avenue, 130
54th Avenue, 150
'5000 Homes Now!' committee, 134, 135, 138

Acadia Camp, 149
Activists. *See* Housing activists in Vancouver
Adams, Thomas, 27, 29, 33, 78
Advisory Committee on Reconstruction, Subcommittee on Housing and Community Planning. *See* Curtis report
Agnew, Mrs. Harvey, 117
Air pollution, 59
Alma Road, 109
Amalgamated Building Workers of Canada, 82
Amputation Club of British Columbia, 27
The Anatomy of Poverty, 164
Anderson, Kay, 165
Andrews, Margaret, 9
Anglican Church, 22
Anthes, Laurence I., 69
Apartment and Rooming House Operators' Association, 138, 153
Apartments: business licences for, 40, 50; census information for (1921), 10, 11; conversion of single dwellings to, 13; and government housing programs, 130, 131, 157; high-rent, 111; increase in, between 1921-31, 17, 18
Architectural Institute of British Columbia, 26, 72, 88, 151
Architecture, domestic, history of, 165, 170-1. *See also* House styles
Argyle Drive, 150
Armstrong lodging house, 21
Army and Navy Veterans of Canada, 132
Asians: discrimination in distribution of relief for, 48; in east end of Vancouver, 20. *See also* Chinese in Vancouver; Japanese in Vancouver
Associated Boards of Trade of the Fraser Valley, 72
Associated Property Owners of Vancouver, 28, 91, 138, 153, 156, 157
Attic lodgings, 58, 109
Aunt Sally, 18, 189 n. 49

Bacher, John, 141, 170
Balfour, C.B., 157
Banks, and Integrated Housing Plan (IHP), 129

Barman, Jean, 9
Barrie, E.J., 147
Bartholomew report. *See* Harland
  Bartholomew and Associates
Bartlett, W.J., 116
Basement lodgings, 58, 109
Bates, Stewart, 159
Bauer, Catherine, 77
BC Building Contractors'
  Association, 72, 74, 137, 142, 151,
  156, 157
BC Committee for NHA and HIP,
  71, 72, 73, 90, 91
The B.C. Federationist, 86
BC Lumber and Shingle
  Manufacturers' Association, 72
Beatty Street, 56, 86
Belshaw, John, 164
Bennett, R.B., 62, 63, 65
Bennett, W.A.C., 154, 157, 168
Bennett and White Construction
  Company, 129
Better Housing Act, 30
Better Housing Scheme, 5, 24, 25,
  27, 28, 31-7, 52, 73, 89, 101, 147,
  167, 168, 183-4 n. 78, 184 n. 86,
  184 n. 89, 184 n. 90
Beveridge, William, 77
Biltmore Construction Company,
  150
Binning, B.C., 74, 77
Blue collar workers. *See* Working
  class
Blue Triangle Residential Club, 113
Board of Inquiry into the Cost of
  Living in Canada, 16
Boardinghouses, 20, 21, 58, 111. *See
  also* Lodging houses
Boathouses, 112. *See also*
  Floathouses; Houseboats; Shacks
Boeing Aircraft of Canada Limited,
  99, 120, 124
Bone, W. Rupert, 46
Bonner, Margerie, 112
Boulevard Heights, 101
Boultbee, Sweet, and Company
  Limited, 142
Boundary Road, 23, 50, 114
Bradbury, Bettina, 164

Bremerton, Washington, 147
British, in Vancouver, 20
British and Foreign Sailors Society,
  22
British Columbia: Department of
  Labour, 55, 154; Department of
  Lands, 33, 34; and Dominion
  Housing Act (DHA), 66; and Home
  Improvement Plan (HIP), 67; and
  housing question, 137; and Little
  Mountain public housing, 158; as
  migration destination for
  Canadians, 40; rent controls in,
  153; and social housing programs,
  167-8
British Columbia Building
  Contractors' Association. *See* BC
  Building Contractors' Association
British Columbia Electric Company,
  17, 109, 110
British Columbia Electric Railway, 60
British Columbia Federation on
  Unemployment, 91
British Columbia Mainland United
  Soldiers, 27
British Columbia Post-War
  Rehabilitation Council, 133, 134
British Columbia Underwriters'
  Association, 72
British Columbia Woman's Suffrage
  League, 86
British Properties, 101
Broadway Avenue, 103, 104, 129,
  130, 142, 157, 161
Brotherhood of Railway Carmen of
  America, 82
Broughton Street, 59
Brown, Everett, 157
Bruce, H.A., 63
Bruce report, 63, 75, 90
Buck, Frank E., 26, 58, 86
Builders' Exchange. *See* Building and
  Construction Industries Exchange
Building and Construction
  Industries Exchange, 28, 69, 70, 91
Building industry. *See* Construction
  industry
Building needs, of major Canadian
  cities (1944), 95

Building permits in Vancouver: (1902-24), 24; (1920-55), 39
Building standards, and government housing programs, 73-4
Building Trades Council, 91
Bungalow Finance and Building Company, 23
Burke, Stanley, 209-10 n. 11
Burkeville, 120, 124, 142
Burnaby, 12, 101, 130, 152, 163
Burnett, John, 169
Burrard Bridge, 51
Burrard Drydock Company Limited, 99, 119
Burrard Inlet, 12, 50, 59, 86, 104
Burrard Street, 12, 50, 56, 57, 86, 102, 104, 106, 143
Business district, of Vancouver: ethnic groups in, 20; lodging houses in, 50; residential living conditions in (1920s), 12
Business licences: for apartments, 18; housing-related, between 1930-7, 40; for lodging houses, 13, 40, 49-50
Buttenweiser, Ann L., 169
Buzelle, S.D., 73

Cabins: disrepair of, 57, 106; as domestic architecture, 165, 166; extant, 179 n. 21; living conditions in, 17, 18, 111, 112; sanitary facilities in, 57
Cambie Street, 13, 111
Cambie Street bridge, 59
Campbell Avenue, 44, 154, 155
Canada: Department of Finance, 65, 67, 68-9, 88, 125, 126, 127, 129, 130, 136, 141, 143, 144, 161; Department of Health, 29; Department of Munitions and Supply, 97-8, 118, 119, 126, 136, 137, 141, 142, 161; Department of National Defence, 136, 141, 143; Department of National Defence relief camps, 45, 60; Department of Pensions and National Health, 136; Department of Reconstruction and Supply, 130,

136, 161; Department of Veterans Affairs (DVA), 116, 131, 132, 136, 144; Dominion Bureau of Statistics, 93
Canada (Central) Mortgage and Housing Corporation (CMHC): and absorption of Emergency Shelter Administration, 140; and construction of housing for veterans, 103, 141; and Fraserview, 150, 151; and hutments from Bremerton, Washington State, 147; and Little Mountain public housing, 157-8; origins of, 116, 130-1; and Renfrew Heights, 147-8; and sale of veterans' housing, 160-1; and social housing in Vancouver, 156, 157; and Strathcona housing survey, 154; as target of protest by housing activists, 139
Canada Permanent Mortgage Corporation, 69, 193 n. 27, 193-4 n. 29
Canadian Bank of Commerce, 71
Canadian Bankers' Association, 67
Canadian Business, 136
Canadian Chamber of Commerce, 63
Canadian Congress of Labour, 153
Canadian Construction Association, 63, 67, 69, 137
Canadian Corps Association, 132
Canadian Daughters' League, 91
Canadian Federation of the Blind, BC Division, 91
Canadian Federation of Mayors and Municipalities (CFMM), 79, 155, 156, 168
Canadian Legion, 132, 133, 135, 144, 147, 149, 153, 159. *See also* Veterans
Canadian Manufacturers' Association, 28, 63
Canadian Memorial Church, 78
Canadian National Railway (CNR), 44, 143
Canadian Pacific Railway (CPR), 12, 143, 144

234 *Index*

Canadian Reconstruction
Association, 35-6
Canton Alley, 21, 48
'Cape Cod style,' 71, 120, 171, 195
n. 62
Capilano Properties, 101, 213 n. 45
Carbon monoxide poisoning, from
gas appliances, 17, 109, 110
Cardero Street, 59
Carrall Street, 12
Carver, Humphrey, 80, 161
Cassiar Street, 147
Cassidy, Harry M., 63, 77, 78, 79, 90
Catholic Women's League of
Canada, 91
CCF. *See* Co-operative
Commonwealth Federation (CCF)
CCF News, 136
Ceiling standards, 109
Census of Canada: (1921), 10-12;
(1931), 11, 51, 55, 58; (1941), 51,
52, 55, 56, 58, 93, 105, 106;
(1951), 93, 97, 106; and working
class living conditions, 164
Central City Mission, 22, 45, 59,
180 n. 39, 180 n. 40
Central Methodist Church, 28
Central Mortgage and Housing
Corporation. *See* Canada (Central)
Mortgage and Housing
Corporation (CMHC)
Central Mortgage Bank, 125, 130
CFMM. *See* Canadian Federation of
Mayors and Municipalities (CFMM)
Chambers, J., 142
Chicago, 24
Children: in cabins, 17;
discrimination against, 113; and
housing shortage, 104; lack of play
space for, 110; in lodging houses,
16-17; of veterans, and move to
Renfrew Heights, 150
Chinatown: fire hazards in, 111; gas
appliances in, 109; and housing
for elderly, 113; living conditions
in, 9, 19, 58, 165; and lodging
houses, 111; as neighbourhood,
12; overcrowding in, 105
Chinese in Vancouver: and

community care of destitute men,
48; and family living conditions,
21; and labourers' living
conditions, 19, 20
Choko, Marc H., 165
Chown United Church, 91
Cincinnati, 169
Citizens' Emergency Housing
Committee, 134
Citizens' Rehabilitation Council of
Greater Vancouver (CRCGV): and
Dunsmuir Hotel as veterans'
hostel, 145; and Hotel Vancouver
as veterans' hostel, 144; and
housing activism, 167; and Little
Mountain barracks as veterans'
housing, 148; and Seaforth
Armories as veterans' housing,
149-50; support for CMHC
housing for veterans, 146; support
for WHL housing for veterans,
141, 142; and Vancouver housing
authority, 156; and veterans'
housing, 132, 133, 136, 138-9
City of Vancouver. *See* Vancouver
city council
City planning: and Curtis report,
128; by Harland Bartholomew and
Associates, 10, 25-6
Civilian Pensions Mother's
Organization, 91
Clark, W.C., 64, 65, 81, 87, 125,
126, 128, 161, 167, 212 n. 31
Clark Drive, 12, 55, 57, 59
CMHC. *See* Canada (Central)
Mortgage and Housing
Corporation (CMHC)
CNR. *See* Canadian National
Railway (CNR)
Coal Harbour, 50, 58, 59
Cockfield, Brown, and Company
Limited, 67
Columbia Street, 59, 130
Commercial Drive, 104
Commission of Conservation, 27, 78
Commissioner Drive, 112
Communist Party of Canada (CPC),
27, 65, 74, 80-1, 82, 131. *See also*
Labor Progressive Party (LPP)

Community groups: and lack of input into Better Housing Scheme, 35; support for social housing, 26-8

Community Planning Association of Canada, 154

The Condition of the Working Class in Toronto, 164

Conservative party. *See* Progressive Conservative party

Construction industry: activity in Vancouver of (1920-9), 12; (1930-7), 38-41; assistance through federal programs for, 62; and construction methods, 120; and Curtis report, 128; and Dominion Housing Act (DHA), 65, 69-70; and federal controls during Second World War, 97-8, 118; and Integrated Housing Plan (IHP), 129; materials of, census information, 12; materials of, shortages during Second World War, 94-5; and National Housing Act (NHA) (1944), 101, 131; opposition to housing activists, 28, 137-38; opposition to Little Mountain public housing, 157; support for housing programs, 4, 63, 83; unemployment in, 41, 73

Consumers' Research Council, 138

Contractors: business licences for, between 1930-7, 40; and financial difficulty, 23

Conversion, of single homes into multiple units, 98, 104, 127, 131, 137. *See also* Apartments; Lodging houses

Cooking facilities, 108. *See also* Gas appliances

Cooper, H.W., 60

Cooper, Reverend Father, 87

Co-operative Commonwealth Federation (CCF): growth in British Columbia of, 80; and Helena Gutteridge, 85, 86; and housing activism, 74, 79, 87, 131, 132, 133-4, 135, 136, 137, 140, 155, 167, 168; leader of, in British Columbia, 23; opposition to

Dominion Housing Act (DHA), 65; opposition to Wartime Housing Limited (WHL) program, 125; in Saskatchewan, 153; and social protest, 82; in Vancouver, 153

Cooperative housing, 3, 128, 133, 134, 161, 171, 212 n. 37

Copp, Terry, 164, 170

Cordova Street, 86, 149

Cornett, J.W., 143

Cost of Living in Canada, Board of Inquiry into the, 16

CPC. *See* Communist Party of Canada (CPC)

CPR. *See* Canadian Pacific Railway (CPR)

Crabgrass Frontier, 165

CRCGV. *See* Citizens' Rehabilitation Council of Greater Vancouver (CRCGV)

Crerar, T.A., 29, 30

Crossley, Alan, 150

Crowding. *See* Overcrowding

Curtis, C.A., 127

Curtis report, 95, 127-8, 133, 135, 171

Daily Province, 136, 157

Dalkeith Place, 130

Damer, Sean, 168

Dania Home, 152

Danish housing project for elderly, 152

Daunton, Martin J., 168

Davenport Rooms, 112

Davidson, Jocelyn, 127, 136

Denman Street, 50

Depression, economic (1930s). *See* Great Depression

DERA. *See* Downtown Eastside Residents' Association (DERA)

Design No. 501 (NHA), 171

Devonshire Apartment Hotel, 18

DHA. *See* Dominion Housing Act (DHA)

Diseases, 20, 60

Dobson, Hugh, 78, 87, 88, 90, 152

Dollarton, 112

Dominion Housing Act (DHA), 64-5,

66, 67, 68-70, 71, 72, 73, 74, 75, 87, 167, 193 n. 27
Dominion Mortgage and Investments Association, 28, 64, 128, 129, 137
Dominion Provincial Conference, Ottawa (1918), 28
Doucet, Michael J., 34, 165
Downpayments. *See* Mortgages
Downtown Eastside: as neighbourhood, 12; residence for elderly in, 113. *See also* East end of Vancouver
Downtown Eastside Residents' Association (DERA), 3, 173 n. 2
Dumbbell design, of multiple unit dwellings, 17, 18
Dunlevy Avenue, 45, 57, 60
Dunromin hostel, 48
Dunsmuir Hotel, 145, 147
Dunsmuir Street, 56, 57, 99, 106
DVA. *See* Canada, Department of Veterans' Affairs (DVA)

East end of Vancouver: building disrepair, 106; ethnic groups, 20; housing shortage, 23; living conditions, 9, 12, 13, 18; overcrowding, 56. *See also* Downtown Eastside
East Hastings (neighbourhood), 12, 73, 101
East Indians, living conditions of, 21
East Vancouver, 23
Eaton's. *See* T. Eaton Company Limited
Edmonton: construction materials in, 12; home ownership in, 11, 46, 52; housing conditions, 10, 11, 12, 56
Elderly: housing activism for, 152-3; housing needs of, 151; housing projects for, 147; housing shortage for, 104, 113, 163; income levels of, 113; living conditions of, 113-14; shelters for, 23; support of Vancouver Housing Association (VHA), 135
Electricity, 59

Elgin Street, 142
Elks Hall, 90
Ellis, J.N., 116
Emergency Shelter Administration, 140, 141, 142, 143, 147, 149
Emergency shelter programs, 160
Employment Service of Canada, 41
Engineering Institute of Canada, 63
Englander, David, 168, 169
Englesea Lodge, 18
English Bay, 59
Erickson, Arthur, 225 n. 172
Erickson, Oscar, 156, 158, 225 n. 172
Esquimalt, 120
Europeans, in east end of Vancouver, 20
Evans, Arthur 'Slim,' 46, 51
Evictions: activist's campaign for suspension of, 139; controls of, 98; freeze of, 132, 140-1; of Malcolm Lowry and Margerie Bonner, 112; protests of, 140-1; of relief recipients, 51; and WPTB, 99, 117, 139, 140-1
Expropriation, of land for Fraserview, 150

Fair Haven project, 152
Fairbanks, Robert B., 169
Fairview, 12, 48, 55, 111
False Creek, 12, 19, 50, 51, 56, 58, 59, 86, 105, 106
Families, lack of affordable housing for, 113
Family Welfare Bureau of Greater Vancouver, 27-8
Federal government: joint responsibility for housing with other levels of government, 121, 123, 156-7, 210 n. 16. *See also* Canada (Central) Mortgage and Housing Corporation (CMHC); Wartime Housing Limited (WHL); *names of boards, bureaus, committees, and commissions; names of government departments under Canada; names of housing programs*
Fell Avenue, 119
Finkel, Alvin, 170

Finnish Association, 82
Finnish loggers, unemployment
among, 41, 44
Fire hazards, 58, 59, 110, 111, 200
n. 130
Firestone, O.J., 127
First Presbyterian Church, 28
First United Church, 28, 78
First United Church Social Housing
Society, 3
Fitzpatrick, Pat, 112
Fleming, Donald, 151
Fleming, Millicent, 118
Floathouses, 18, 19, 51, 111, 112
Fort Camp, 149
Fourth Avenue, 103, 109, 129, 130,
157, 161
Fraser River, 12, 50, 59
Fraser Street, 142
Fraserview, 105, 150-1, 152, 160,
161, 163, 168, 170
Fraserview Golf Course, 150

Ganong, Arthur, 64
Garden City design, 129
Gas appliances, 17, 49, 108, 109-10
Gauldie, Enid, 169
Genevro, Rosalie, 169
Georgia Hotel, 70, 71, 84
Georgia Medical-Dental Building, 90
Georgia Strait, 12
Georgia Street, 50, 143
Georgia Viaduct, 44, 60
Gilford Court, 18
Gitterman, Sam, 147
Glasgow, Scotland, 24, 159, 170
Glen Drive, 114
Goodwill Activities Association, 91
Gore Street, 86, 151, 154
Gosling, G.K., 147
Government. *See* British Columbia;
Canada; Federal government;
Vancouver city council
Grand Army United Veterans,
Vancouver branch, 27
Grand Union Rooms, 17
Grandview Chamber of Commerce,
71
Grandview Highway, 101, 130, 147

Grandview (neighbourhood), 8, 12
Granville Street, 143
Grauer, A.E., 33
Great Britain: 'homes for heroes'
program in, 30, 129; housing
activism in, 6, 168, 169; social
housing programs in, 75
Great Depression, and housing in
Vancouver, 38-92
Great Northern Railway, 45, 59
Great War Veterans' Association of
Canada, 27, 28
Greater Vancouver and New
Westminster Youth Council, 86,
87, 91
Greater Vancouver Health League,
91
Green, Howard, 90
Green, Jim, 173 n. 2
Green spaces, lack of, 110
Gunderson, Eric, 157
Gutteridge, Helena: and housing
activism, 28, 85-6; and housing
activist successors, 134; and
low-rent housing campaign, 87;
and National Housing Act (NHA),
Part II, 88, 89, 90, 92; political
defeat of, 92, 138; retirement of,
111; and work with displaced
Japanese Canadians, 138

H.A. Roberts Limited, 40
Haggart, Andrew J., 184 n. 93
Hale, Fred J., 69, 71
Halifax: housing shortage in, 38, 99;
population growth in, (1940s), 95;
V-E Day riots, 132
Hamilton: construction materials
in, (1931), 12; emergency shelter
regulations in, (1944), 140;
evictions in, 141; home ownership
in, 11, 46, 52; housing conditions,
10, 11, 12, 56; and Wartime
Housing Limited (WHL), 126
Harland Bartholomew and
Associates: and city plan for
Vancouver, 10; and re-zoning of
Vancouver, 13, 26
Harris, Richard, 165

Harrison, A.J., 86, 88, 138
Harry Ablowitz Realty Limited, 130
Hart, John, 90
Hastings Park camp, as shelter for homeless, 22
Hastings Street, 17, 151, 154
Health Department of City of Vancouver. *See* Vancouver health department
Heathcote, Francis, 90
Heating systems, 107, 108, 109
HEC. *See* Housing Enterprises of Canada Limited (HEC)
Helmcken Street, 50
Henderson, Jack, 133
Henry Hudson School Parent-Teacher Association, 104
Heritage issues, and housing, 107, 166, 171
HEV. *See* Housing Enterprises of Vancouver Limited (HEV)
Hill, Octavia, 79
Hines, Thomas S., 169
HIP. *See* Home Improvement Plan (HIP)
Hobo camps, during Great Depression, 44-5, 60
Hodgetts, Charles A., 27
Hogan's Alley, 90
Holdsworth, Deryck, 8-12, 19-20, 25, 162, 164
Home Conversion Plan, 127, 131
Home Improvement Loans Guarantee Act, 67, 68
Home Improvement Plan (HIP), 66-7, 67-8, 70-3, 97, 116, 126-7, 167
Home Life, 121
Home owners, 11, 46, 52, 85, 157
Home ownership: in Edmonton, 11, 46, 52; in Hamilton, 11, 46, 52; and income, 52; and National Housing Act (NHA) (1938), Part I, 128; and National Housing Act (NHA), (1944), Part I, 101; and shelter allowances, 55; supported by CCF, 133; in Toronto, 11, 46, 52; in Vancouver, 4, 8, 11, 45, 46, 51-5, 100-1, 162; in Victoria, 11,

46, 52; in Winnipeg, 11, 46, 52
Homeless: missed by census surveys, 59; prevalence of, during 1930s, 42, 44, 45, 59-60, 163; shelters for, 22-3, 45, 59, 60, 180 n. 39, 180 n. 40; social protest about, 83-4; and substandard housing in Vancouver, 166
'Homes for heroes' program, 30, 129
Hotel Vancouver: campaign to preserve, 144; home building exhibition in, 72, 90; new building for, 38; occupation by veterans of, 144, 145; as shelter for homeless, 140, 143, 144, 145, 146, 147, 148, 160; as shelter for veterans, 132
Hotels: business licences between 1930-7 for, 40; as residences, 13, 17, 44, 106, 111, 113, 163, 164; and social architectural history, 165; in Strathcona, 154-5. *See also* Lodging houses
House Owners' Association, 85
House repairs. *See* Repairs, to buildings
House styles, 16, 33, 34, 35, 74, 75, 76, 77, 120, 122, 129, 147, 151, 152, 157, 171. *See also* Architecture
Houseboats, 50, 58-9, 89. *See also* Boathouses; Floathouses; Shacks
Housewives' League, 138
Housing. *See* Apartments; Boathouses; Cabins; Floathouses; Hotels; Lodging houses; Market housing programs; Rooms; Shacks; Single dwellings; Social housing programs
Housing activists in Vancouver, 3, 4, 5, 7, 25-8, 37, 74-86, 92, 131-8, 154, 155, 159, 160, 166-8, 169, 170, 172; achievements of, 159, 160, 161; and community organizations' support (1940s), 215 n. 74; lessons of, 171-2; opposition to, 28, 85, 91, 137-8, 157, 168; reasons for success of (1940s), 159-60; and trade union support (1940s), 215-16 n. 73; and women's organizations' support

(1940s), 216 n. 74

Housing Enterprises of Canada Limited (HEC), 103, 116, 129, 131

Housing Enterprises of Vancouver Limited (HEV), 129, 130, 131, 157, 161

Housing reform. *See* Housing activists in Vancouver

Housing registries, 98, 99, 100, 117-18, 133

Housing shortages in Vancouver, 23-4, 31, 38-41, 93-100, 112-14

Housing standards, 89, 137

Howe, C.D., 118, 120, 126, 130, 137, 142, 143, 146, 147, 155, 167

Hudson's Bay Company, 71, 72

Hulchanski, David, 170

Hull, 140

Hullah, N.W., 157

IHP. *See* Integrated Housing Plan (IHP)

Immigrants, 8, 13, 96

Income: and home ownership, 52, 100; personal, in Canada (1926-40), 42, 43; and rents (1944), 102; sources of, during Great Depression, 54-5

Independent Labour Party, 82

Industrial growth, in Vancouver (1940s), 95

Inflation: and rent increases, after Second World War, 103; and Vancouver housing market, 23, 24

Insect infestations, 58

Inspectors, health. *See* Vancouver health department

Integrated Housing Plan (IHP), 101, 116, 129

International Union of Mine, Mill and Smelter Workers, 134

International Woodworkers of America, 134, 159

Isley, J.L., 117, 126, 130, 137, 144

Italian Home Owners' and Electors' Association, 85

Italians, labourers' living conditions, 13, 21-2

J.G. James and Son, 130

Jackson, Kenneth T., 165

Jail, as shelter for homeless, 22, 180 n. 40

Jamieson, Laura, 28, 134, 156, 170

Japanese in Vancouver, living conditions of, 21

Jervis Street, 50

Johnson, Byron, 72, 153-4, 155, 156, 160, 168

Joint Committee on Unemployment, 82

Jones, A.E., 30, 33

Jones, Gareth Stedman, 169

Jones, J.A., 131, 156

Jopson, John, 88, 90

Journals, on housing conditions, 136

Jungles. *See* Hobo camps

Kaslo Street, 59

Katz, Michael B., 165

Keefer Street, 113, 155

Keen, J.F., 69, 71

Kerrisdale, 12

King, William Lyon Mackenzie, 30, 62, 66, 67, 81, 87, 137

Kinsmen Club, 159

Kitsilano, 8, 12, 35, 48, 49, 50, 55, 56, 73, 75, 104, 105, 106, 108, 109, 110, 111, 113, 165

Kitsilano Chamber of Commerce, 157

Kitsilano Indian Reserve, 50

Kiwanis Club, 72

Knight, Rolf, 112

Knight Road, 130

Korean War, 101-2, 151

Labor Progressive Party (LPP), 131, 132, 133, 134, 135, 136, 138, 139, 140, 147, 149, 153, 159, 167. *See also* Communist Party of Canada (CPC)

Labour Gazette, 86

Laing, Arthur, 151

Landlords: discrimination against children, 113; discrimination against elderly, 113, 114; and eviction controls, 117; refusal to

repair dwellings, 106, 112
Lansdowne Park, Ottawa, 149
Laski, Mrs. Harold J., 195 n. 66
Lasserre, Fred, 154
Lawson, Robert, 169
LCW. *See* Local Council of Women (LCW)
League for Social Reconstruction (LSR), 63, 74, 78, 79, 80, 81
Leasehold Regulations Act, 154
Lebowitz, Neil H., 169
Lecky, R.J., 69, 70, 71, 88, 90
Lemon Creek relocation project, 138
Leonard, T. D'Arcy, 64
Liberal party, 65, 66, 81, 155, 160, 168
Life insurance companies, and Housing Enterprises of Canada Limited (HEV), 129
Light, lack of, 17, 57-8, 109, 111
Lindenlea, 32
Lions Club of Vancouver, 153
Little, Maddock, and Meirte Limited, 130
'Little Haven,' 114, 208 n. 128
Little Mountain, 73, 101
Little Mountain barracks, 148, 149
Little Mountain public housing, 5, 116, 156-9, 161, 167, 168
Loans, for housing, 66-7, 125, 126, 129. *See also* Mortgages
Local Council of Women (LCW), 26-7, 70, 72, 83, 87, 90, 151, 153
Lodging and Restaurant Keepers' Association, 85
Lodging houses: basement and attic lodgings, 109; business licences for, 13, 40, 49-50; and Canadian social architectural history, 165, 166; for Chinese labourers, 20-1; conversion of houses to, 48-50; disrepair of, 57, 106; including rooms, cheap hotels, and cabins, 17; inspection of, 13, 25; lack of light and ventilation in, 58; living conditions in, 16-17; and relief system and landlords, 85; sanitary facilities in, 57, 107-8, 109, 111; in West End, 13, 16, 49, 50, 58, 106,

107, 108, 109, 110, 111, 113. *See also* Boardinghouses; Cabins; Hotels; Rooms
London, England, 24
Lonsdale Avenue, 119
Low-income groups: housing shortage for, 23, 60-1, 62, 131, 163; not helped by federal housing programs, 33-4, 35, 66, 67, 73, 123; rents of, 102-3
Lowry, Malcolm, 112
LPP. *See* Labor Progressive Party (LPP)
LSR. *See* League for Social Reconstruction (LSR)
Lubove, Roy, 169
Lulu Island, 131
Lulu Island Camp, 149
Lumbermen's Association, 28
Lun Yick Company Limited, 21

McCarter and Nairne, 120, 142
McCririck, Donna, 9, 11
McDonald, R.A.J., 9, 165
Macdonald Commission, 60
McEwen, Bob, 144, 212 n. 132
McEwen, Tom, 84
McGeer, Gerry, 146, 147, 155
MacInnis, Angus, 28, 79, 80, 134, 135, 146
MacInnis, Grace, 79, 89, 134, 136, 140, 150, 154
MacKenzie, Ian, 87, 144
MacKenzie, Larry, 149, 154
Maclean, A.K., 29, 30
Maclean's, 136
Macmillan, H.R., 147
MacNeil, Grant, 88, 134, 140
McPeake, John, 134, 135, 138
Main Street, 17, 50, 57, 86, 142, 156
Maitland, R.L., 139
Malkin, W.H., 38
Manhattan Apartments, 18
Manitoba Street, 130
Mansions in West End, conversion into multiple unit dwellings, 12, 13, 49, 165
Mansur, David, 125, 146, 147, 156
Marcuse, Peter, 169

Marine Drive, 142, 150
Marine Workers' and Boilermakers' Union, 82
Market Alley, 58
Market housing programs, definition of, 4-5. *See also* Better Housing Scheme; Dominion Housing Act (DHA); National Housing Act; Home Improvement Plan (HIP); Integrated Housing Plan (IHP)
Marrion, Robert, 21, 25
Marsh, Betty, 154
Marsh, Leonard C., 77, 78, 79, 127, 136, 154, 171
Marshall Wells Limited, 111
Massey, Vincent, 81
Mathers, T.G., 29
Mayhew, R.H., 143
Media, on housing shortage, 136
Meighen, Arthur, 27, 30
Melling, Joseph, 168
Merritt, Cecil, 146
Migration, to British Columbia from the Prairie provinces, 31, 40, 95-6
Miller, George C., 71, 146, 155
Mixed-income projects, 158-9
Montreal: evictions in, 141; housing conditions in, 24, 38; and Housing Enterprises of Canada Limited (HEC), 129; rents in, 16; reports on housing problems in, 38, 63, 77
Mooney, George S., 78-9, 88
Mortgage and Trust Companies Association of British Columbia, 69, 137-8
Mortgages: and Better Housing Scheme, 24, 33, 34-5, 36-7; Dominion Housing Act (DHA), 64-5, 193-4 n. 29; and financial hardship, 23, 24, 52-5; and National Housing Act (NHA), 68, 128
Moscovitch, Alan, 170
Mothers' Council, 82
Mount Pleasant, 8, 12, 48, 49, 50, 55, 73
Mount Pleasant Women's Christian Temperance Union, 91

Multiple unit dwellings. *See* Apartments; Lodging houses
Municipal governments, joint responsibility for housing with other levels of government, 121, 123. *See also* Vancouver city council
Murray, Stewart, 110
Mutual Life of Canada, 69

Nanaimo, 120
Nanaimo Street, 101
National Construction Council, 63, 64, 69, 125
National Council of Jewish Women, 91
National Council of Women, 67
National Employment Commission (NEC), 66, 67, 81, 88
National Harbour Board, 45
National House Builders' Association, 129, 137
National Housing Act (NHA) (1938), 68, 71, 72, 73, 74, 97, 101, 116, 125, 126, 128
National Housing Act (NHA) (1938), Part II, 81-2, 88, 89, 90, 91, 92
National Housing Act (NHA) (1944), 101-2, 103, 116, 128, 129, 130, 131, 153
National Housing Act (NHA) (1949), amendment to, 156
National Housing Act (NHA) (1973), amendment to, 161
National Housing Administration, 68, 74, 76, 98, 124, 125, 126, 127, 131, 136, 153, 171, 194 n. 49
National Housing and Planning Association (NHPA), 79, 88
National Industrial Conference, 30
National Industrial Recovery Act (U.S. 1933), 75
Natives, and housing, 19, 165
NEC. *See* National Employment Commission (NEC)
Neighbourhoods, before the Great Depression, 8
'New Deal' program, 65
New Era League, 28, 82, 91

'New social history,' 6
New Veterans' Branch, of the Canadian Legion, 144, 145, 148, 150
New Vista Society, 151, 152
New Westminster, 101, 130, 131, 140, 152
New York, 24, 169
News-Herald, 136
Newspapers, on housing shortage, 136
NHA. *See* National Housing Act (NHA)
NHPA. *See* National Housing and Planning Association (NHPA)
Nicolls, F.W., 74, 88, 89, 125, 126, 127
Non-Partisan Association (NPA), 133, 138, 160
Norgate, 101
North Van Ship Repairs Limited, 99, 119
North Vancouver, 101, 119, 120, 121, 123, 124, 126, 130, 131, 133, 163
Norwegian loggers, unemployment among, 44
NPA. *See* Non-Partisan Association (NPA)

Oak Street, 111
Occupancy rates, in Vancouver (1930s), 40-1. *See also* Vacancy rates, in Vancouver (1940s)
Old Age Pensioners' Organization Foundation, 153
Old Peoples' Home, 23, 114
On-to-Ottawa trek, 70
One-room dwellings, 11
Ontario: and Dominion Housing Act (DHA), 66; and federal housing program (1919), 28, 29, 30; and Home Improvement Plan (HIP), 67; and rent controls, 153
Ontario Street, 12, 73, 156
Orchard Park, 161
Order No. 200, 117, 137
Order No. 537, 140-1
Overcrowding: as shown in census

(1921), 11-12; (1931), 55-6; (1941), 56, 105, 108; (1951), 105, 108; in Edmonton, 56; in Hamilton, 56; standard of, 127, 179 n. 10; in Toronto, 56; in Vancouver, 11-12, 13, 19, 20-1, 24, 55-6, 58, 108, 163; in Victoria, 56; in Winnipeg, 56
Owen, W.S., 88, 90
Ownership, home. *See* Home ownership

Pacific Advocate (Tribune), 136
Pacific Command, 140
Pacific Tribune, 136, 145
Parent-Teachers' Association, 91
Parliamentary Special Committee on Housing (1935), 63-4
Pattullo, Duff, 31, 69, 83, 87, 89-90
'Peewee' houses, 97
Pemberton and Sons Limited, 18
Pender Street, 13, 19, 111, 112, 155
Pickersgill, J.W., 225 n. 180
Pickersgill, T.B., 157, 225 n. 180
Piggott, Joseph M., 119, 120, 127
Pioneer Political Equality League, 86
Piva, Michael, 164, 170
Planning. *See* City planning
Point Grey, 9-10, 11, 23, 26, 32, 34, 36, 78, 162
Point Grey relief camps, 45, 60
Point Grey Road, 109
Point Grey Town Planning Commission, 26
Pollution, 59
Population growth, 40, 95-6
Port Alberni, 147
Portuguese Joe, 18
Portuguese Pete, 18
Powell Rooms, 17
Pratt, N.E., 154
Prices of houses, increase between 1939-46, 100
Prince Rupert, 120
Prior Street, 44, 60, 86, 154
Pritchett, Harold, 134
Privy Council, 29
Progressive Conservative party, 155, 160, 168

Progressive Women's Federation, 91

Property tax arrears and sales, 53-5, 190 n. 60

Property values, and government housing projects, 125

Prostitutes, 48

Protest. *See* Housing activists in Vancouver

Provincial government (BC). *See* British Columbia

Public housing. *See* Social housing programs

Public library, as shelter for homeless, 22, 180 n. 40

Purvis, Arthur B., 66

Pyke and White Construction Limited, 157

Quadra Club, 90

Quality Homes Corporation, 138

Quebec: and Dominion Housing Act (DHA), 66; housing conditions in, compared with BC before the Great Depression, 9; support for rent controls in, 153

Queen Elizabeth Park, 156

Queensborough, 131

Radios, 108

Ralston, J.L., 141

Rat infestation, 58, 60

Raymur Place, 161

Real estate, and business licences between 1930-7, 40

Real Estate Exchange, 28, 70, 72, 91, 99

Reconstruction, and housing programs, 127

Reconstruction and Development Committee of Canada, 29

Reform, housing. *See* Housing activists in Vancouver

Refrigeration, 58, 107, 108

Regina Manifesto, 80

Relief camps, 45, 60

Relief Projects Workers' Union, 91

Relief recipients. *See* Welfare

Renfrew Heights, 105, 109, 146, 147-8, 150, 160, 161, 163, 170

Renfrew Street, 59, 101, 130, 147

Rent controls: in British Columbia, 153-4, 160; federal regulations of, 98, 103, 116-17, 167; litigation of, 153-4

Rent strikes, 145, 221 n. 121

Rental housing: campaign for low-cost units in late 1930s, 85-92; census information on (1921), 11, 16; cost of (*see* rents); living conditions in, 16-18, 19-20, 55-8, 103-12; for low-income groups, 102-3; regulation of, 25, 49

Rents: in Canada (1926-40), 42, 43; (1929-39), 43; controls of (*see* rent controls); disproportionate, definition of, 204 n. 54; for housing built under federal programs, 123, 147-8, 149, 151, 159; protests over, 145; in Vancouver (1900-13), 16; (1921), 11-12; (1929-39), 43; (1931-41), 45; (1944), 102-3

Repairs, to buildings: encouraged by Home Improvement Plan (HIP), 70-1; need for, 56, 57, 106, 108, 111

Richmond, 120, 124, 131, 170

Riverview, 114

Robertson, G.D., 29

Robinson, Norman B., 120

Robson Street, 13, 50

Roddan, Andrew, 78, 87

Rogers, Norman, 81

Rooms, 17, 112. *See also* Lodging houses

Rooms per person, as a standard of overcrowding, 12

Rose, Albert, 170

Row houses (1921), 10-11

Rowell, N.W., 29, 30

Royal Architectural Institute of Canada *Journal*, 136

Royal Bank, 70

Royal Columbian Hospital, 152

Royal Commission of Industrial Releations, 29

Royal Commission on Chinese and Japanese Immigration, 21

Royal Commission on
   Dominion-Provincial Relations, 33
Royal Trust Company, 18
Ruddell, Elgin, 134, 136
Ryan Contracting Company, 69

Salvation Army, 22, 153, 180 n. 39,
   180 n. 40
St. James Social Services, 3
Sam Kee Building, 21
Sanders, Byrne Hope, 117
Sanitary facilities, 16, 56-7, 58, 59,
   60, 107, 108, 109, 111, 112
Saturday Night, 136
Sawmills, 59
Scanlon, E.S., 135
Schools, 119, 124
Schwartz, Joel, 169
Scott, Frank, 80
Scott, Lionel, 121
Sea Island, 120, 126, 160
Sea Island Camp No. 1, 140, 142
Sea Island Camp No. 2, 142-3
Seafarers' Industrial Union, 82
Seaforth Armories, 149-50
Seaforth Village, 148, 150
Second Narrows, 50
Selman, Laura, 118, 133, 158
Semi-detached dwellings (1921), 10,
   11
Senior citizens. *See* Elderly
Sewage disposal, 59
Sewage system, 124
Sexton, J., 73
Shacks, 18, 19, 50, 51, 58-9, 89, 111,
   112, 113, 137, 165, 166
Shanghai Alley, 21, 58, 111
Sharp, George L. Thornton, 26
Sharp and Thompson, 26
Sharp and Thompson, Berwick,
   Pratt, 129, 157
Shaughnessy, 73
Shaughnessy Heights, 12, 13
Shaughnessy Heights Restriction
   Act, 117
Shaughnessy United Church, 91
Shelter: allowance for home owners,
   55; allowance for homeless, 45-8;
   bedtickets for homeless, 22, 44,

45, 48; hostels for homeless, 22-3,
   45, 59-60, 180 n. 39, 180 n. 40
Simpson, Michael, 33, 34
Sinclair, James, 133, 146
Sinclair Homesites Limited, 130
Single dwellings: census
   information of (1921), 10, 11, 16;
   as percentage of homes in
   Vancouver, 8
Single Unemployed Protective
   Association, 82, 84
Sisters of Service Residential Club,
   113
Site planning, 34, 120-1, 124, 148,
   150-1
Smalley, Thomas R., 75, 193 n. 27
Smart, Russel, 127
Smith Brothers and Wilson, 120
Social control, 29-30, 34, 70, 83,
   121, 133, 141, 160, 169
Social engineering, and housing
   programs, 121
Social gospel, 78
Social housing programs: definition
   of, 5. *See also* Cooperative housing;
   Elderly, housing projects for; Little
   Mountain public housing
Social Planning for Canada, 80
Social protest. *See* Housing activists
   in Vancouver
Social Services Council of Canada,
   87
Socialist Party of Canada, 80
South Granville, 111
South Little Mountain Community
   Association, 149
South Vancouver, 9-10, 11, 23, 26,
   32, 33, 34, 101, 152, 162
Southern View, 101
Squatters: and housing activists,
   148-9, 221 n. 132; in Stanley Park,
   18, 50, 189 n. 49; on Vancouver
   waterfront, 18, 19. *See also* Shacks
Standard-of-living debate, 164
Stanley Park, 12, 18, 50, 110, 189 n.
   49
Startup, R., 56, 57, 200 n. 124
Steeves, Dorothy Gretchen, 26, 79,
   80, 90, 134

Stevens, H.H., 63, 65, 133
Stevenson, Leigh F., 140, 143, 160
Strathcona: cabins in, 90, 111; facilities, conveniences in, 108; gas appliances in, 108, 109; housing survey of, 107, 136, 154-5; living conditions in, 108, 110, 111, 165; lodging houses in, 111; need of building repairs in, 106-7, 108; as a neighbourhood, 12; overcrowding in, 105, 108; rents in, 103; residence for elderly in, 113
Stratton, P.R.U., 76, 77, 88, 89, 135, 154, 156, 158, 172
Subdivisions, 120, 121, 124, 129-30, 131, 147, 150-1
Suburban Property Owners' Association, 157
Suburbs, 165. *See also* Subdivisions
Suncrest, 101
Supreme Court of Canada, and rent controls, 153
Sutherland, Mary, 67
Swedish loggers, unemployment among, 41, 44
Sylvia Court, 18

T. Eaton Company Limited, 144
Tarn, John N., 169
Taylor, Louis D., 84
Taylor Manor, 23, 114, 180-1 n. 42
Telephones, 107, 108
Telford, Lyle, 58, 90
Tenant relations, as part of housing management, 120-1
Tents, 18, 19
Terminal Avenue, 12
Thompson, Charles E., 151, 155, 156
Thompson, E.P., 164
Thompson, Berwick and Pratt, 157
Thurlow Street, 13
Toilets. *See* Sanitary facilities
'Tom Thumb' houses, 97
Topping, Coral W., 77-8, 79, 87
Toronto: construction materials in (1931), 12; emergency shelter regulations in (1944), 140; evictions in, 141; home ownership in, 11, 46, 52; housing conditions in, 10, 11, 12, 24, 56; and Housing Enterprises of Canada Limited (HEC), 129; housing shortage in, 38, 155; population growth in (1940s), 95; rents in, 12, 16
Toronto Board of Trade, 28
Toronto Housing Company, 79
Town planning. *See* City planning
Town Planning Institute of Canada (TPIC), 26, 78, 79
TPIC. *See* Town Planning Institute of Canada (TPIC)
Trades and Labour Congress of Canada, 63
Trades and Labour Congress of Canada *Journal*, 136
Trafalgar Street, 109
Transitional Powers Act, 153
Trout Lake project, 26, 89, 90

UBC. *See* University of British Columbia
Ukranian Association, 82
Underhill, Frank, 80
Underhill, Frederick T., 25, 27, 35
Unemployed and Part-time Workers' Organization, 78
Unemployed Women's Protective Association, 82
Unemployed Workers' Association, 82, 84
Unemployment: in Canada (1926-40), 43; in construction industry, 73; and housing activism, 82-5; and housing problem, 163; in Vancouver (1931-2), 41-2; (1941), 41
Union of British Columbia Municipalities, 156
Union of Canadian Municipalities, 88
United Church, 78, 83, 152
United Kingdom. *See* Great Britain
United Services Bureau, 118
United States: housing activism in, 168, 169; housing policy in, 6; 'New Deal' legislation and social housing programs in, 75

United Suffrage Societies of Vancouver, 86
University Club of Vancouver, 27
University of British Columbia (UBC): and Emergency Shelter Administration, 149; and Endowment lands relief camps, 45; and housing surveys, 77-8, 154; and veterans' student housing, 149
University students, and housing shortages, 97, 99
University Women's Club, 28, 159
Unwin, Raymond, 60, 61, 76-7, 90
Urban History Review / Revue d'histoire urbaine, 6

V-E Day riots, 132
Vacancy rates, in Vancouver (1940s), 99-100. *See also* Occupancy rates, in Vancouver (1930s)
Van Norman, C.B.K., 154, 195 n. 62
Vancouver and District Trades and Labour Council, 136
Vancouver Art Gallery, 70, 84
Vancouver Board of Trade, 26, 91
Vancouver City Central Woman's Suffrage Campaign Association, 86
Vancouver city council: and building bylaws, 49; and Emergency Shelter Administration, 140; and Helena Gutteridge, 86-7; and housing authority, 156; housing committees of, 86-7, 137, 138; and housing standards bylaw, 89, 137; housing survey of (1937), 26, 78, 87; and joint responsibility for housing with other levels of government, 84-85, 121, 123, 137, 156-7; and Little Mountain public housing, 156-8; and loss of tax revenue from WHL houses, 141-2; and National Housing Act (NHA) (1938), Part II, 89-92; reluctance to participate in housing programs, 167-8; and rental housing for veterans, 146; and shelter

allowance, 45-8; and social housing, 155, 167; and zoning bylaws, 49. *See also* Vancouver health department
Vancouver Council of Social Agencies (VCSA), 70, 82-3, 87, 91, 121
Vancouver Council of Women. *See* Local Council of Women (LCW)
Vancouver East. *See* East Vancouver
Vancouver Emergency Refuge, 45, 59, 70
Vancouver Federated Ratepayers' Association, 85, 91
Vancouver Freehomes Limited, 23
Vancouver health department: appointment of full-time medical health officer, 25; campaign to improve Vancouver's public health, 25; and Chinese lodging houses, 21; inspection of apartments, 17-18; inspection of lodging houses, 13, 16-17; and reported need of building repairs, 106; and surveys of lodging houses, 105
Vancouver Housing Association (VHA): closing of, 172; founding of, 87-8; and Fraserview, 151; and housing activism, 131, 132, 133, 135-6, 139, 154, 167, 170; and housing surveys, 56-7, 89, 104, 105, 108-9, 110, 154-5; and Little Mountain public housing, 157; and rent controls, 153, 154; report on National Housing Act (NHA) program, 73; support of construction industry, 72; and Vancouver housing authority, 155-6; support of housing for veterans, 112, 146; and visit of Sir Raymond Unwin, 90
Vancouver Housing Authority, 158
Vancouver Junior Board of Trade, 159
Vancouver Labour Council, 136
Vancouver Loan and Mortgage Association, 72
Vancouver, New Westminster, and

District Trades and Labour Council, 82, 87, 91
Vancouver Parks Board, 51
Vancouver Police Women, 48
Vancouver Real Estate Board, 153, 157
Vancouver Real Estate Exchange. *See* Real Estate Exchange
Vancouver Sun, 71, 94, 136, 144, 148, 149, 157
Vancouver Titles Limited, 138
Vancouver Town Planning Commission, 26
Vancouver Trades and Labour Council, 27
Vancouver Veterans' Council, 132
Vancouver Welfare Foundation, 45
VCSA. *See* Vancouver Council of Social Agencies (VCSA)
Veiller, Lawrence, 27
Ventilation, lack of, 17, 57-8, 109-10, 111
Vermin infestation, 58, 109, 110, 111
Veterans: assistance for, in buying housing, 131; attempt to purchase hutments from U.S., 147; and Better Housing Scheme, 24, 25, 31-7; current housing projects for, 161; evictions of, under WPTB regulations, 139; and groups in support of veterans' housing, 27; and Hotel Vancouver, 144-6; housing programs for, 28-30, 98, 116, 170; housing shortage for, 95-7, 99-100, 112-13, 163; organizations, and housing, 131, 132-3; postwar training in Vancouver, 97; public sympathy for, 159; and sale of designated housing by CMHC, 160, 161; and Wartime Housing Limited (WHL) programs, 141
Veterans' Land Act, 131
VHA. *See* Vancouver Housing Association (VHA)
Victoria: construction materials in, 11-12; emergency shelter regulations in (1944), 140; home

ownership in, 11, 46, 52; housing conditions in, 10, 11, 56
Victory Heights, 101, 213 n. 45

Wagner Steagall Act (U.S. 1937), 75
Walker, J. Alexander, 26, 79, 88
Walker, J.G., 116, 117, 140
War Amputations Association, 132
War Measures Act, 28-9, 116, 119-20, 153
War Supply Board, 118
War workers: housing for, 118-121; housing shortage for, 113, 163; and sale of designated housing by CMHC, 160, 161
Wartime Housing Limited (WHL): board of directors of, 209 n. 7; construction of rental homes in Vancouver, 141-2, 143; and house styles, 122, 171; and housing for veterans, 139, 140, 141, 142, 143; and housing for war workers, 99, 116, 119-26; opposition to, by housing industry groups, 138; and sale of veterans' housing, 161; take-over of, by CMHC, 131; and veterans' demands for housing, 132; and waiting list for housing, 100
Wartime Prices and Trade Board (WPTB): and emergency shelter regulations, 139-40; and evictions freeze, 142; and Hotel Vancouver as temporary shelter, 143; and housing availability, 98; opposition to WHL, 124; Order No. 200, 137; Order No. 537, 140-1; powers of, 116-18
Water supply, 56-7, 59, 60, 111-12
Weaver, John, 9, 34
Weir, G.M., 90
Welfare: cases (1931-38), 42; recipients, and housing activism, 82-3; and shelter allowance, 45-8
Welfare Council of Greater Vancouver, 138
West End: conversion of single homes into multiple units in, 13, 165; firehazards in, 111; gas

appliances in, 109-10; lack of green spaces in, 110; living conditions in, 12; lodging houses in, 13, 16, 49, 50, 58, 106, 107, 108, 109, 110, 111, 113; as neighbourhood, 12

West End Chamber of Commerce, 72

White, Thomas, 28, 29

White-collar workers. *See* Working class

Whittaker, Henry, 33, 34

WHL. *See* Wartime Housing Limited (WHL)

Willingdon Heights, 101, 213 n. 45

Wilson, Halford D., 155

Winch, Ernest E., 23, 80, 134, 151

Winch, Harold, 134, 147

Windermere bathing pool, 51

Windermere District Improvement Association, 85

Windsor, population growth in (1940s), 95

Windsor Street, 33

Winnipeg: and Better Housing Scheme, 32-3, 36; construction materials in, 12; evictions in, 141; home ownership in, 11, 46, 52; housing conditions in, 10, 11, 12, 56; housing shortage in, 38; population growth in (1940s), 95

Winnipeg General Strike, 29

Winters, Robert H., 151, 156

Wohl, Anthony S., 169

Women: and Better Housing Scheme, 35-6; Boeing aircraft workers, and housing shortage, 99; of CCF, and housing activism, 134; and cooperative houses, 134; of groups supporting low-cost rental housing, 91; housewives as advertising target of NEC program, 67; as housing activists, 79; housing shortage for, 104, 113, 163; lack of shelters for, 22-3; of organizations, and housing activism, 136, 170; and property tax arrears and sales, 54; and relief (1931-8), 42; shelter allowance for, 48; social protest of, 82; support of Vancouver Housing Association (VHA), 135; unemployment of, in Vancouver (1931-2), 42

Women's Employment League, 86

Women's International League for Peace and Freedom, 82

Women's Minimum Wage League, 86

Wood, J.S., 157

'Work for taxes' scheme, 54, 85

Workers' Alliance of British Columbia, 84, 87

Workers' Party of Canada, 80

Workers' Unity League, 80, 84

Working class: and Better Housing Scheme, 34; and housing activism, 169; housing shortage for, 23; and suburbs, studies of, 165

WPTB. *See* Wartime Prices and Trade Board (WPTB)

Yaletown, 12, 50

Yee, Paul, 165

Yip family, 48

Young, H.E., 25, 90

Young Women's Christian Association (YWCA), 48, 113, 117

Yun Ho Chang, 21

YWCA. *See* Young Women's Christian Association (YWCA)

Zoning bylaws, 25, 26, 117

Set in Stone by Vancouver Desktop Publishing Centre

Printed and bound in Canada by D.W. Friesen & Sons Ltd.

Copy-editor: Camilla Jenkins

Indexer: Annette Lorek

Cartographer: Eric Leinberger